Author's Message:

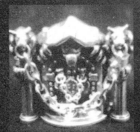

Production—Sands. Creative Assist—MAD TOYZ

NOBUYUKI ANZAI PRESENTS 安西信行

Maybe I should invoke it...

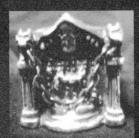

Production—DEVIL'S FACTORY

MÄR
Vol. 6
Story and Art by Nobuyuki Anzai

English Adaptation/Gerard Jones
Translation/Kaori Inoue
Touch-up Art & Lettering/James Gaubatz
Design/Izumi Evers
Editor/ Pancha Diaz

Managing Editor/Annette Roman
Director of Production/Noboru Watanabe
Vice President of Publishing/Alvin Lu
Sr. Director of Acquisitions/Rika Inouye
Vice President of Sales & Marketing/Liza Coppola
Publisher/Hyoe Narita

Printed in Canada

Published by VIZ Media, LLC
P.O. Box 77010
San Francisco, CA 94107

10 9 8 7 6 5 4 3 2 1
First printing, March 2006

www.viz.com
store.viz.com

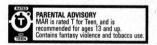

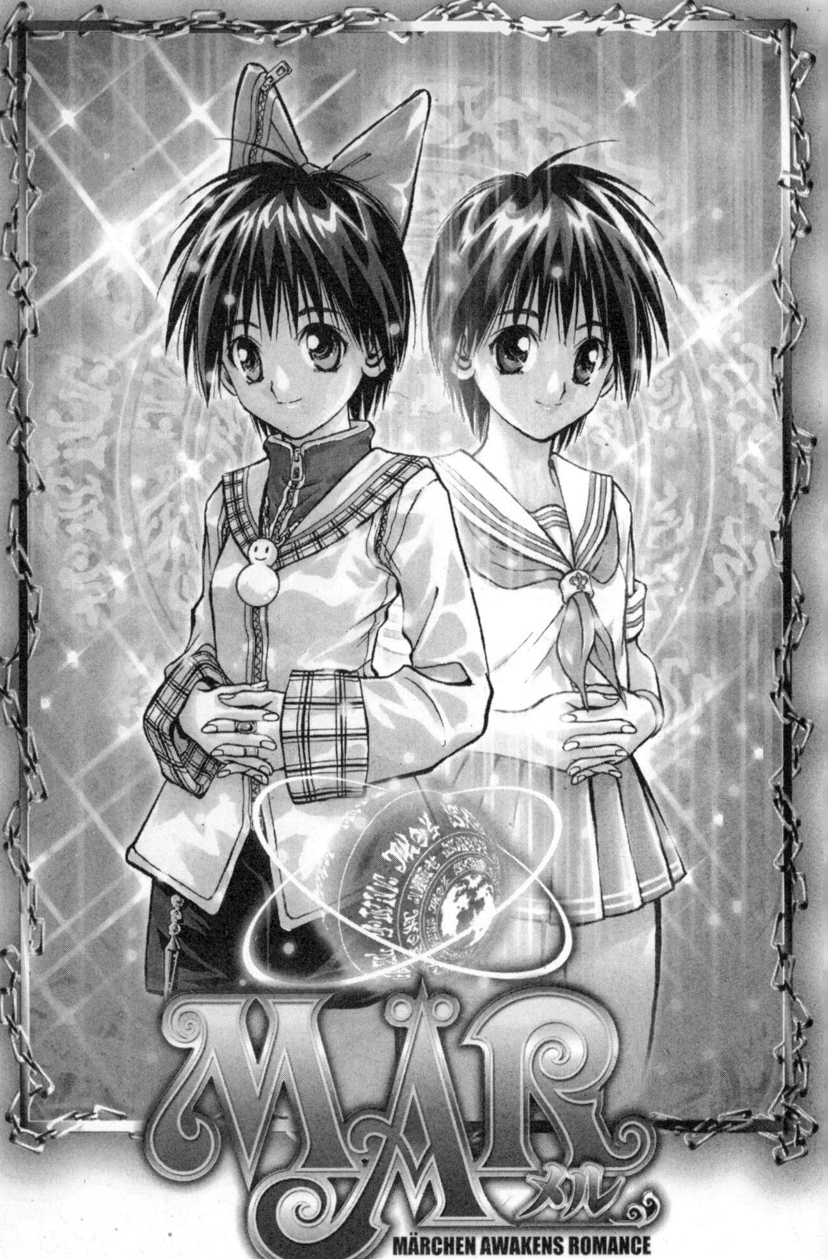
MÄR
MÄRCHEN AWAKENS ROMANCE

Vol.6

Nobuyuki Anzai

Characters

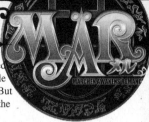

Edward (Human)

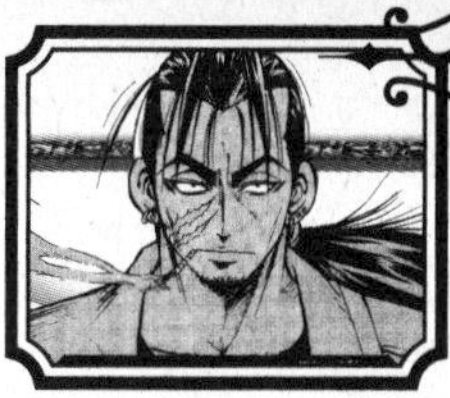

He was once a warrior named Alan who played a major role in the war of six years ago. But then a curse trapped him in the form of a dog.

Snow

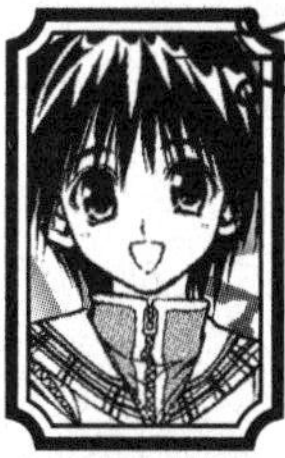

The Princess of the Great Kingdom of Lestava, freed from a frozen state by Ginta.

Edward (Canine)

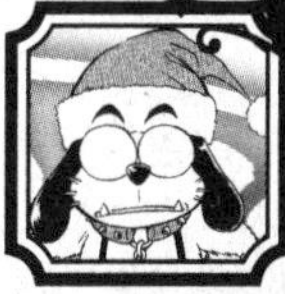

Devotedly serves Princess Snow. He returns to human form after falling asleep three times.

Alviss

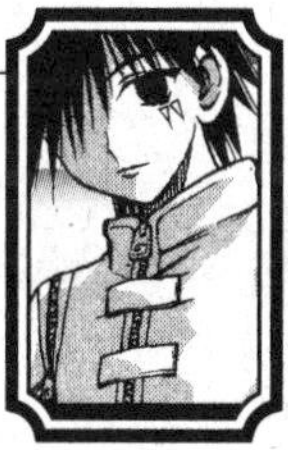

Using the Dimensional ÄRM called the “Gate Keeper Clown,” he is the one who brought Ginta to MÄR Heaven.

Dorothy

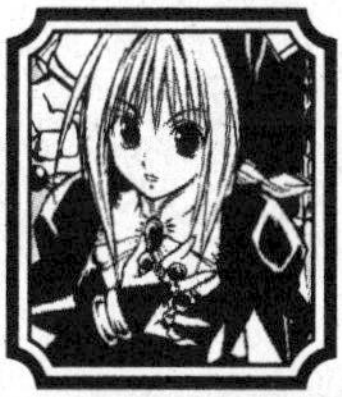

A witch. Although she used Ginta to help her find Babbo, could she have some real feelings for him…?

Babbo

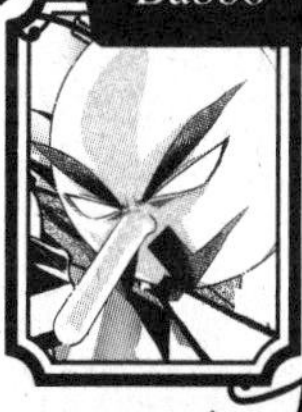

A rare talking ÄRM who once belonged to Phantom.

Jack

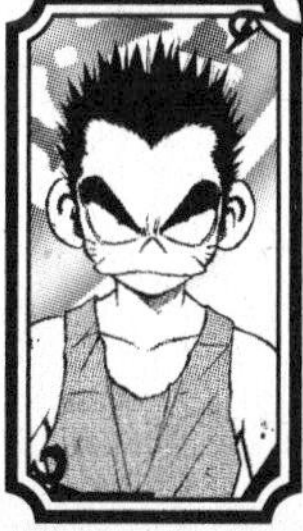

A farmboy whom Ginta helped to defeat the Rogalu brothers. Now he’s left his mother and his farm to go on an adventure with Ginta.

Ginta Toramizu

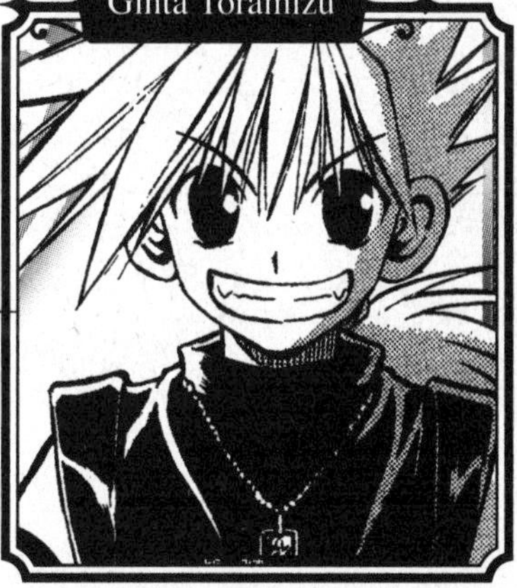

A second year middle school student who dreams about the world of fairy tales—and suddenly finds himself there!

Previous Volume

Ginta jumps through a "door" that suddenly appears in his classroom a finds himself in Märchen, the magical world of his dreams. Now, at th "request" of the Chess Pieces, the War Games have begun—and Ginta and his friends, calling themselves "Mär," must battle the Chess warri The Mär team is victorious in its first battle, and Snow wins the first match of the second battle—but then Nanashi meets a shocking defeat the hands of Loco! The final outcome of the battle now rests on the w Dorothy…

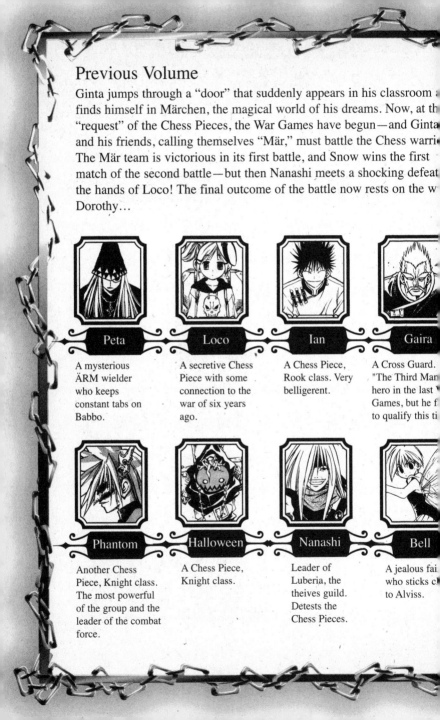

Peta
A mysterious ÄRM wielder who keeps constant tabs on Babbo.

Loco
A secretive Chess Piece with some connection to the war of six years ago.

Ian
A Chess Piece, Rook class. Very belligerent.

Gaira
A Cross Guard. "The Third Man hero in the last Games, but he f to qualify this ti

Phantom
Another Chess Piece, Knight class. The most powerful of the group and the leader of the combat force.

Halloween
A Chess Piece, Knight class.

Nanashi
Leader of Luberia, the theives guild. Detests the Chess Pieces.

Bell
A jealous fai who sticks c to Alviss.

CONTENTS

AKT.53/ Dorothy vs. Maira ①..7

AKT.54/ Dorothy vs. Maira ②..23

AKT.55/ Rolan..39

AKT.56/ HOPE..55

AKT.57/ The Man Who Came Late...............................71

AKT.58/ Ed vs. Alibaba...87

AKT.59/ Jack vs. Pano (Rematch) ①..........................103

AKT.60/ Jack vs. Pano (Rematch) ②..........................121

AKT.61/ Snow vs. Mr. Hook.......................................137

AKT.62/ Ginta vs. Kannochi ①...................................153

AKT.63/ Ginta vs. Kannochi ② 169

AKT.53/ Dorothy vs. Maira①

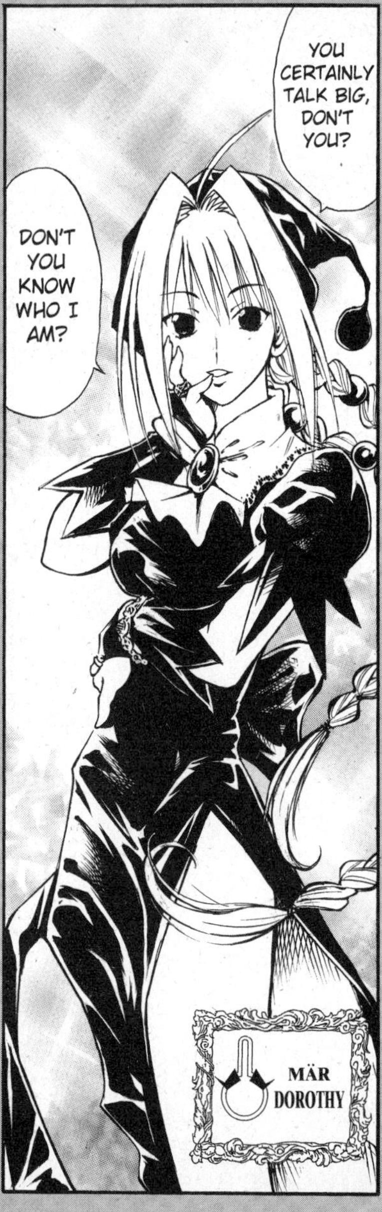
YOU CERTAINLY TALK BIG, DON'T YOU?
DON'T YOU KNOW WHO I AM?
MÄR
DOROTHY

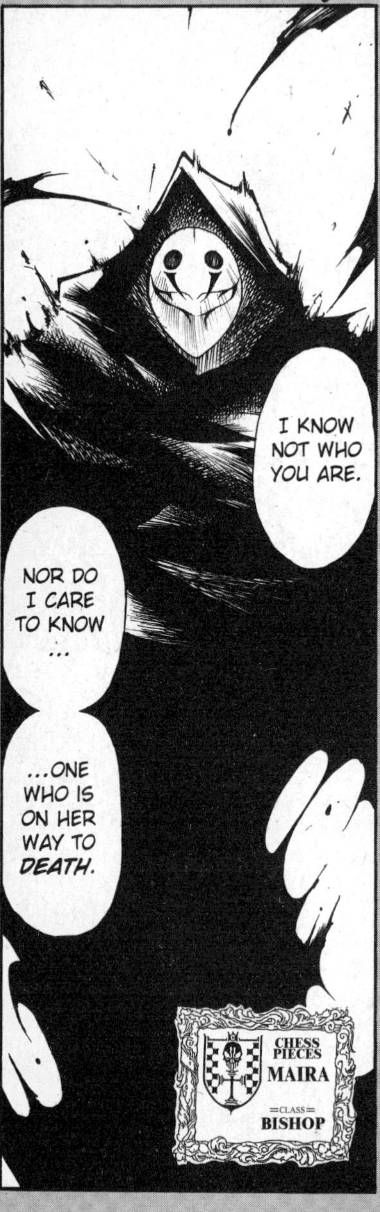
I KNOW NOT WHO YOU ARE.
NOR DO I CARE TO KNOW ...
...ONE WHO IS ON HER WAY TO *DEATH*.
CHESS PIECES
MAIRA
CLASS
BISHOP

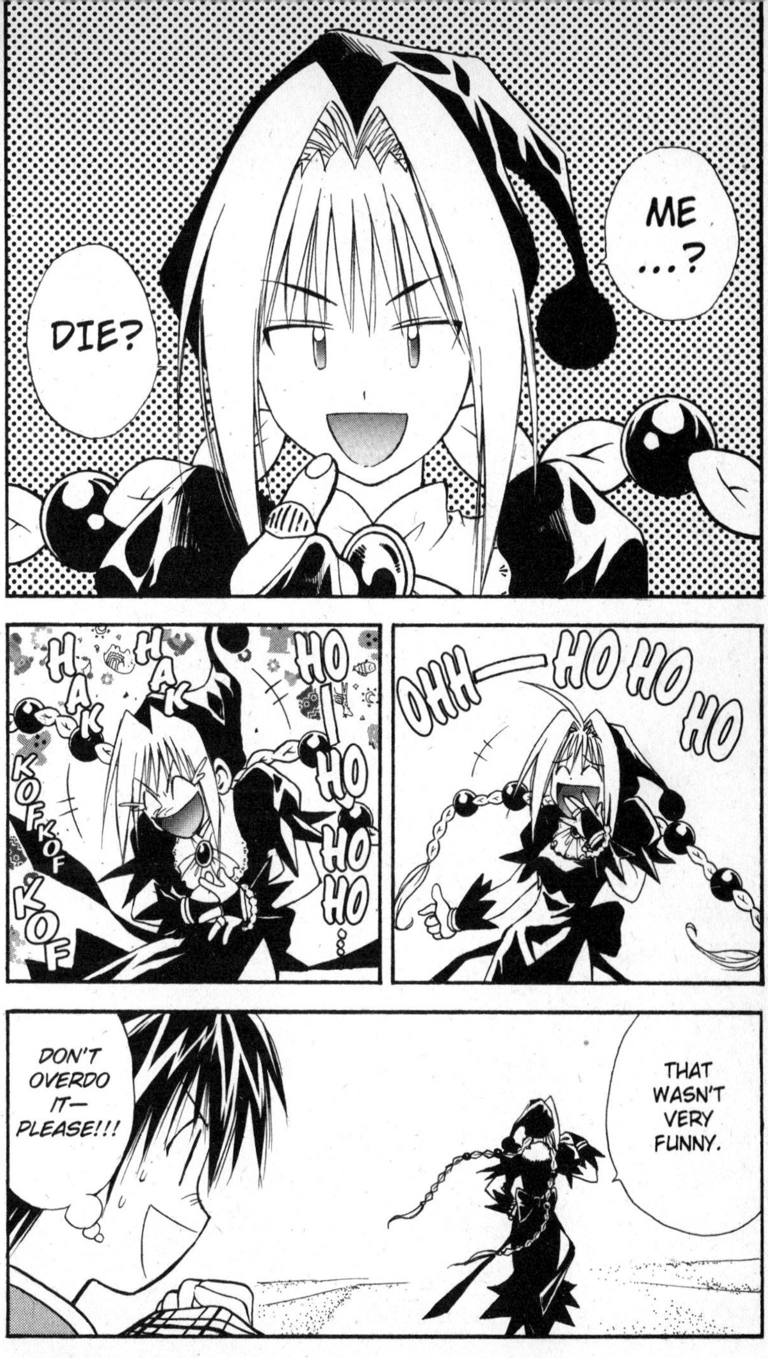
ME ...?
DIE?
OHH—HO HO HO HO
HO HO HO HO...
HAK HAK
KOF KOF KOF KOF
THAT WASN'T VERY FUNNY.
DON'T OVERDO IT—PLEASE!!!

AKT.53/ Dorothy vs. Maira①

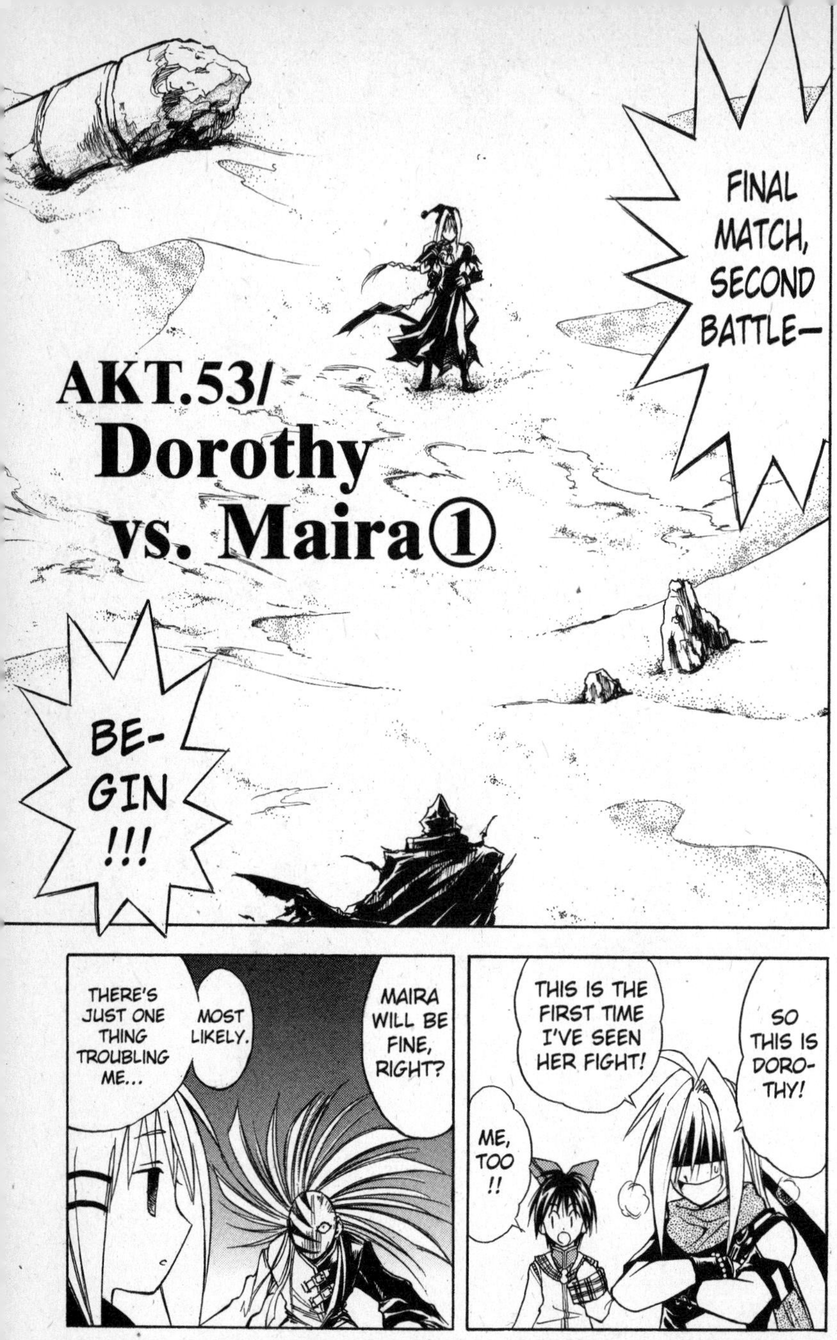
FINAL MATCH, SECOND BATTLE—
BE-GIN!!!
SO THIS IS DORO-THY!
THIS IS THE FIRST TIME I'VE SEEN HER FIGHT!
ME, TOO!!
MAIRA WILL BE FINE, RIGHT?
MOST LIKELY.
THERE'S JUST ONE THING TROUBLING ME...

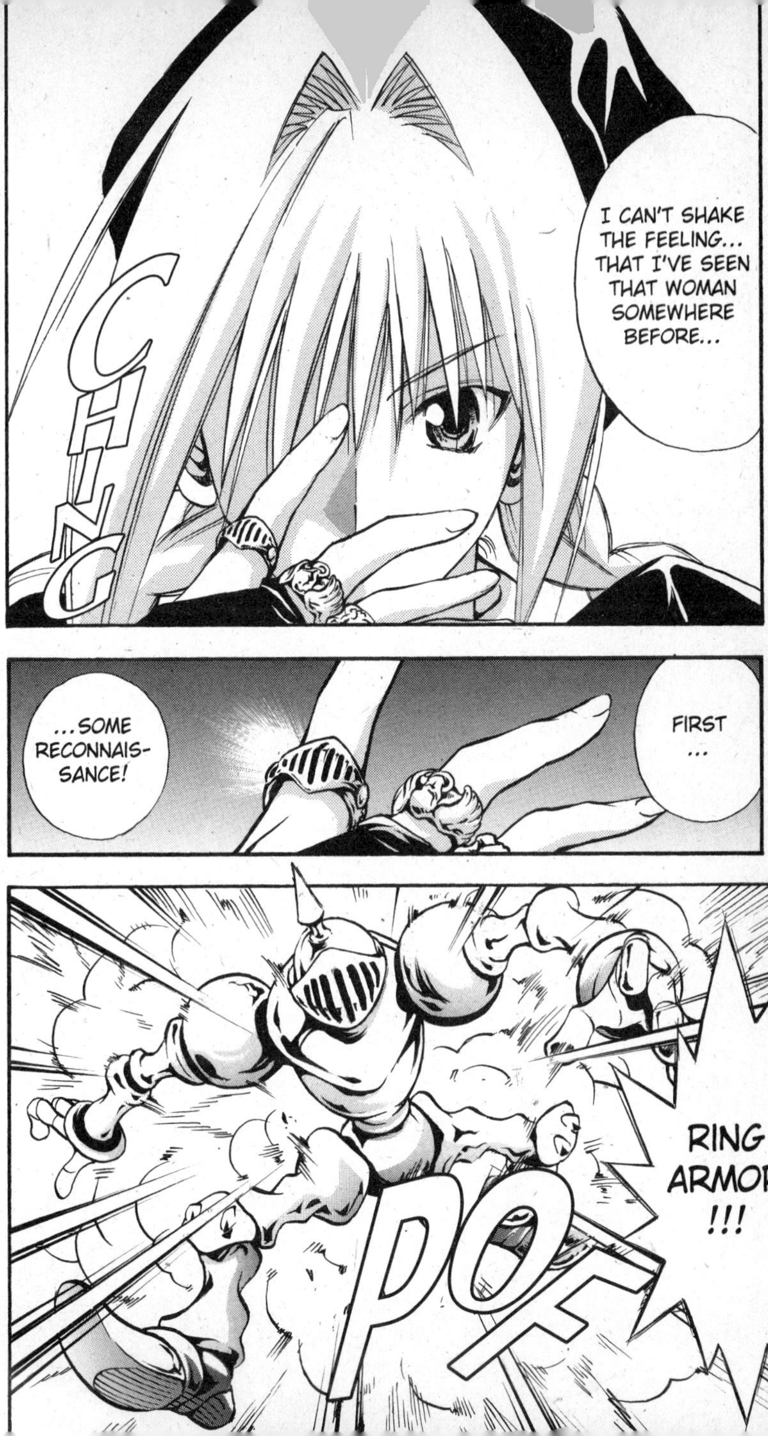
I CAN'T SHAKE THE FEELING... THAT I'VE SEEN THAT WOMAN SOMEWHERE BEFORE...
CHING
FIRST ...
...SOME RECONNAIS-SANCE!
RING ARMOR !!!
POF

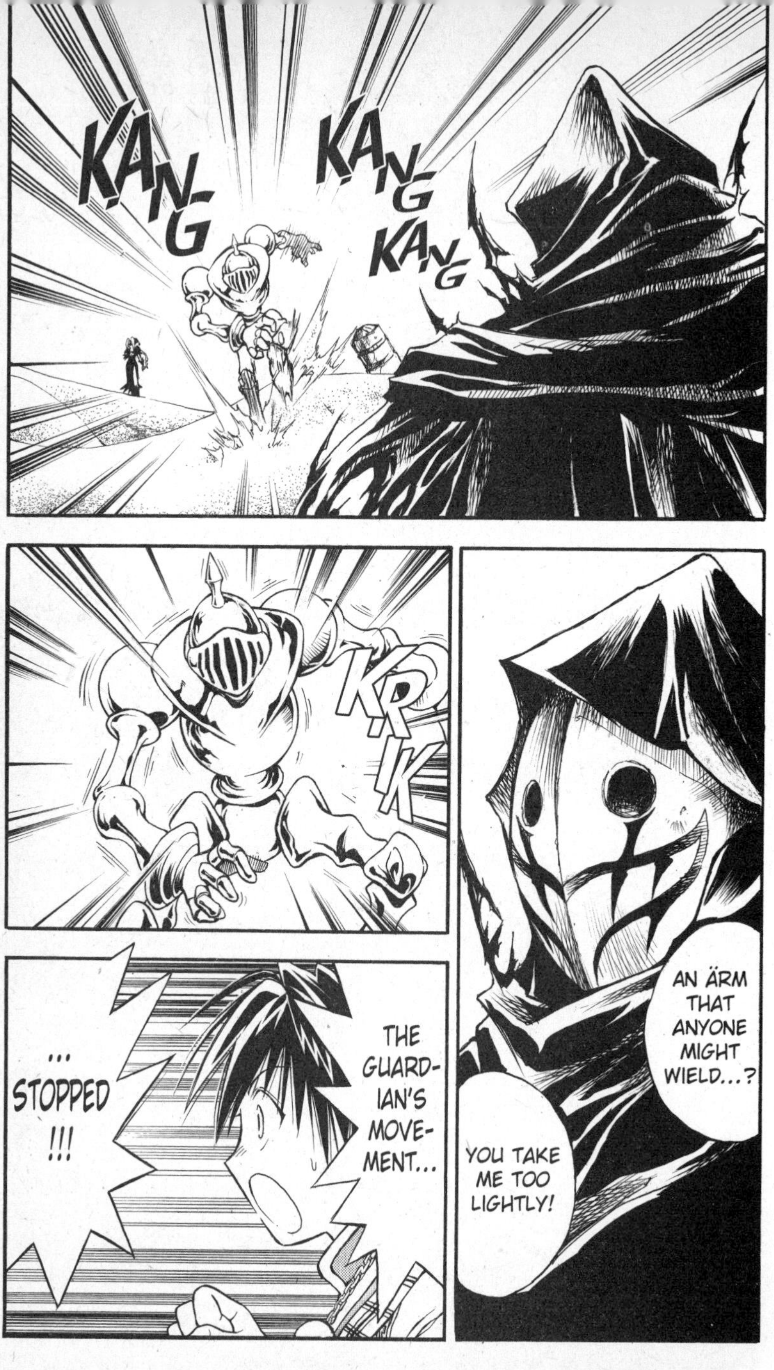
KANG KANG
KANG
KANG
AN ÄRM THAT ANYONE MIGHT WIELD...?
YOU TAKE ME TOO LIGHTLY!
KRIK
THE GUARD-IAN'S MOVE-MENT...
... STOPPED !!!

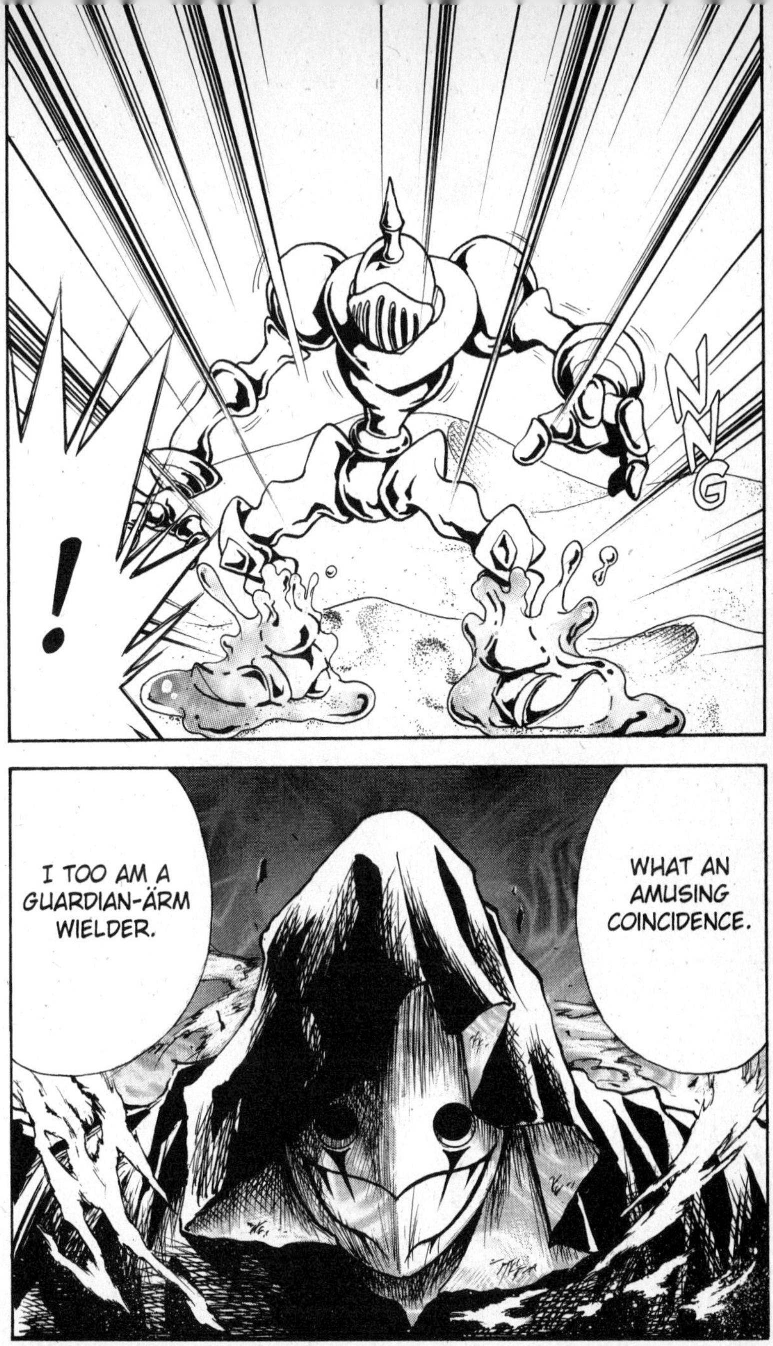
NNG
!
WHAT AN AMUSING COINCIDENCE.
I TOO AM A GUARDIAN-ÄRM WIELDER.

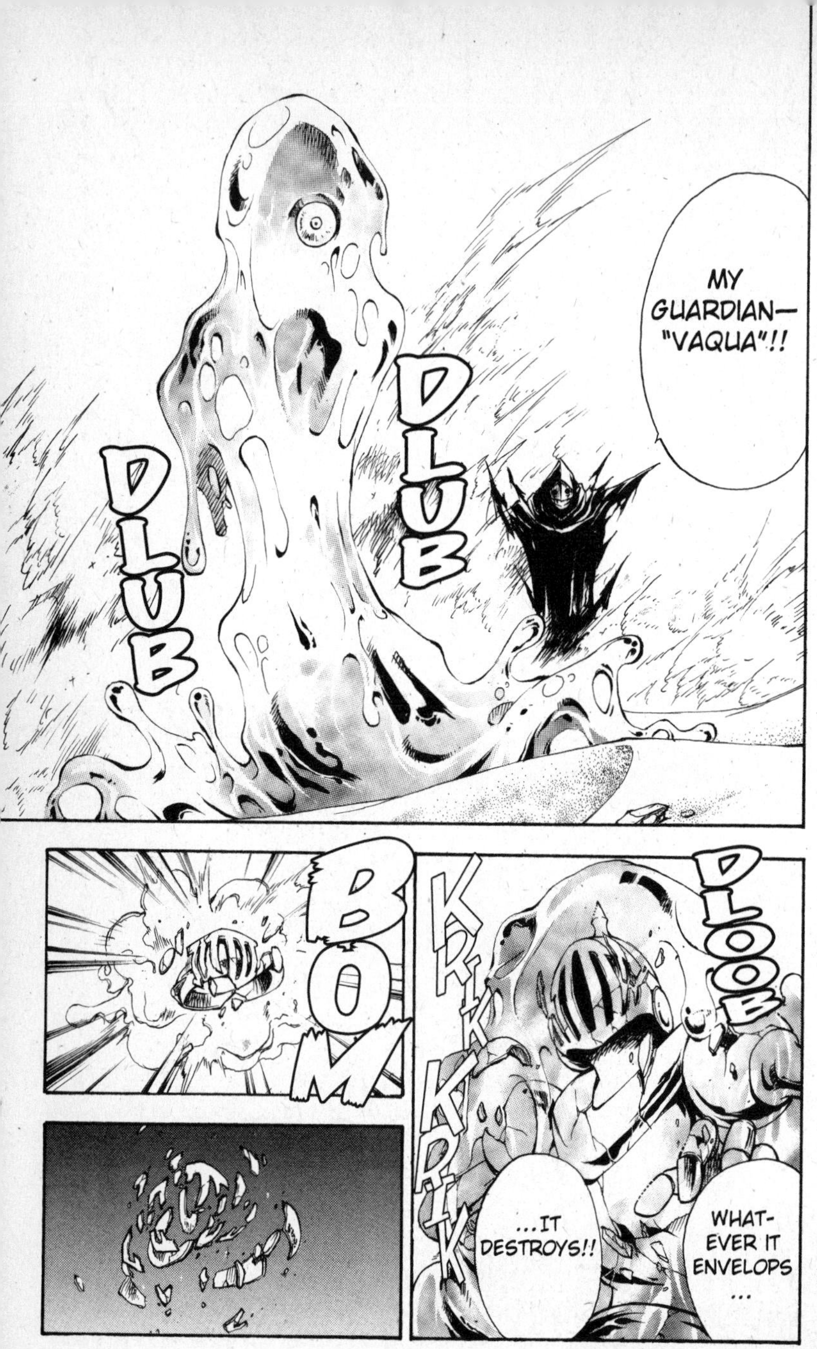
MY GUARDIAN— "VAQUA"!!
DLUB
DLUB
DLOOB
KRIK KRIK
KRIK KRIK
WHAT-EVER IT ENVELOPS ...
...IT DESTROYS!!
BOM

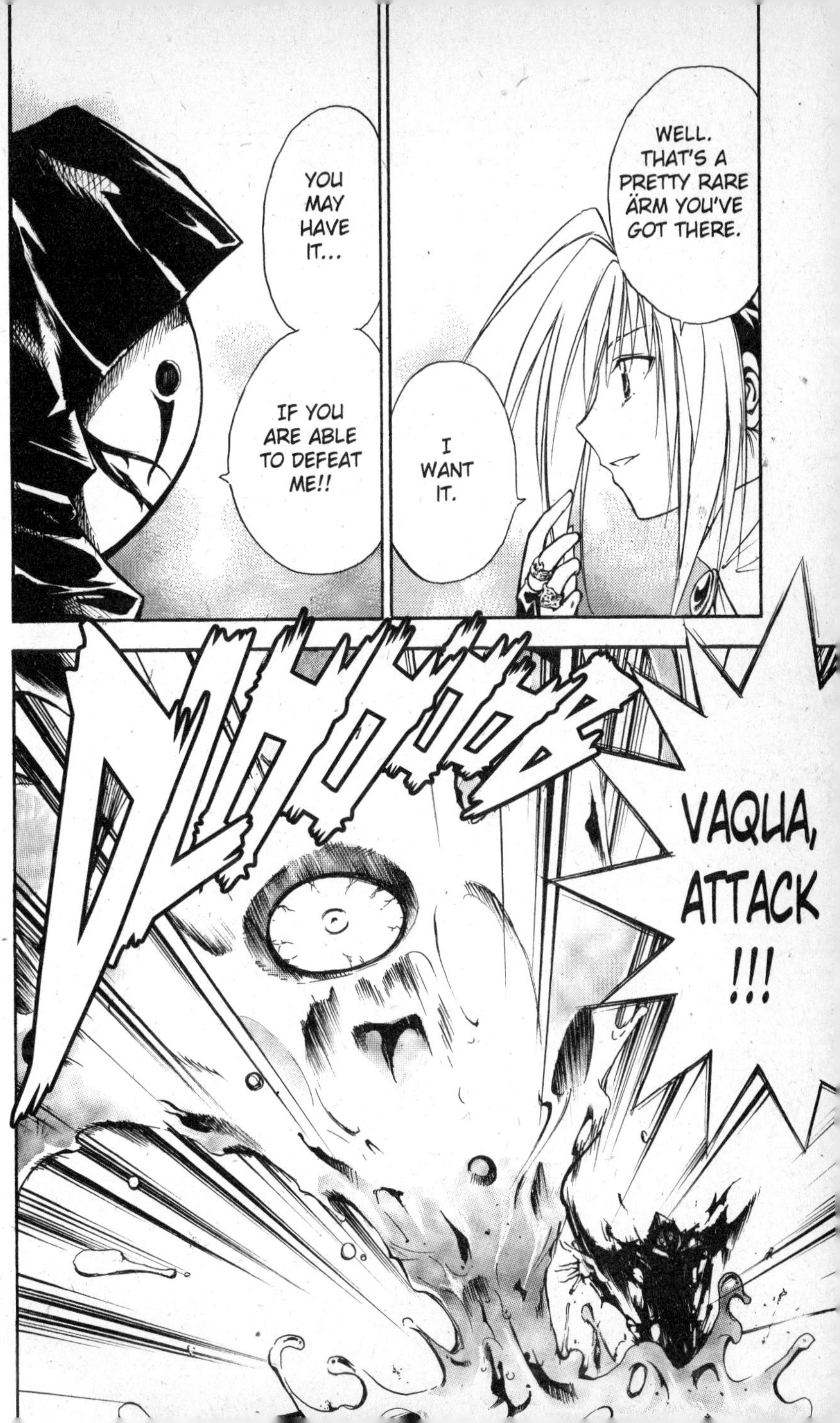
WELL. THAT'S A PRETTY RARE ÄRM YOU'VE GOT THERE.
I WANT IT.
YOU MAY HAVE IT...
IF YOU ARE ABLE TO DEFEAT ME!!
VAQUA, ATTACK!!!

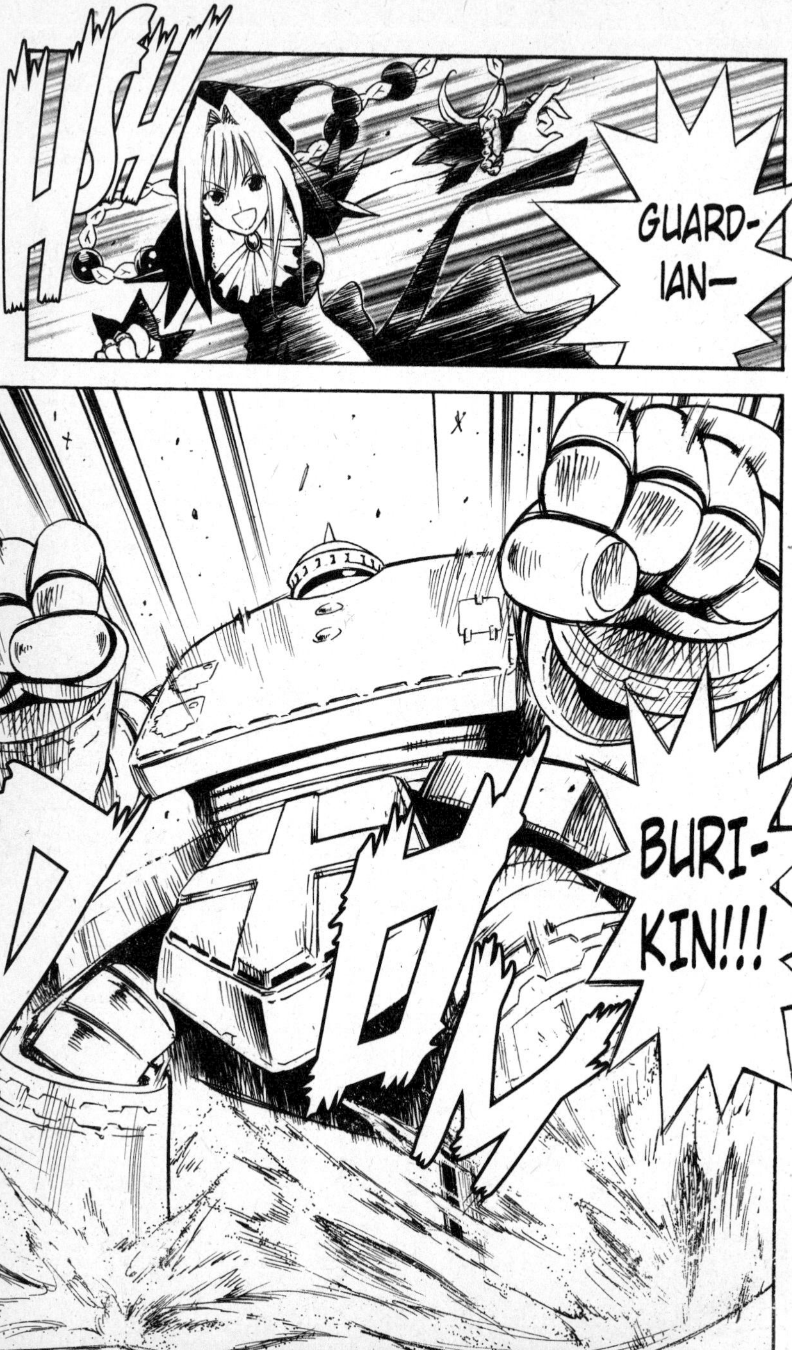
GUARD-IAN–
BURI-KIN!!!

AH. EVEN LARGER THAN GINTA'S GARGOYLE!
THAT WOULD BE DIFFICULT TO ENVELOP, INDEED.
HOW-EVER ...
HHHH

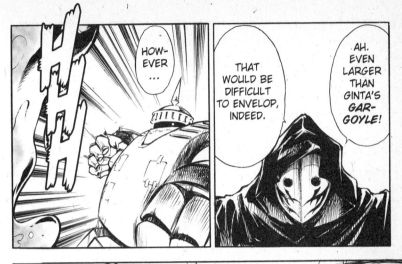

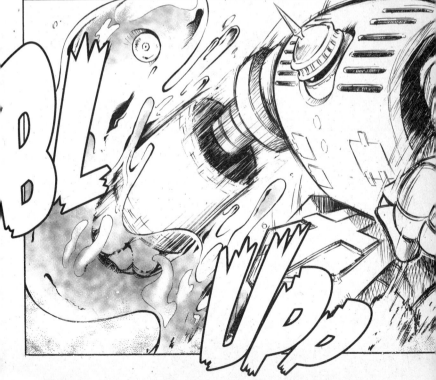

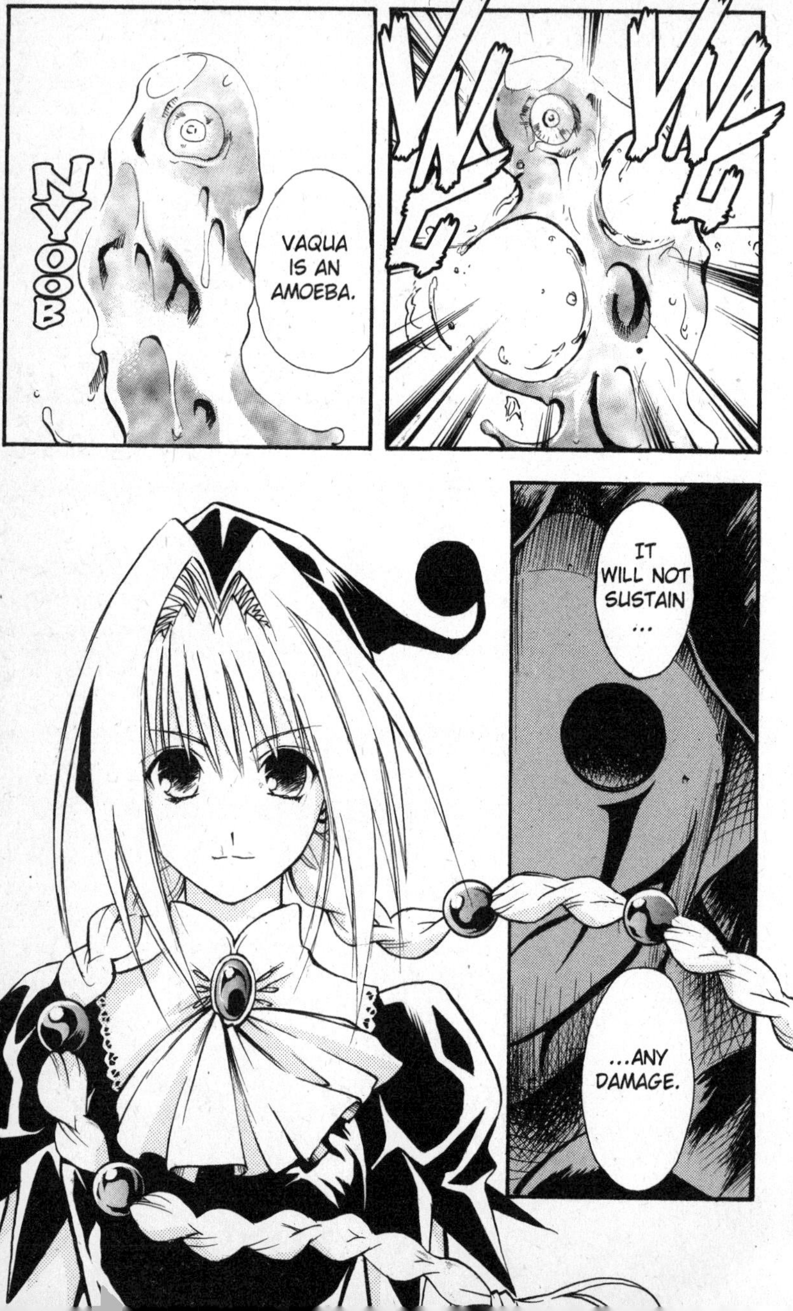
NYOOB
VAQUA IS AN AMOEBA.
IT WILL NOT SUSTAIN...
...ANY DAMAGE.

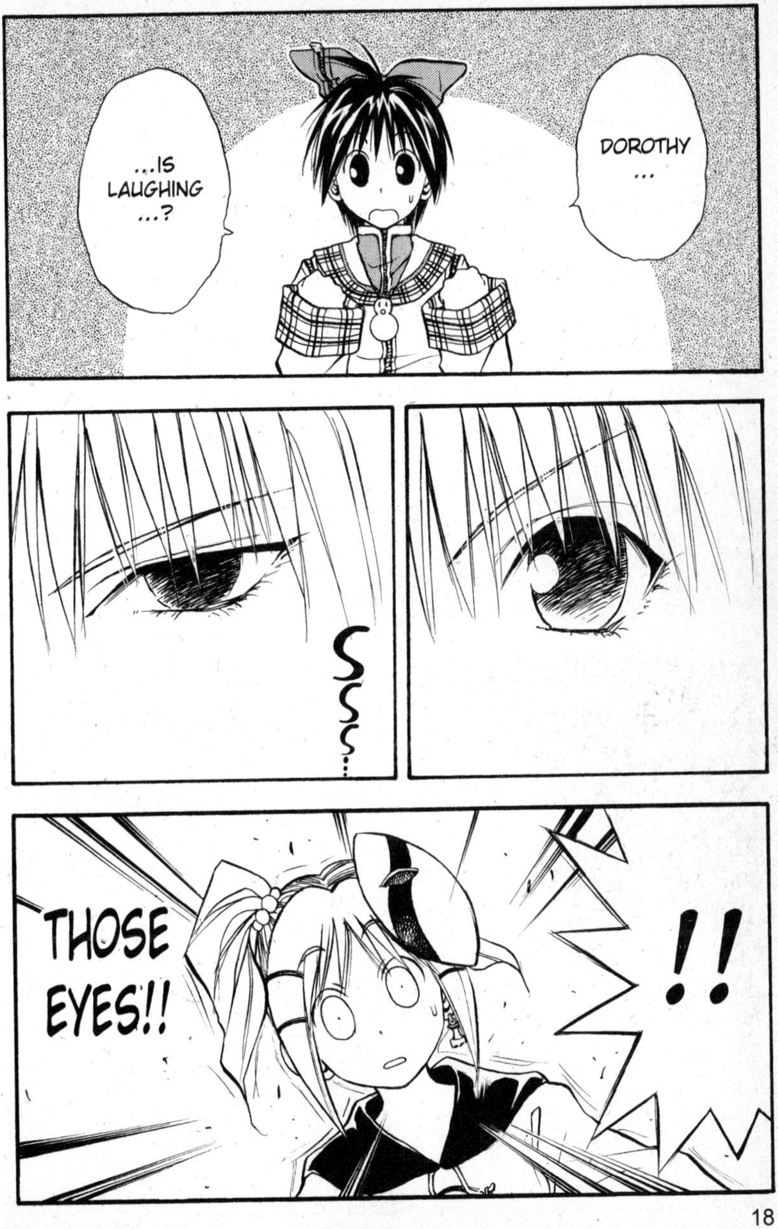
DOROTHY ...
...IS LAUGHING ...?
SSS...
!!
THOSE EYES!!

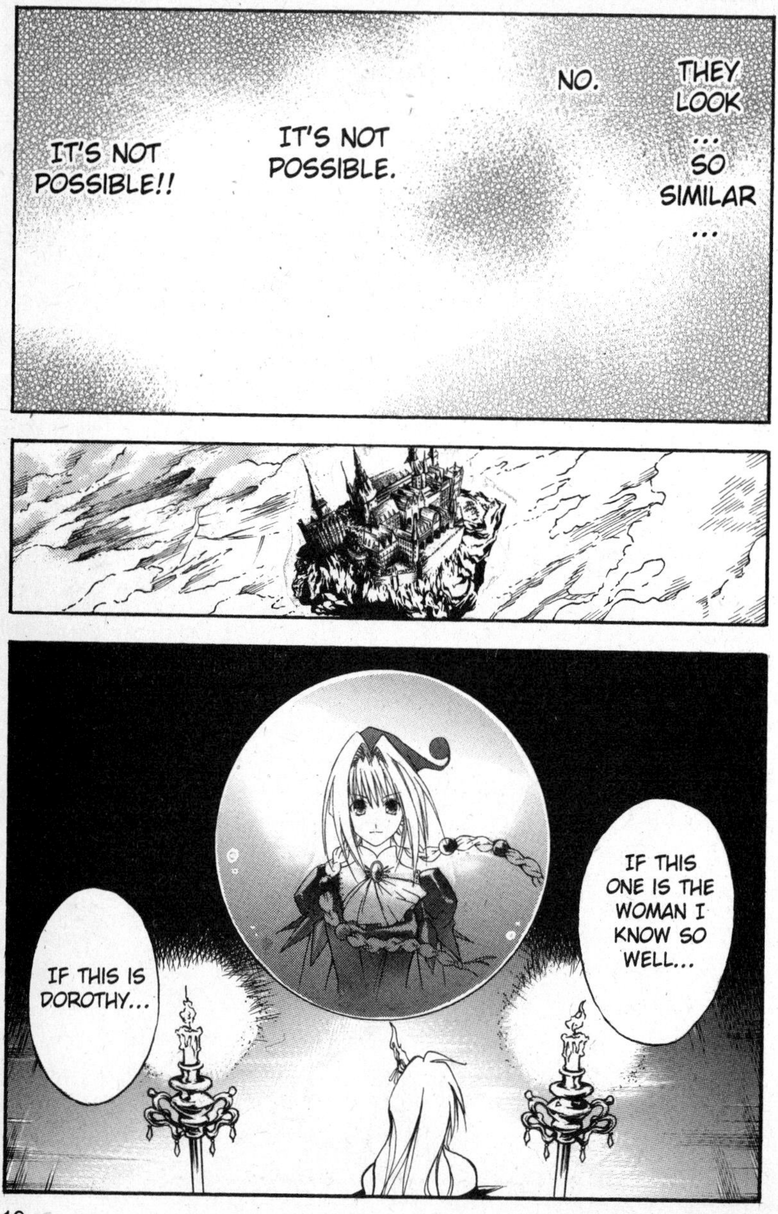
THEY LOOK... SO SIMILAR...
NO.
IT'S NOT POSSIBLE.
IT'S NOT POSSIBLE!!
IF THIS ONE IS THE WOMAN I KNOW SO WELL...
IF THIS IS DOROTHY...

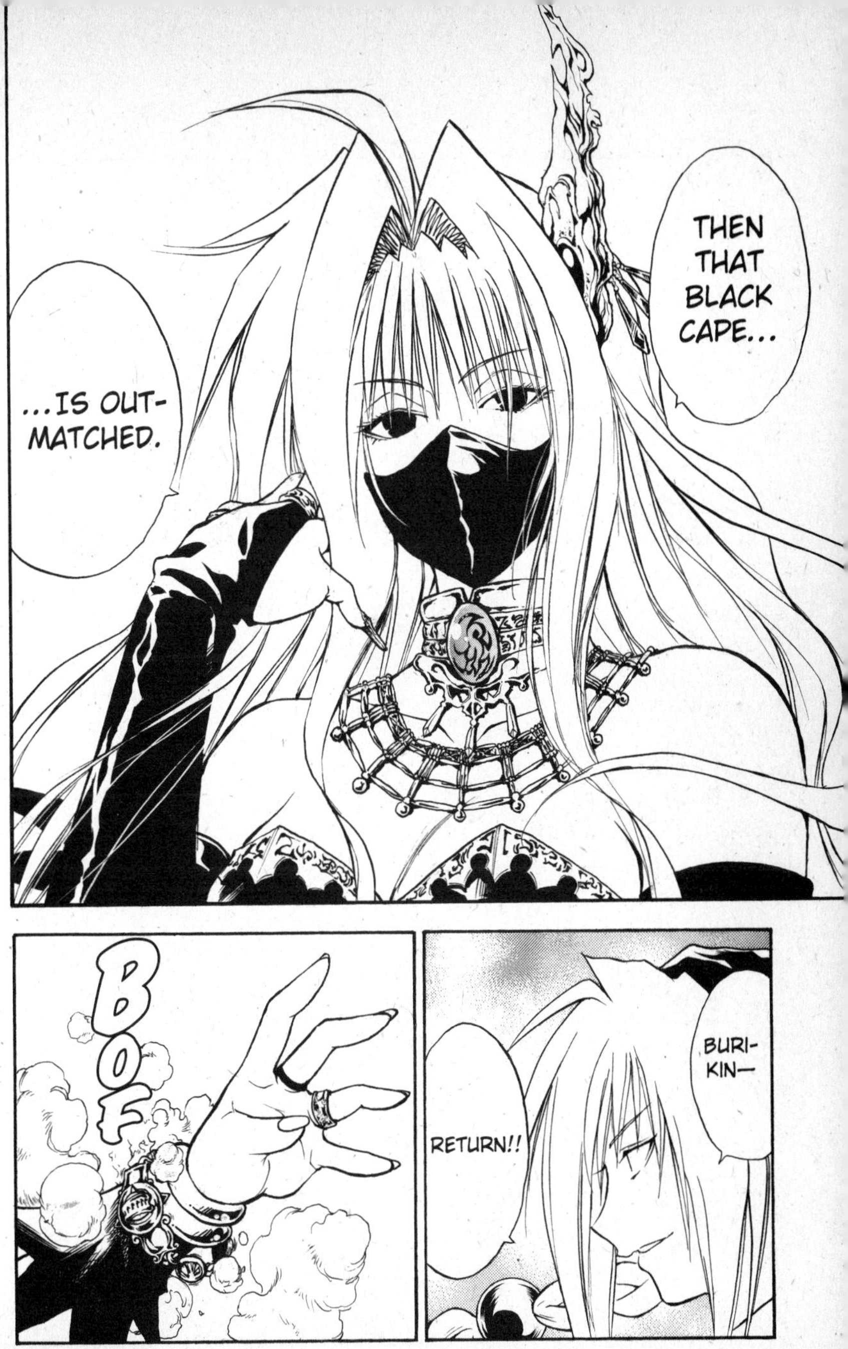
THEN THAT BLACK CAPE...
...IS OUT-MATCHED.
BURI-KIN—
RETURN!!
BOF

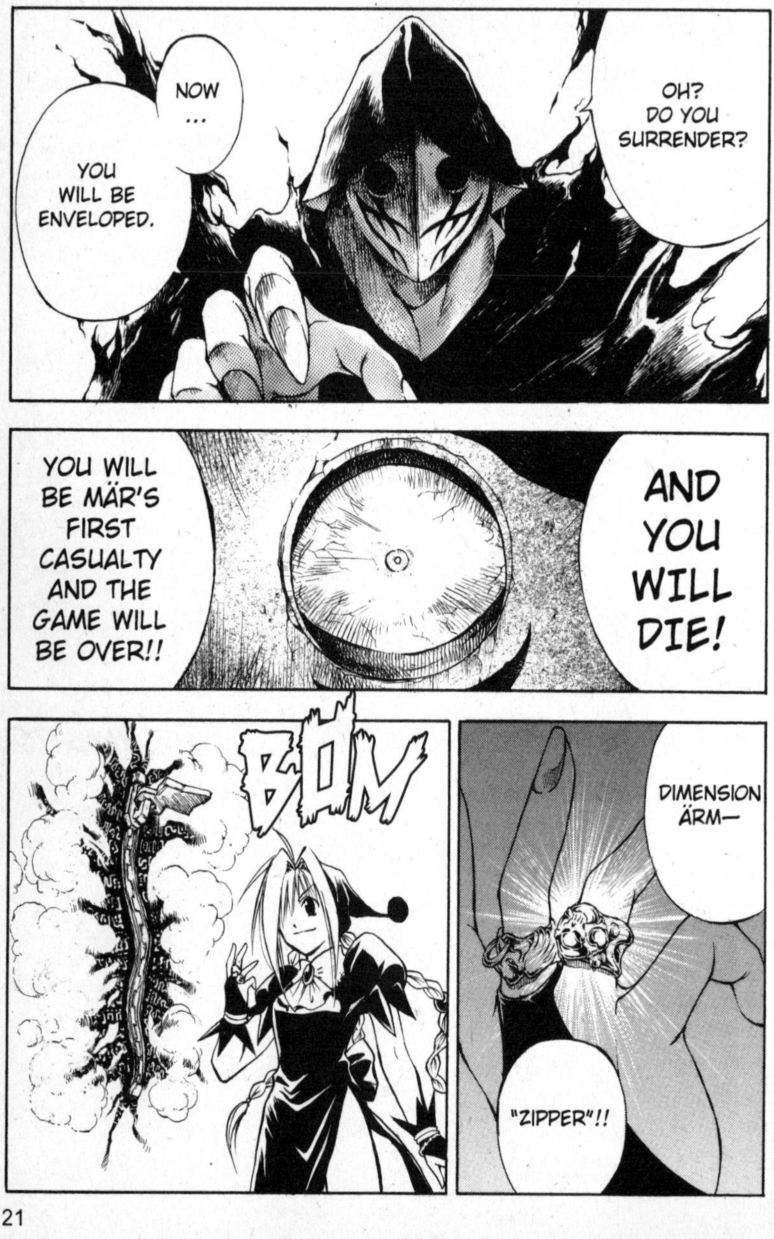
OH? DO YOU SURRENDER?
NOW ...
YOU WILL BE ENVELOPED.
AND YOU WILL DIE!
YOU WILL BE MÄR'S FIRST CASUALTY AND THE GAME WILL BE OVER!!
DIMENSION ÄRM—
"ZIPPER"!!
BOM

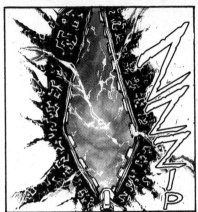

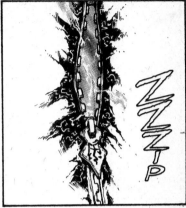

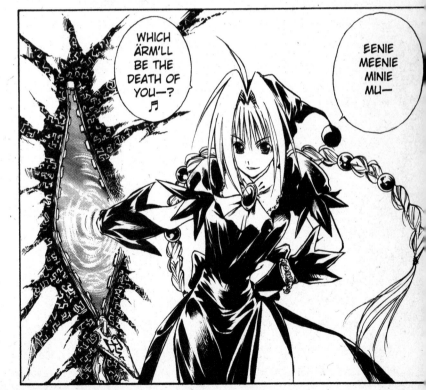

ZZZIP
ZZZZZIP
EENIE MEENIE MINIE MU—
WHICH ÄRM'LL BE THE DEATH OF YOU—? ♬

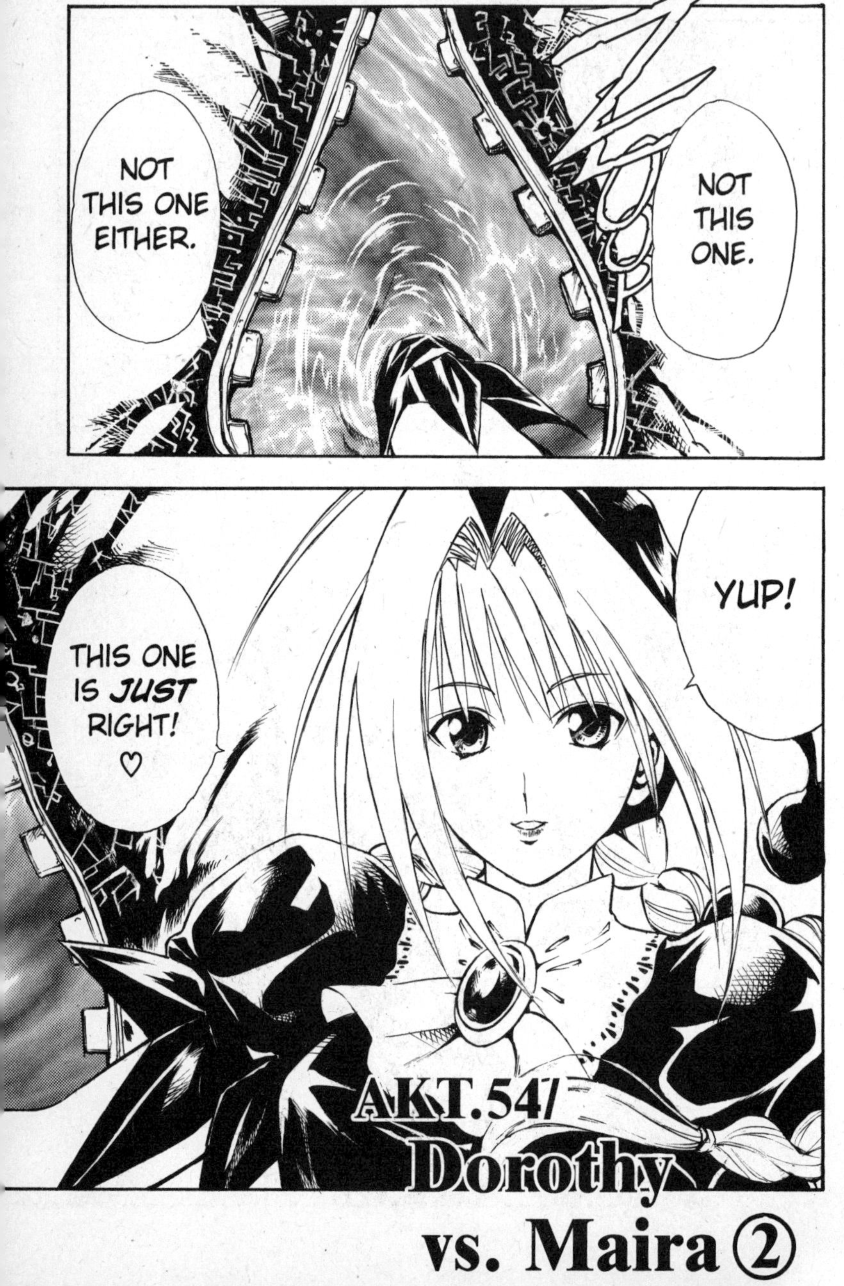
NOT THIS ONE.
NOT THIS ONE EITHER.
YUP!
THIS ONE IS *JUST* RIGHT! ♡

AKT.54/ Dorothy vs. Maira ②

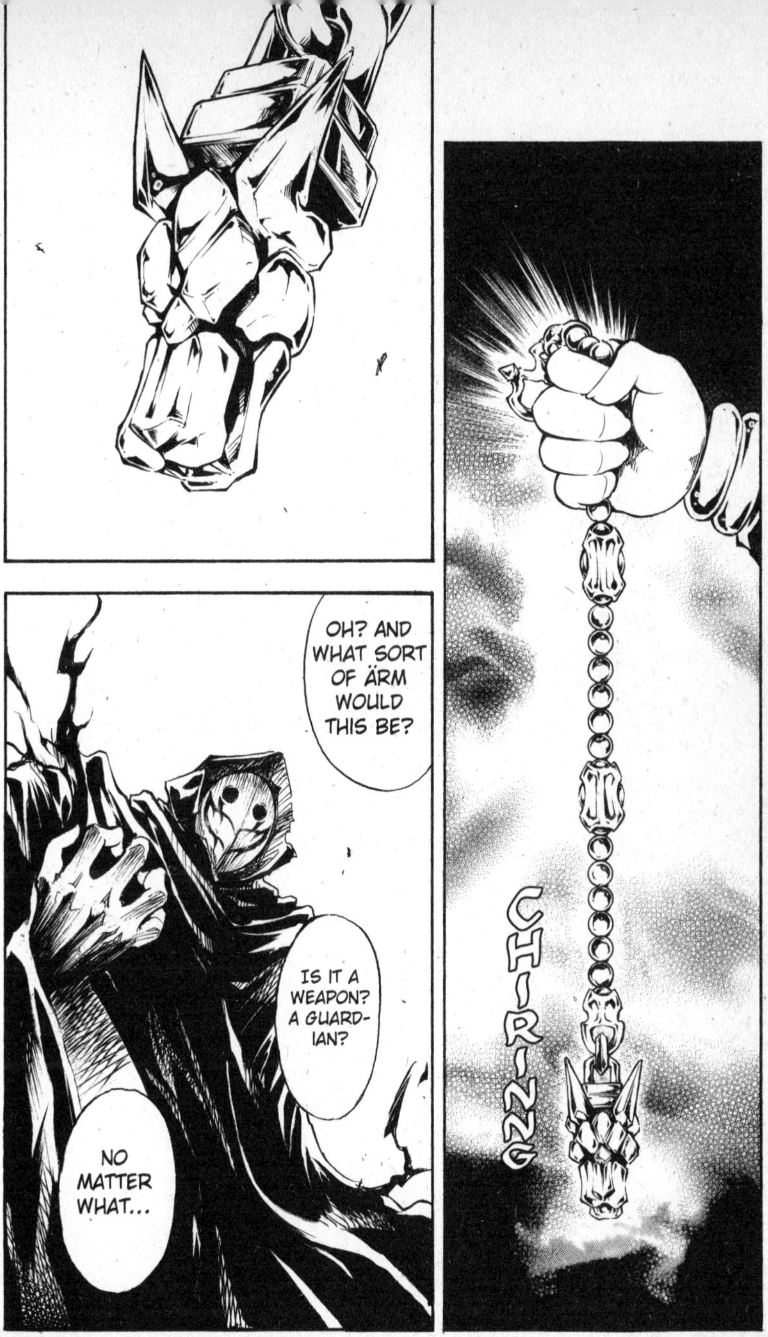
CHIRING
OH? AND WHAT SORT OF ÄRM WOULD THIS BE?
IS IT A WEAPON? A GUARDIAN?
NO MATTER WHAT...

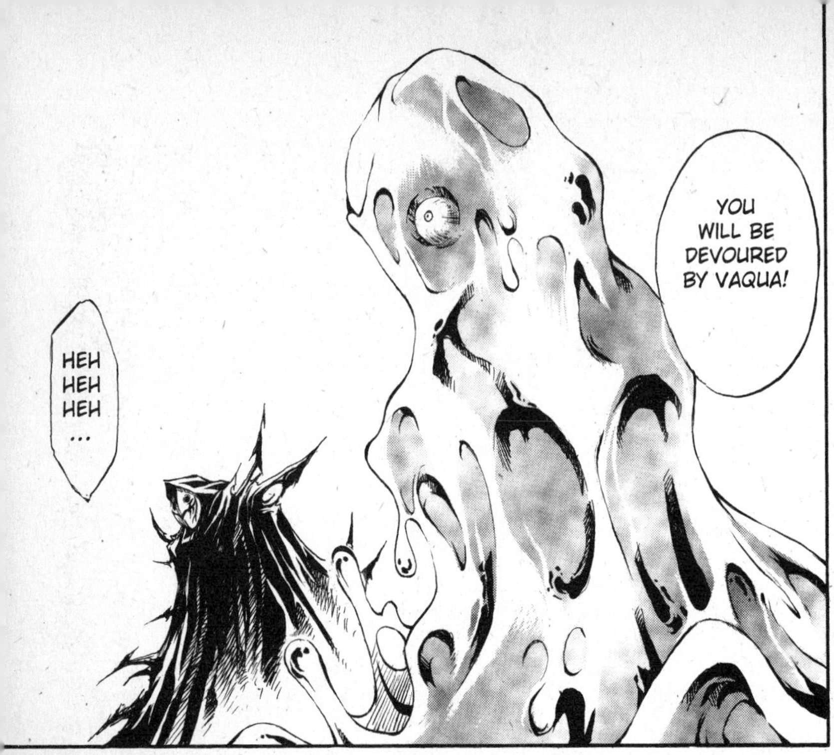
YOU WILL BE DEVOURED BY VAQUA!
HEH HEH HEH ...

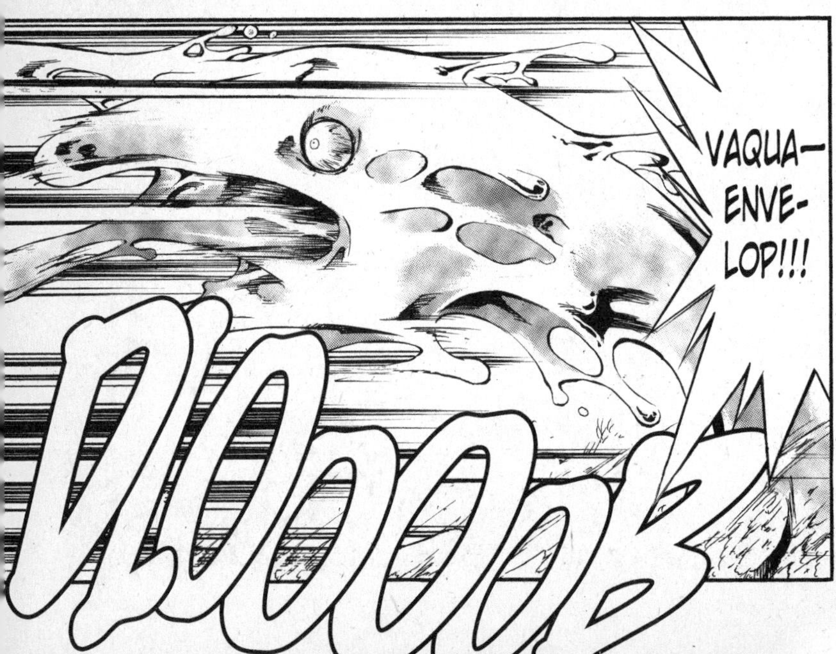
VAQUA-ENVELOP!!!

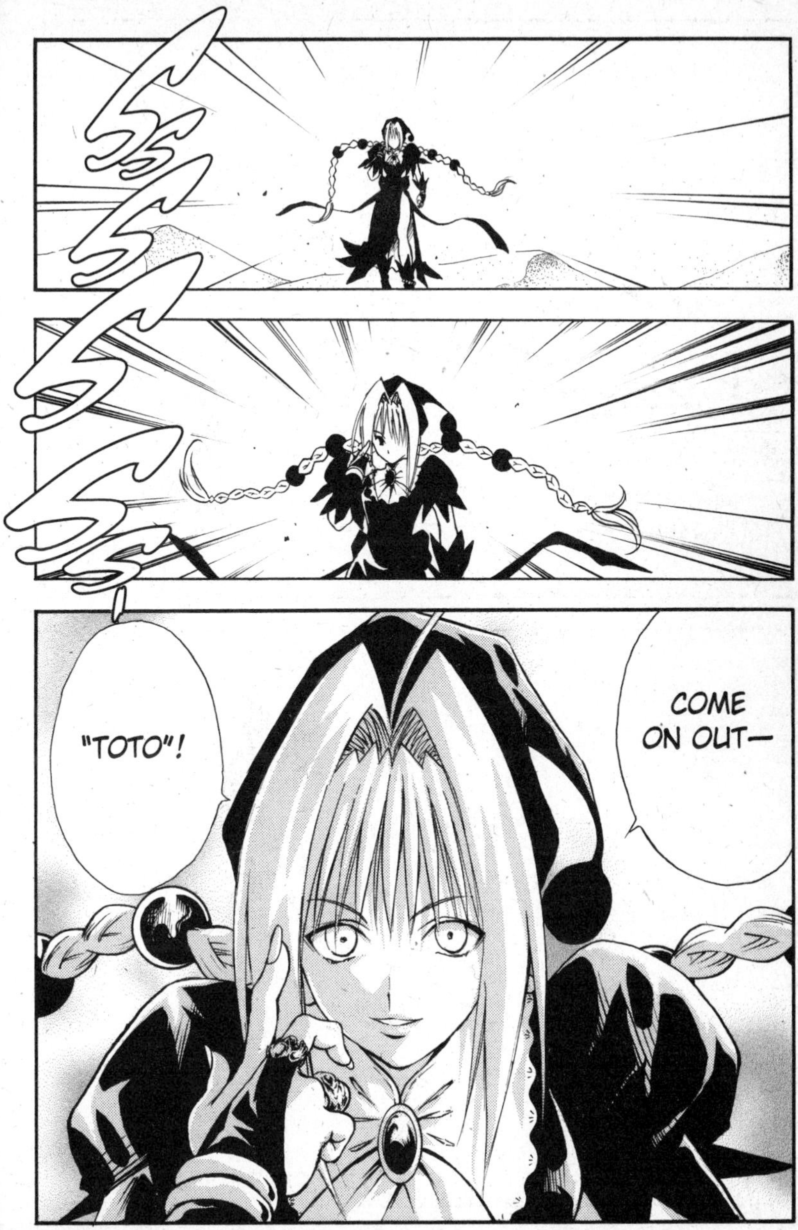
COME ON OUT—
"TOTO"!

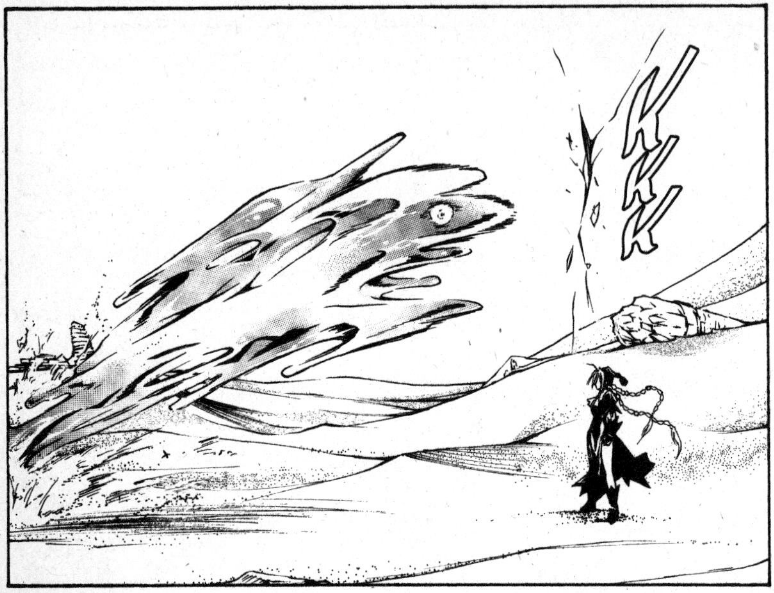

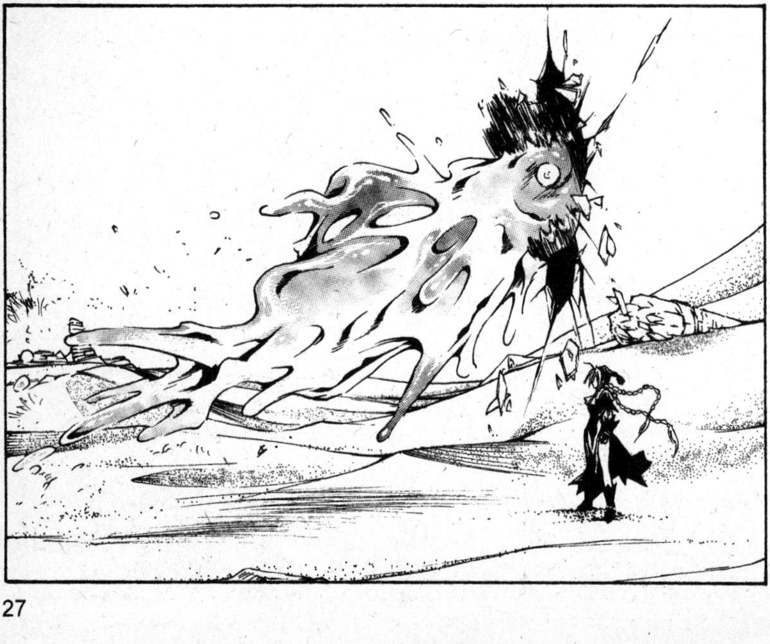

ZLOOP
?!!
KRUNCH
KRUNCH
ZLURP
GLUMP

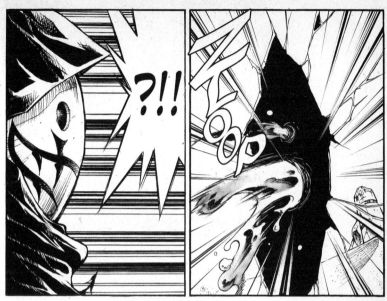

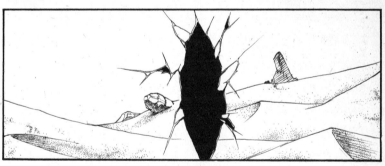

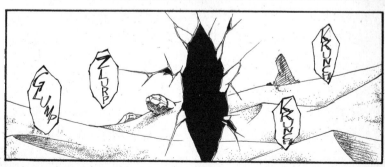

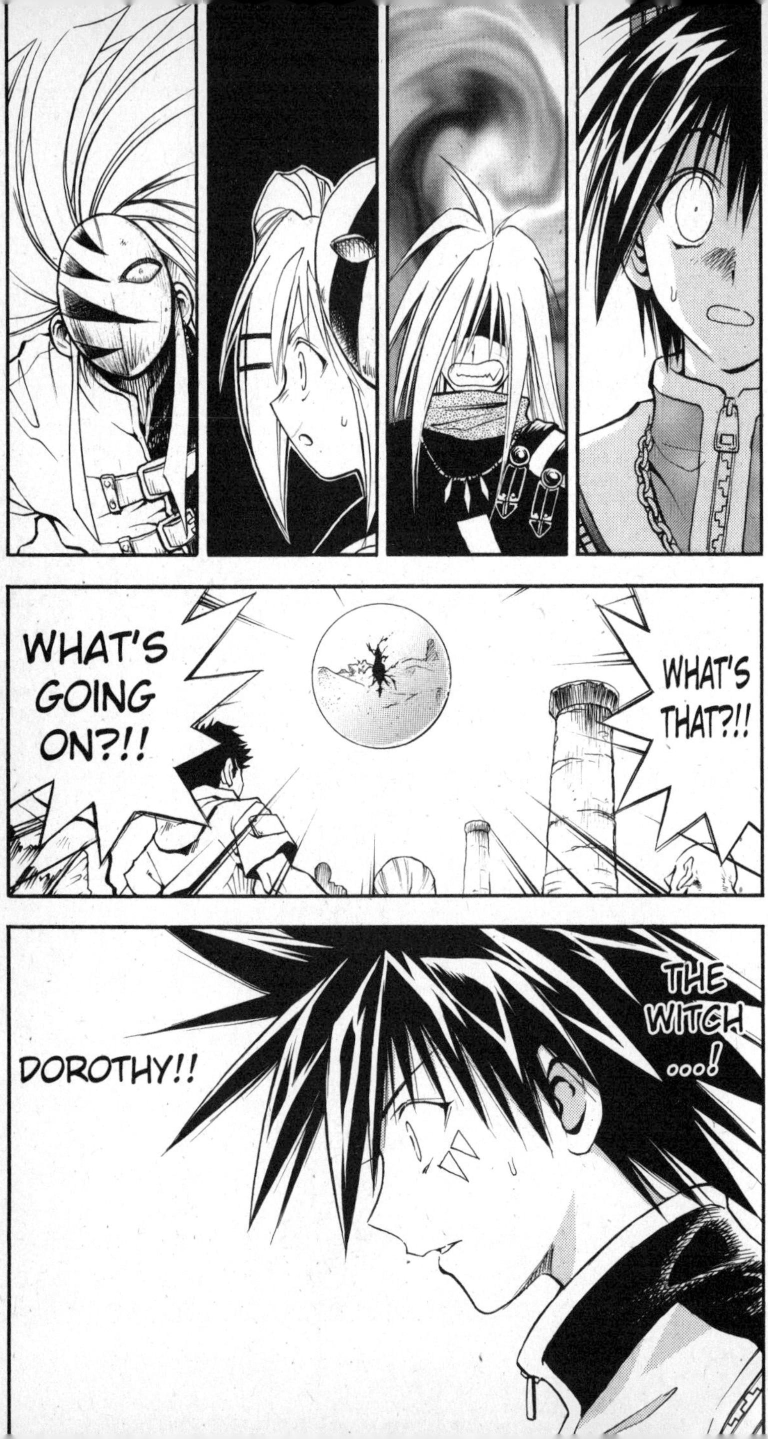
WHAT'S THAT?!!
WHAT'S GOING ON?!!
THE WITCH ...!
DOROTHY!!

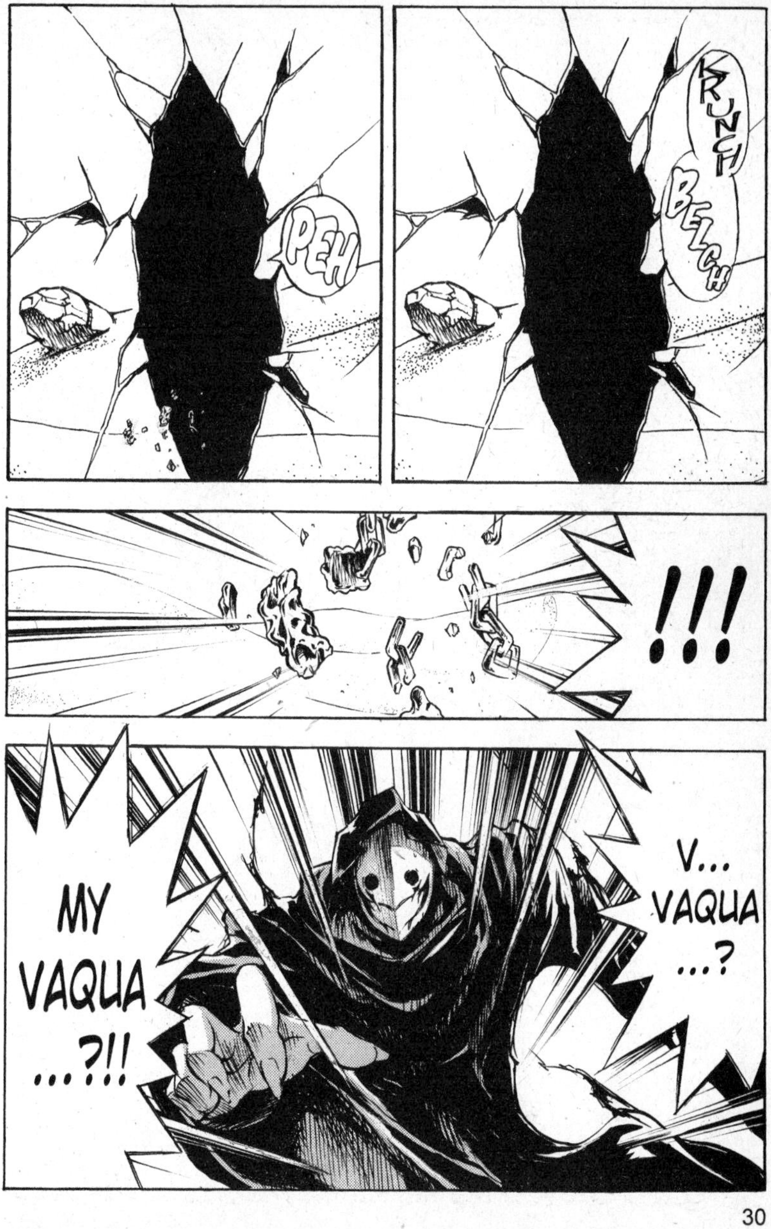
KRUNCH
BELCH
PEH
!!!
V... VAQUA ...?
MY VAQUA ...?!!

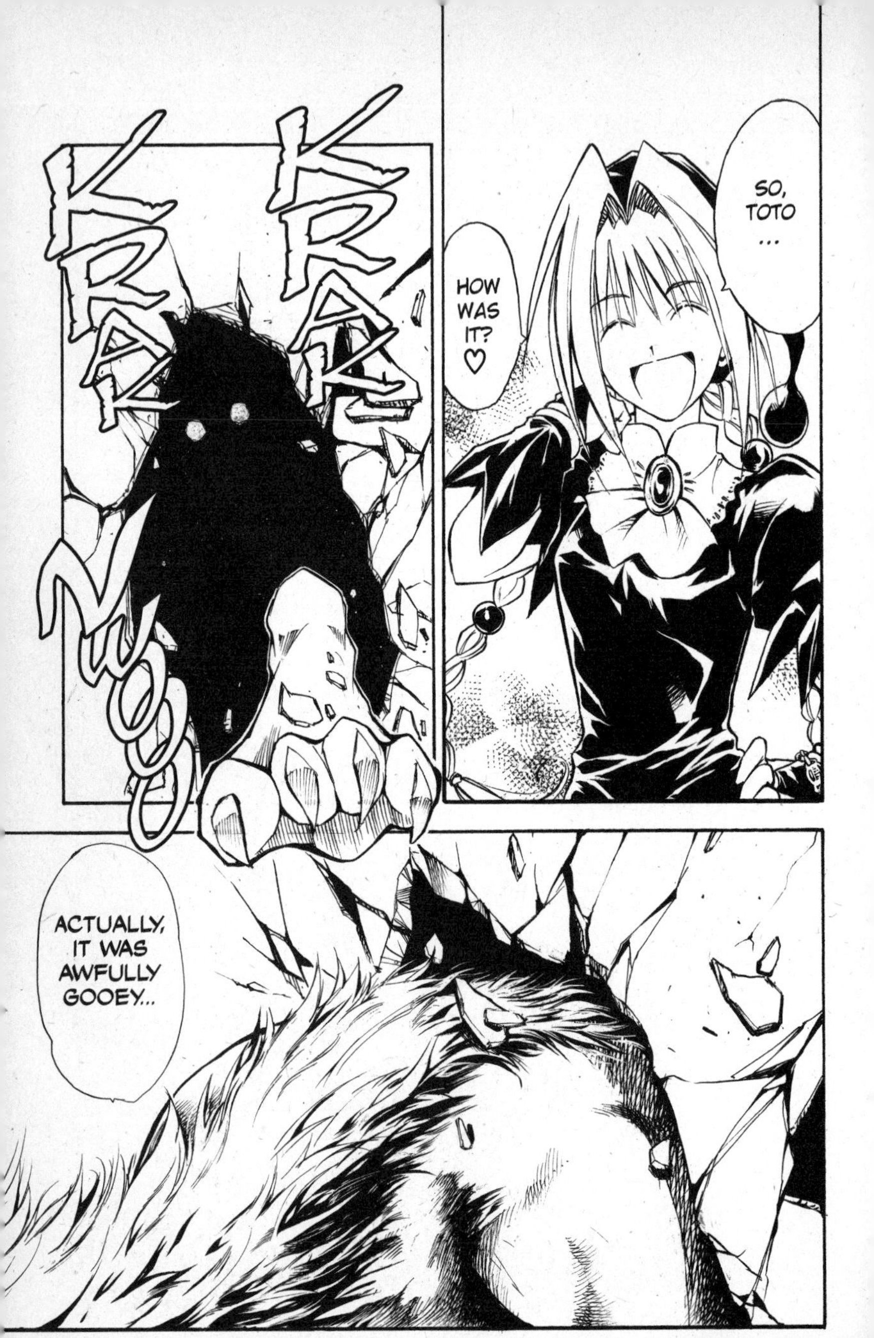
SO, TOTO ...
HOW WAS IT? ♡
KRAK
KRAK
ZWOOOO
ACTUALLY, IT WAS AWFULLY GOOEY...

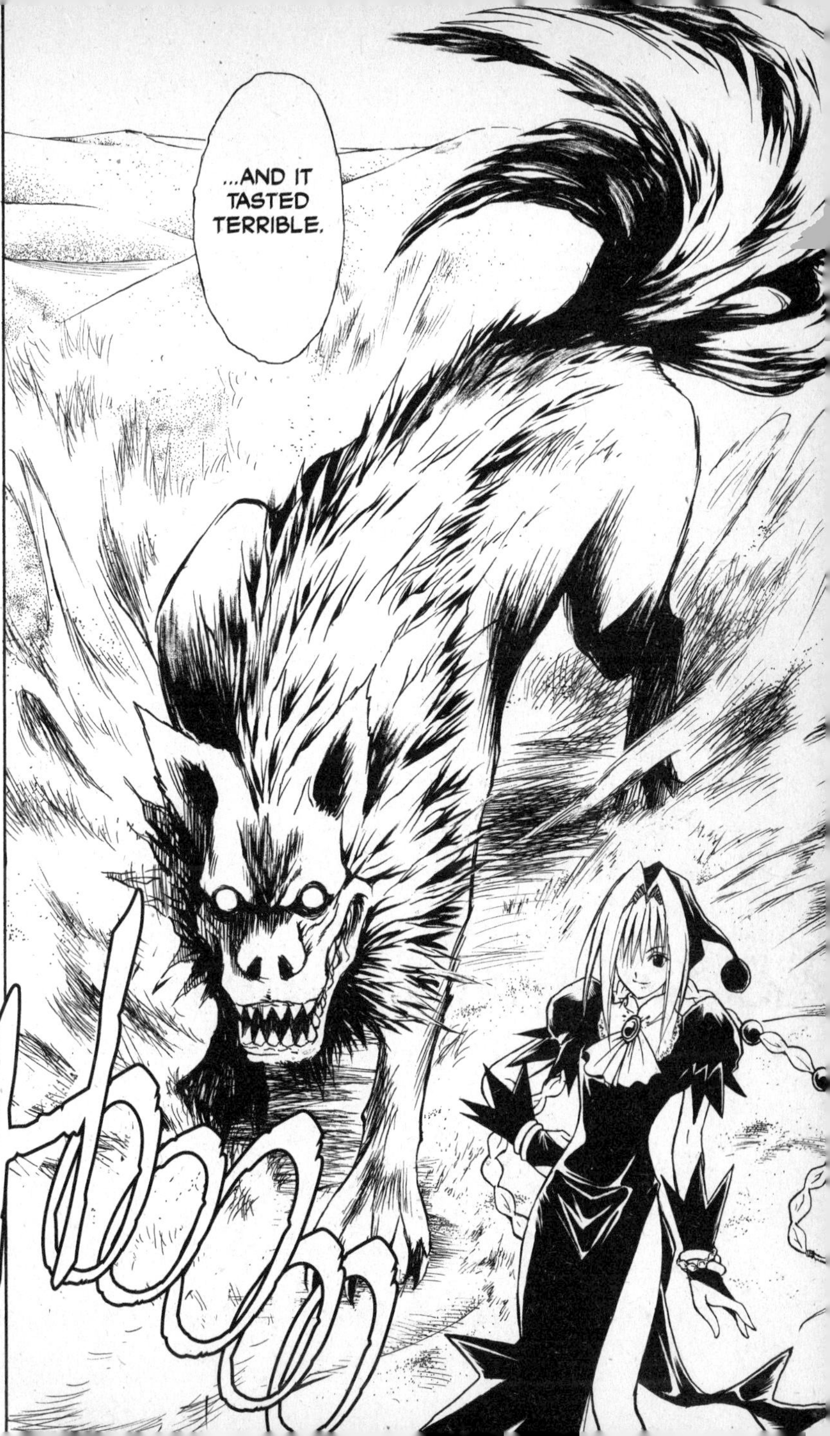
...AND IT TASTED TERRIBLE.
Fsooom

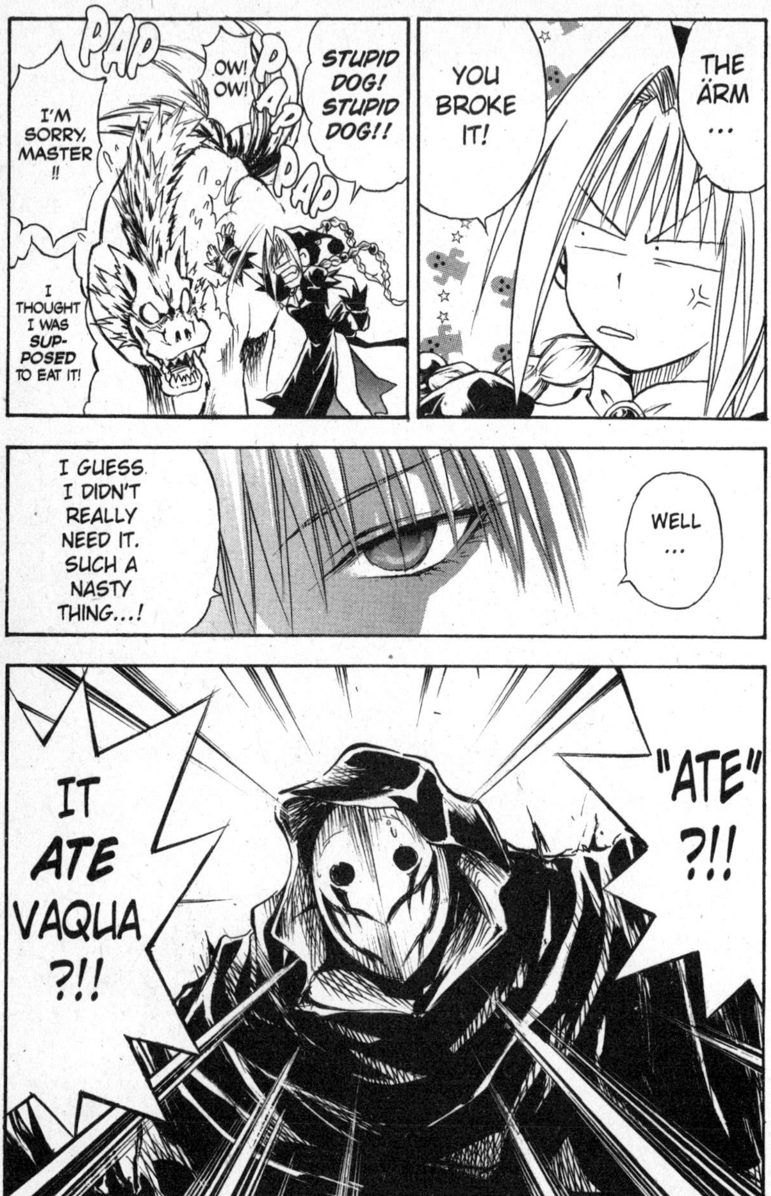
THE ÄRM...
YOU BROKE IT!
STUPID DOG! STUPID DOG!!
PAP PAP PAP PAP
OW! OW!
I'M SORRY, MASTER!!
I THOUGHT I WAS SUPPOSED TO EAT IT!
WELL...
I GUESS I DIDN'T REALLY NEED IT. SUCH A NASTY THING...!
"ATE"?!!
IT ATE VAQUA?!!

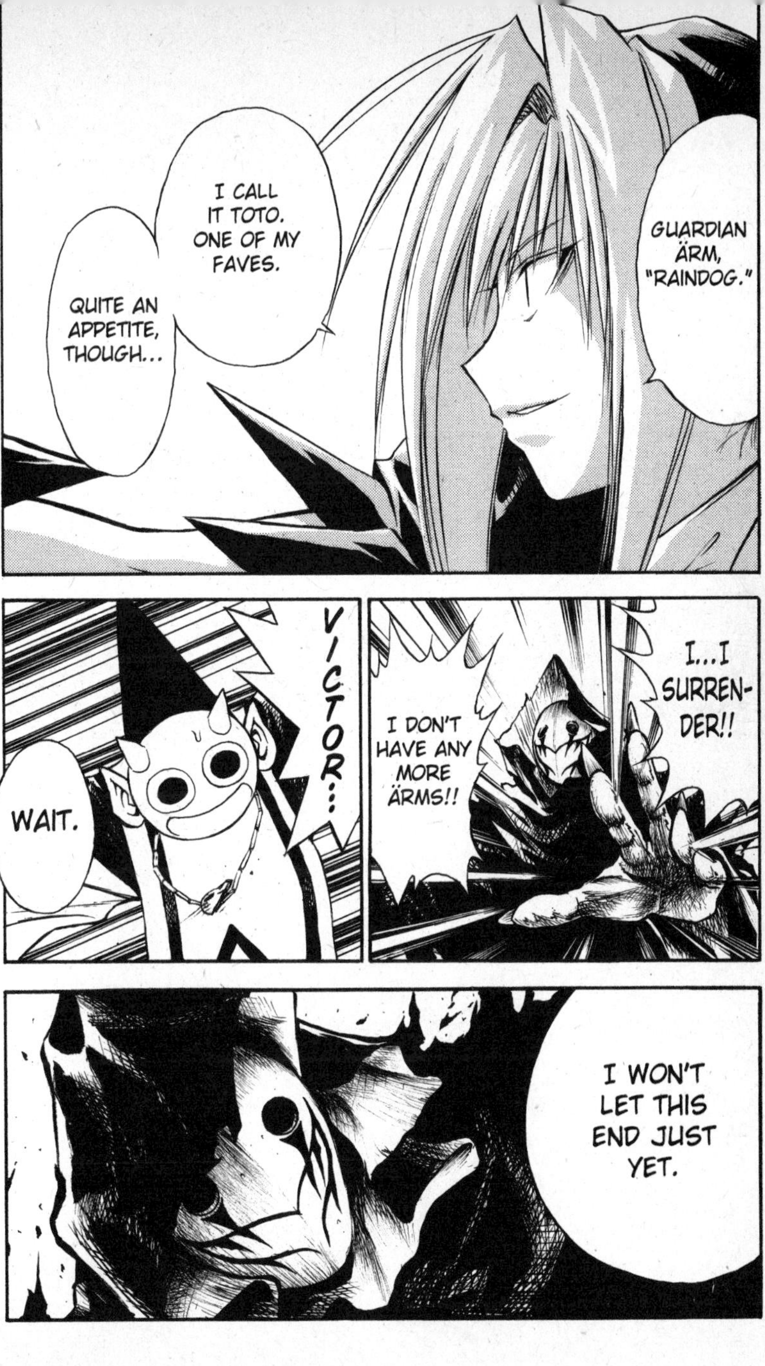
GUARDIAN ÄRM, "RAINDOG."
I CALL IT TOTO. ONE OF MY FAVES.
QUITE AN APPETITE, THOUGH...
I...I SURREN-DER!!
I DON'T HAVE ANY MORE ÄRMS!!
VICTOR...
WAIT.
I WON'T LET THIS END JUST YET.

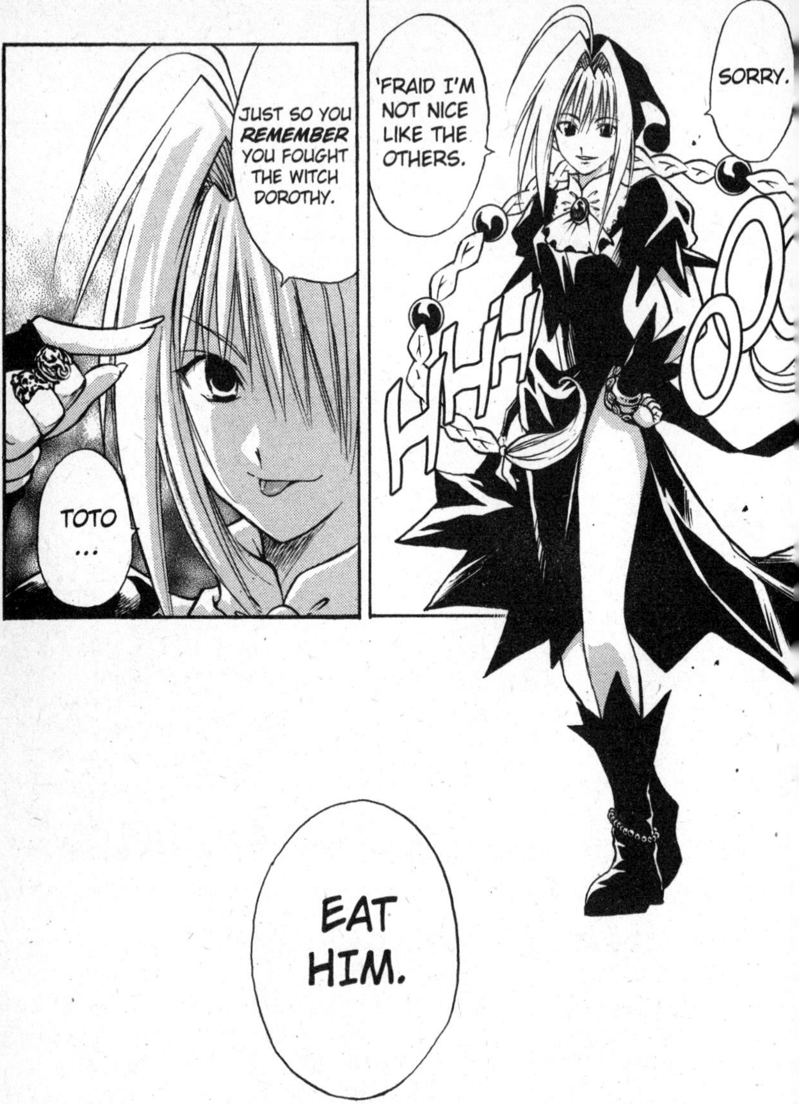
SORRY.
'FRAID I'M NOT NICE LIKE THE OTHERS.
JUST SO YOU **REMEMBER** YOU FOUGHT THE WITCH DOROTHY.
TOTO ...
EAT HIM.

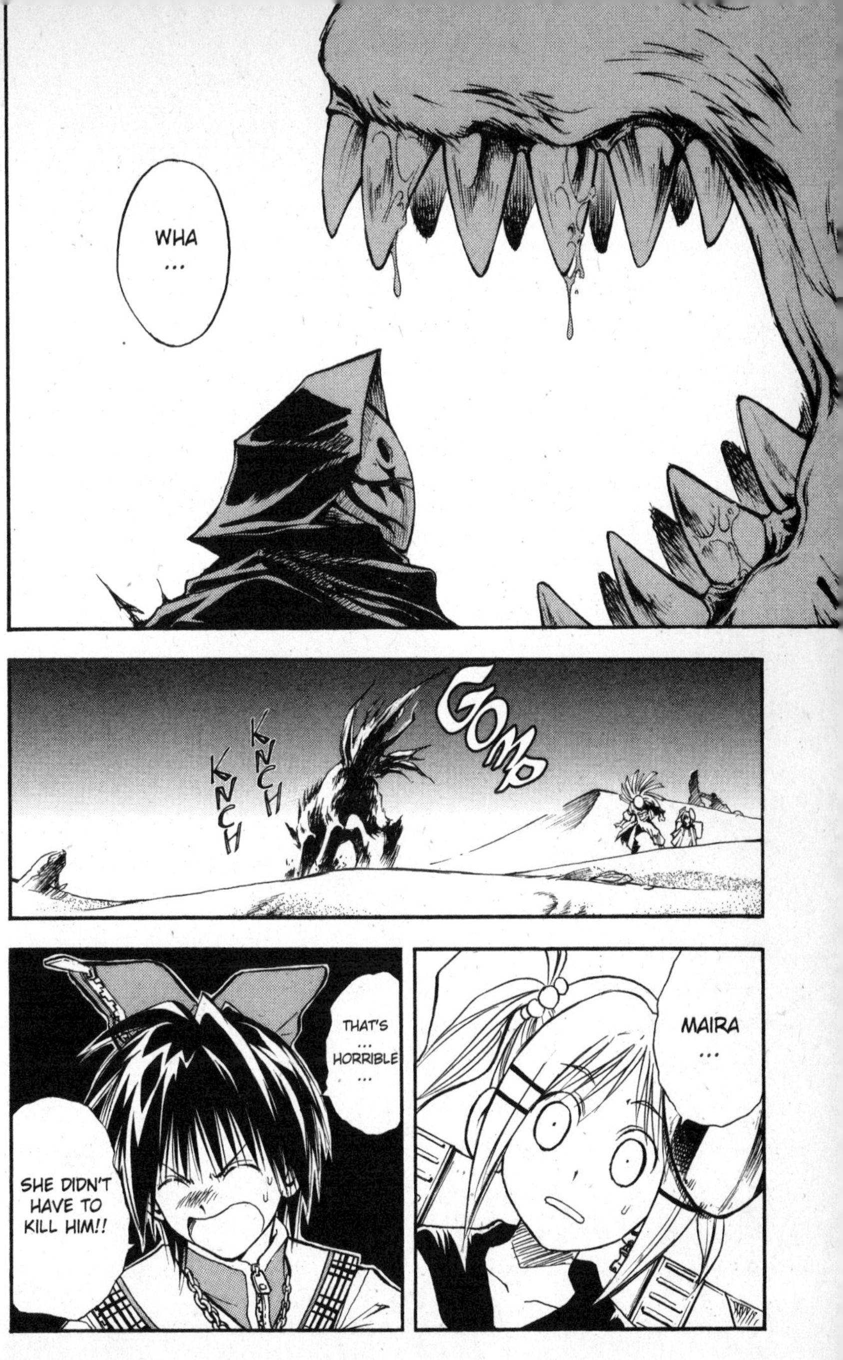
WHA ...
GOMP
KNCH
KNCH
MAIRA ...
THAT'S ... HORRIBLE ...
SHE DIDN'T HAVE TO KILL HIM!!

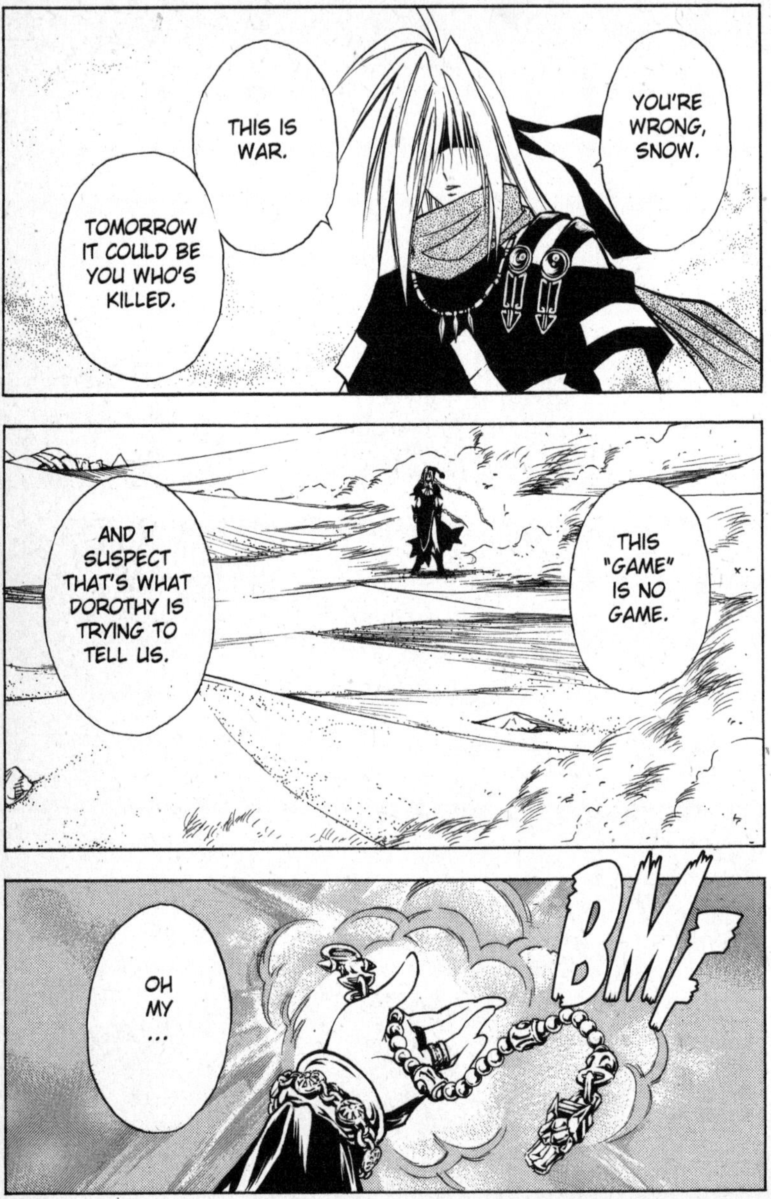
YOU'RE WRONG, SNOW.
THIS IS WAR.
TOMORROW IT COULD BE YOU WHO'S KILLED.
THIS "GAME" IS NO GAME.
AND I SUSPECT THAT'S WHAT DOROTHY IS TRYING TO TELL US.
BMF
OH MY ...

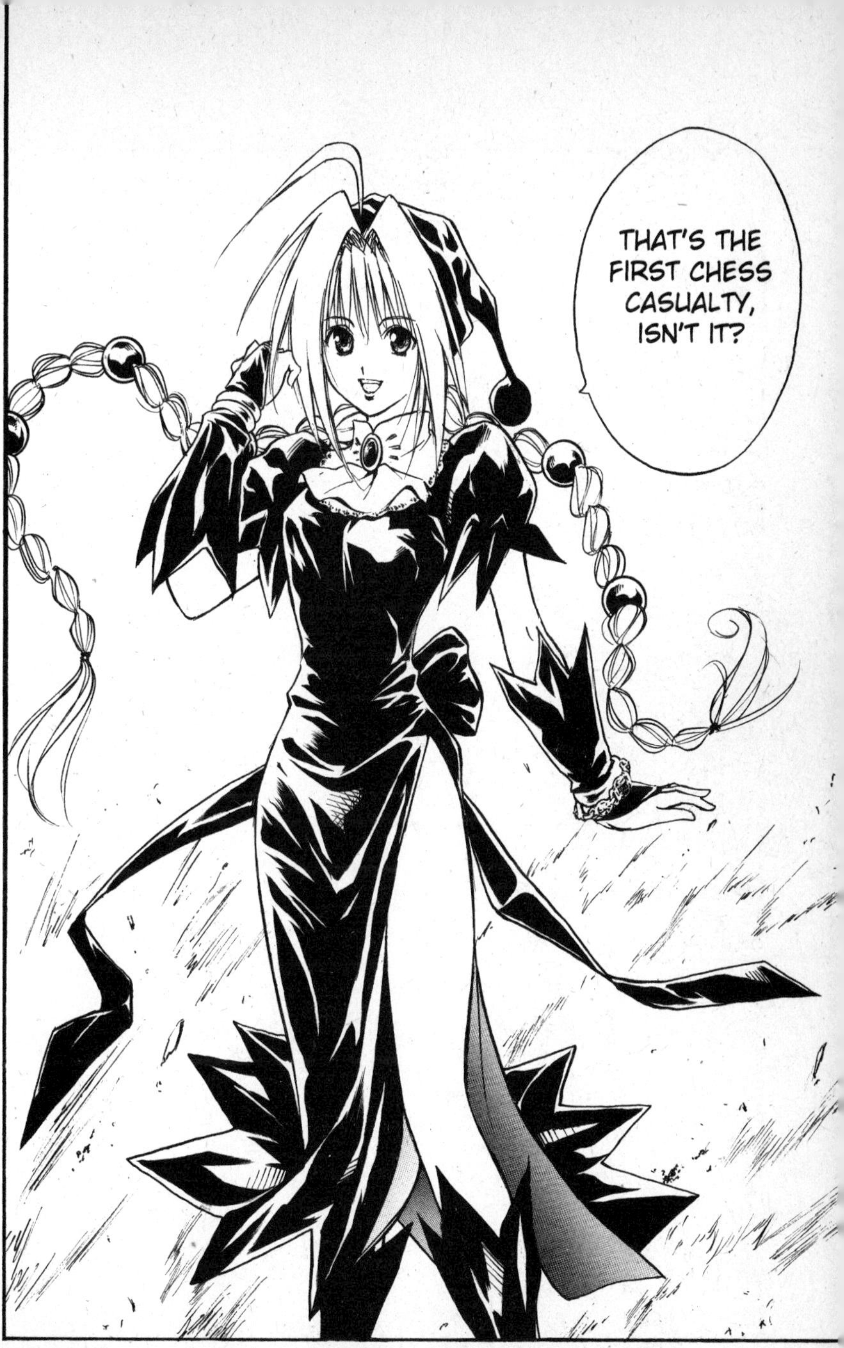
THAT'S THE FIRST CHESS CASUALTY, ISN'T IT?

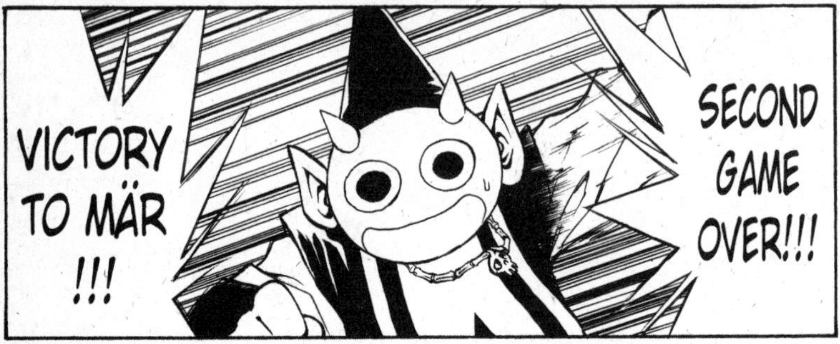
SECOND GAME OVER!!!
VICTORY TO MÄR !!!

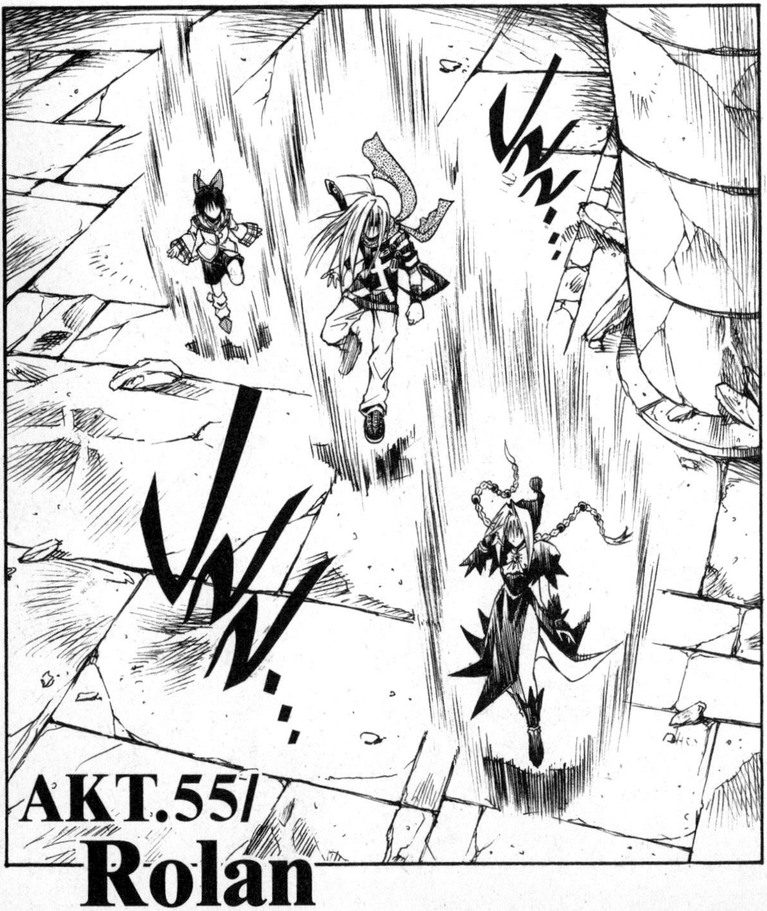

AKT.55/ Rolan

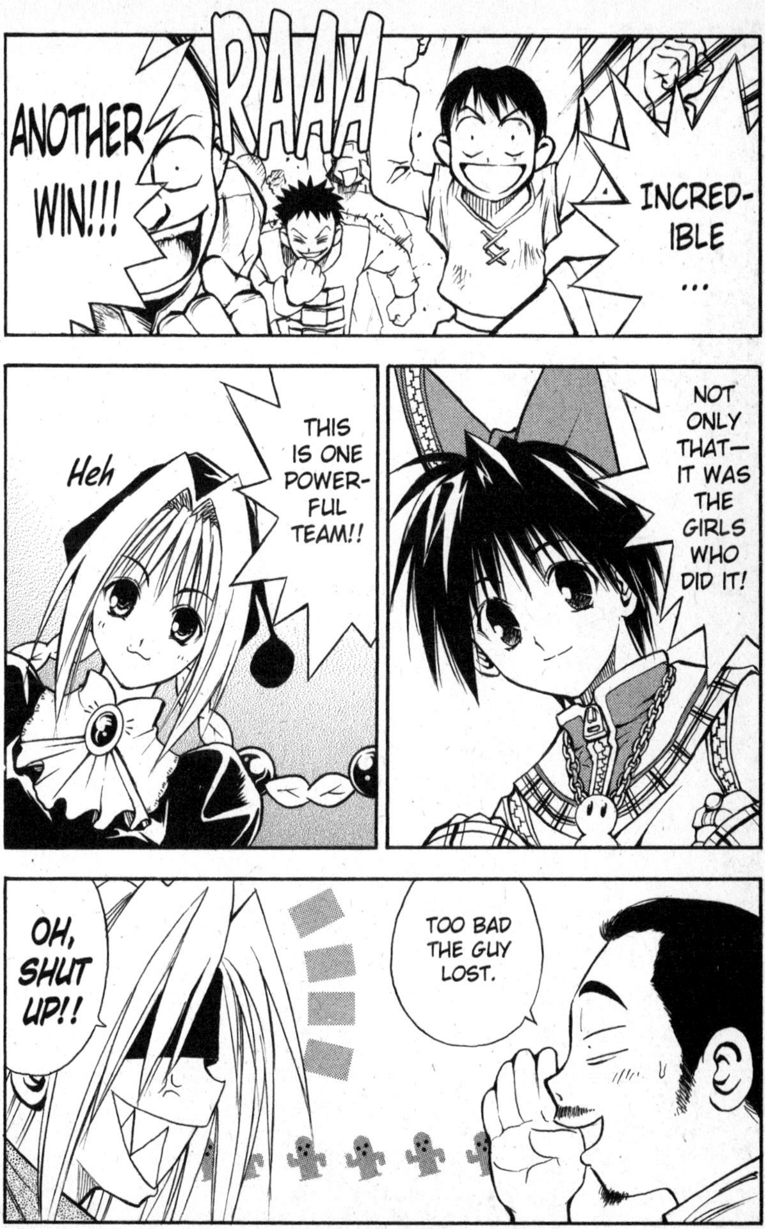
ANOTHER WIN!!!
RAAA
INCRED-IBLE ...
Heh
THIS IS ONE POWER-FUL TEAM!!
NOT ONLY THAT— IT WAS THE GIRLS WHO DID IT!
TOO BAD THE GUY LOST.
OH, SHUT UP!!

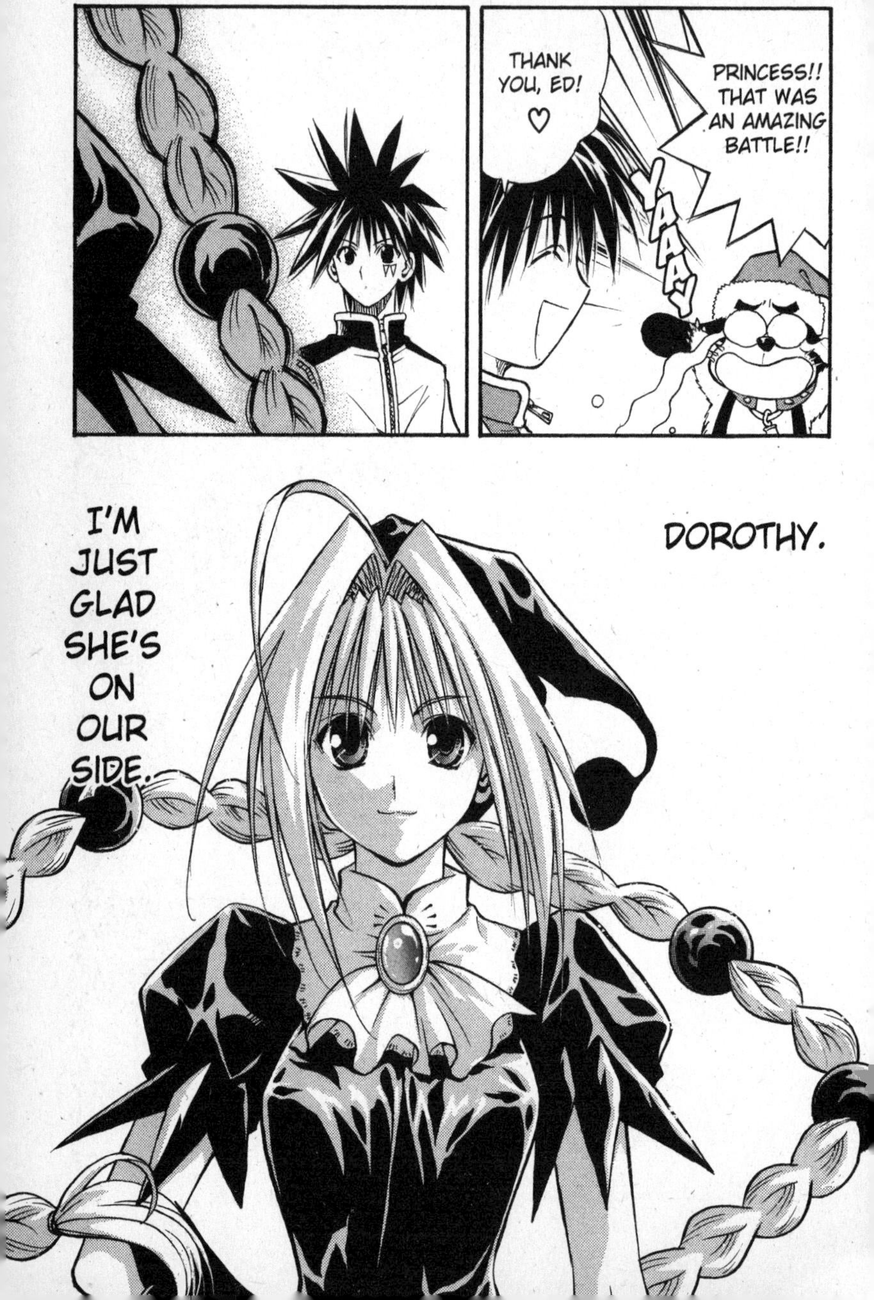
PRINCESS!! THAT WAS AN AMAZING BATTLE!!
THANK YOU, ED! ♡
YAAAY
DOROTHY.
I'M JUST GLAD SHE'S ON OUR SIDE.

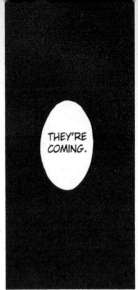

THEY'RE COMING.

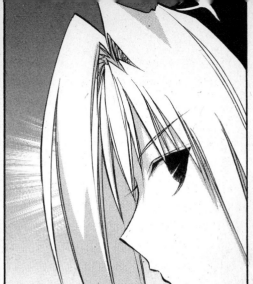

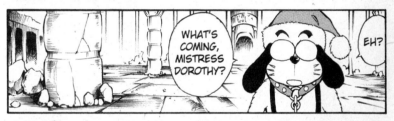

WHAT'S COMING, MISTRESS DOROTHY?

EH?

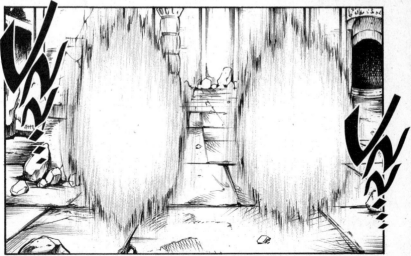

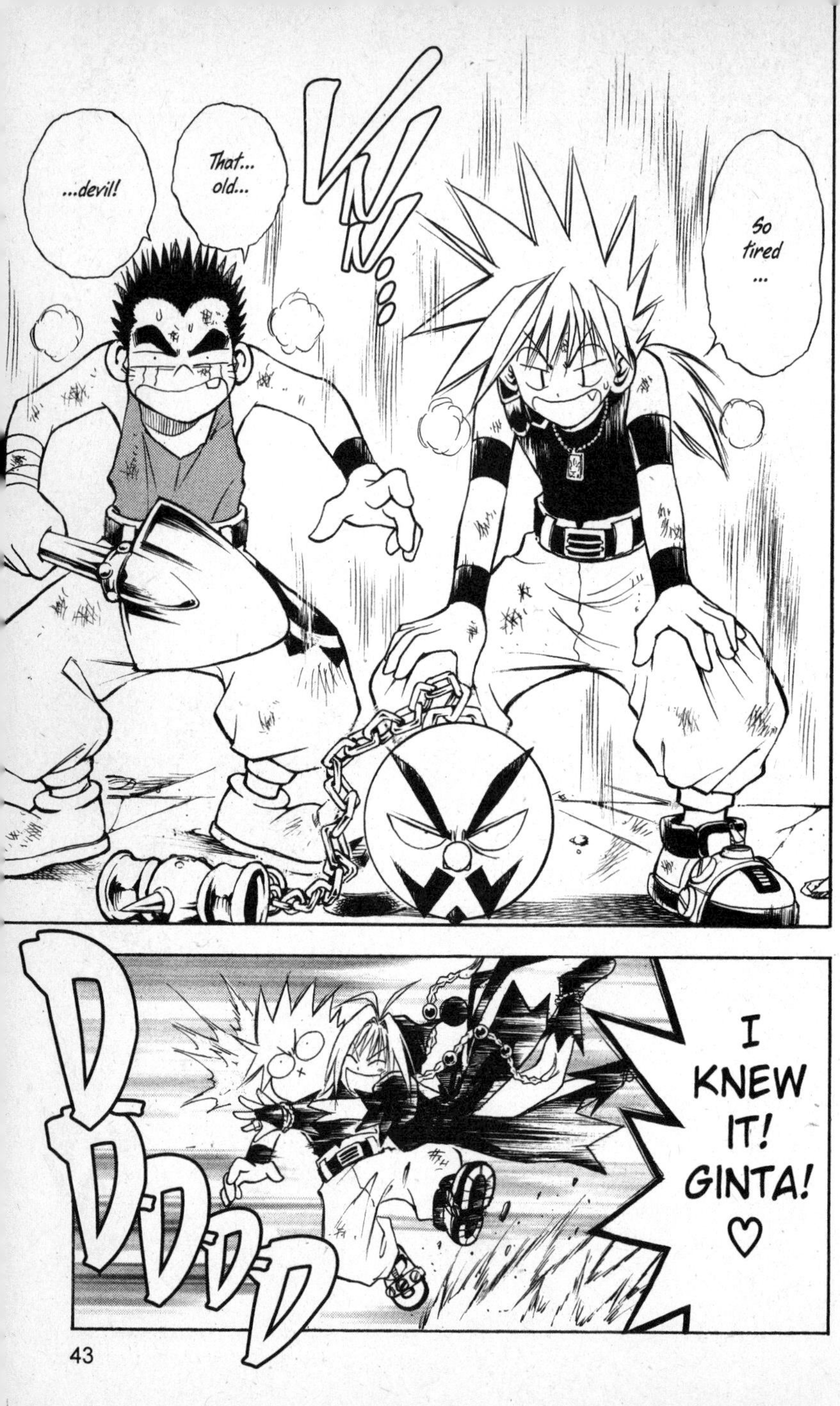
So tired ...
That... old...
...devil!
I KNEW IT! GINTA! ♡

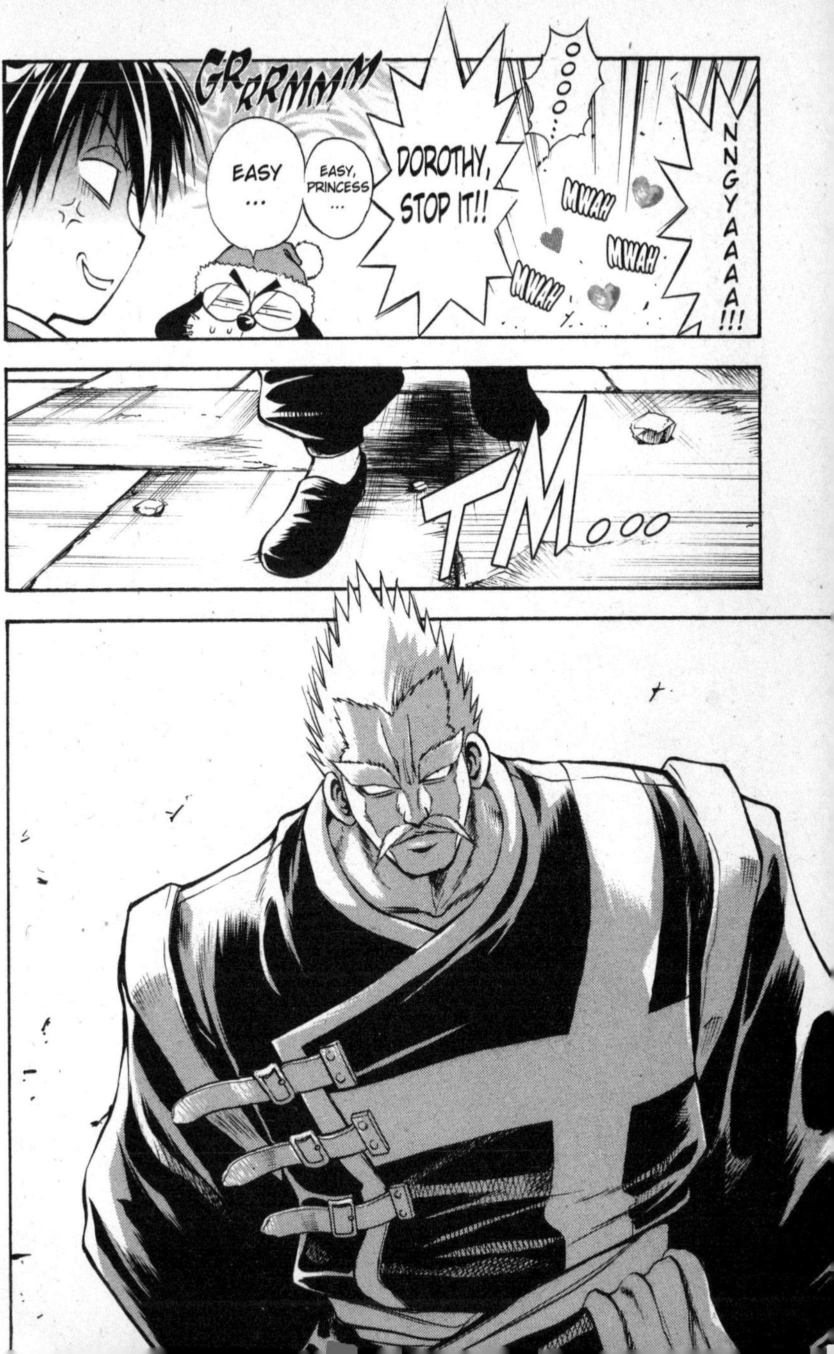
NNGYAAAAA!!!
MWAH
MWAH
MWAH
OOOO...
DOROTHY, STOP IT!!
EASY, PRINCESS...
EASY...
GRRRMMM
TMOOO

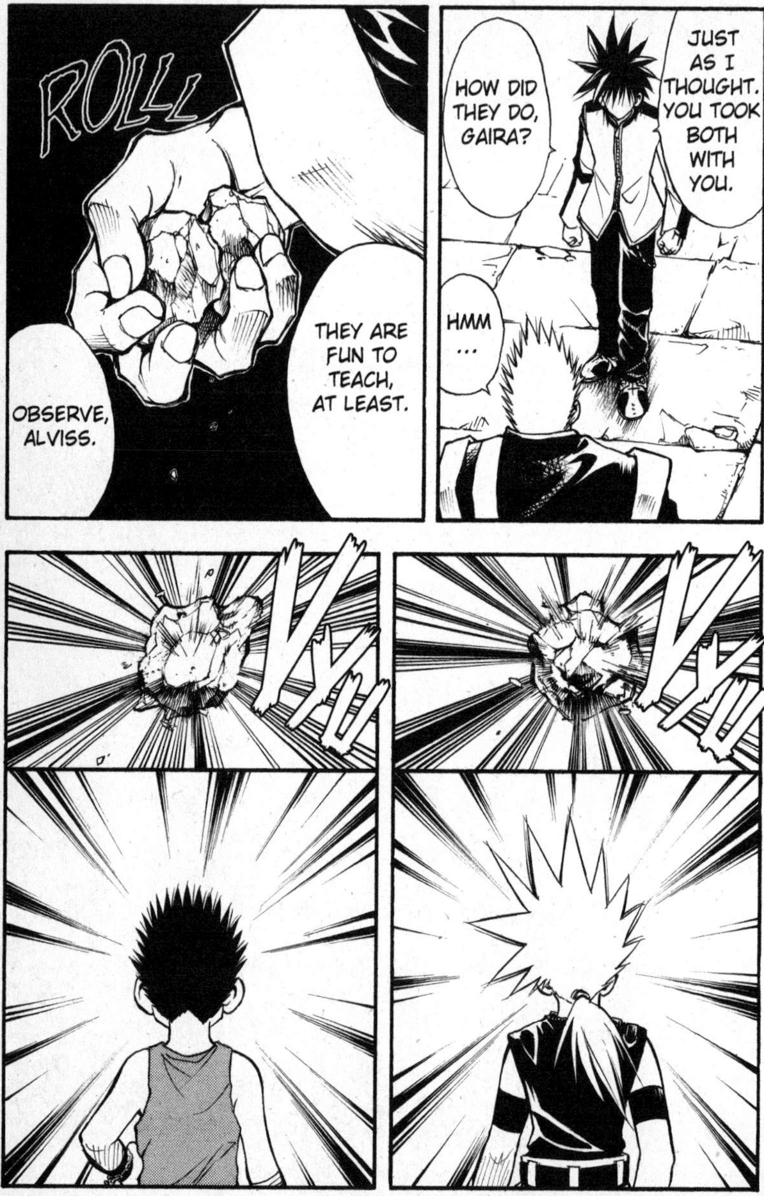
JUST AS I THOUGHT. YOU TOOK BOTH WITH YOU.
HOW DID THEY DO, GAIRA?
HMM ...
ROLL
THEY ARE FUN TO TEACH, AT LEAST.
OBSERVE, ALVISS.
VYU
VYU

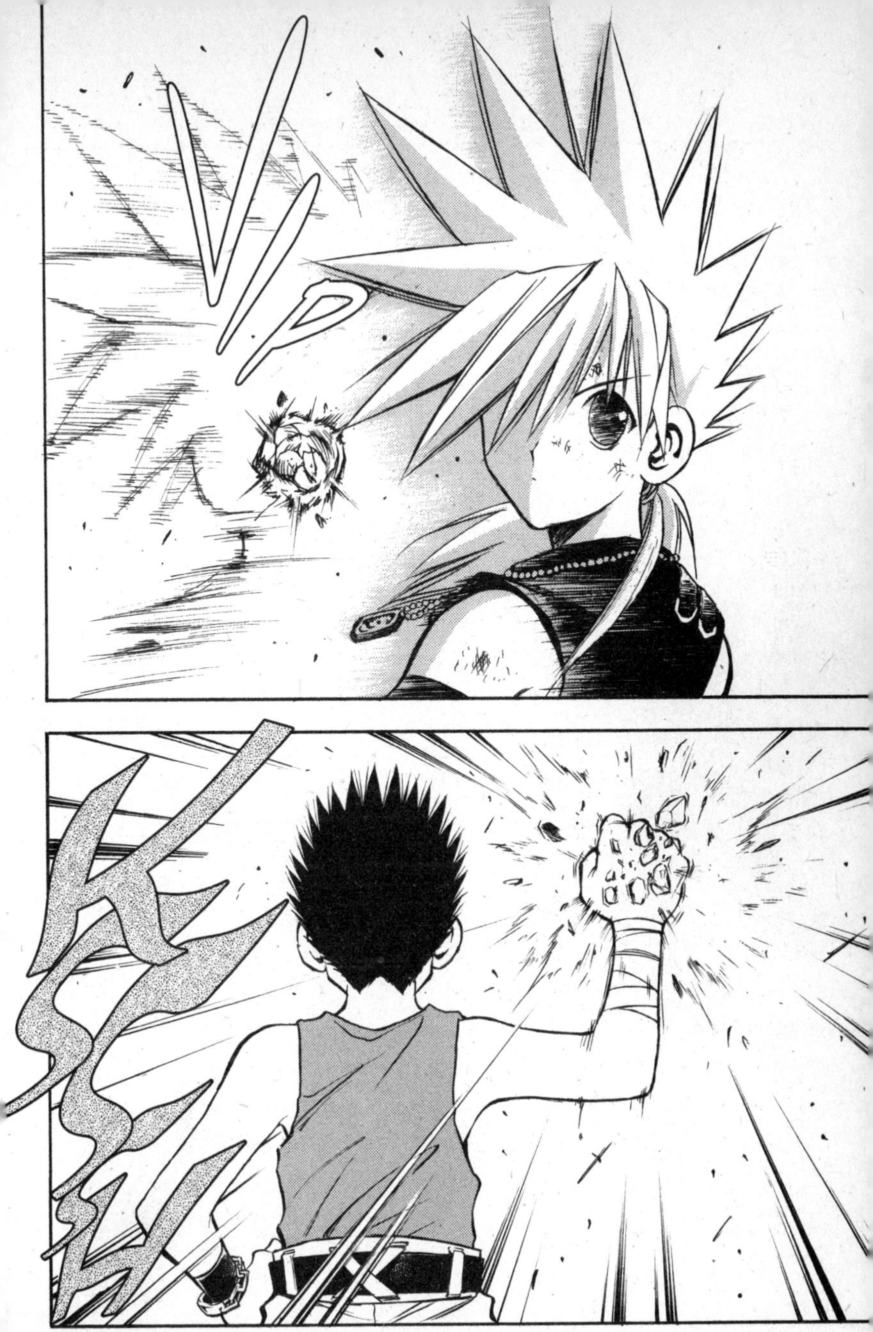
VIP
KSSH

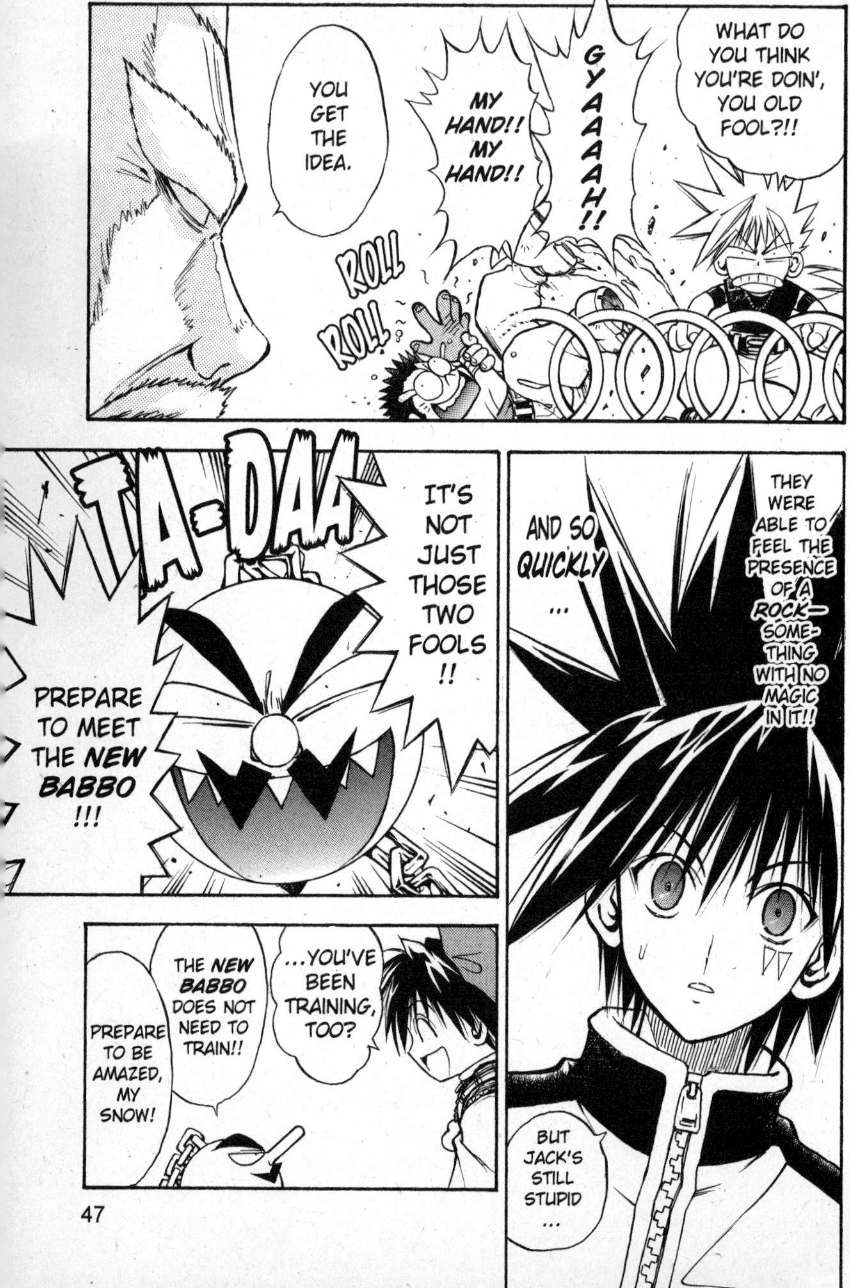
WHAT DO YOU THINK YOU'RE DOIN', YOU OLD FOOL?!!
GYAAAAAH!!
MY HAND!! MY HAND!!
ROLL ROLL
YOU GET THE IDEA.
THEY WERE ABLE TO FEEL THE PRESENCE OF A ROCK— SOMETHING WITH NO MAGIC IN IT!!
AND SO QUICKLY...
BUT JACK'S STILL STUPID...
IT'S NOT JUST THOSE TWO FOOLS!!
TA-DAA
PREPARE TO MEET THE NEW BABBO!!!
...YOU'VE BEEN TRAINING, TOO?
THE NEW BABBO DOES NOT NEED TO TRAIN!!
PREPARE TO BE AMAZED, MY SNOW!

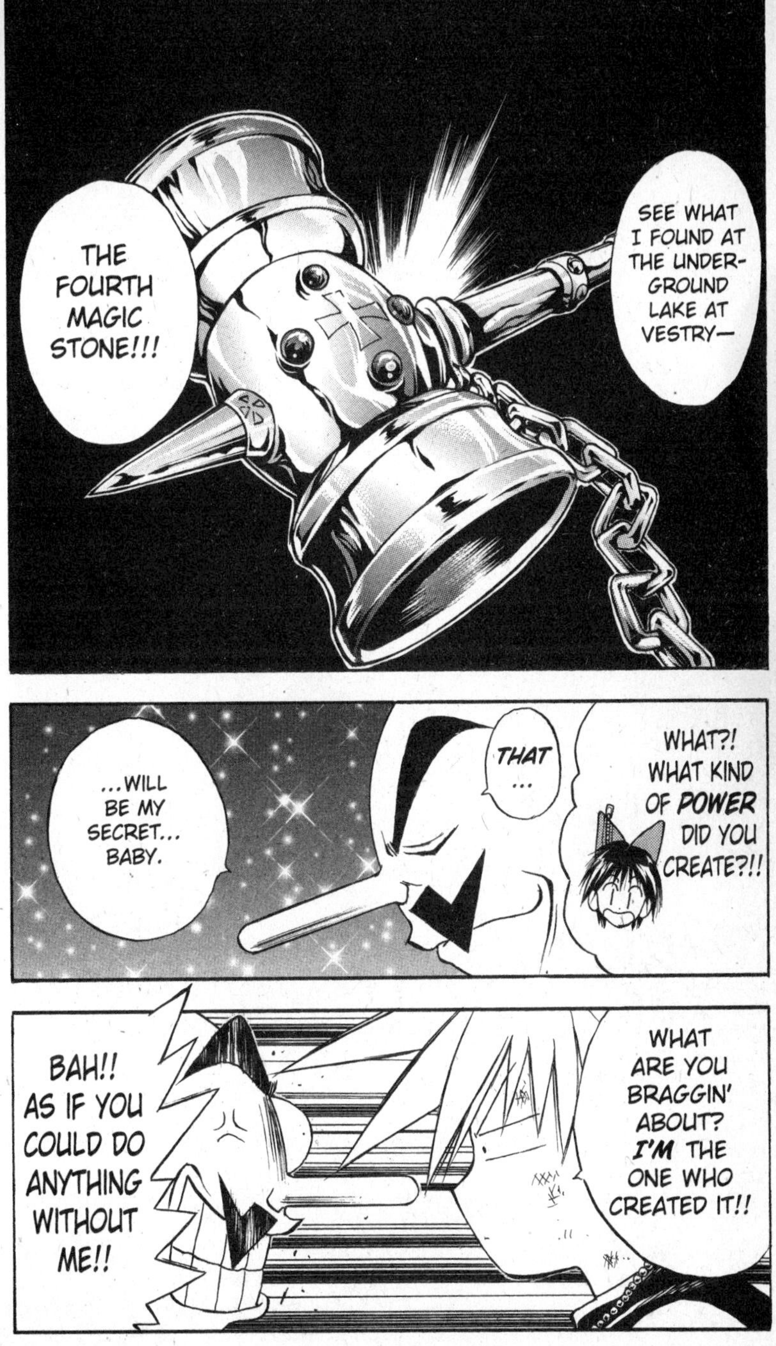
SEE WHAT I FOUND AT THE UNDER-GROUND LAKE AT VESTRY—
THE FOURTH MAGIC STONE!!!
WHAT?! WHAT KIND OF **POWER** DID YOU CREATE?!!
THAT ...
...WILL BE MY SECRET... BABY.
WHAT ARE YOU BRAGGIN' ABOUT? ***I'M*** THE ONE WHO CREATED IT!!
BAH!! AS IF YOU COULD DO ANYTHING WITHOUT ME!!

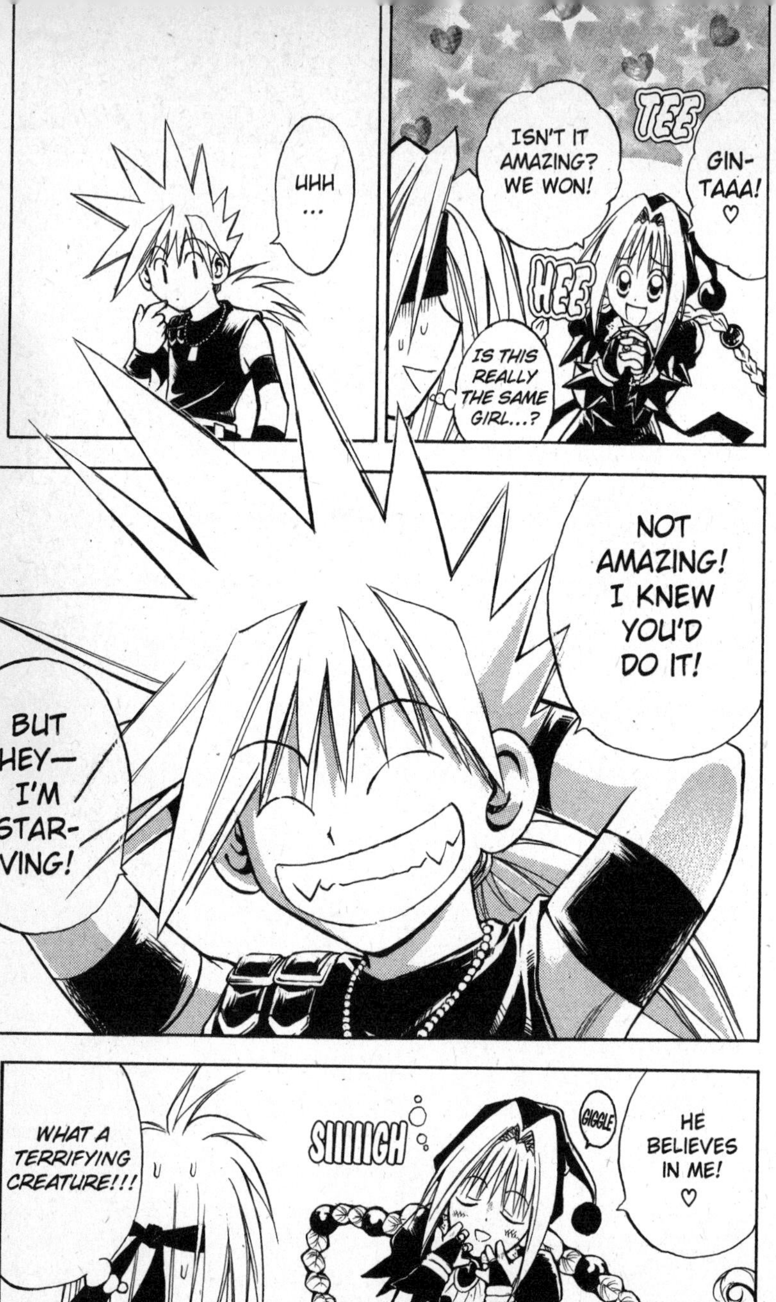
GIN-TAAA! ♡
TEE
ISN'T IT AMAZING? WE WON!
HEE
IS THIS REALLY THE SAME GIRL...?
UHH ...
NOT AMAZING! I KNEW YOU'D DO IT!
BUT HEY— I'M STAR-VING!
HE BELIEVES IN ME! ♡
GIGGLE
SIIIIIGH
WHAT A TERRIFYING CREATURE!!!

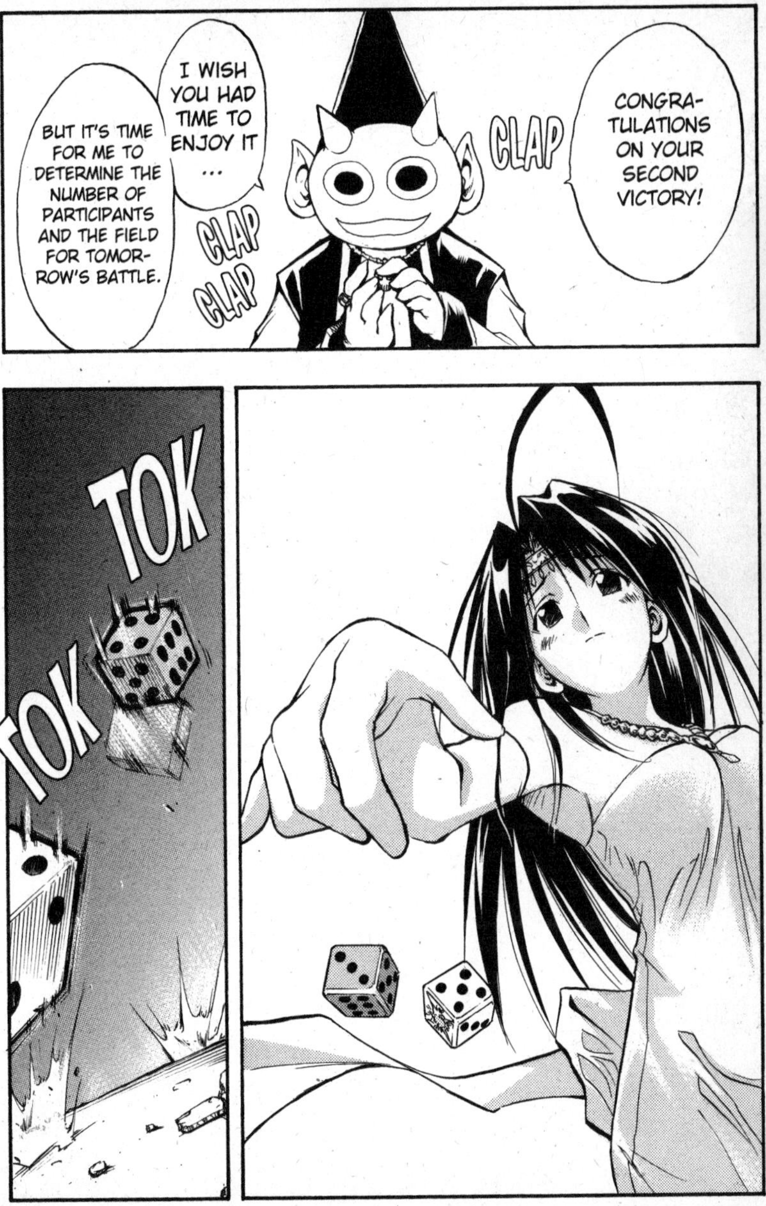
CONGRATULATIONS ON YOUR SECOND VICTORY!
CLAP
CLAP CLAP
I WISH YOU HAD TIME TO ENJOY IT ...
BUT IT'S TIME FOR ME TO DETERMINE THE NUMBER OF PARTICIPANTS AND THE FIELD FOR TOMORROW'S BATTLE.
TOK TOK

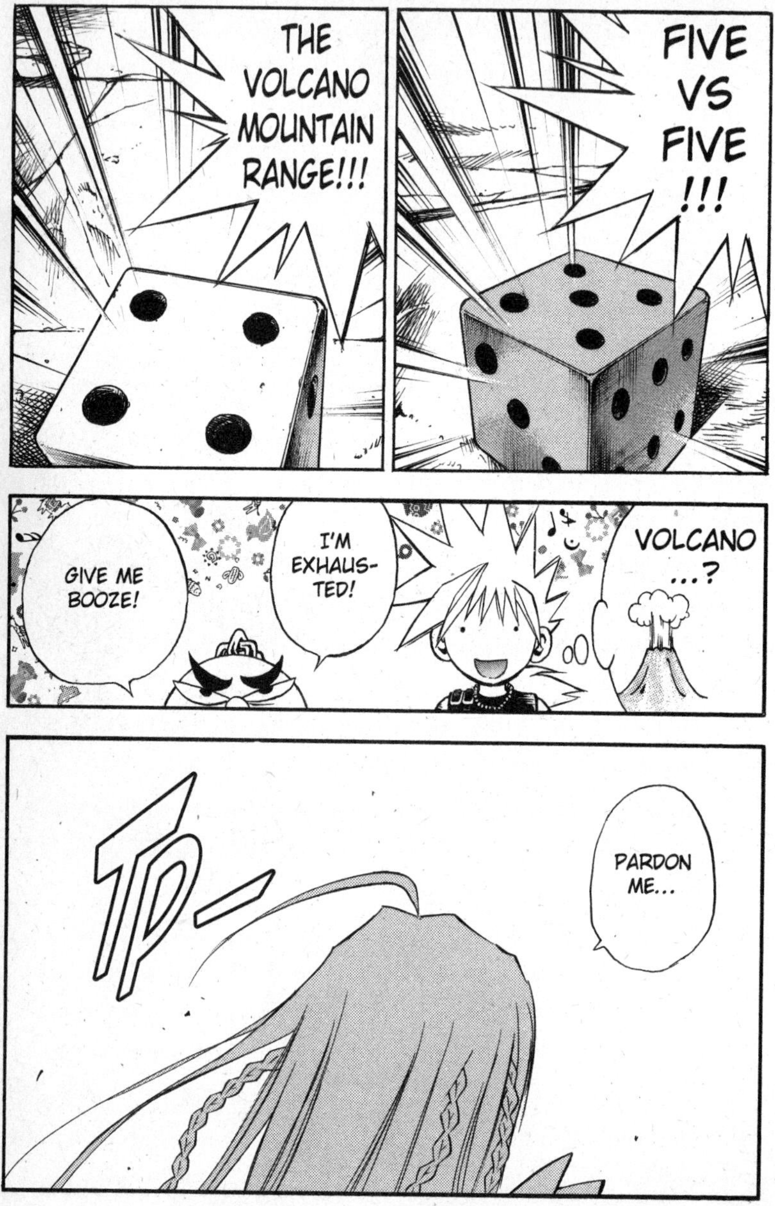
FIVE VS FIVE!!!
THE VOLCANO MOUNTAIN RANGE!!!
VOLCANO ...?
I'M EXHAUS-TED!
GIVE ME BOOZE!
PARDON ME...
Tp–

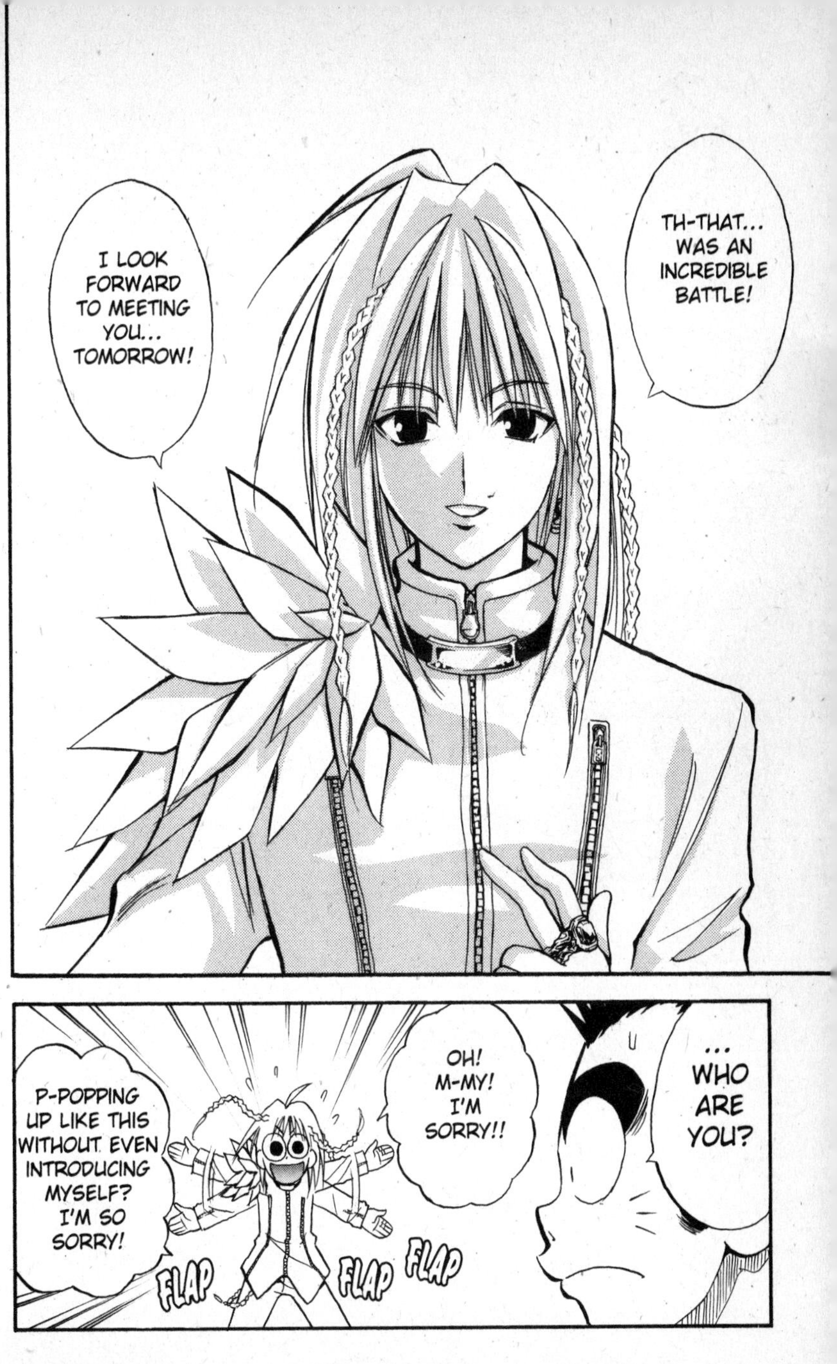
TH-THAT... WAS AN INCREDIBLE BATTLE!
I LOOK FORWARD TO MEETING YOU... TOMORROW!
... WHO ARE YOU?
OH! M-MY! I'M SORRY!!
FLAP
FLAP
FLAP
P-POPPING UP LIKE THIS WITHOUT EVEN INTRODUCING MYSELF? I'M SO SORRY!

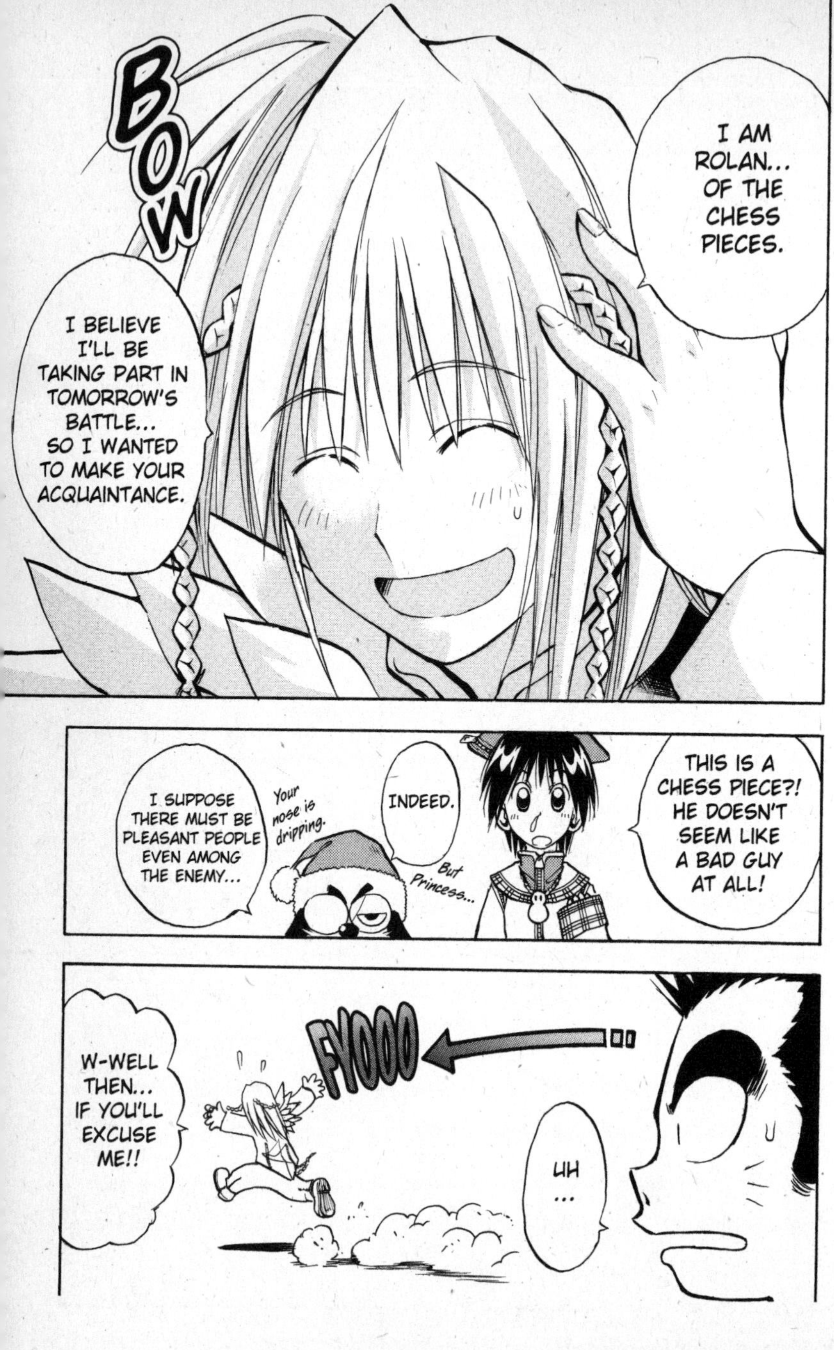
I AM ROLAN... OF THE CHESS PIECES.
BOW
I BELIEVE I'LL BE TAKING PART IN TOMORROW'S BATTLE... SO I WANTED TO MAKE YOUR ACQUAINTANCE.
THIS IS A CHESS PIECE?! HE DOESN'T SEEM LIKE A BAD GUY AT ALL!
But Princess...
INDEED.
Your nose is dripping.
I SUPPOSE THERE MUST BE PLEASANT PEOPLE EVEN AMONG THE ENEMY...
UH ...
FYOOO
W-WELL THEN... IF YOU'LL EXCUSE ME!!

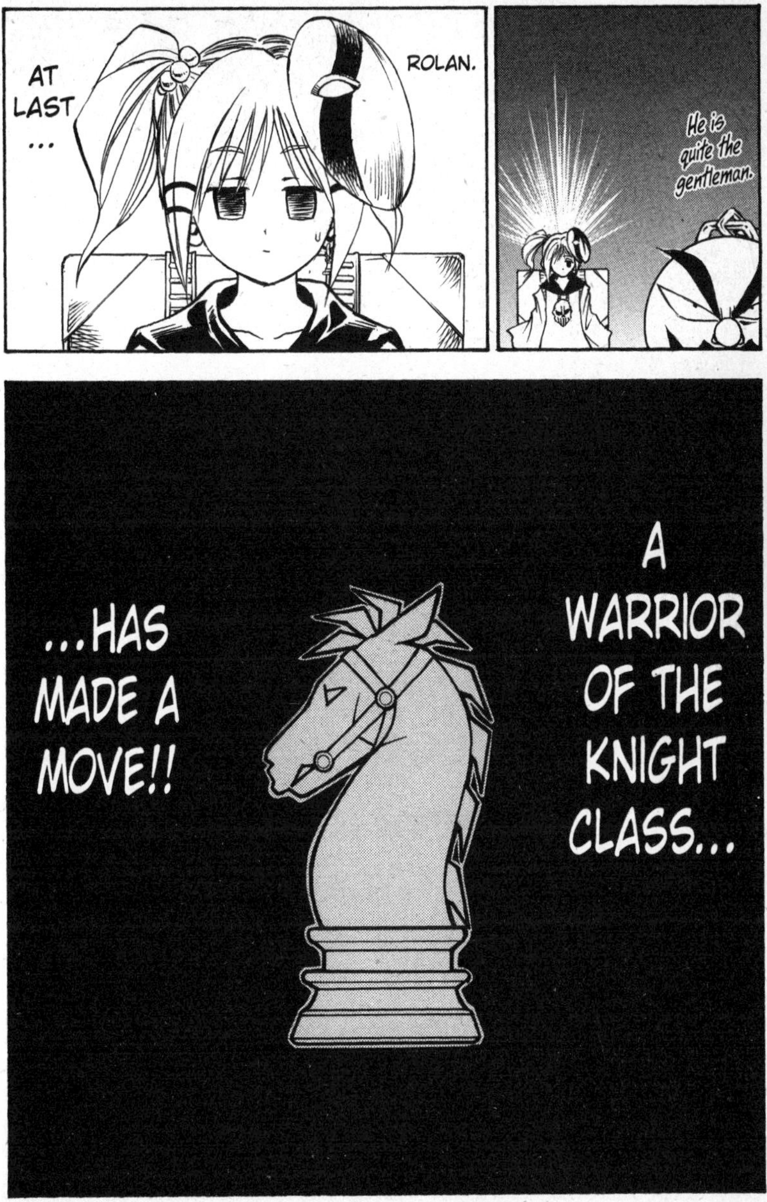
He is quite the gentleman.
ROLAN.
AT LAST ...
A WARRIOR OF THE KNIGHT CLASS...
...HAS MADE A MOVE!!

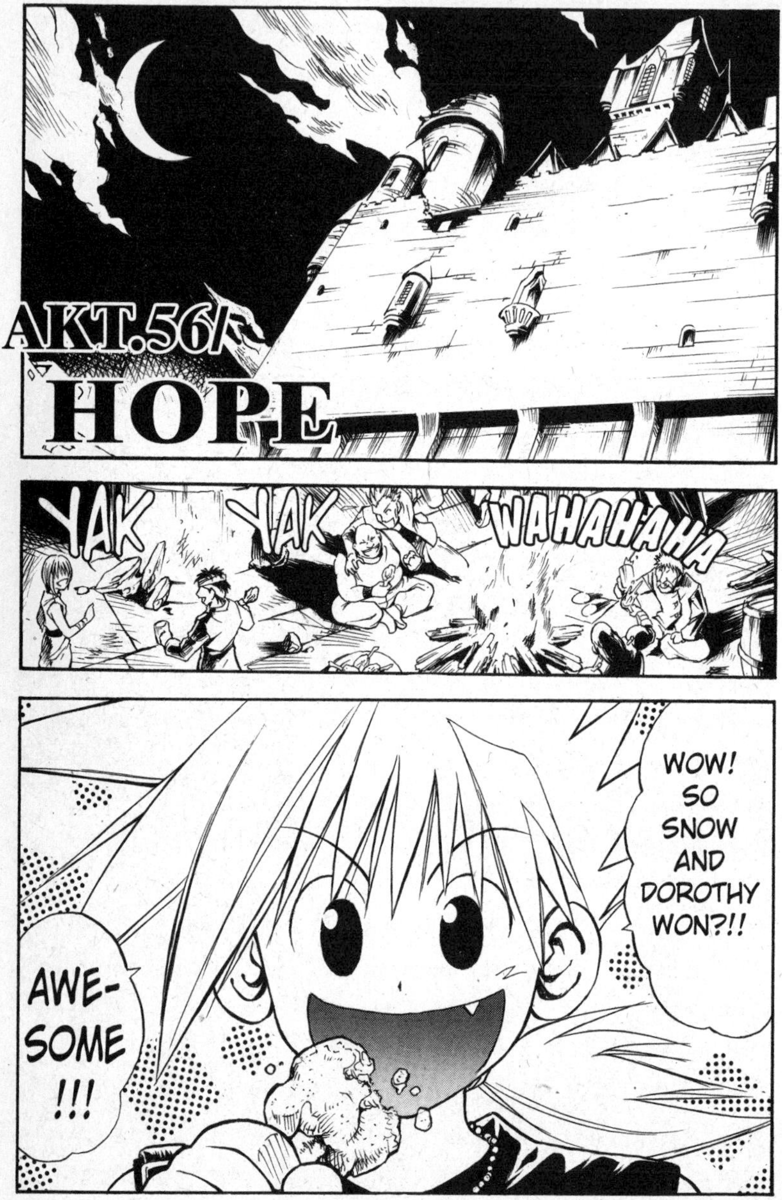
AKT.56/ HOPE
WAHAHAHA
YAK YAK
WOW! SO SNOW AND DOROTHY WON?!!
AWE-SOME!!!

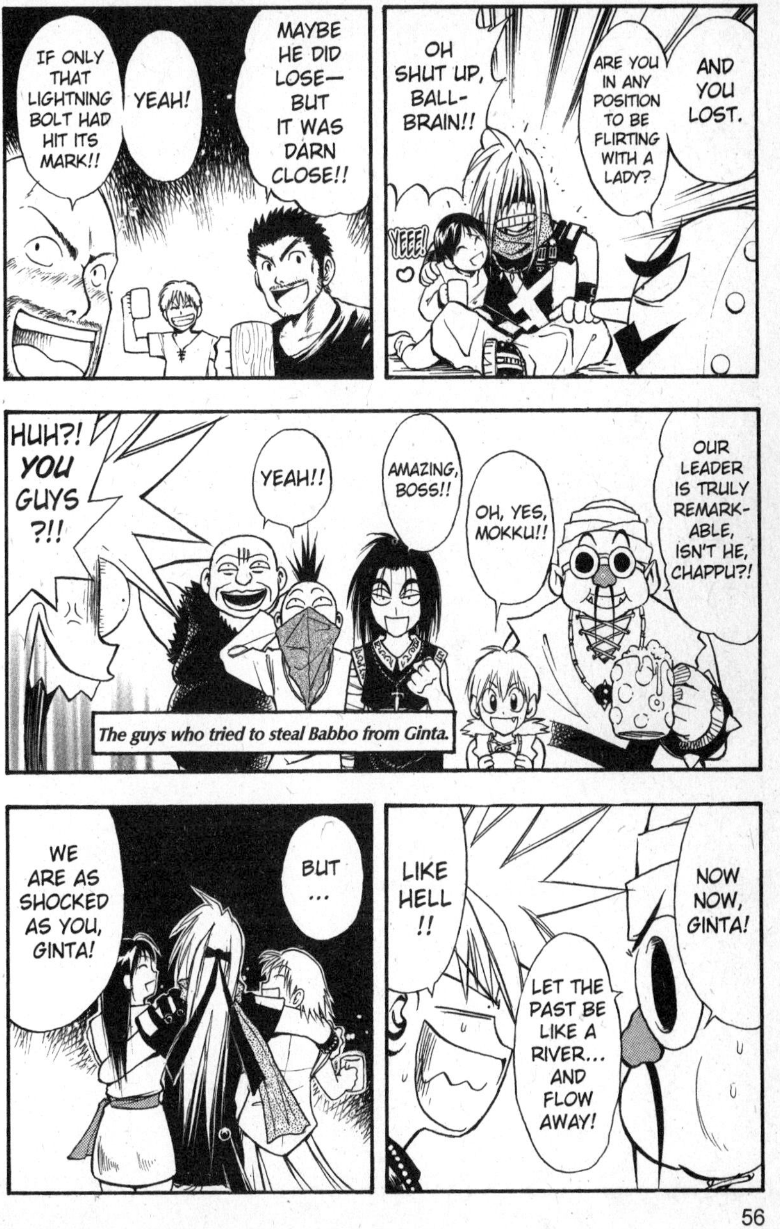
AND YOU LOST.
ARE YOU IN ANY POSITION TO BE FLIRTING WITH A LADY?
OH SHUT UP, BALL-BRAIN!!
YEEE!
MAYBE HE DID LOSE— BUT IT WAS DARN CLOSE!!
YEAH!
IF ONLY THAT LIGHTNING BOLT HAD HIT ITS MARK!!
OUR LEADER IS TRULY REMARKABLE, ISN'T HE, CHAPPU?!
OH, YES, MOKKU!!
AMAZING, BOSS!!
YEAH!!
HUH?! *YOU* GUYS ?!!
The guys who tried to steal Babbo from Ginta.
NOW NOW, GINTA!
LIKE HELL !!
LET THE PAST BE LIKE A RIVER... AND FLOW AWAY!
BUT ...
WE ARE AS SHOCKED AS YOU, GINTA!

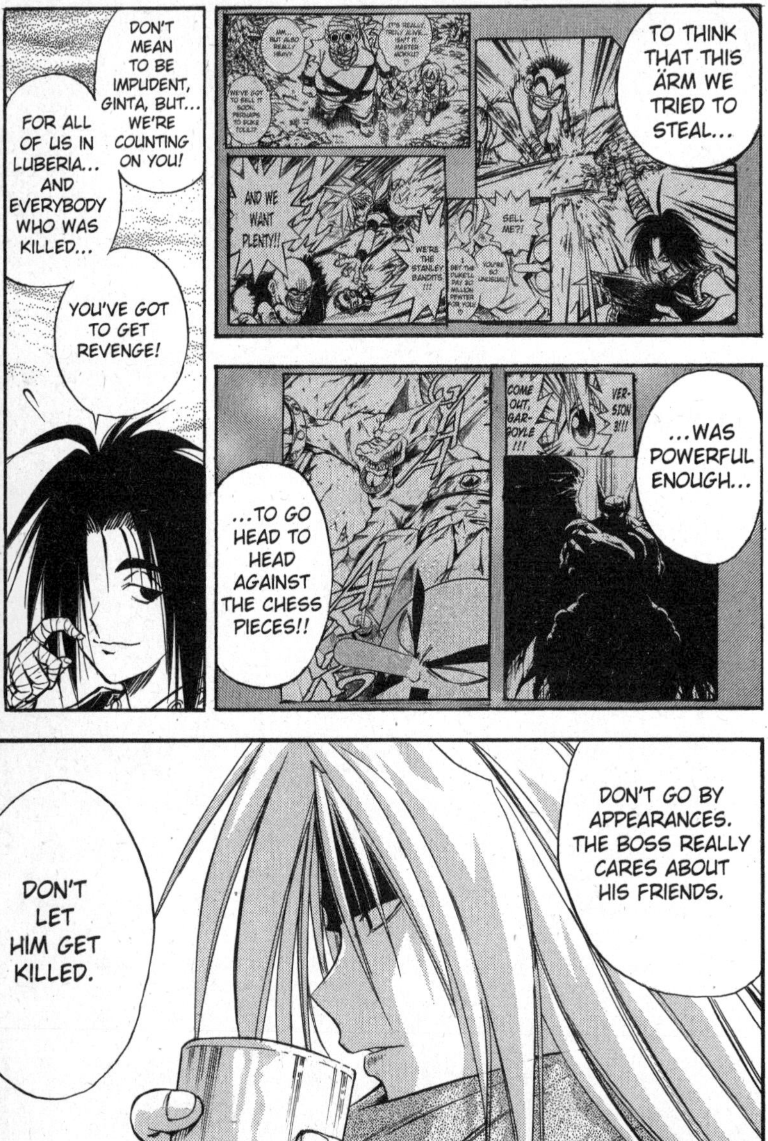
TO THINK THAT THIS ÄRM WE TRIED TO STEAL...
SELL ME?!
YOU'RE SO UNUSUAL!
WE'RE THE STARLEY BANDITS!!!
AND WE WANT PLENTY!!
VERSION 3!!!
COME OUT, GARGOYLE!!!
...WAS POWERFUL ENOUGH...
...TO GO HEAD TO HEAD AGAINST THE CHESS PIECES!!
DON'T MEAN TO BE IMPUDENT, GINTA, BUT... WE'RE COUNTING ON YOU!
FOR ALL OF US IN LUBERIA... AND EVERYBODY WHO WAS KILLED...
YOU'VE GOT TO GET REVENGE!
DON'T GO BY APPEARANCES. THE BOSS REALLY CARES ABOUT HIS FRIENDS.
DON'T LET HIM GET KILLED.

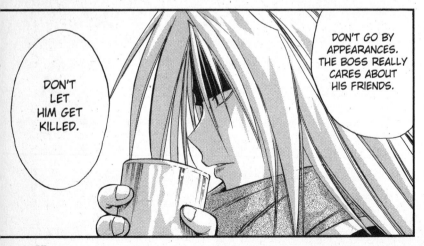

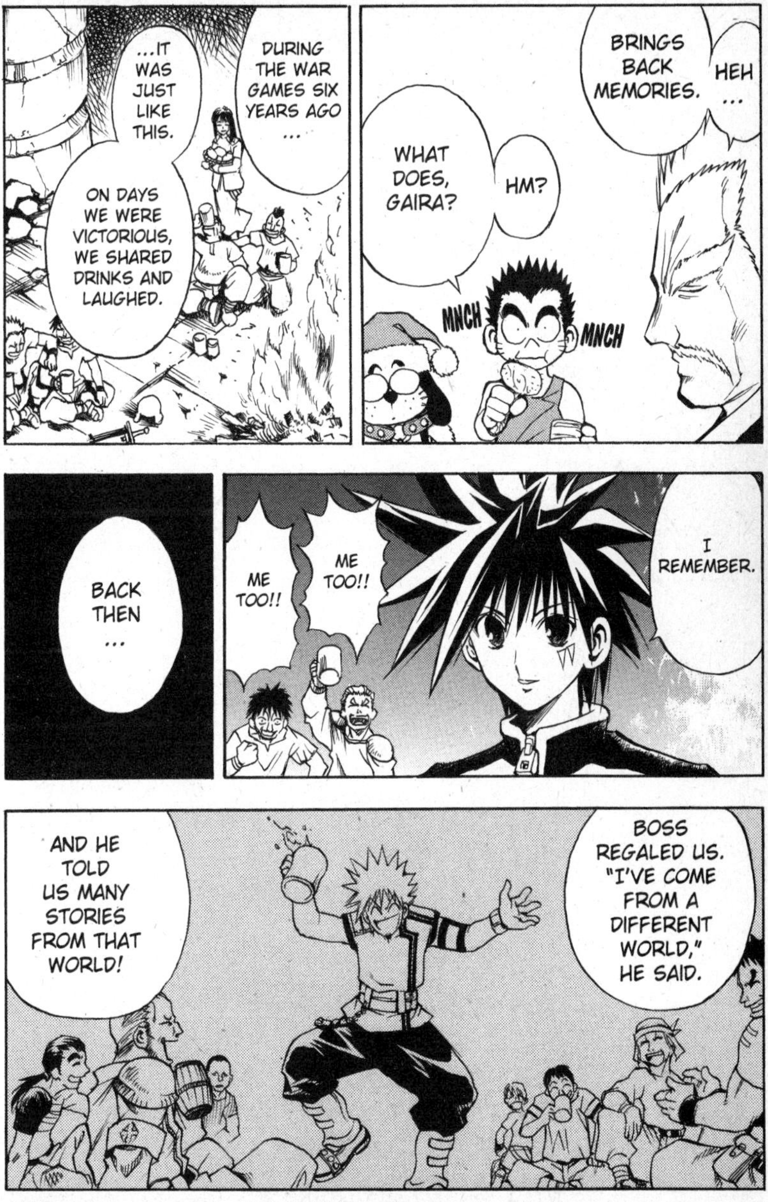
HEH ...
BRINGS BACK MEMORIES.
HM?
WHAT DOES, GAIRA?
MNCH
MNCH
DURING THE WAR GAMES SIX YEARS AGO ...
...IT WAS JUST LIKE THIS.
ON DAYS WE WERE VICTORIOUS, WE SHARED DRINKS AND LAUGHED.
I REMEMBER.
ME TOO!!
ME TOO!!
BACK THEN ...
BOSS REGALED US. "I'VE COME FROM A DIFFERENT WORLD," HE SAID.
AND HE TOLD US MANY STORIES FROM THAT WORLD!

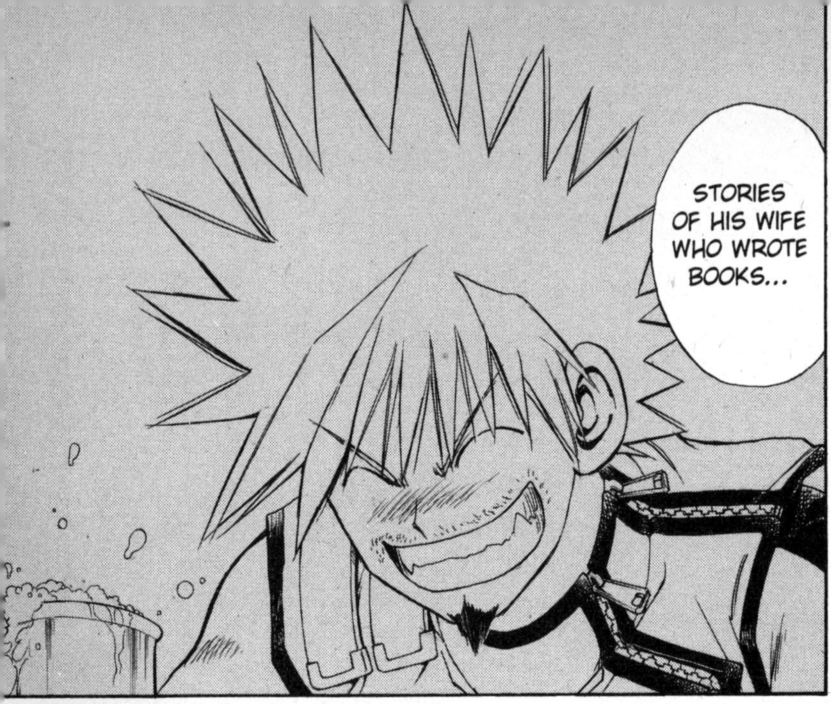
STORIES OF HIS WIFE WHO WROTE BOOKS...
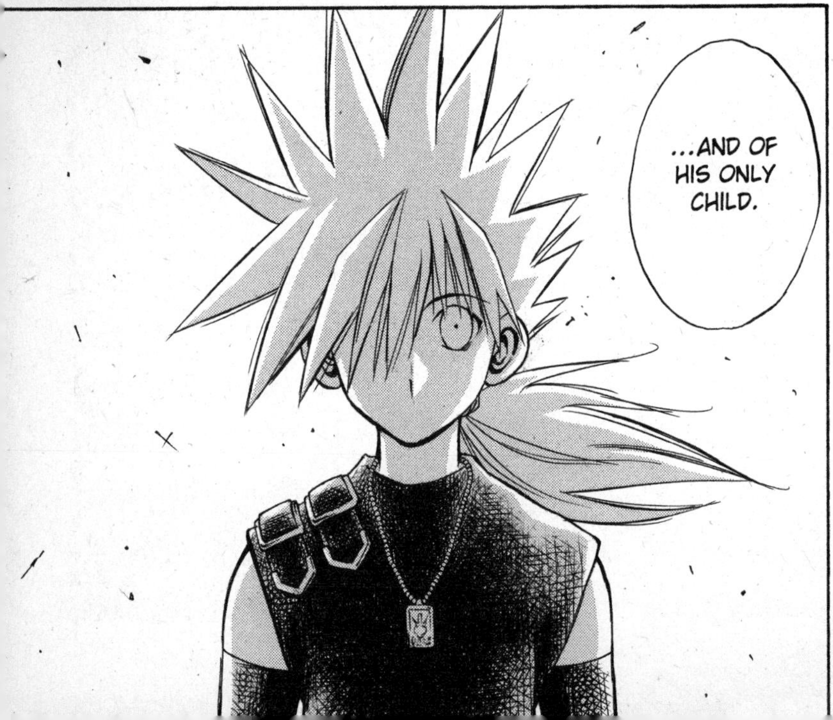
...AND OF HIS ONLY CHILD.

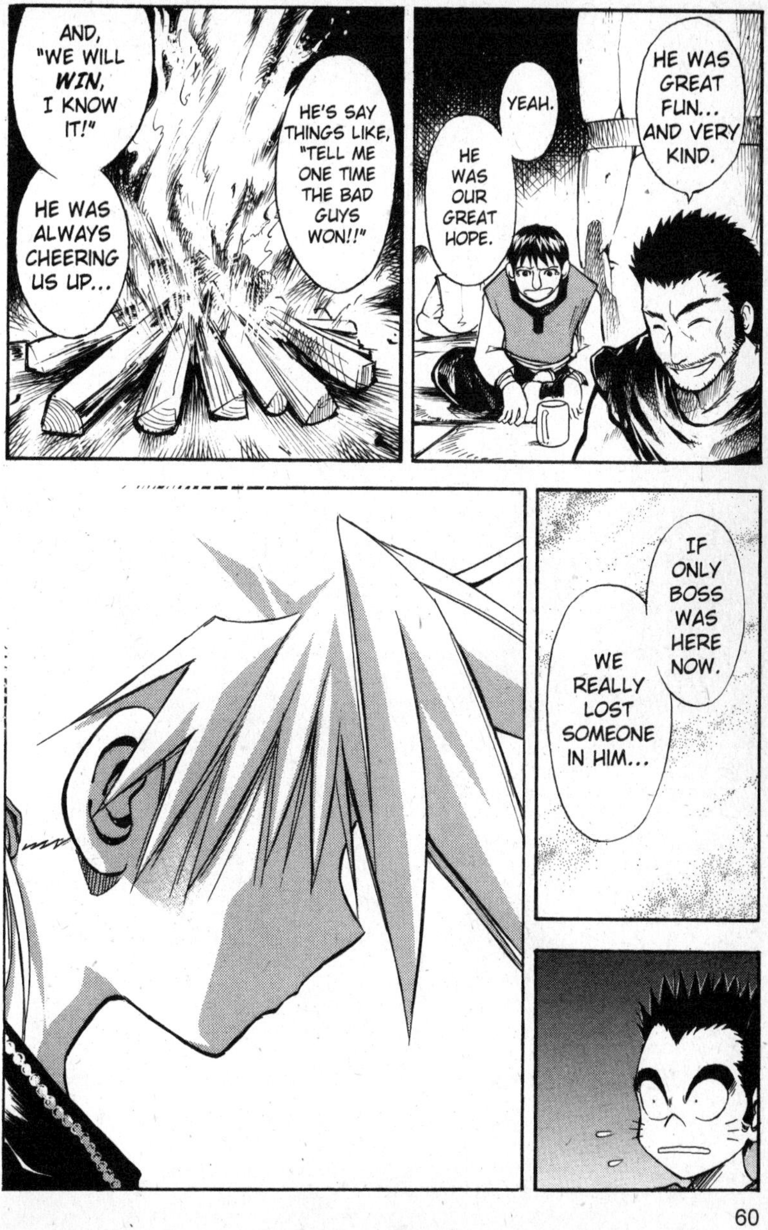
HE WAS GREAT FUN... AND VERY KIND.
YEAH.
HE WAS OUR GREAT HOPE.
HE'S SAY THINGS LIKE, "TELL ME ONE TIME THE BAD GUYS WON!!"
AND, "WE WILL *WIN*, I KNOW IT!"
HE WAS ALWAYS CHEERING US UP...
IF ONLY BOSS WAS HERE NOW.
WE REALLY LOST SOMEONE IN HIM...

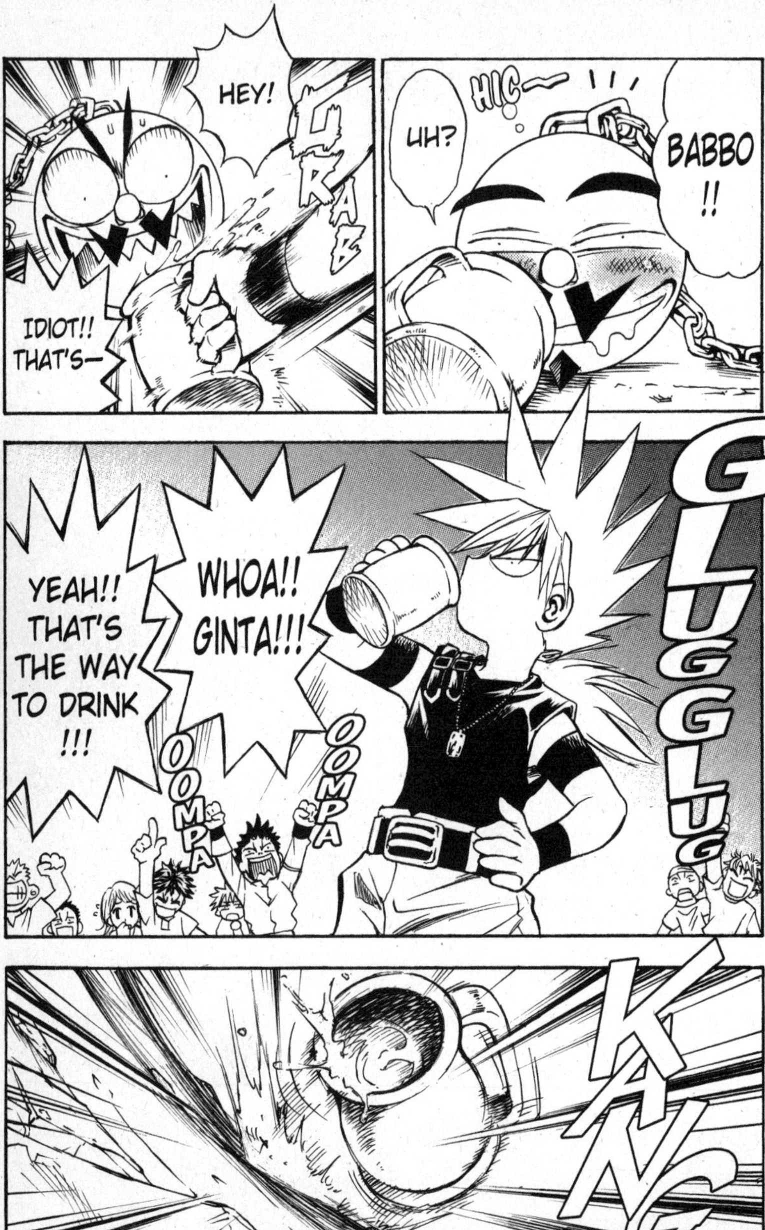
BABBO!!
HIC~
UH?
HEY!
GRAB
IDIOT!! THAT'S—
GLUGGLUG
OOMPA
WHOA!! GINTA!!!
OOMPA
YEAH!! THAT'S THE WAY TO DRINK!!!
KANG

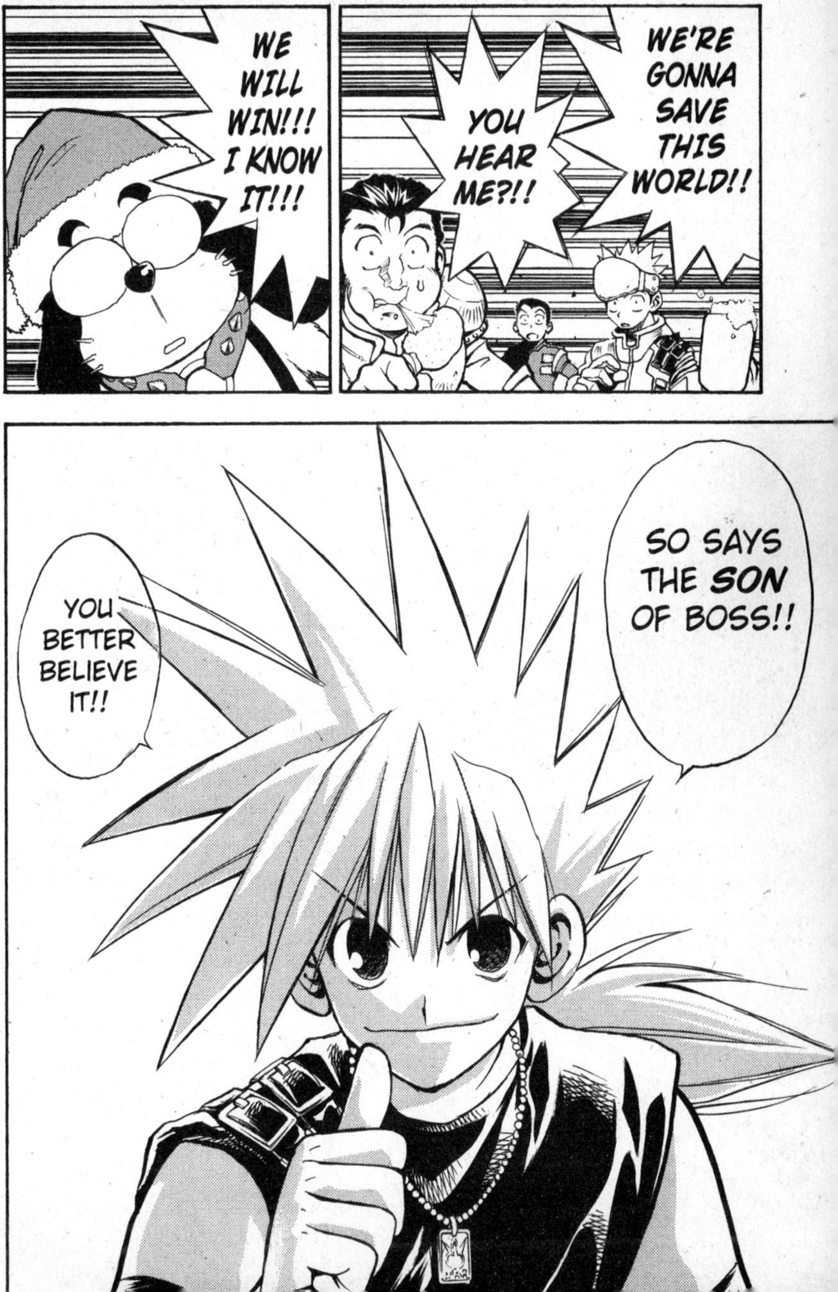
WE'RE GONNA SAVE THIS WORLD!!
YOU HEAR ME?!!
WE WILL WIN!!! I KNOW IT!!!
SO SAYS THE *SON* OF BOSS!!
YOU BETTER BELIEVE IT!!

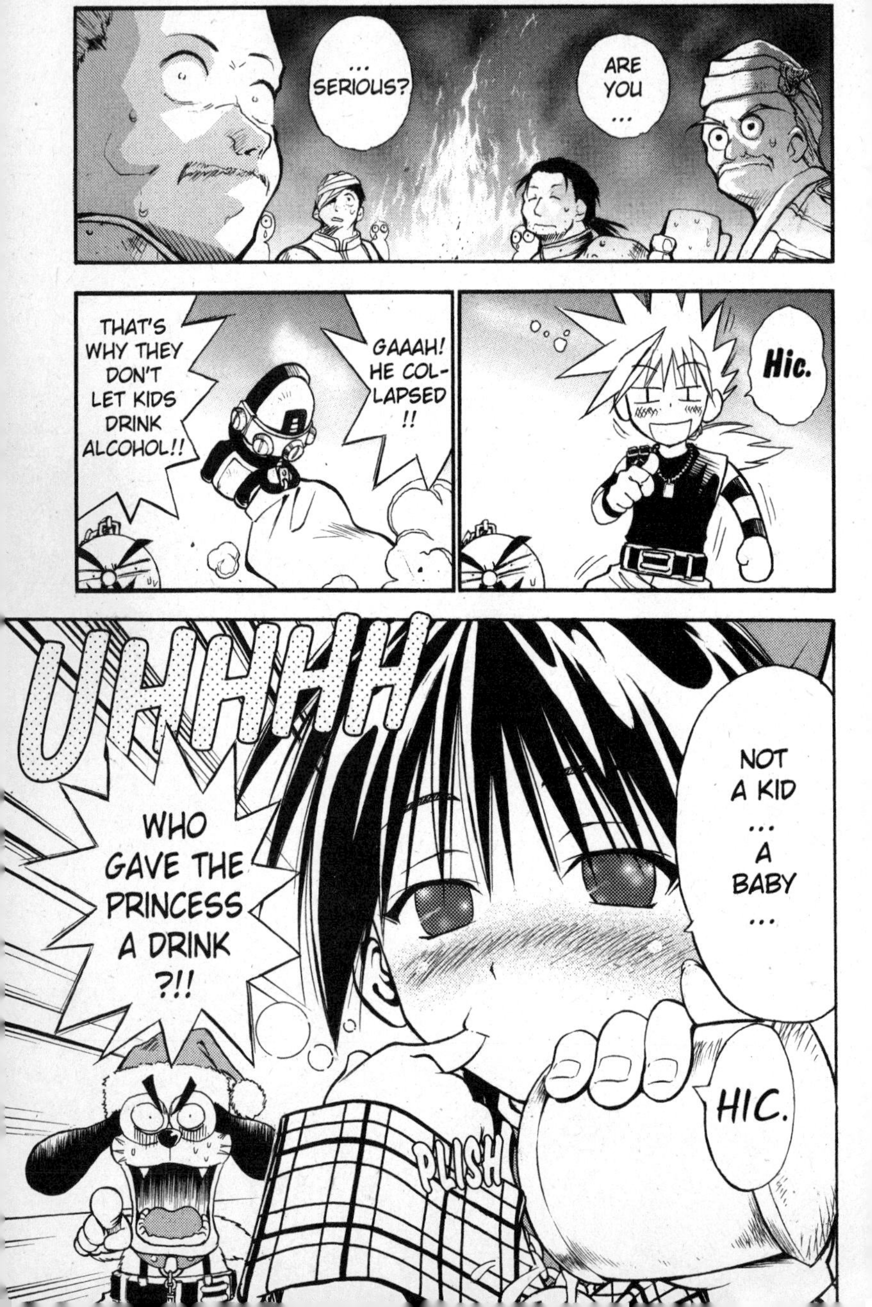
ARE YOU ...
... SERIOUS?
Hic.
GAAAH! HE COL-LAPSED!!
THAT'S WHY THEY DON'T LET KIDS DRINK ALCOHOL!!
NOT A KID ... A BABY ...
UHHHH
WHO GAVE THE PRINCESS A DRINK ?!!
HIC.
PLISH

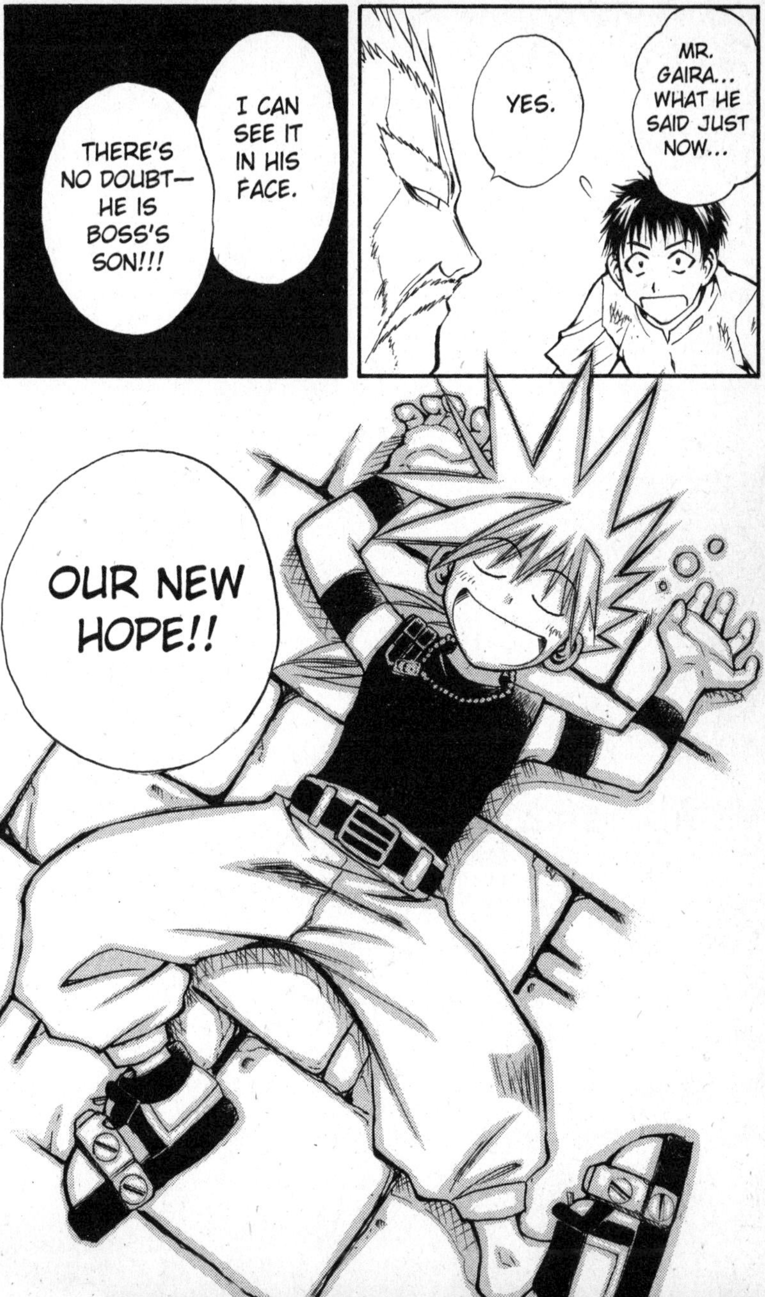
MR. GAIRA... WHAT HE SAID JUST NOW...
YES.
I CAN SEE IT IN HIS FACE.
THERE'S NO DOUBT—HE IS BOSS'S SON!!!
OUR NEW HOPE!!

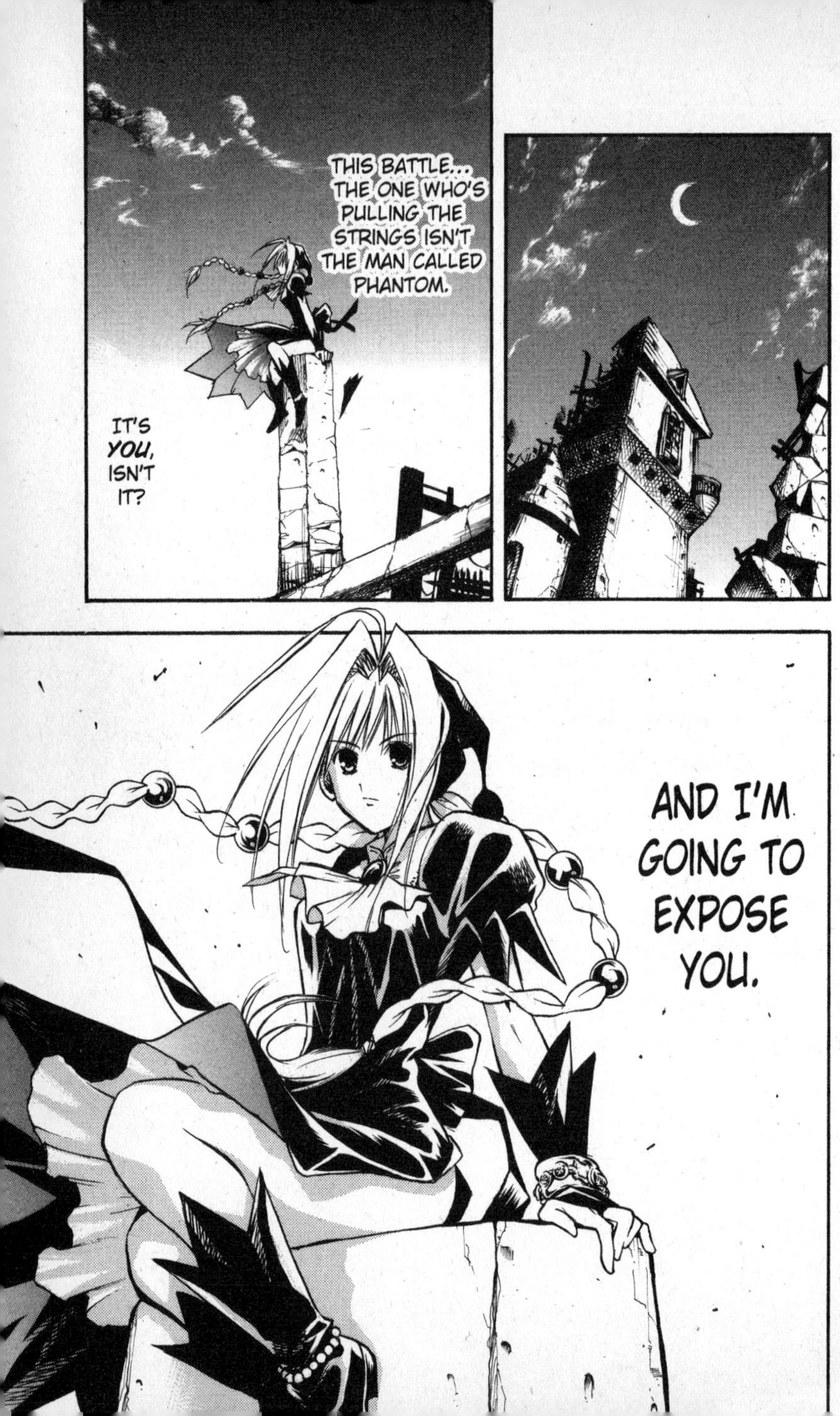
THIS BATTLE... THE ONE WHO'S PULLING THE STRINGS ISN'T THE MAN CALLED PHANTOM.
IT'S *YOU*, ISN'T IT?
AND I'M GOING TO EXPOSE YOU.

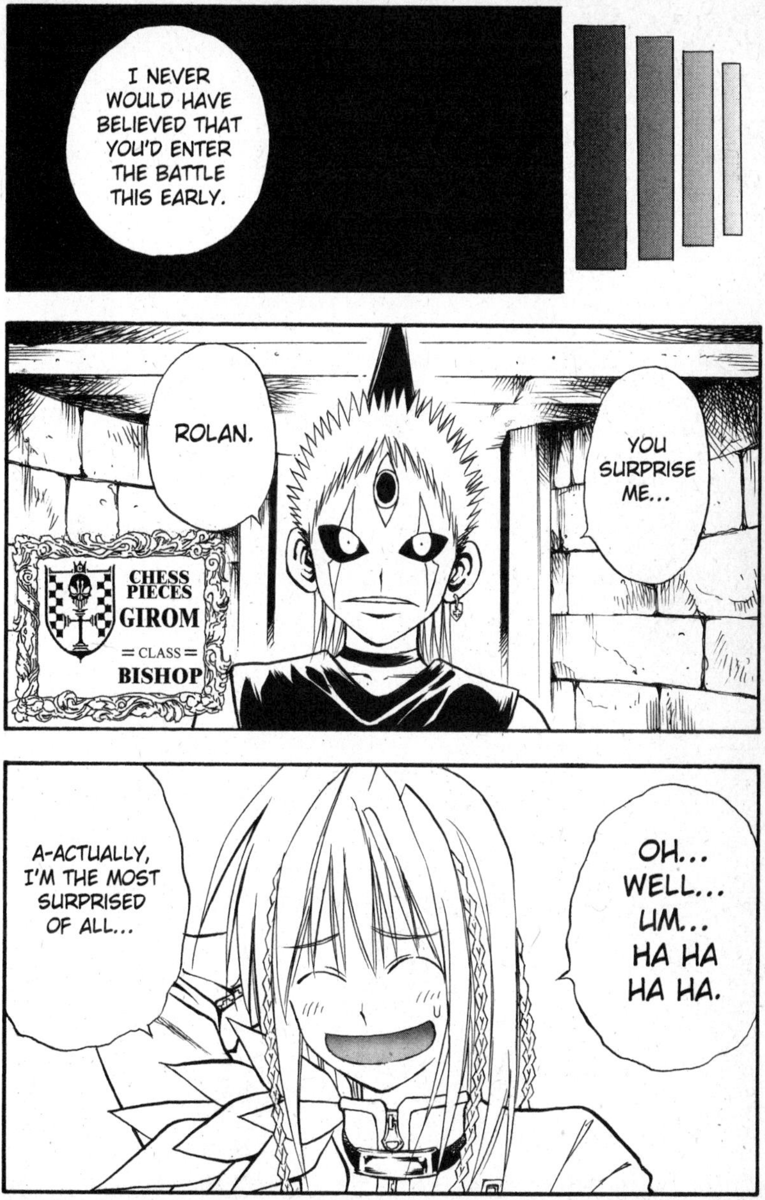
I NEVER WOULD HAVE BELIEVED THAT YOU'D ENTER THE BATTLE THIS EARLY.
YOU SURPRISE ME...
ROLAN.
CHESS PIECES GIROM
=CLASS= BISHOP
OH... WELL... UM... HA HA HA HA.
A-ACTUALLY, I'M THE MOST SURPRISED OF ALL...

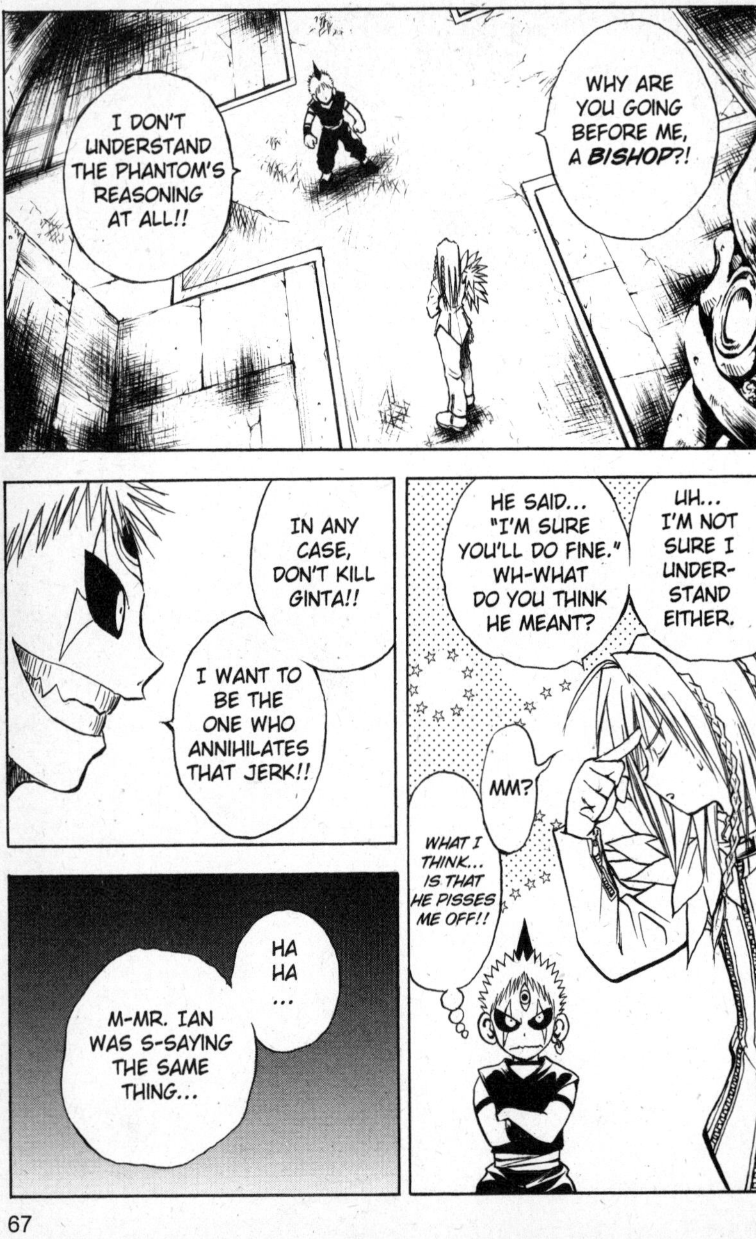
WHY ARE YOU GOING BEFORE ME, A *BISHOP*?!
I DON'T UNDERSTAND THE PHANTOM'S REASONING AT ALL!!
UH... I'M NOT SURE I UNDER-STAND EITHER.
HE SAID... "I'M SURE YOU'LL DO FINE." WH-WHAT DO YOU THINK HE MEANT?
MM?
WHAT I THINK... IS THAT HE PISSES ME OFF!!
IN ANY CASE, DON'T KILL GINTA!!
I WANT TO BE THE ONE WHO ANNIHILATES THAT JERK!!
HA HA ...
M-MR. IAN WAS S-SAYING THE SAME THING...

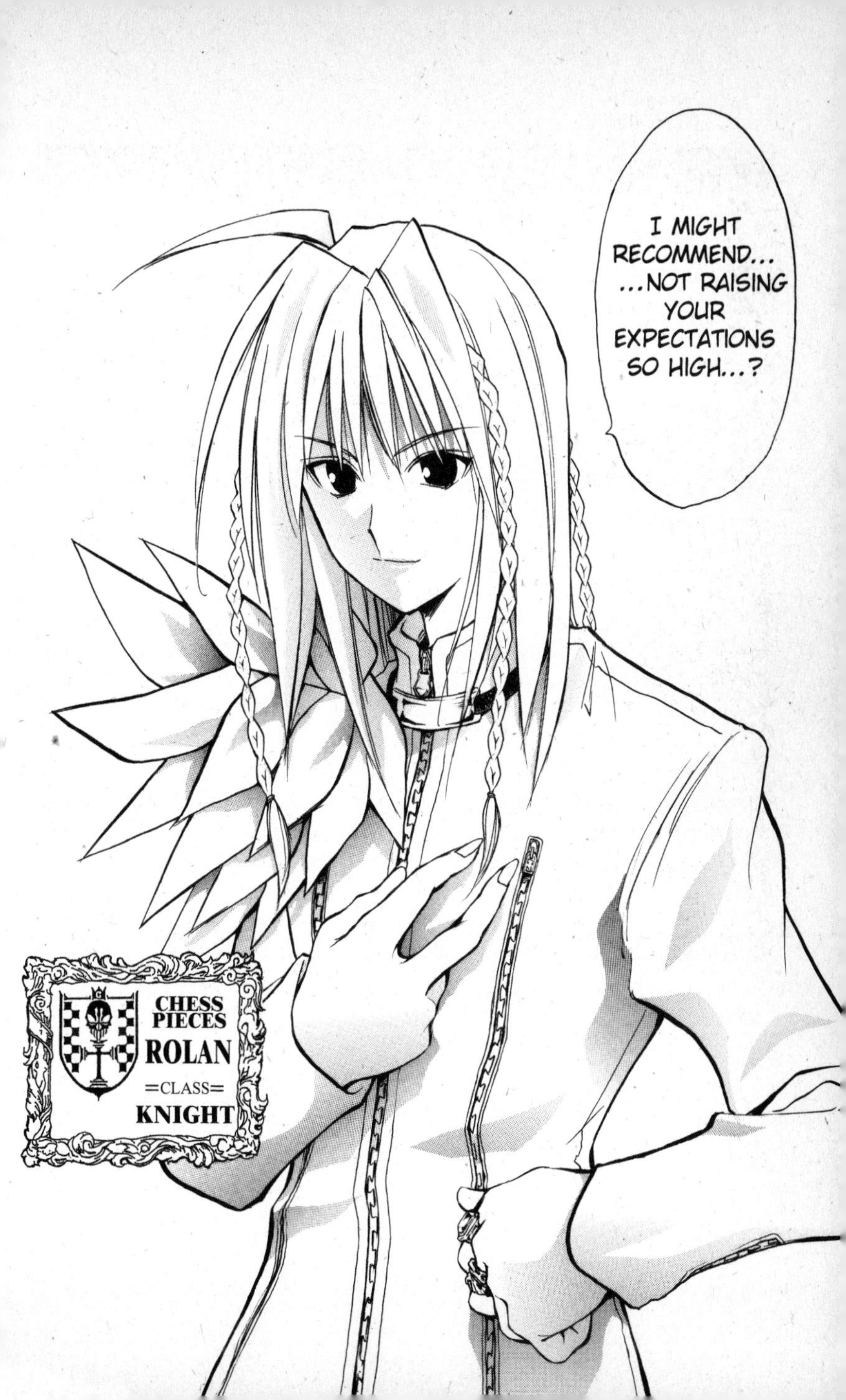
I MIGHT RECOMMEND... ...NOT RAISING YOUR EXPECTATIONS SO HIGH...?
CHESS PIECES
ROLAN
=CLASS=
KNIGHT

Those in the Knight Class of the Chess Pieces...

...Are also known by a group alias.

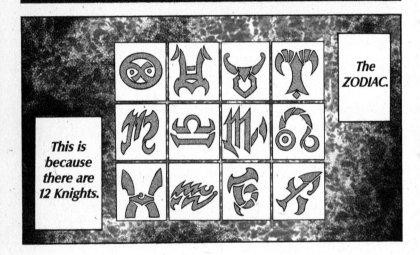

The ZODIAC.

This is because there are 12 Knights.

One of whom...

...is Rolan.

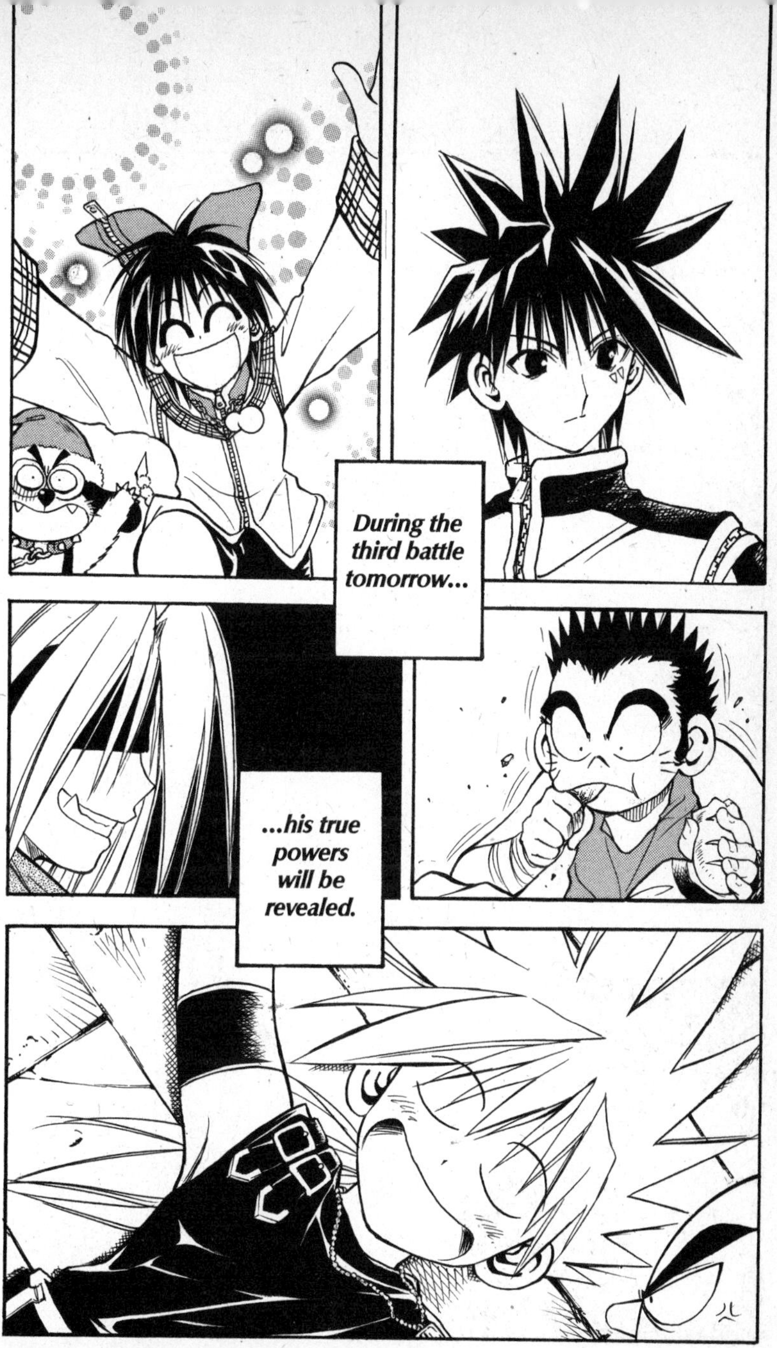
During the third battle tomorrow...
...his true powers will be revealed.

AKT.57/ The Man Who Came Late

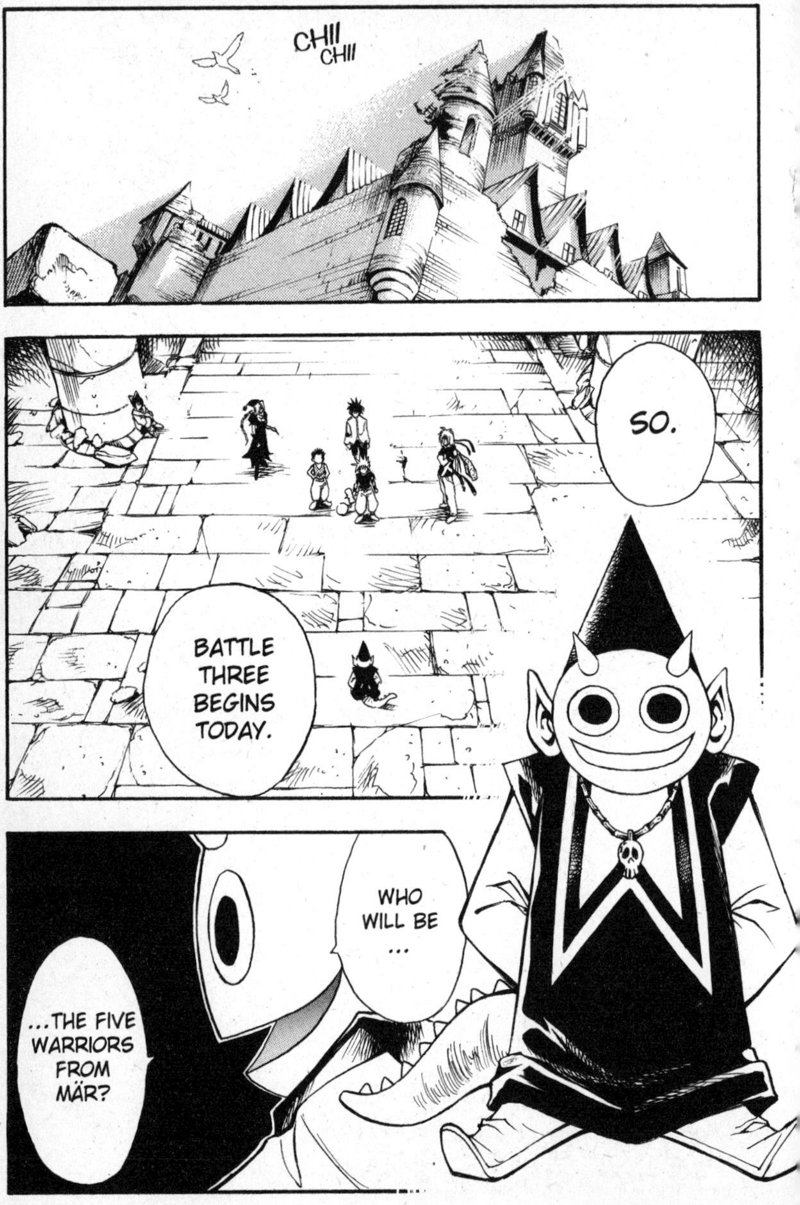
CHII CHII
SO.
BATTLE THREE BEGINS TODAY.
WHO WILL BE ...
...THE FIVE WARRIORS FROM MÄR?

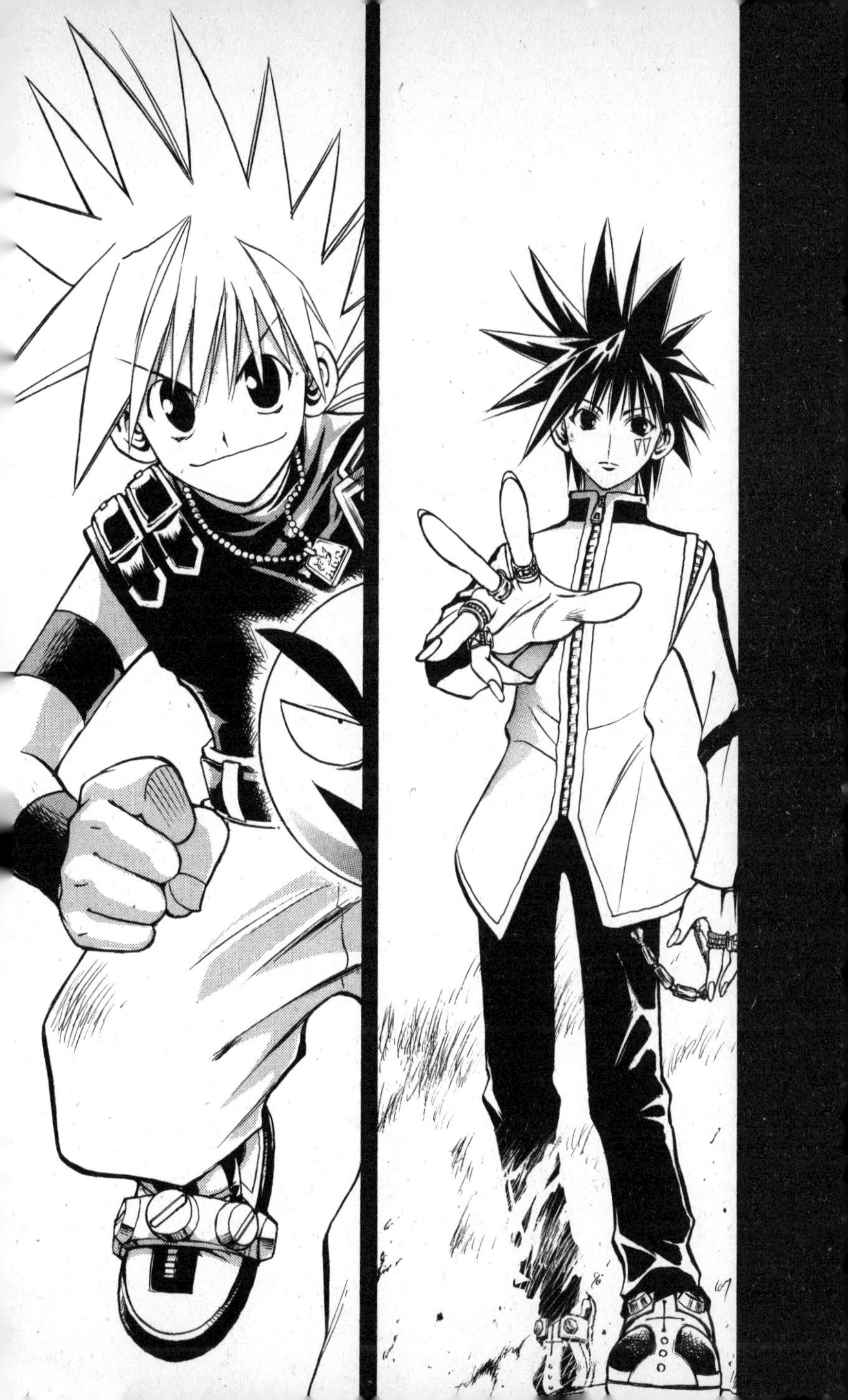

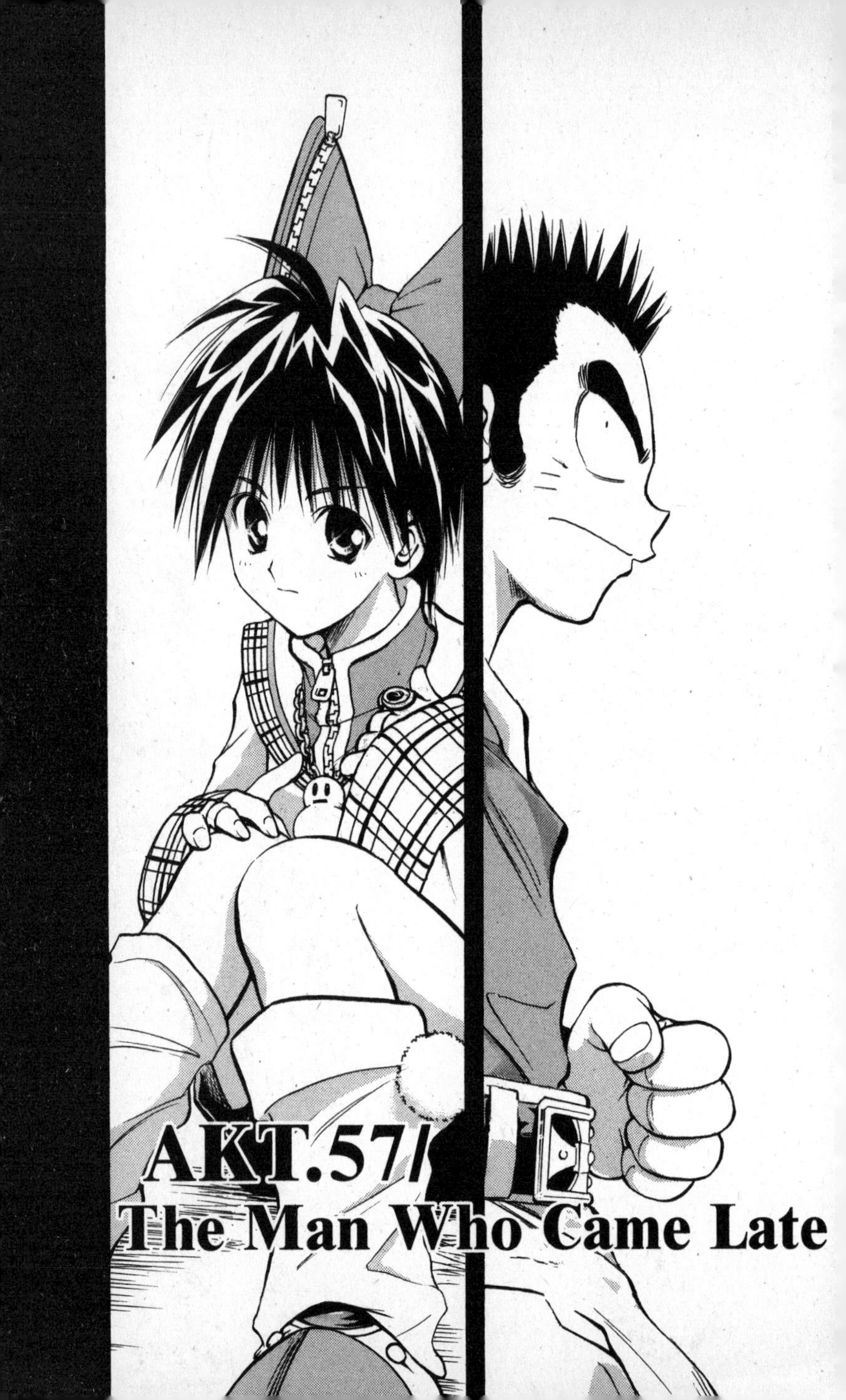
AKT.57/
The Man Who Came Late

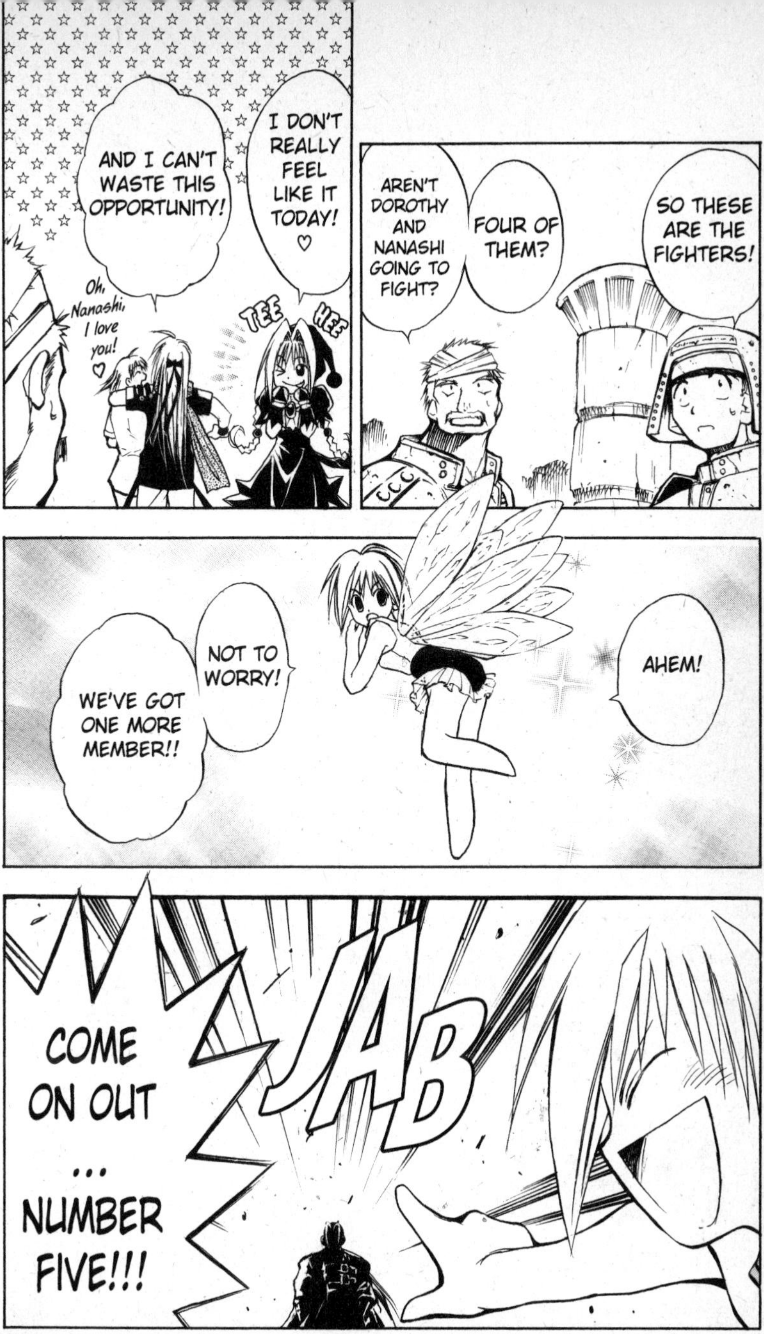
SO THESE ARE THE FIGHTERS!
FOUR OF THEM?
AREN'T DOROTHY AND NANASHI GOING TO FIGHT?
I DON'T REALLY FEEL LIKE IT TODAY! ♡
TEE HEE
AND I CAN'T WASTE THIS OPPORTUNITY!
Oh, Nanashi, I love you! ♡
AHEM!
NOT TO WORRY!
WE'VE GOT ONE MORE MEMBER!!
JAB
COME ON OUT ... NUMBER FIVE!!!

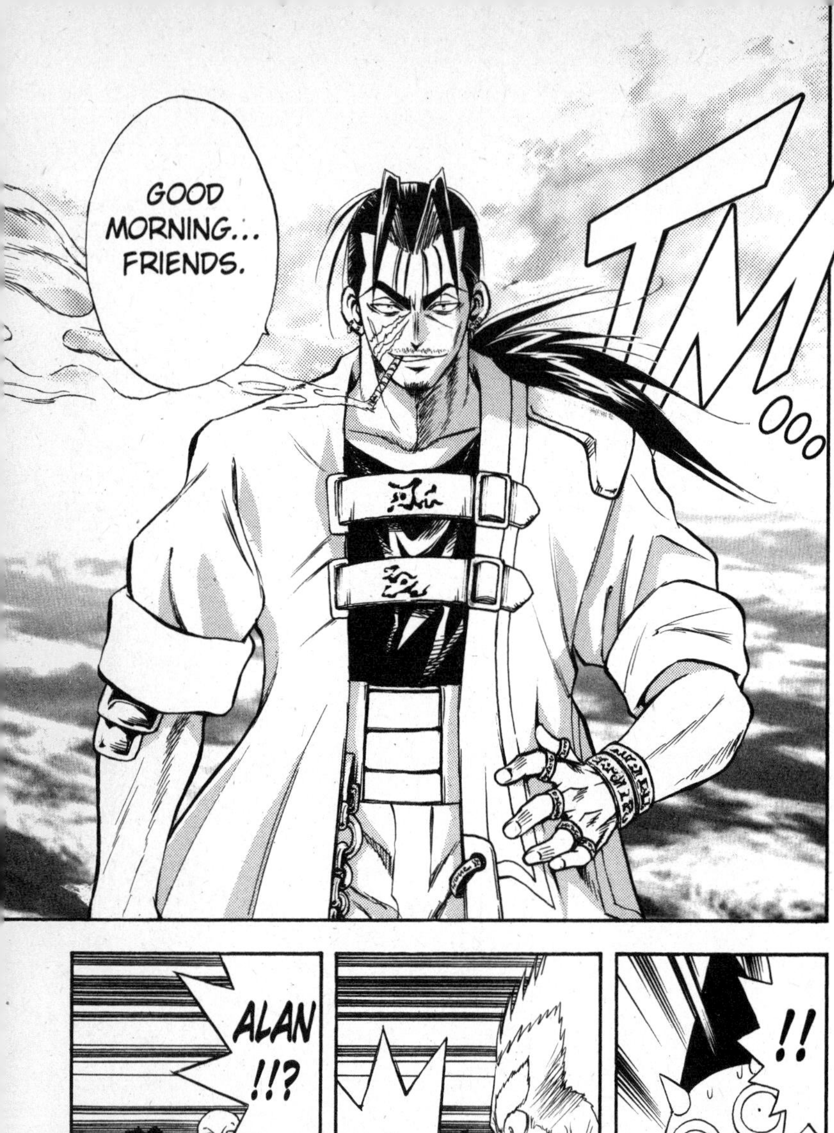
GOOD MORNING... FRIENDS.
TMOOO
!!
A ...
ALAN !!?

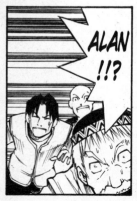

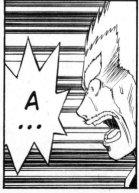

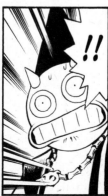

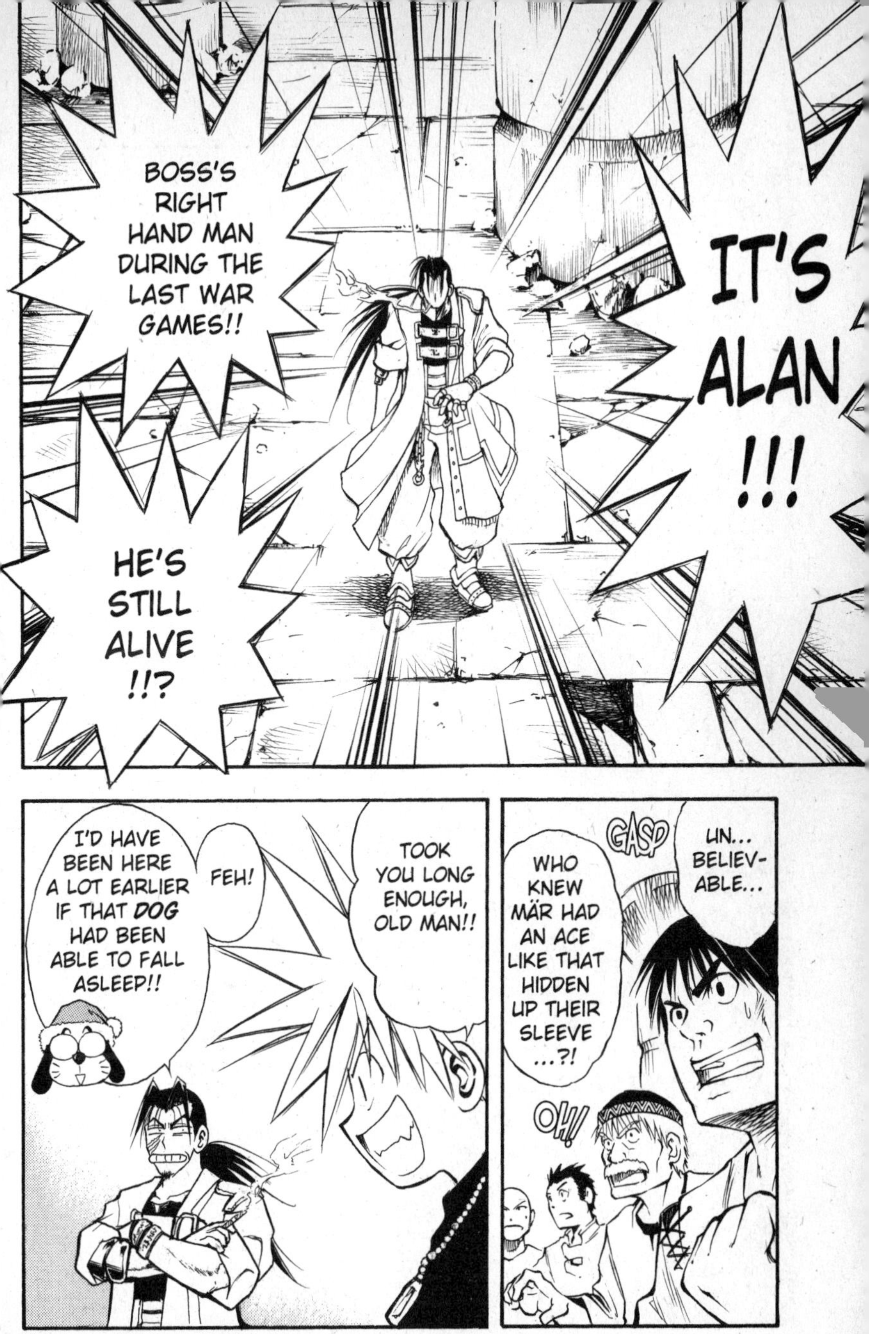
IT'S ALAN!!!
BOSS'S RIGHT HAND MAN DURING THE LAST WAR GAMES!!
HE'S STILL ALIVE!!?
GASP
UN... BELIEV-ABLE...
WHO KNEW MÄR HAD AN ACE LIKE THAT HIDDEN UP THEIR SLEEVE...?!
OH!
TOOK YOU LONG ENOUGH, OLD MAN!!
FEH!
I'D HAVE BEEN HERE A LOT EARLIER IF THAT *DOG* HAD BEEN ABLE TO FALL ASLEEP!!

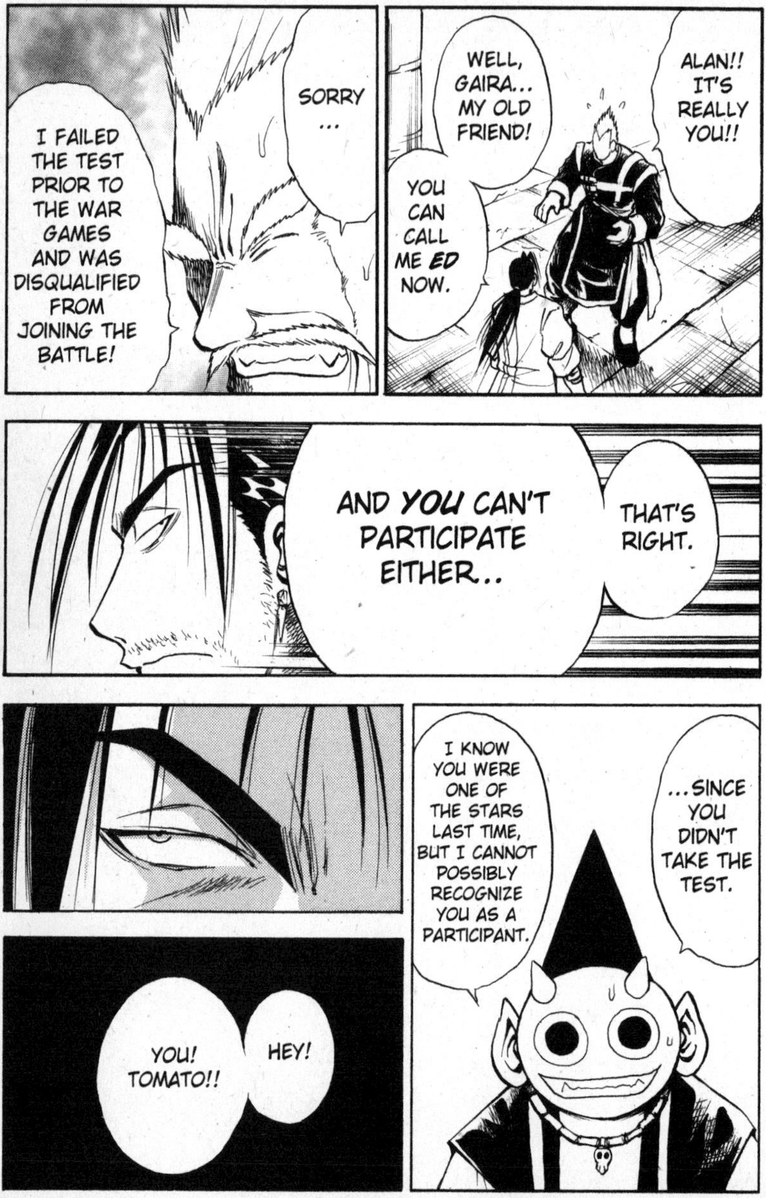
ALAN!! IT'S REALLY YOU!!
WELL, GAIRA... MY OLD FRIEND!
YOU CAN CALL ME ED NOW.
SORRY ...
I FAILED THE TEST PRIOR TO THE WAR GAMES AND WAS DISQUALIFIED FROM JOINING THE BATTLE!
THAT'S RIGHT.
AND YOU CAN'T PARTICIPATE EITHER...
...SINCE YOU DIDN'T TAKE THE TEST.
I KNOW YOU WERE ONE OF THE STARS LAST TIME, BUT I CANNOT POSSIBLY RECOGNIZE YOU AS A PARTICIPANT.
HEY!
YOU! TOMATO!!

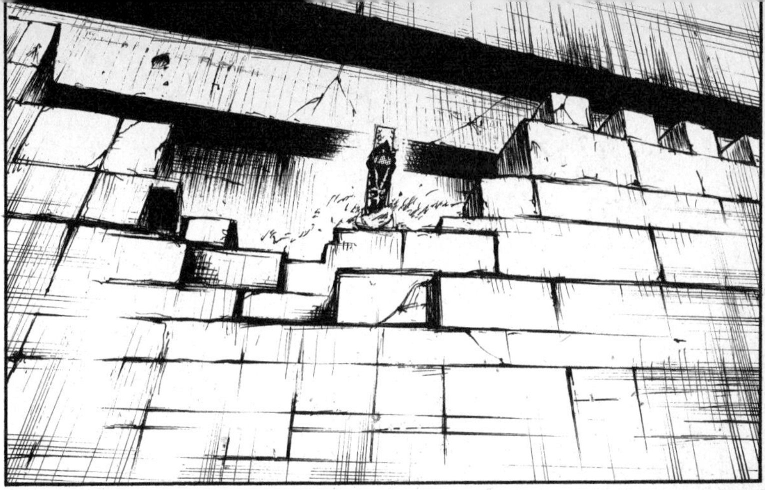

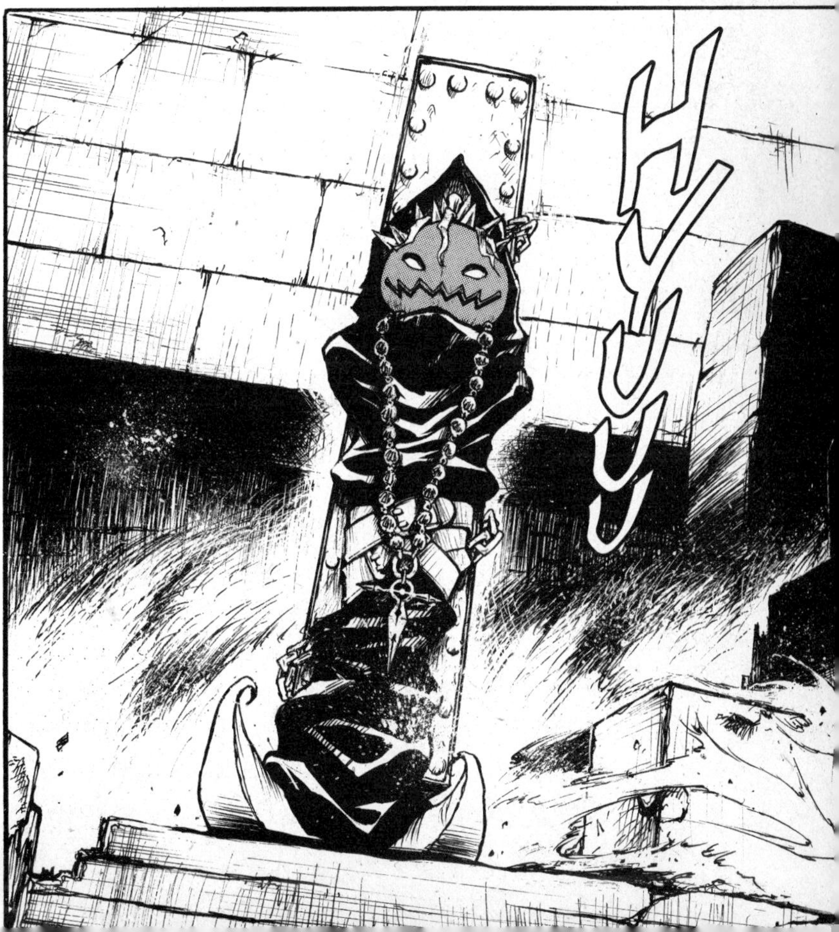
HYUU

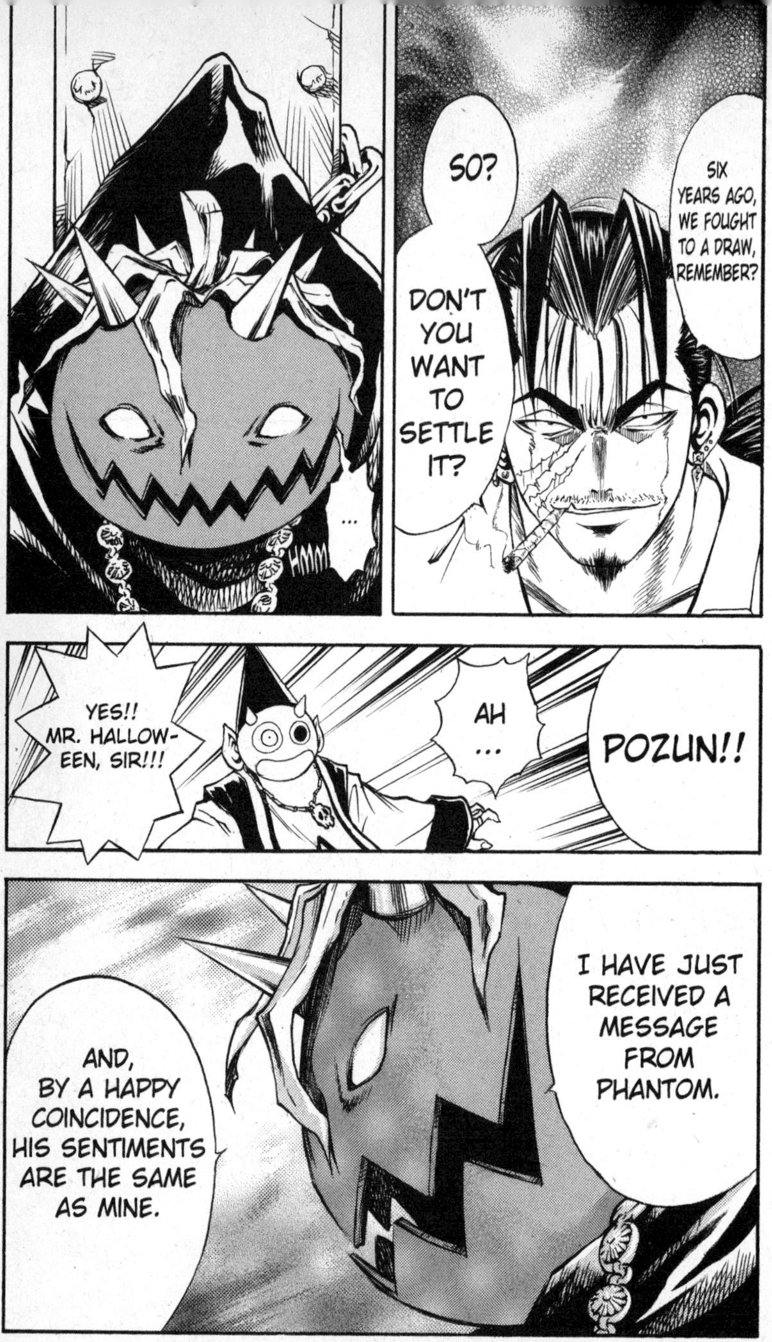
SIX YEARS AGO, WE FOUGHT TO A DRAW, REMEMBER?
SO?
DON'T YOU WANT TO SETTLE IT?
...
HMM
POZUN!!
AH ...
YES!! MR. HALLOW-EEN, SIR!!!
I HAVE JUST RECEIVED A MESSAGE FROM PHANTOM.
AND, BY A HAPPY COINCIDENCE, HIS SENTIMENTS ARE THE SAME AS MINE.

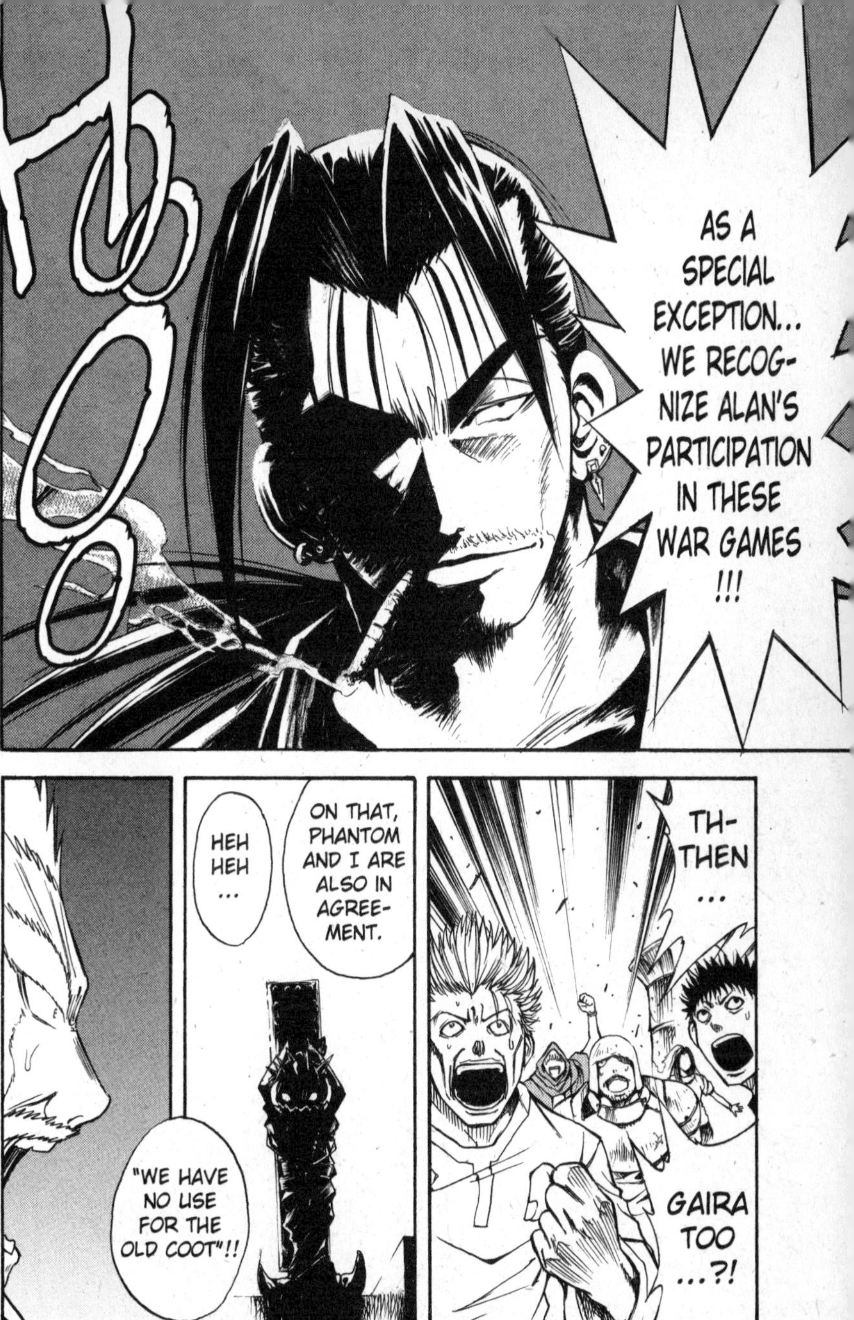
AS A SPECIAL EXCEPTION... WE RECOG-NIZE ALAN'S PARTICIPATION IN THESE WAR GAMES !!!
TH-THEN ...
GAIRA TOO ...?!
ON THAT, PHANTOM AND I ARE ALSO IN AGREE-MENT.
HEH HEH ...
"WE HAVE NO USE FOR THE OLD COOT"!!

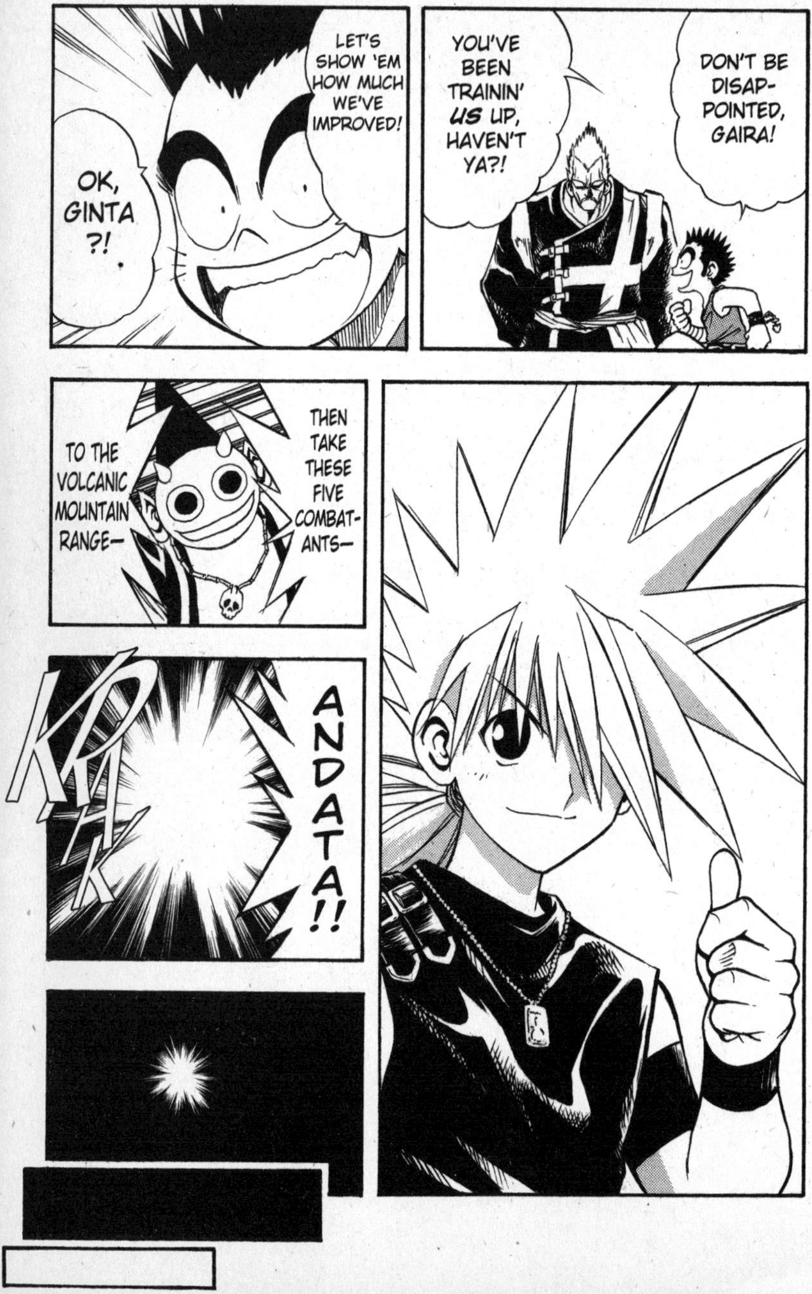
DON'T BE DISAP-POINTED, GAIRA!
YOU'VE BEEN TRAININ' US UP, HAVEN'T YA?!
LET'S SHOW 'EM HOW MUCH WE'VE IMPROVED!
OK, GINTA?!
THEN TAKE THESE FIVE COMBAT-ANTS—
TO THE VOLCANIC MOUNTAIN RANGE—
ANDATA!!
KRAK

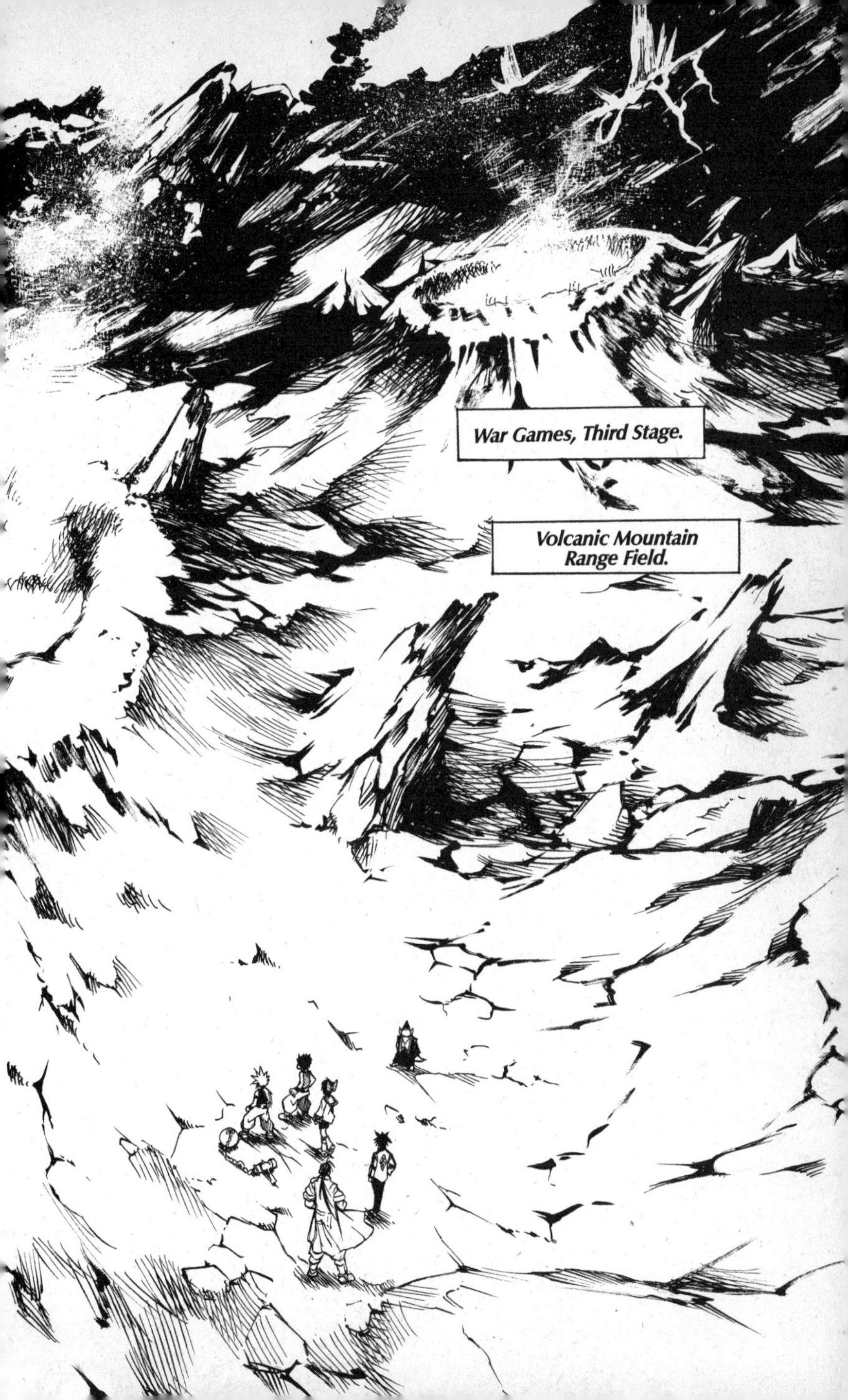
War Games, Third Stage.
Volcanic Mountain Range Field.

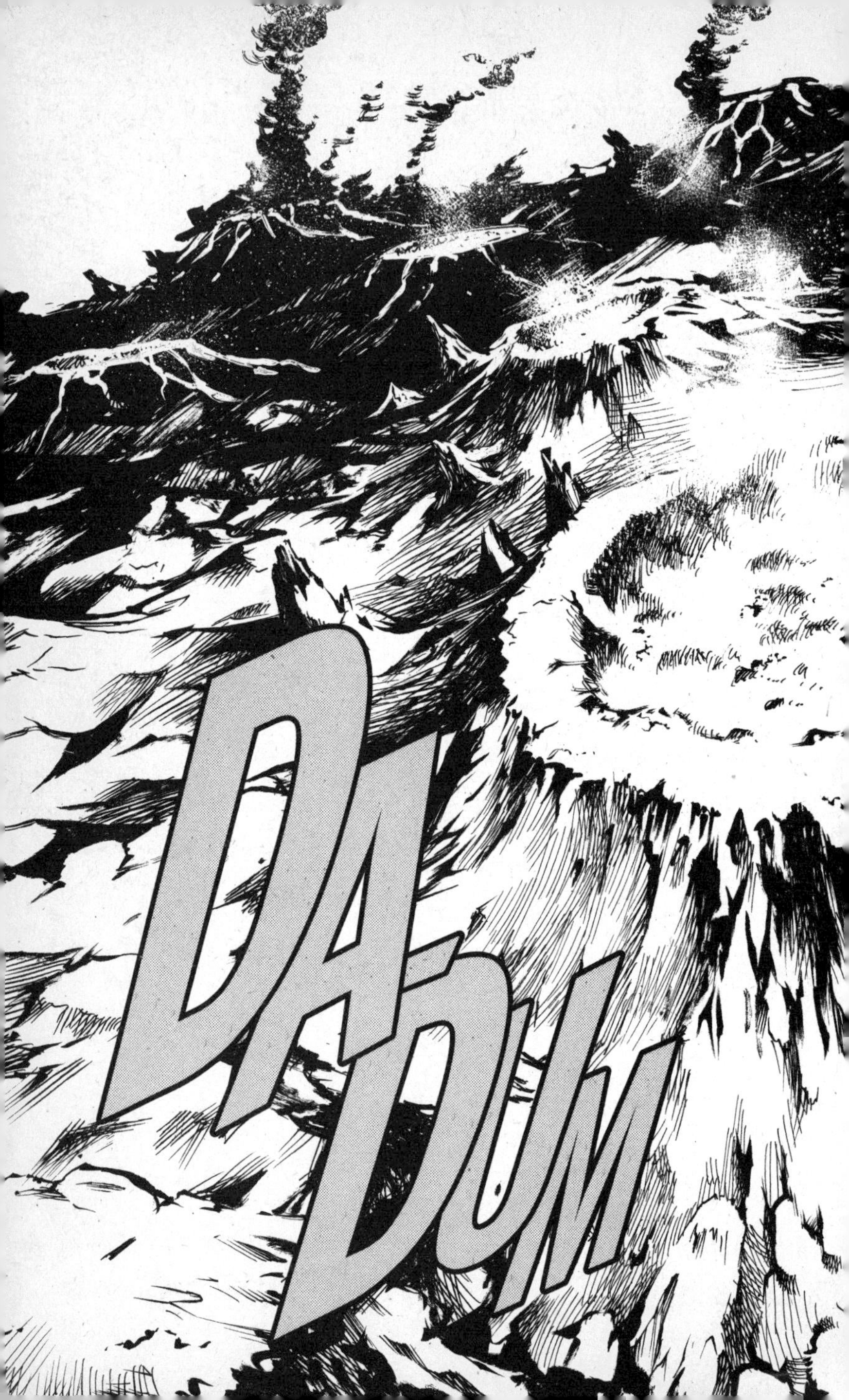
DA DUM

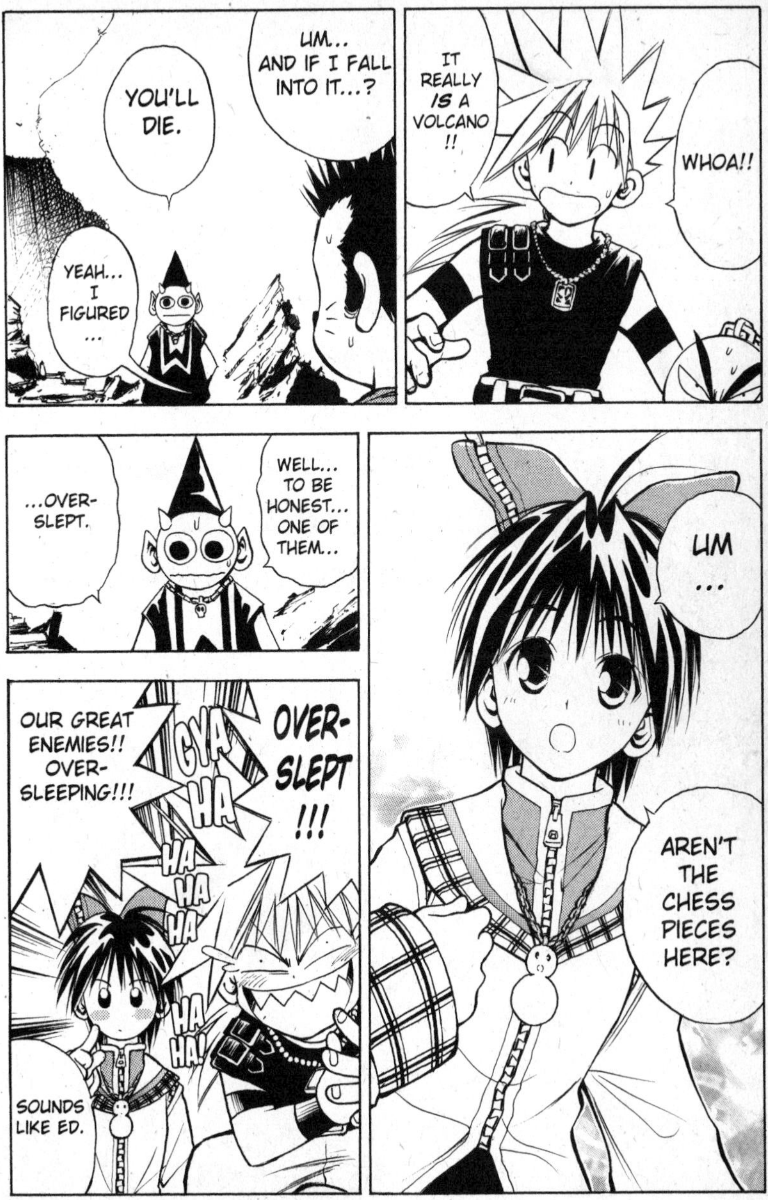
WHOA!!
IT REALLY IS A VOLCANO!!
UM... AND IF I FALL INTO IT...?
YOU'LL DIE.
YEAH... I FIGURED...
UM...
AREN'T THE CHESS PIECES HERE?
WELL... TO BE HONEST... ONE OF THEM...
...OVER-SLEPT.
OVER-SLEPT!!!
GYAHA HA HA HA HA HA HA!
OUR GREAT ENEMIES!! OVER-SLEEPING!!!
SOUNDS LIKE ED.

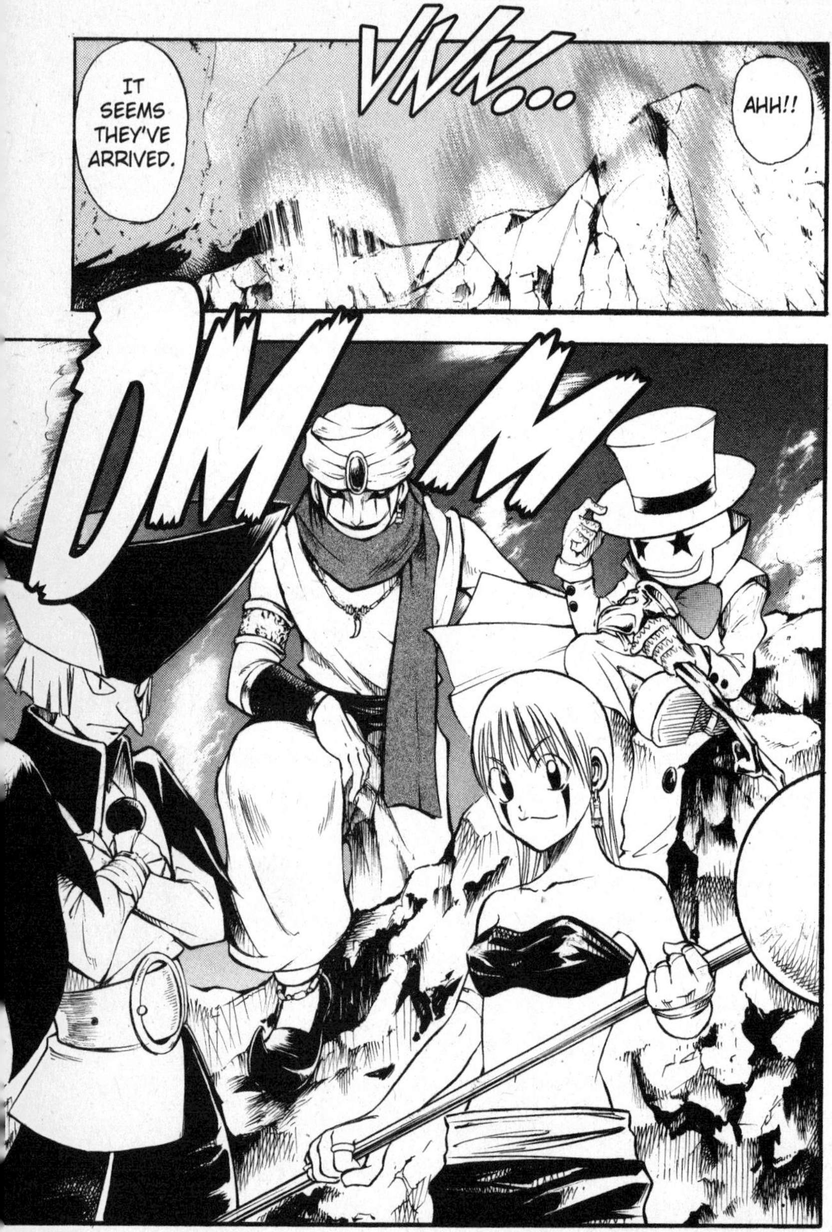
AHH!!
VNVVooo
IT SEEMS THEY'VE ARRIVED.
DMM

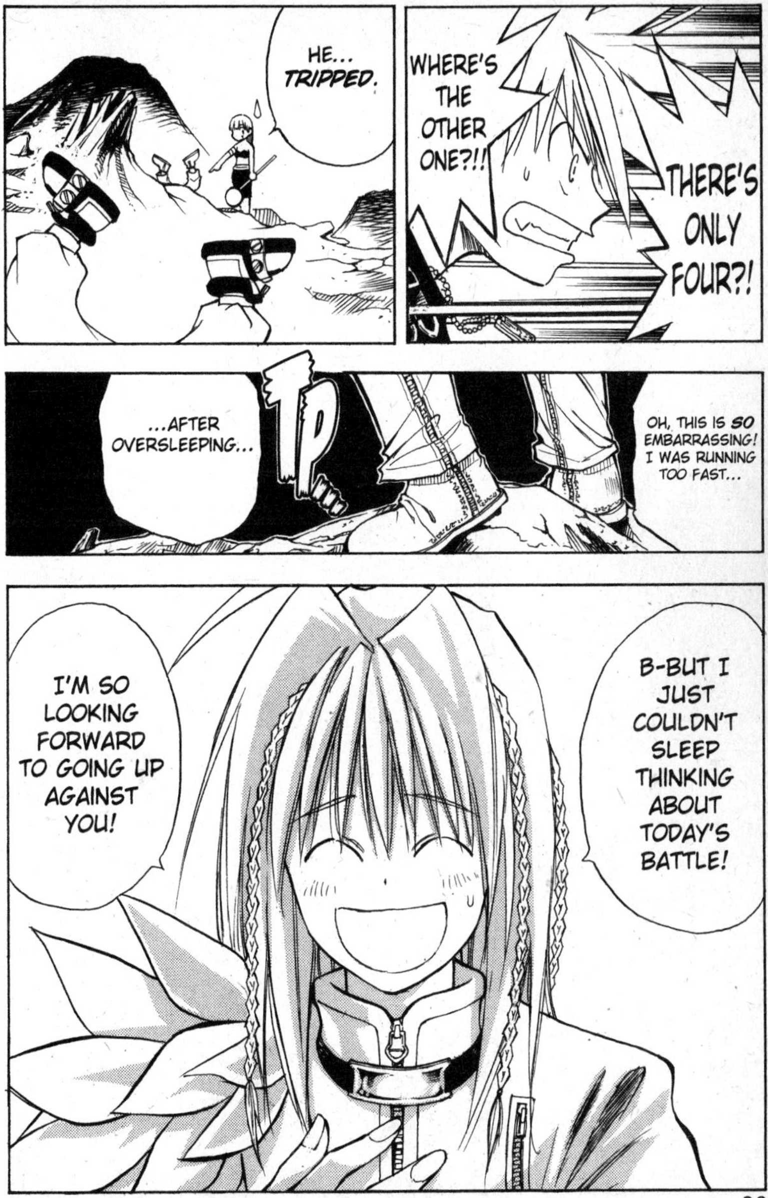
WHERE'S THE OTHER ONE?!!
THERE'S ONLY FOUR?!
HE... TRIPPED.
OH, THIS IS SO EMBARRASSING! I WAS RUNNING TOO FAST...
TP
...AFTER OVERSLEEPING...
B-BUT I JUST COULDN'T SLEEP THINKING ABOUT TODAY'S BATTLE!
I'M SO LOOKING FORWARD TO GOING UP AGAINST YOU!

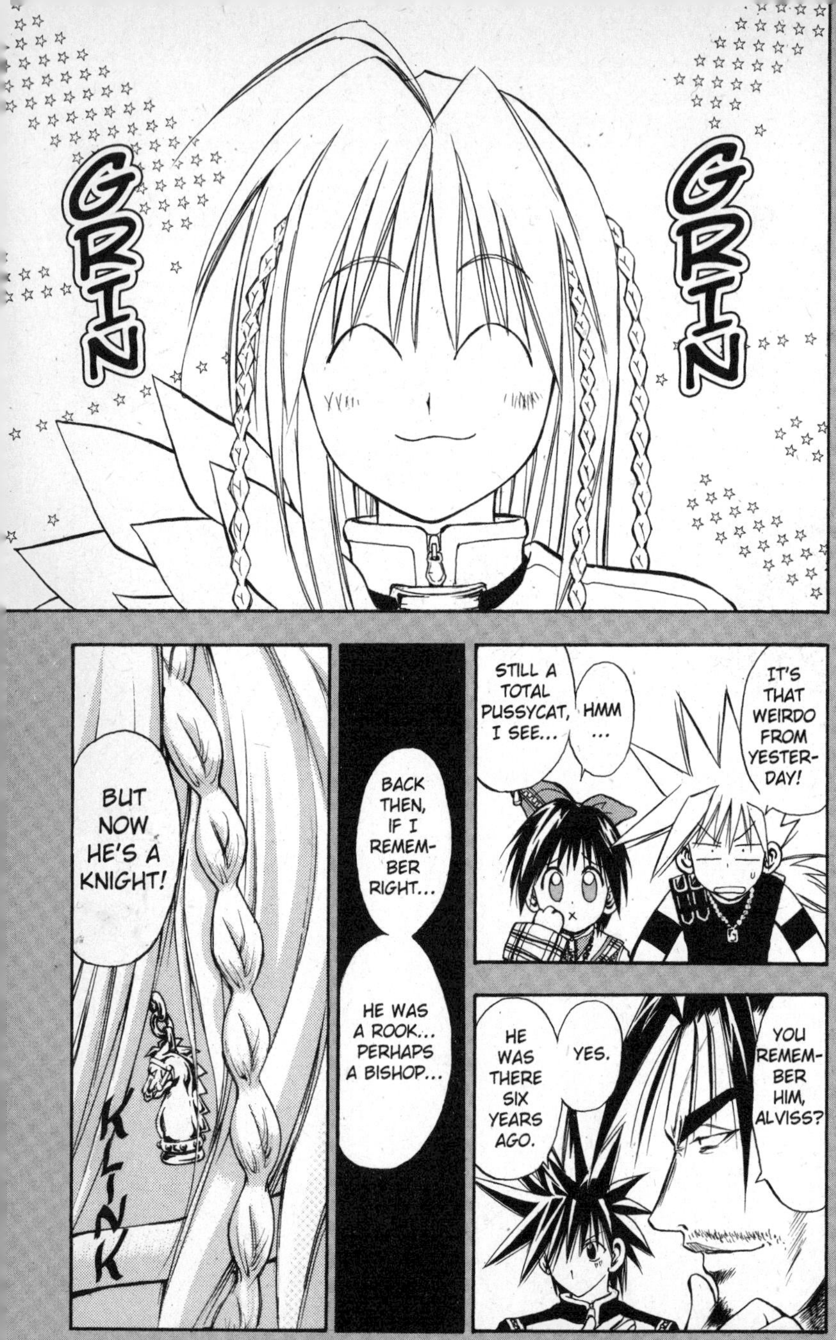
GRIN
GRIN
IT'S THAT WEIRDO FROM YESTERDAY!
HMM...
STILL A TOTAL PUSSYCAT, I SEE...
YOU REMEMBER HIM, ALVISS?
YES.
HE WAS THERE SIX YEARS AGO.
BACK THEN, IF I REMEMBER RIGHT...
HE WAS A ROOK... PERHAPS A BISHOP...
BUT NOW HE'S A KNIGHT!
KLINK

AKT.58/ Ed vs. Alibaba

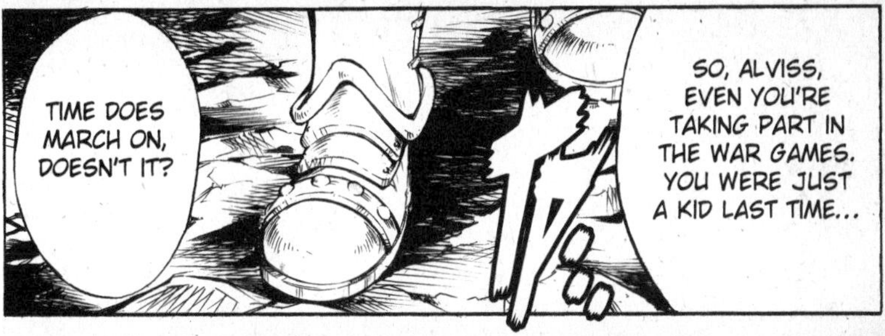
SO, ALVISS, EVEN YOU'RE TAKING PART IN THE WAR GAMES. YOU WERE JUST A KID LAST TIME...
TIME DOES MARCH ON, DOESN'T IT?

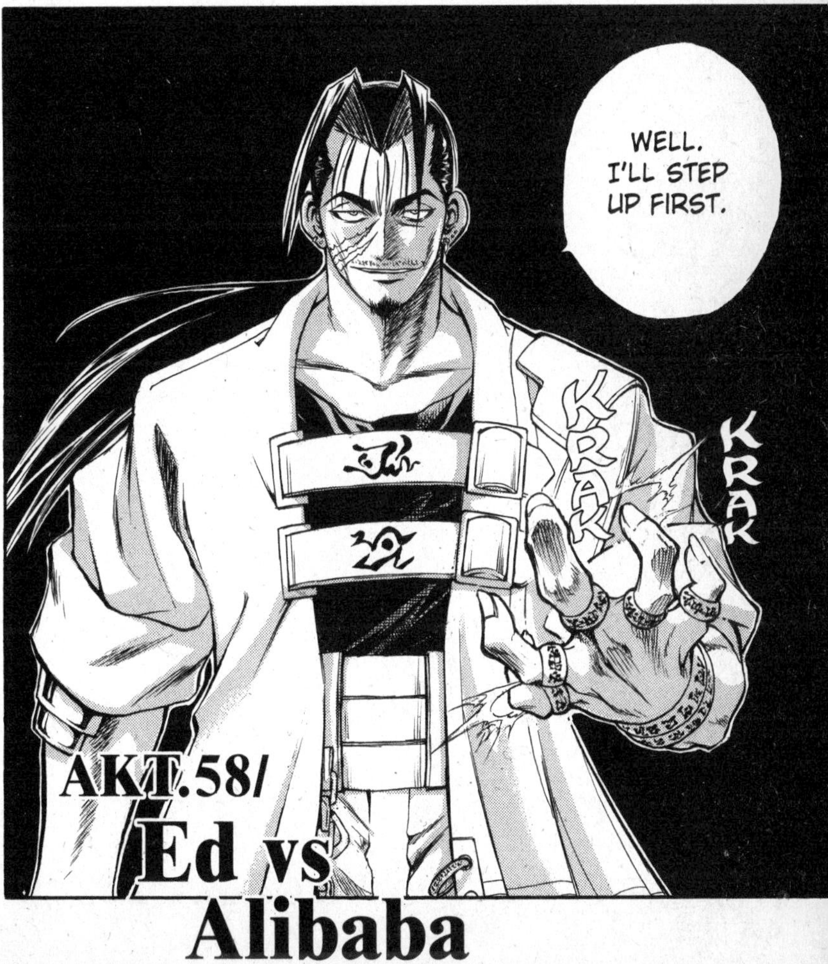
WELL. I'LL STEP UP FIRST.
KRAK
KRAK

AKT.58/ Ed vs Alibaba

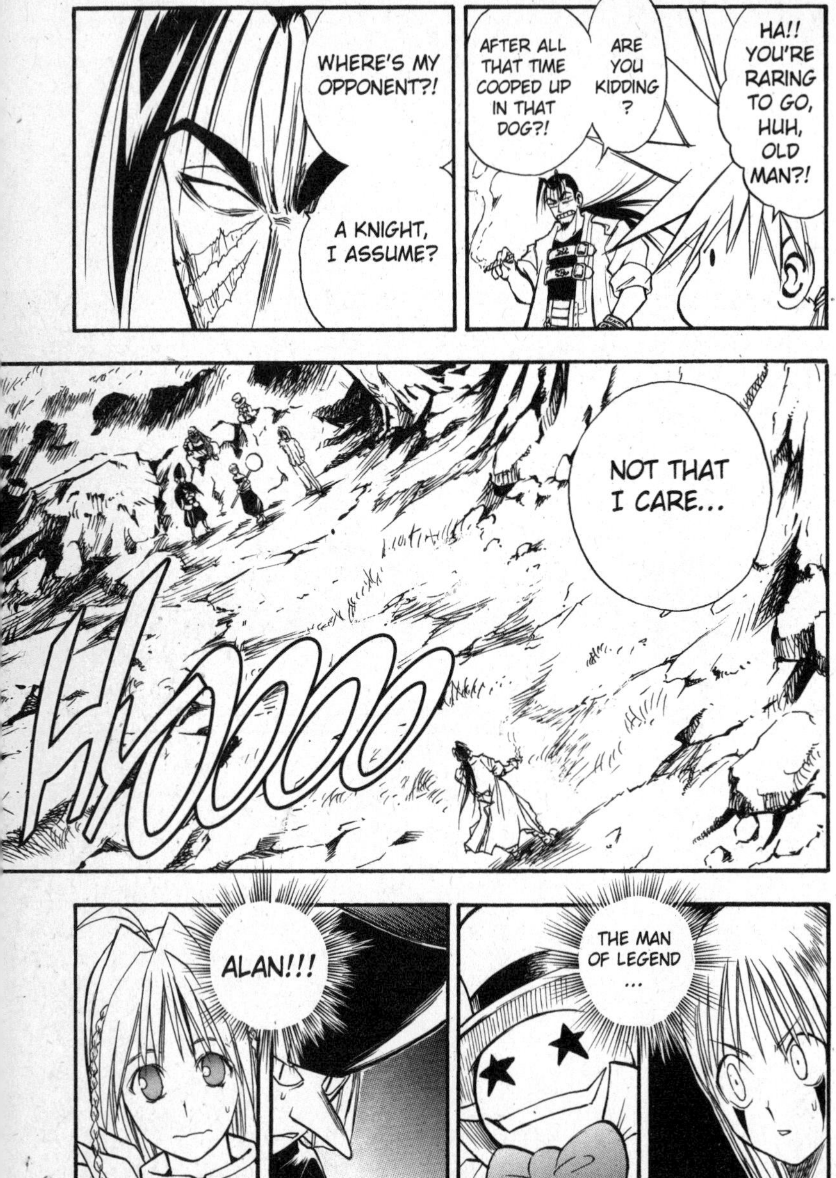
HA!! YOU'RE RARING TO GO, HUH, OLD MAN?!
ARE YOU KIDDING?
AFTER ALL THAT TIME COOPED UP IN THAT DOG?!
WHERE'S MY OPPONENT?!
A KNIGHT, I ASSUME?
NOT THAT I CARE...
THE MAN OF LEGEND ...
ALAN!!!

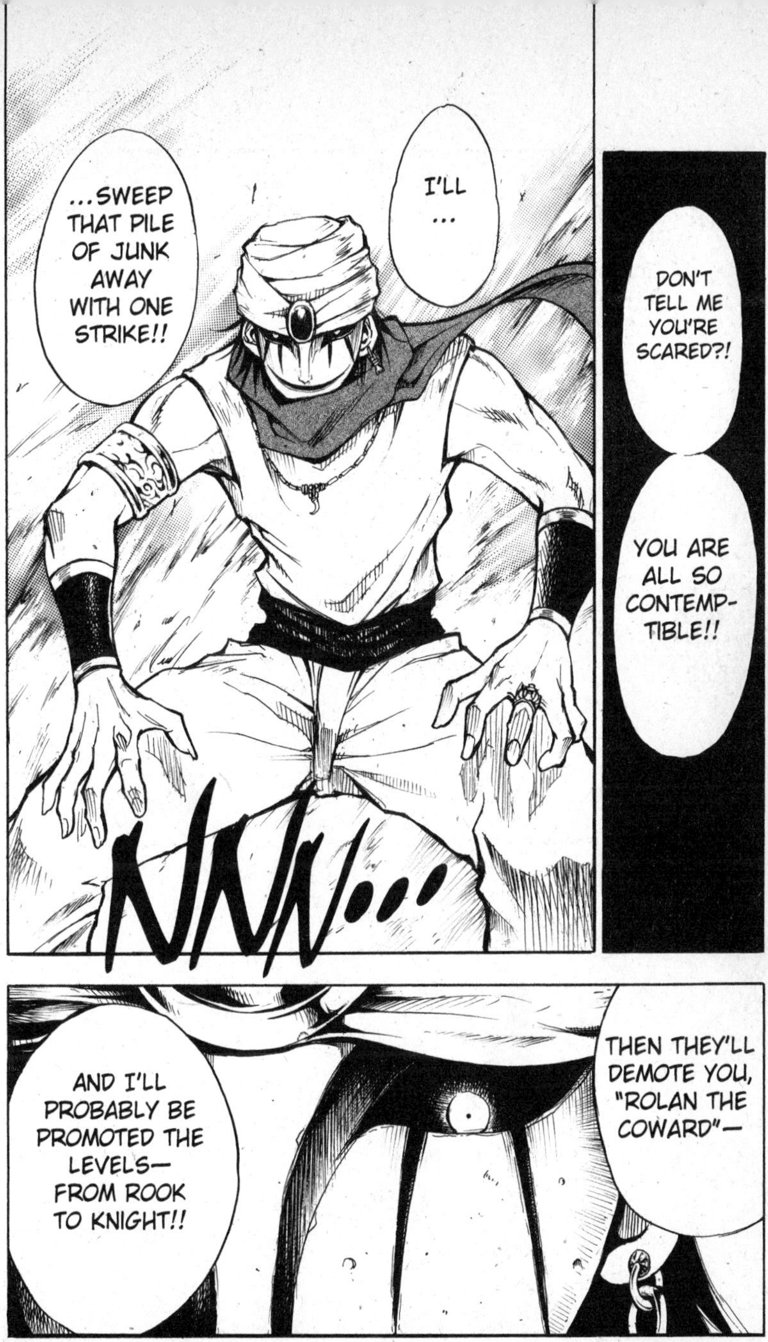
DON'T TELL ME YOU'RE SCARED?!
YOU ARE ALL SO CONTEMP-TIBLE!!
I'LL ...
...SWEEP THAT PILE OF JUNK AWAY WITH ONE STRIKE!!
NNN...
THEN THEY'LL DEMOTE YOU, "ROLAN THE COWARD"—
AND I'LL PROBABLY BE PROMOTED THE LEVELS— FROM ROOK TO KNIGHT!!

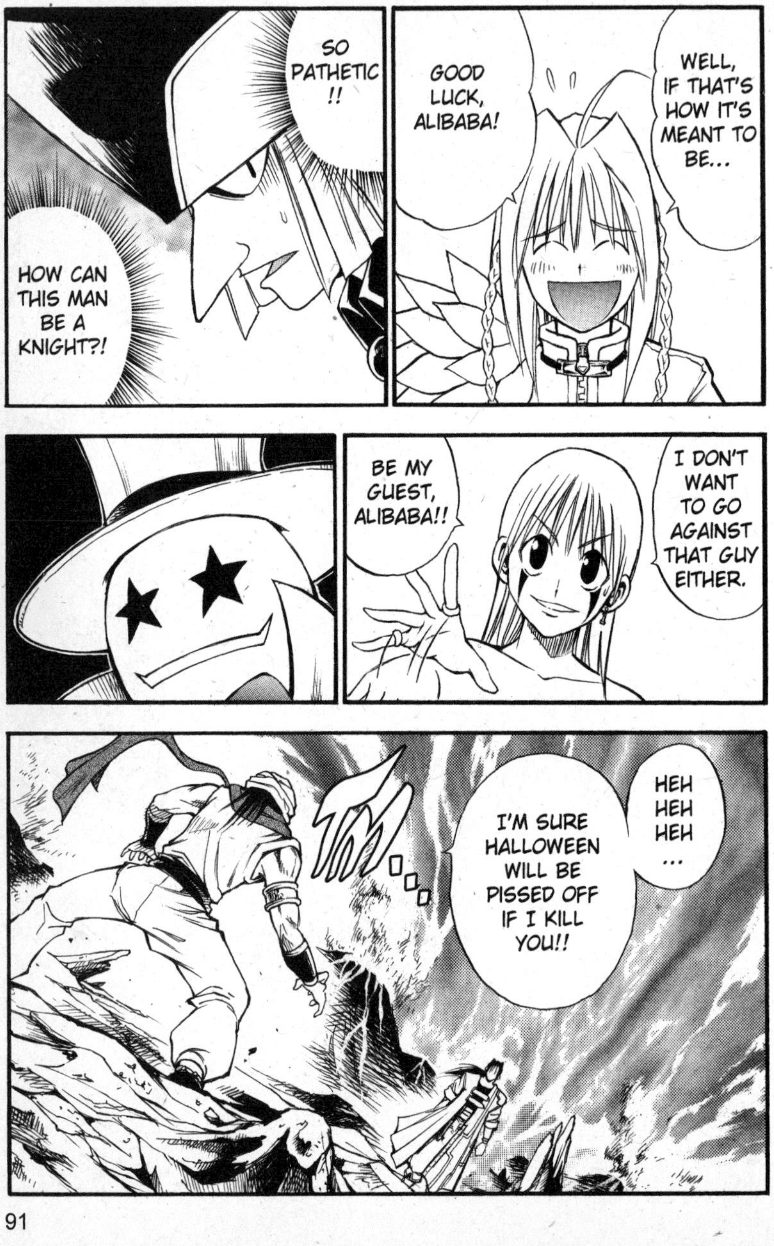
WELL, IF THAT'S HOW IT'S MEANT TO BE...
GOOD LUCK, ALIBABA!
SO PATHETIC!!
HOW CAN THIS MAN BE A KNIGHT?!
I DON'T WANT TO GO AGAINST THAT GUY EITHER.
BE MY GUEST, ALIBABA!!
HEH HEH HEH...
I'M SURE HALLOWEEN WILL BE PISSED OFF IF I KILL YOU!!

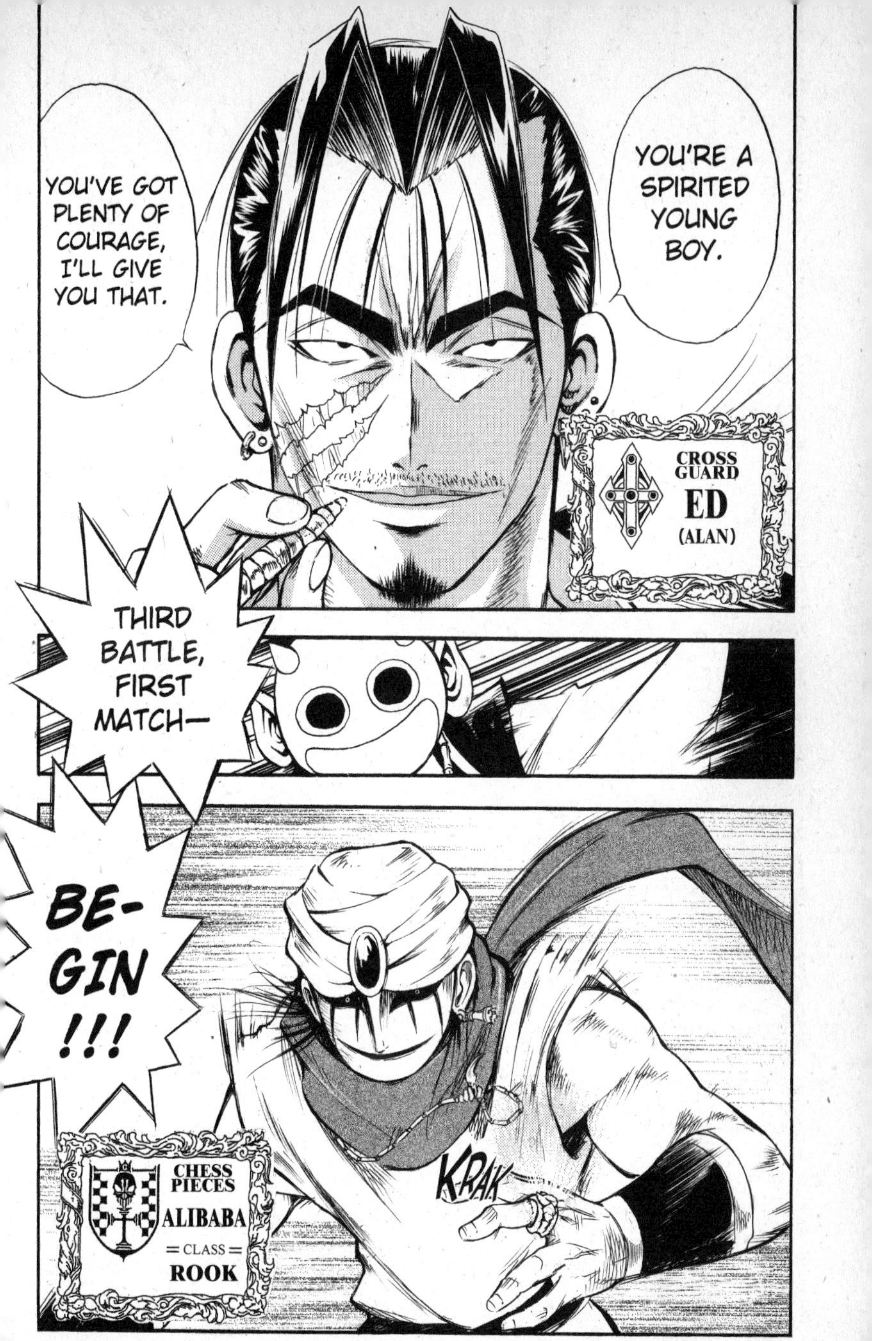
YOU'RE A SPIRITED YOUNG BOY.
YOU'VE GOT PLENTY OF COURAGE, I'LL GIVE YOU THAT.
CROSS GUARD
ED
(ALAN)
THIRD BATTLE, FIRST MATCH—
BE-GIN!!!
KRAK
CHESS PIECES
ALIBABA
=CLASS=
ROOK

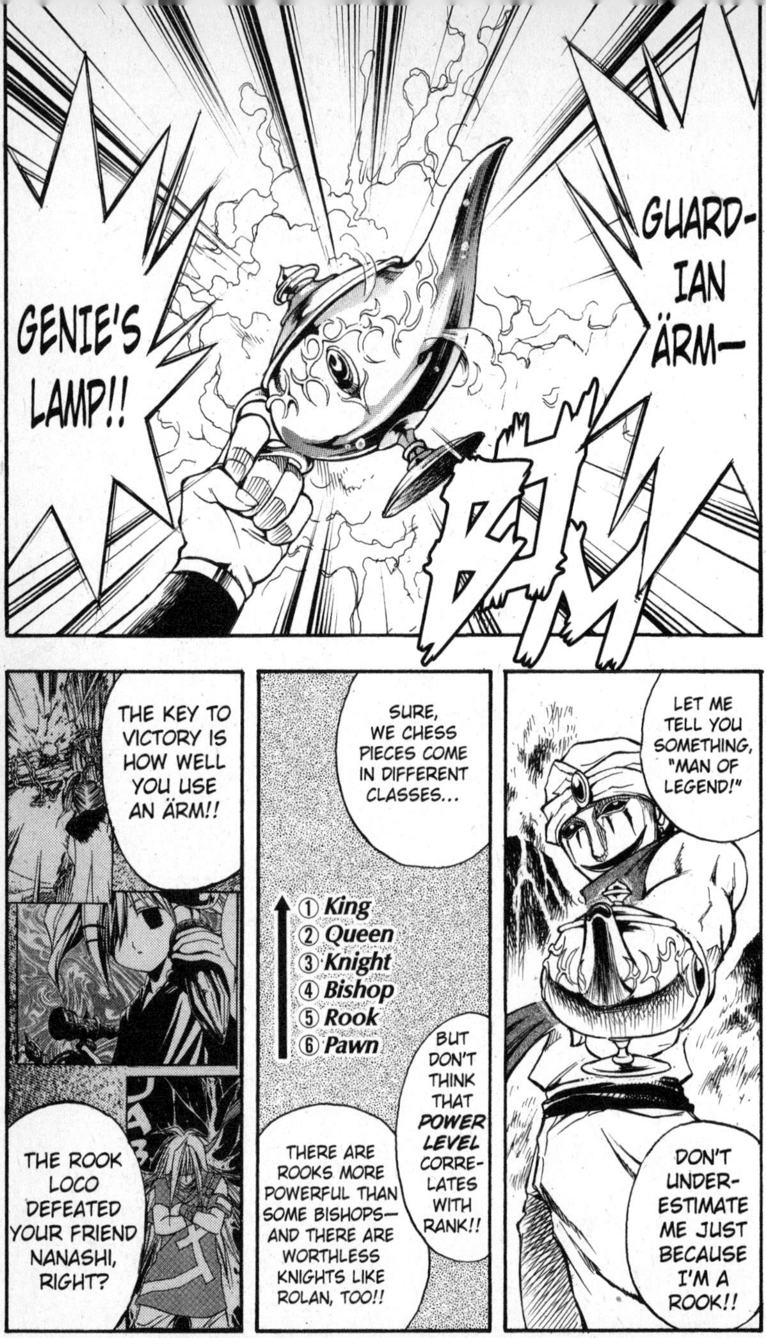
GUARDIAN ÄRM—
GENIE'S LAMP!!
BAM
LET ME TELL YOU SOMETHING, "MAN OF LEGEND!"
DON'T UNDERESTIMATE ME JUST BECAUSE I'M A ROOK!!
SURE, WE CHESS PIECES COME IN DIFFERENT CLASSES...
① King ② Queen ③ Knight ④ Bishop ⑤ Rook ⑥ Pawn
BUT DON'T THINK THAT POWER LEVEL CORRELATES WITH RANK!!
THERE ARE ROOKS MORE POWERFUL THAN SOME BISHOPS—AND THERE ARE WORTHLESS KNIGHTS LIKE ROLAN, TOO!!
THE KEY TO VICTORY IS HOW WELL YOU USE AN ÄRM!!
THE ROOK LOCO DEFEATED YOUR FRIEND NANASHI, RIGHT?

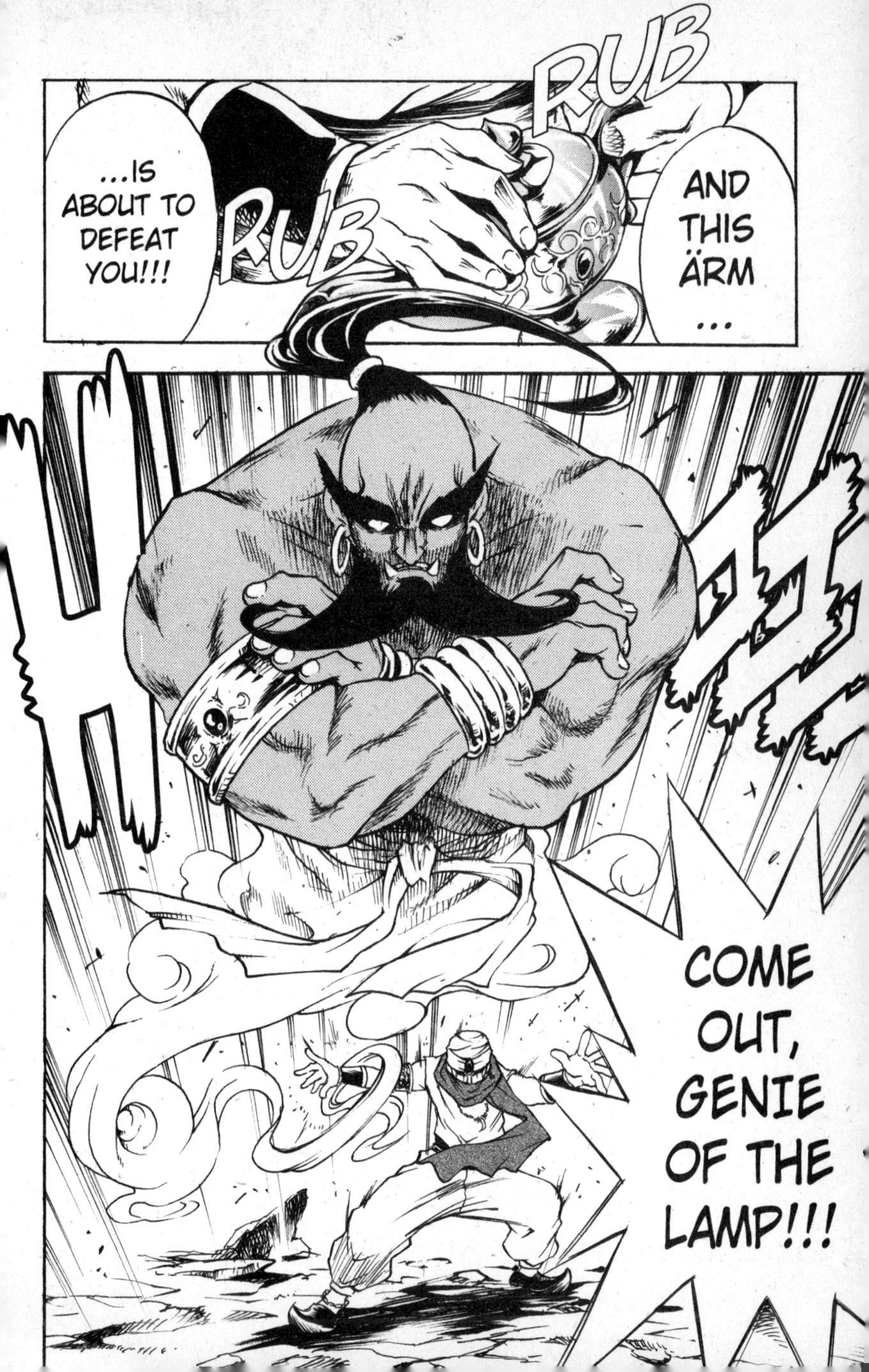
AND THIS ÄRM ...
RUB
RUB
...IS ABOUT TO DEFEAT YOU!!!
COME OUT, GENIE OF THE LAMP!!!

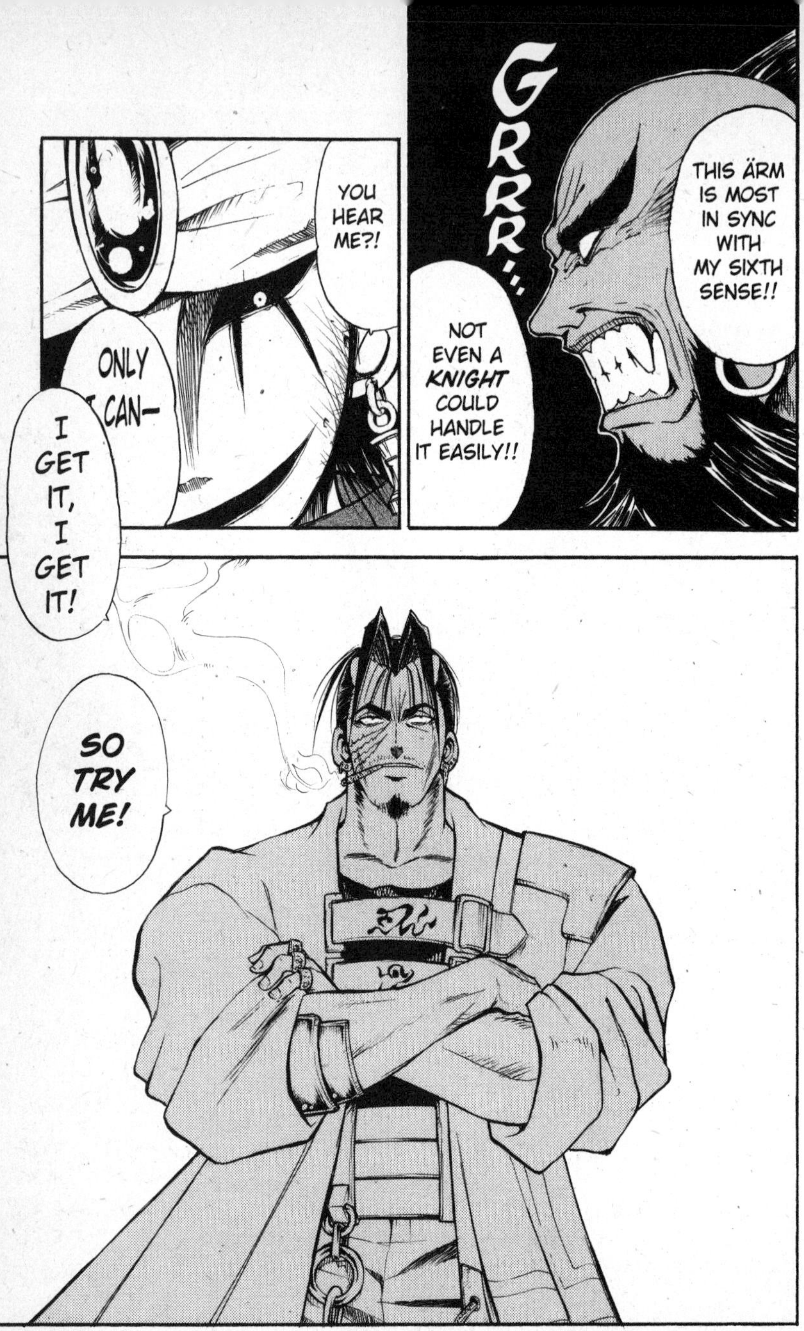
GRRR...
THIS ÄRM IS MOST IN SYNC WITH MY SIXTH SENSE!!
NOT EVEN A KNIGHT COULD HANDLE IT EASILY!!
YOU HEAR ME?!
ONLY I CAN—
I GET IT, I GET IT!
SO TRY ME!

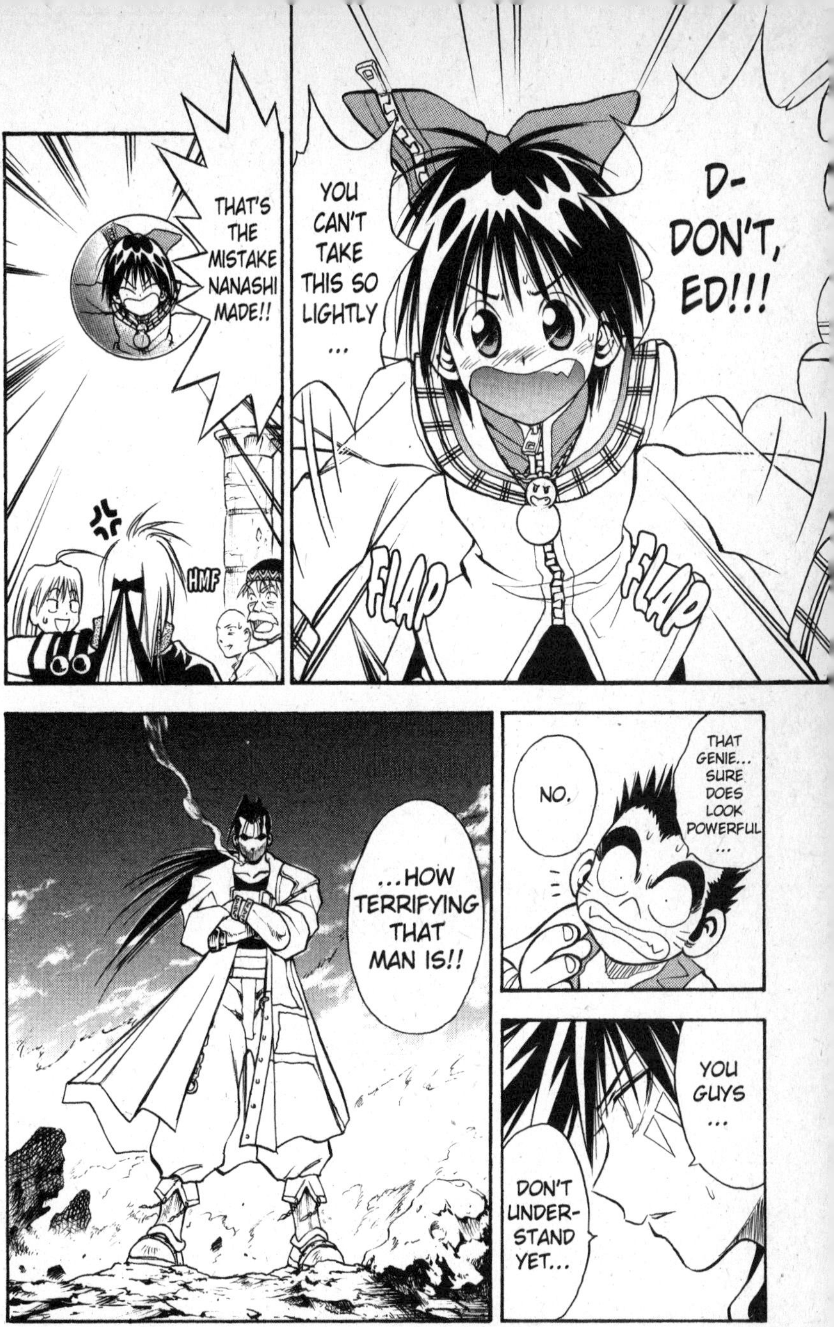
D-DON'T, ED!!!
YOU CAN'T TAKE THIS SO LIGHTLY...
FLAP
FLAP
THAT'S THE MISTAKE NANASHI MADE!!
HMF
THAT GENIE... SURE DOES LOOK POWERFUL...
NO.
YOU GUYS...
DON'T UNDER-STAND YET...
...HOW TERRIFYING THAT MAN IS!!

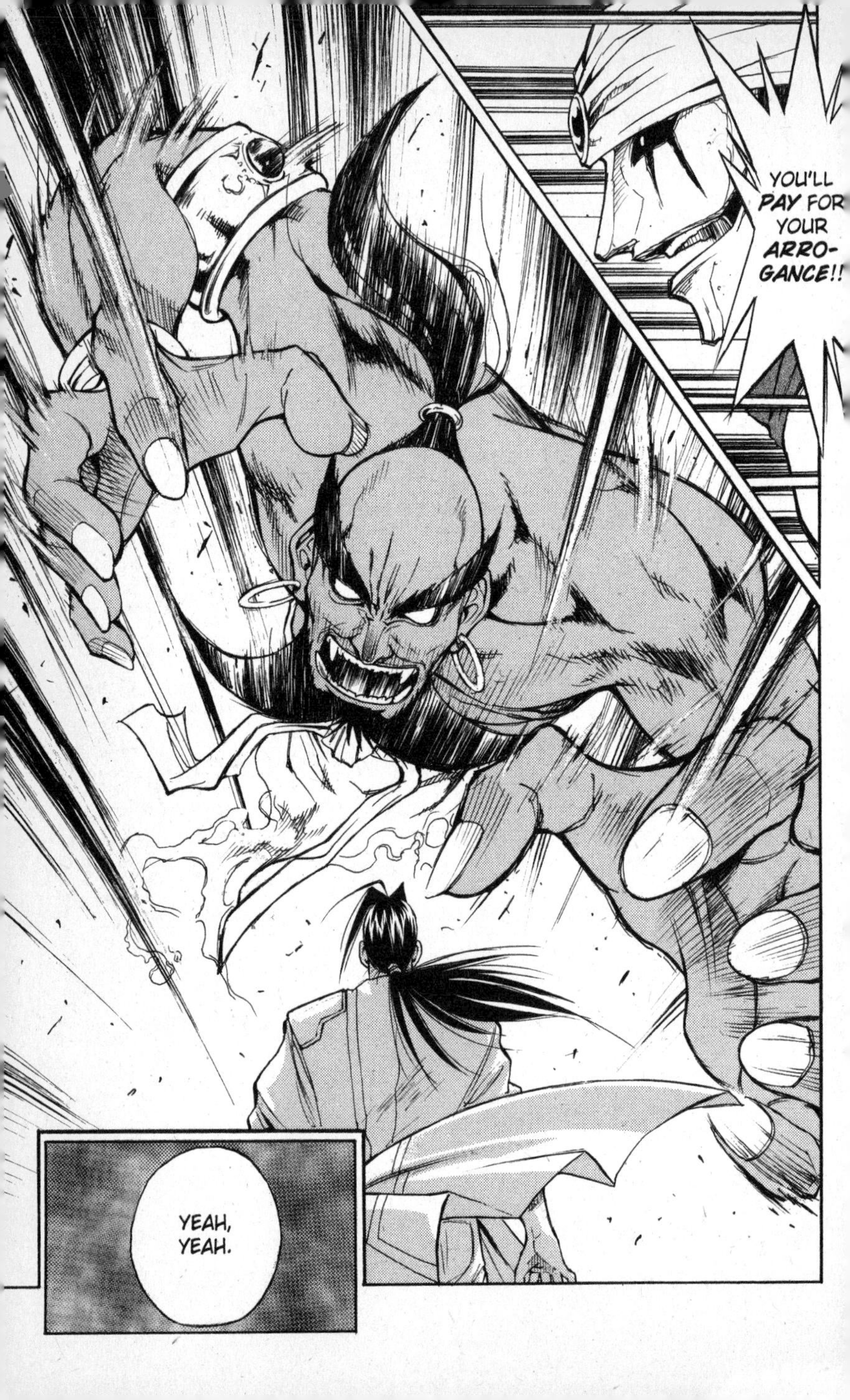
YOU'LL **PAY** FOR YOUR **ARROGANCE!!**
YEAH, YEAH.

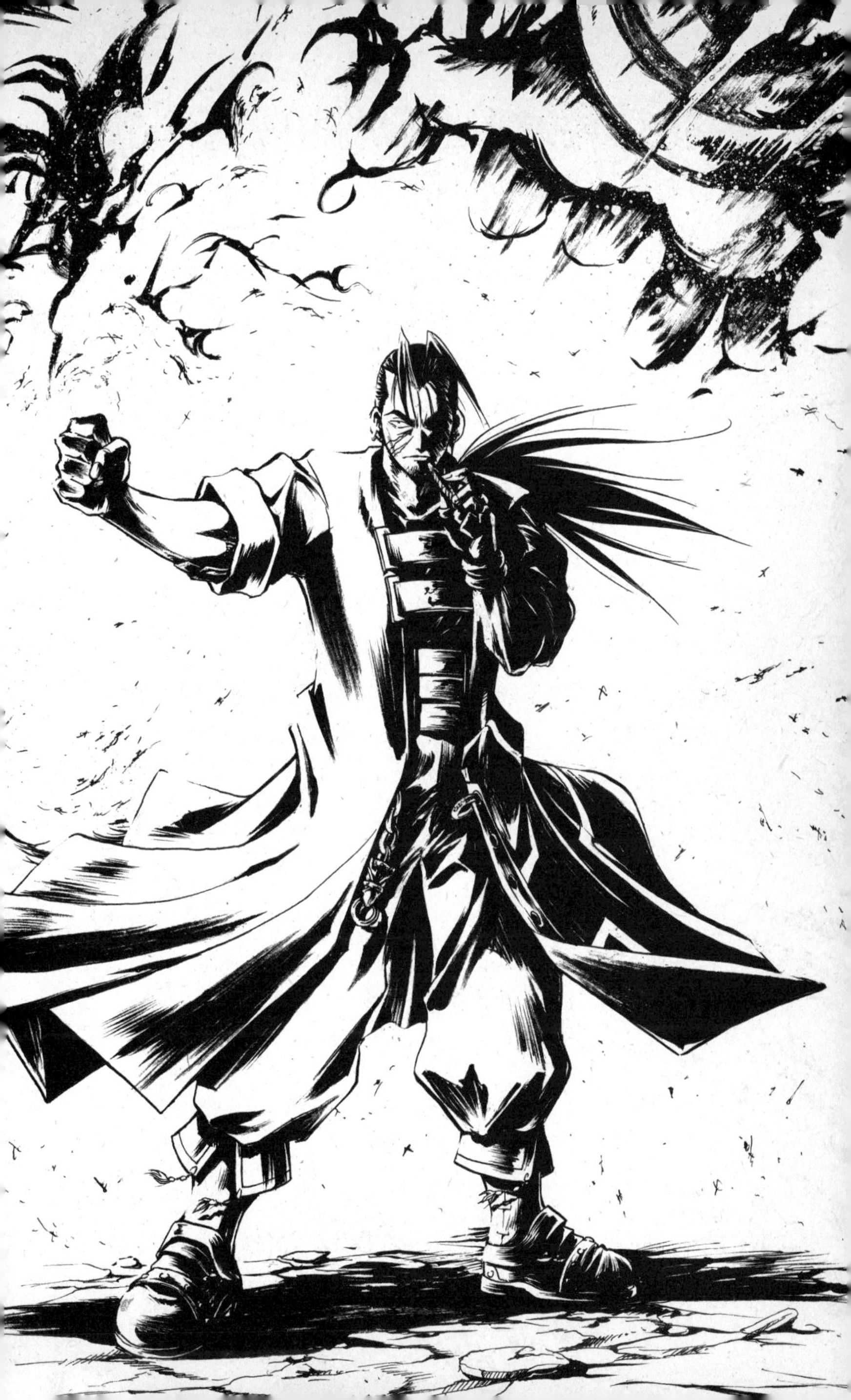

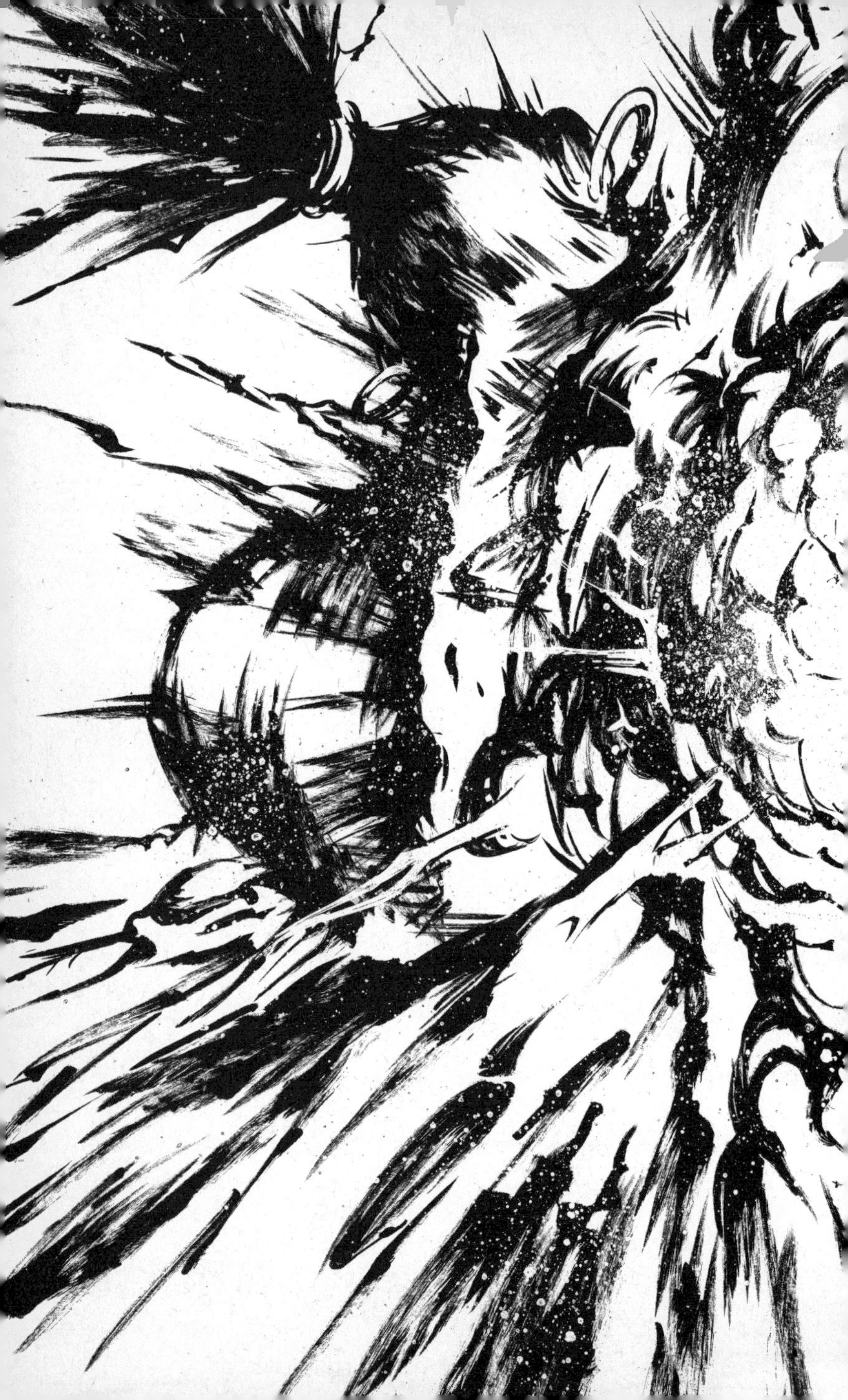

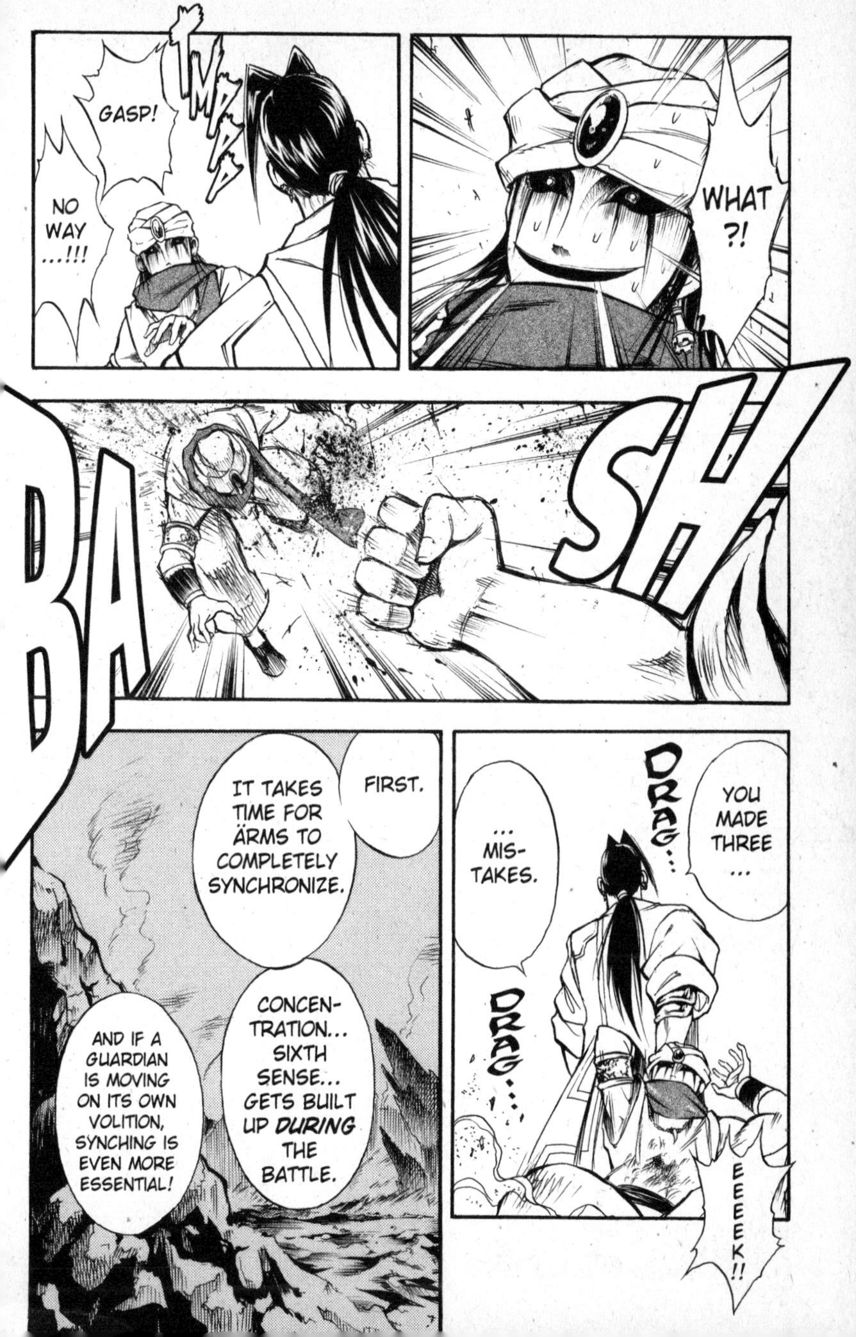
WHAT ?!
TMPPP
GASP!
NO WAY ...!!!
SH
BA
YOU MADE THREE ...
DRAG...
... MIS-TAKES.
DRAG...
EEEEK!!
FIRST.
IT TAKES TIME FOR ÄRMS TO COMPLETELY SYNCHRONIZE.
CONCEN-TRATION... SIXTH SENSE... GETS BUILT UP *DURING* THE BATTLE.
AND IF A GUARDIAN IS MOVING ON ITS OWN VOLITION, SYNCHING IS EVEN MORE ESSENTIAL!

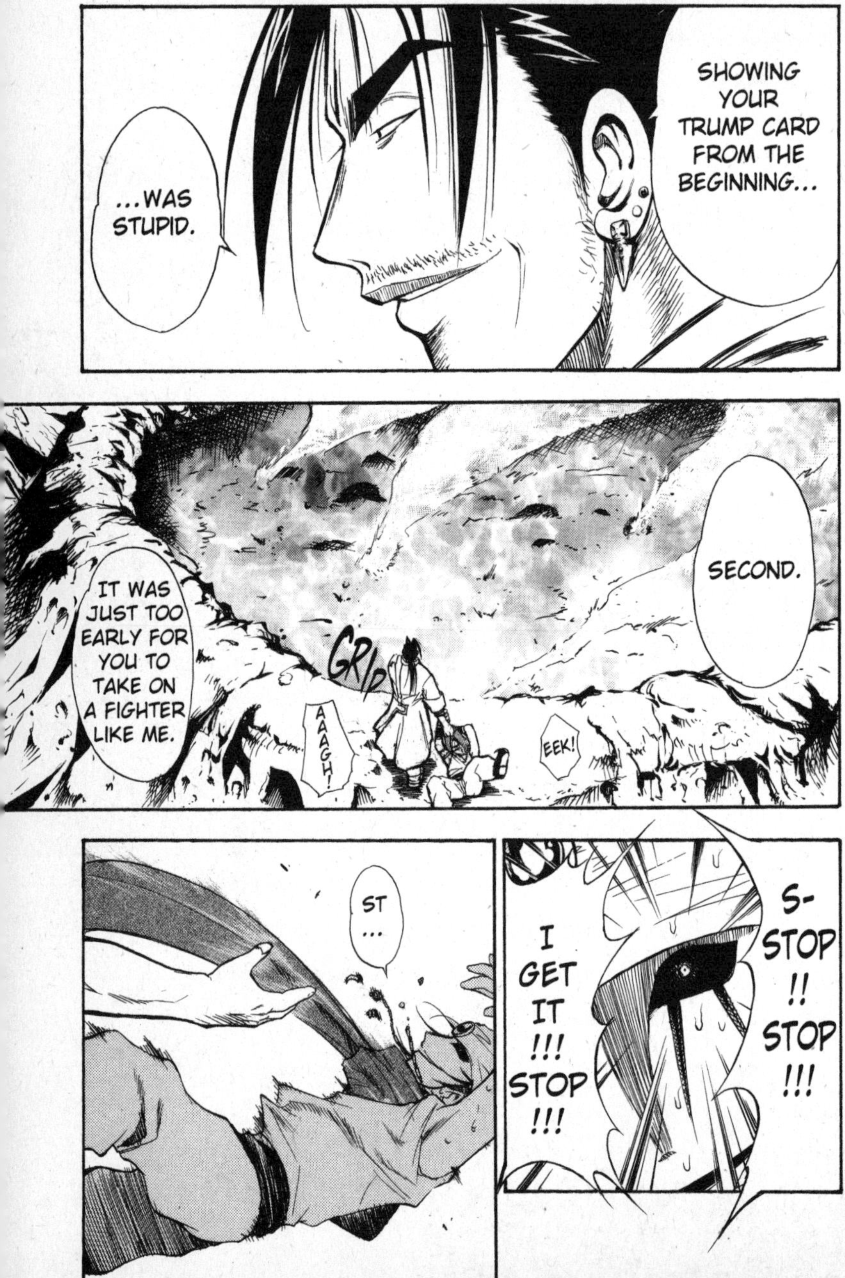
SHOWING YOUR TRUMP CARD FROM THE BEGINNING...
...WAS STUPID.
SECOND.
EEK!
GRIP
AAAGH!
IT WAS JUST TOO EARLY FOR YOU TO TAKE ON A FIGHTER LIKE ME.
S-STOP!! STOP!!!
I GET IT!!! STOP!!!
ST...

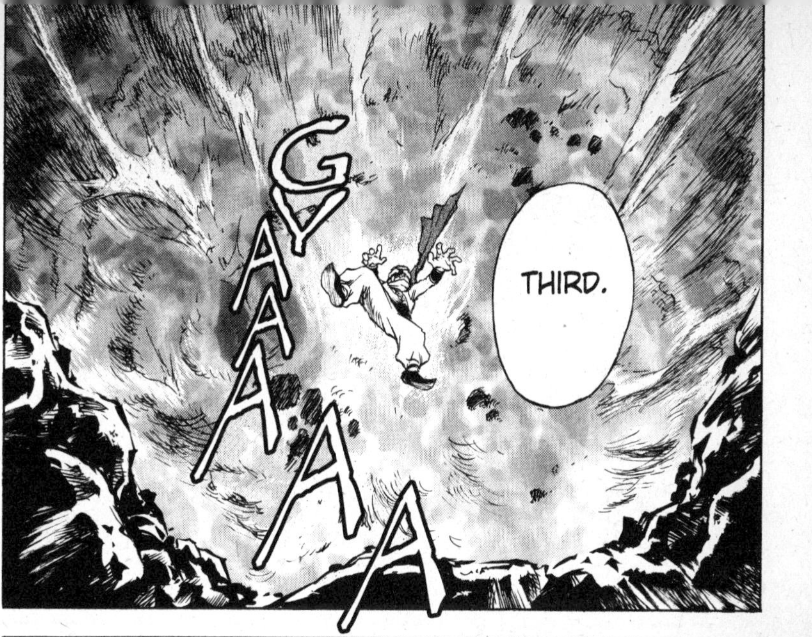
THIRD.
GYAAAAAA
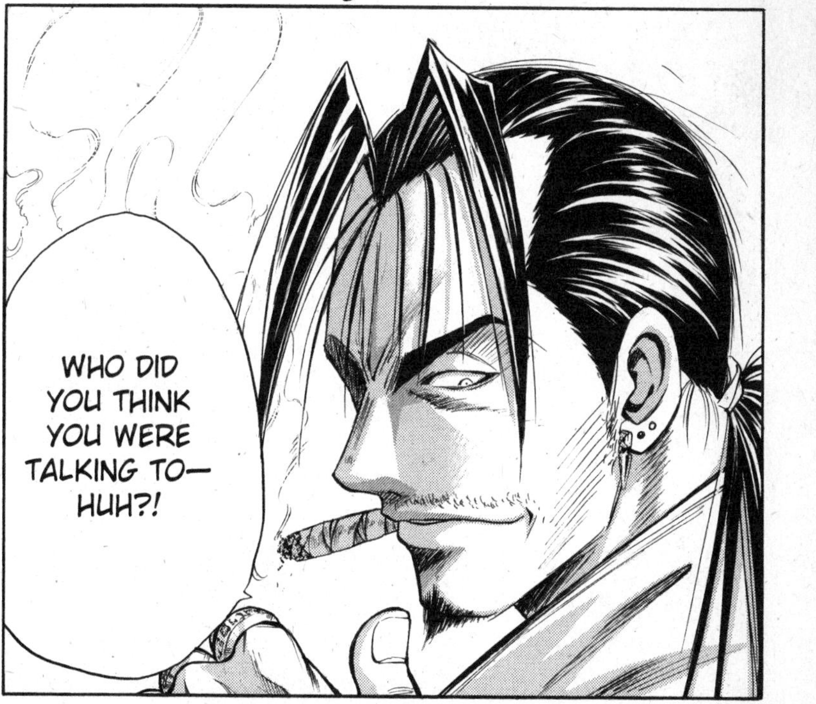
WHO DID YOU THINK YOU WERE TALKING TO—HUH?!

AKT.59/ Jack vs. Pano (Rematch) ①

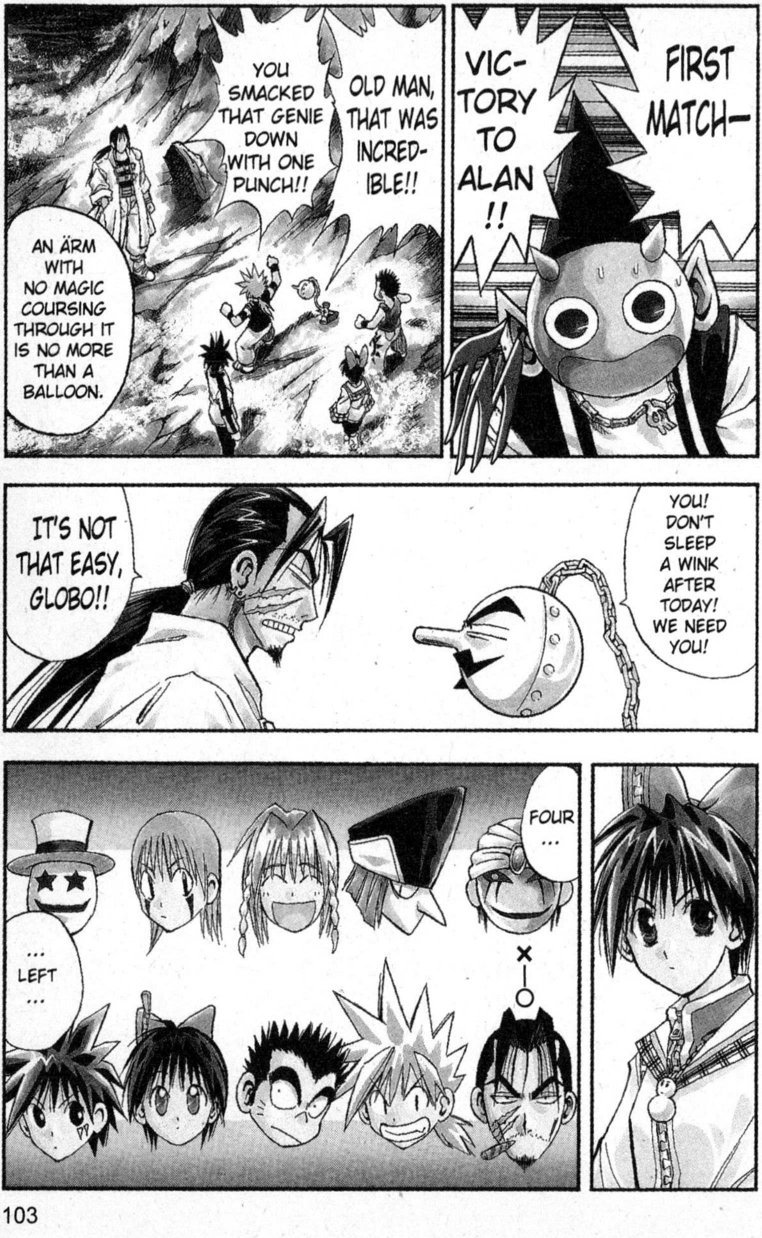
FIRST MATCH—
VICTORY TO ALAN!!
OLD MAN, THAT WAS INCREDIBLE!!
YOU SMACKED THAT GENIE DOWN WITH ONE PUNCH!!
AN ÄRM WITH NO MAGIC COURSING THROUGH IT IS NO MORE THAN A BALLOON.
YOU! DON'T SLEEP A WINK AFTER TODAY! WE NEED YOU!
IT'S NOT THAT EASY, GLOBO!!
FOUR ...
... LEFT ...

CONTEST RESULTS!!

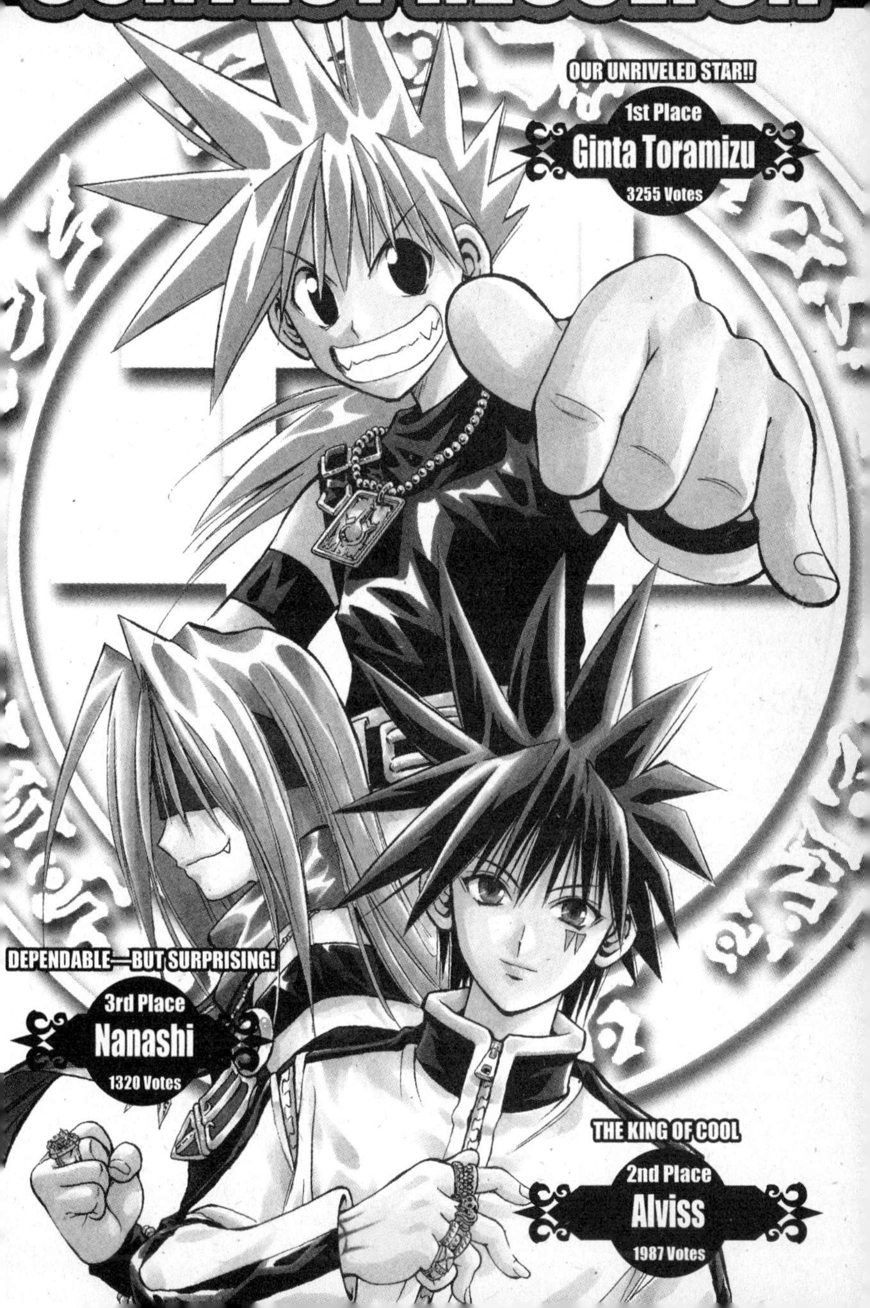
OUR UNRIVELED STAR!!
1st Place
Ginta Toramizu
3255 Votes
THE KING OF COOL
2nd Place
Alviss
1987 Votes
DEPENDABLE—BUT SURPRISING!
3rd Place
Nanashi
1320 Votes

AT LAST!!

CHARACTER POPULARITY

THE WITCH OF MYSTERY!
4th Place
Dorothy
821 Votes
A PRINCESS OF MÄR HEAVEN!
5th Place
Snow
798 Votes
THE RAREST OF ÄRMS!
6th Place
Babbo
742 Votes
THE LEADER OF THE CHESS PIECES!
7th Place
Phantom
440 Votes
THE MAN WHO BURNS WITH VENGEANCE!
8th Place
Ian
390 Votes
A MAN OF SHARP SKILLS!
9th Place
Edward (Alan)
374 Votes
STILL WAITING FOR GINTA!
10th Place
Koyuki
370 Votes

11th Place	Boss	339 Votes
12th Place	Jack	282 Votes
13th Place	Edward (Dog)	168 Votes
14th Place	Garon	139 Votes
15th Place	Girom	101 Votes
16th Place	Loco	99 Votes
17th Place	Ginta's Mom	96 Votes
18th Place	Peta	93 Votes
19th Place	Halloween	81 Votes
20th Place	Merilo	54 Votes
21th Place	Bumoru	51 Votes
22nd Place	Pano	48 Votes
23rd Place	Jack's Mom	44 Votes
	Gaira	44 Votes
25th Place	Chimera	37 Votes
26th Place	Gido	31 Votes
27th Place	Bell	28 Votes
28th Place	Mokku	27 Votes
29th Place	Orco	19 Votes
30th Place	Stanley	12 Votes
31th Place	Chappu	10 Votes
32nd Place	Leno	8 Votes
33rd Place	Rugelu Brothers	1 Vote
	Talking Boulders	1 Vote

AKT.59/

Jack vs. Pano (Rematch) ①

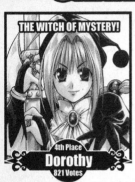

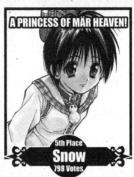

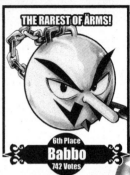

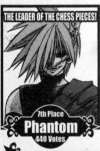

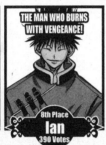

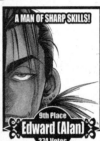

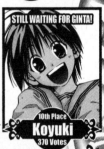

MÄR
MÄRCHEN AWAKENS ROMANCE

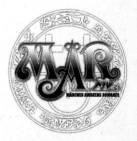

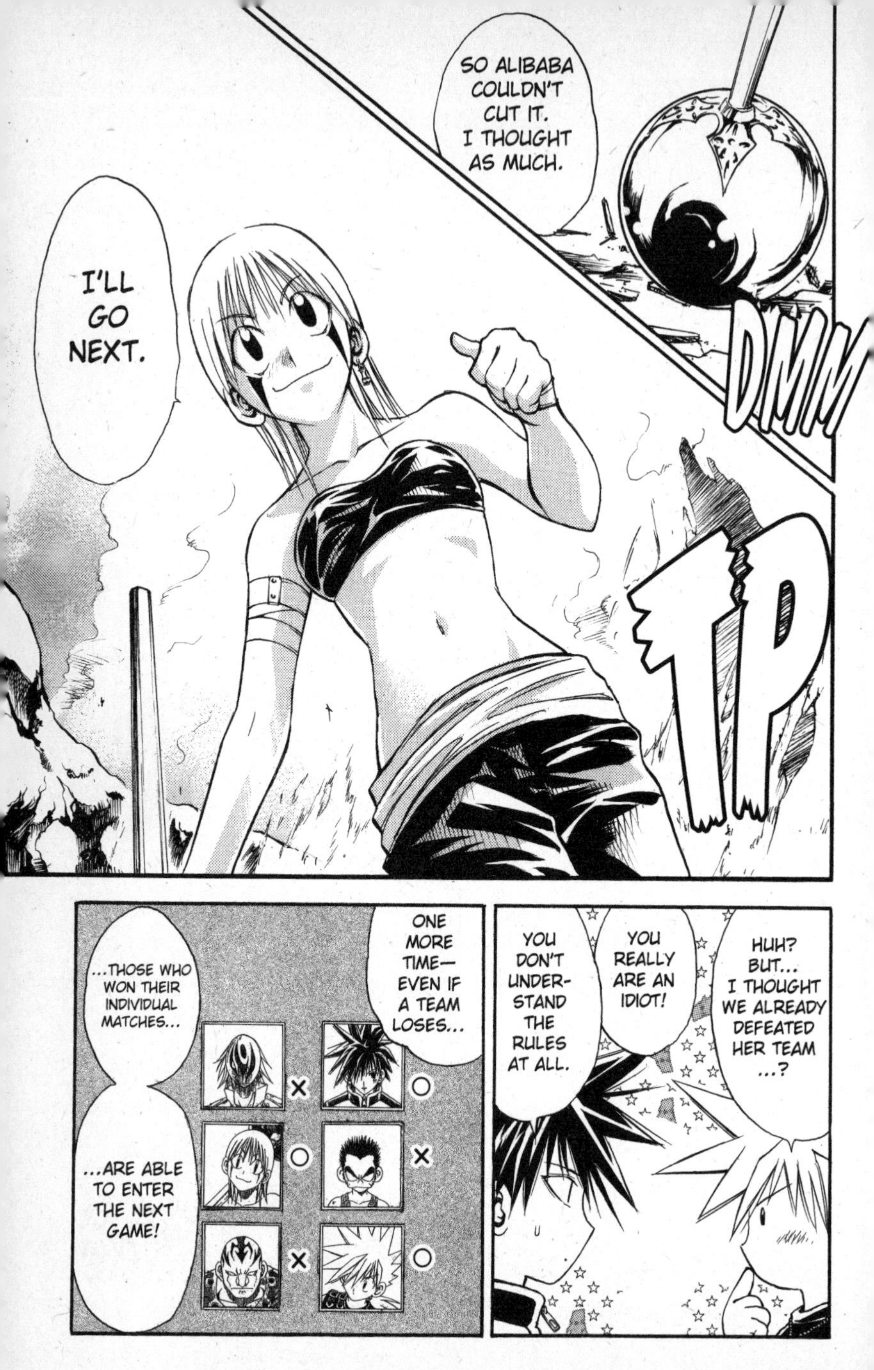
SO ALIBABA COULDN'T CUT IT. I THOUGHT AS MUCH.
DMMM
TP
I'LL GO NEXT.
HUH? BUT... I THOUGHT WE ALREADY DEFEATED HER TEAM ...?
YOU REALLY ARE AN IDIOT!
YOU DON'T UNDER-STAND THE RULES AT ALL.
ONE MORE TIME— EVEN IF A TEAM LOSES...
...THOSE WHO WON THEIR INDIVIDUAL MATCHES...
...ARE ABLE TO ENTER THE NEXT GAME!

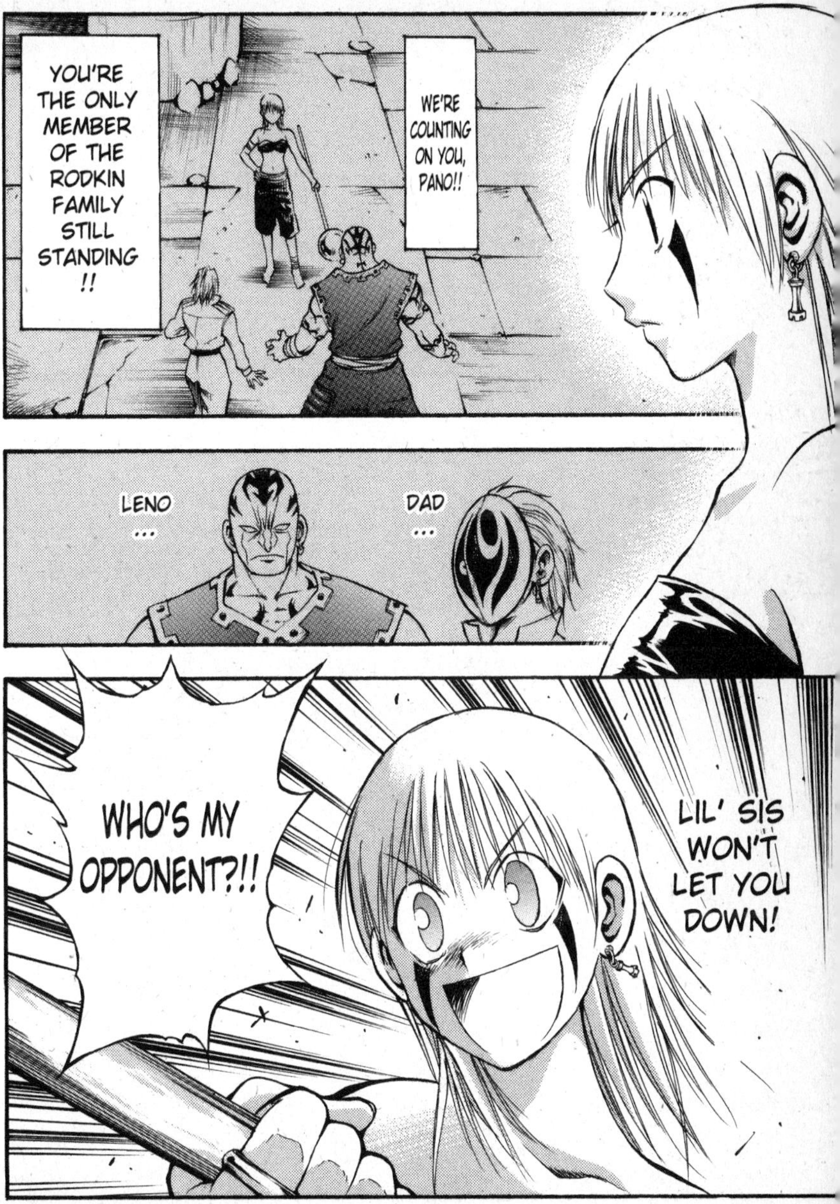
WE'RE COUNTING ON YOU, PANO!!
YOU'RE THE ONLY MEMBER OF THE RODKIN FAMILY STILL STANDING!!
DAD...
LENO...
LIL' SIS WON'T LET YOU DOWN!
WHO'S MY OPPONENT?!!

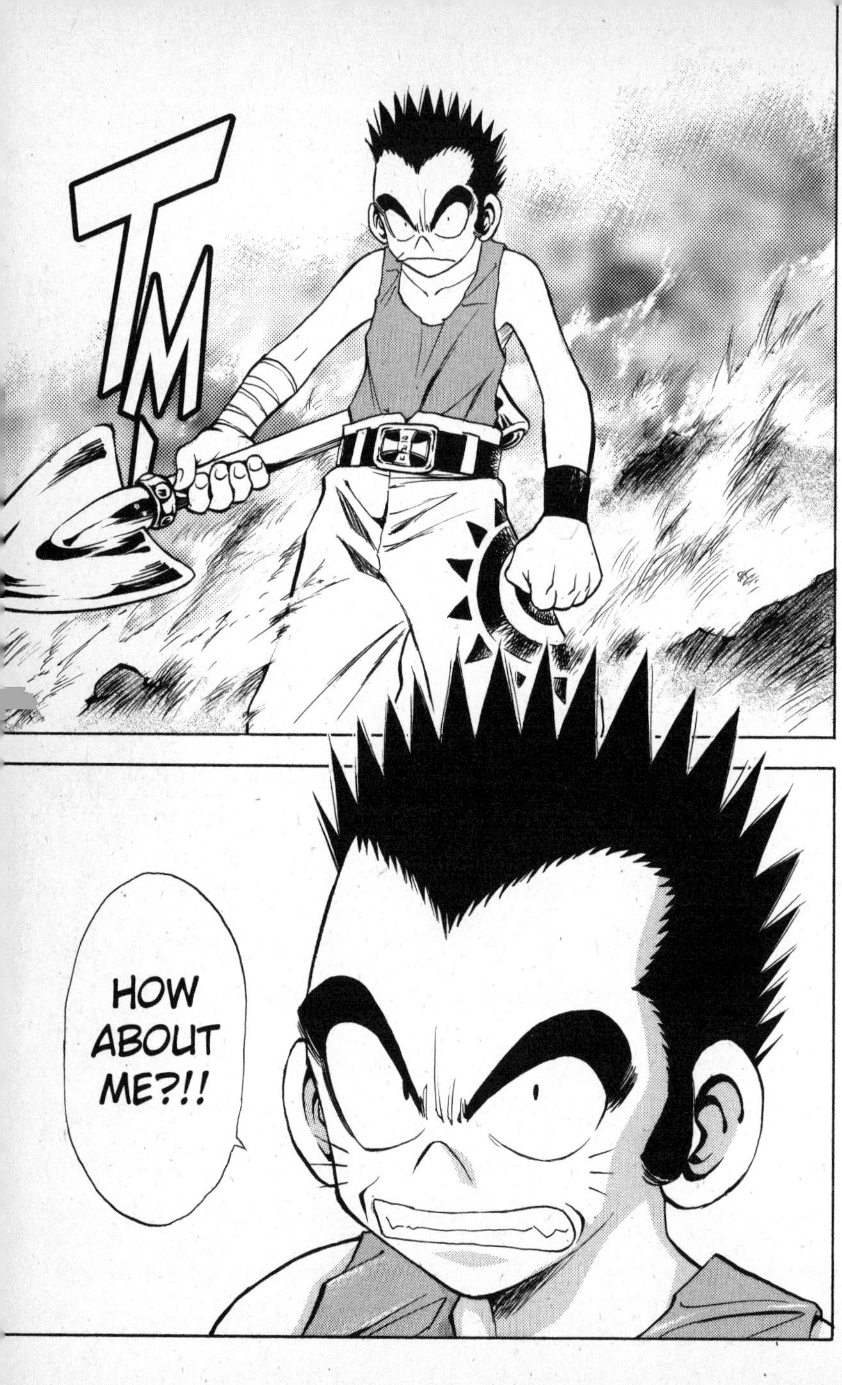
TMM
HOW ABOUT ME?!!

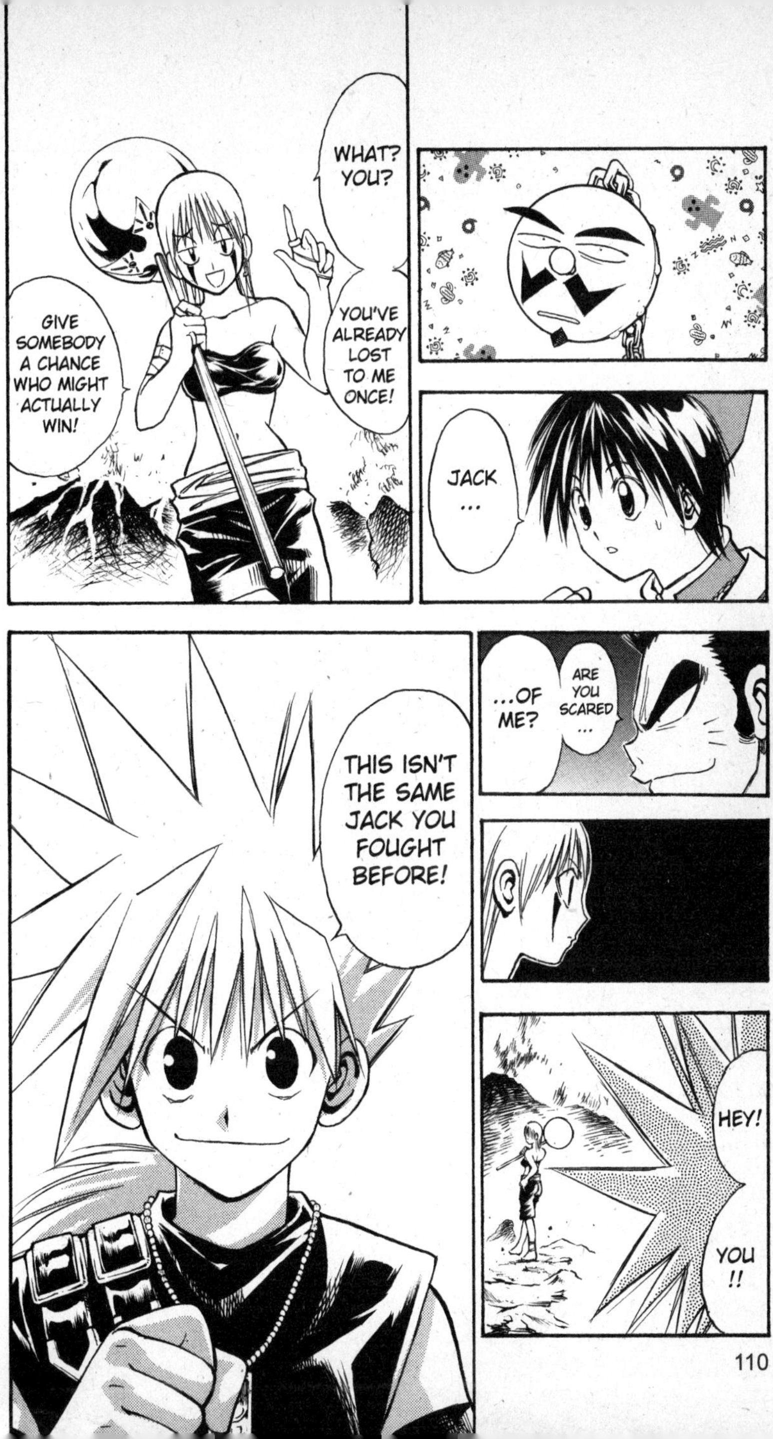
JACK ...
WHAT? YOU?
YOU'VE ALREADY LOST TO ME ONCE!
GIVE SOMEBODY A CHANCE WHO MIGHT ACTUALLY WIN!
ARE YOU SCARED ...
...OF ME?
HEY!
YOU !!
THIS ISN'T THE SAME JACK YOU FOUGHT BEFORE!

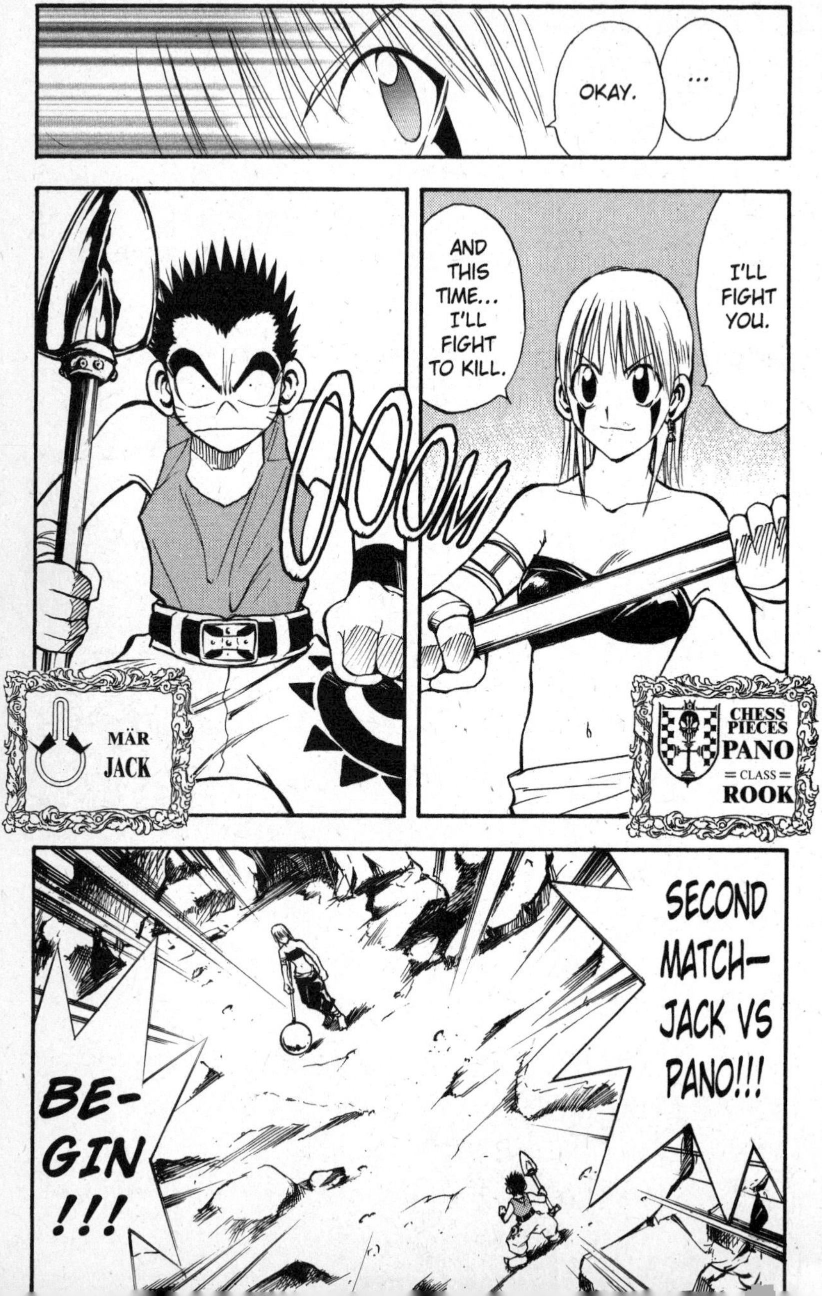
...
OKAY.
I'LL FIGHT YOU.
AND THIS TIME... I'LL FIGHT TO KILL.
OOOM
CHESS PIECES PANO CLASS ROOK
MÄR JACK
SECOND MATCH— JACK VS PANO!!!
BE-GIN!!!

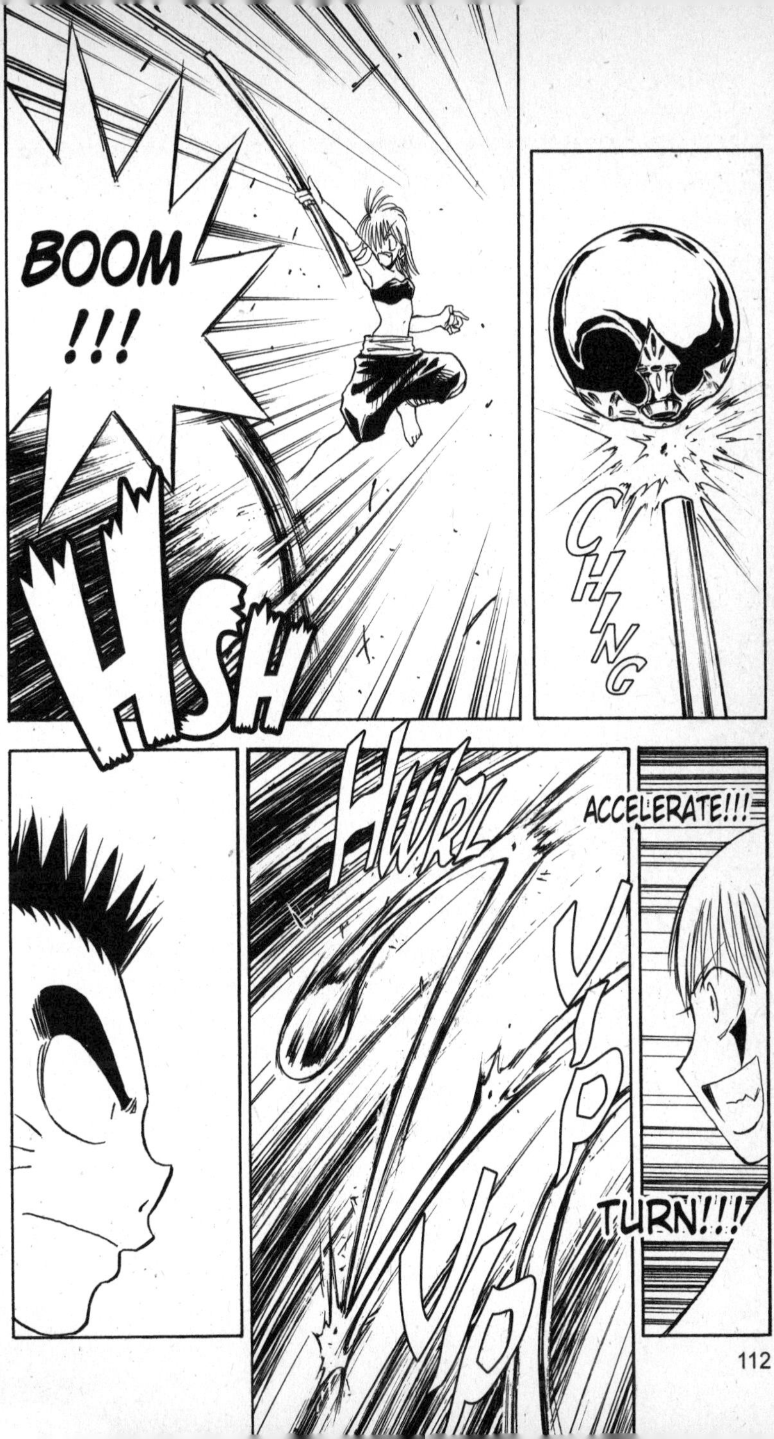
CHING
BOOM !!!
HSH
ACCELERATE!!!
TURN!!!
HURL
YUP

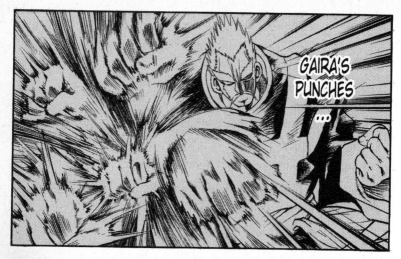

GAIRA'S PUNCHES ...

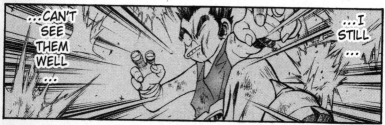

...CAN'T SEE THEM WELL ...

...I STILL ...

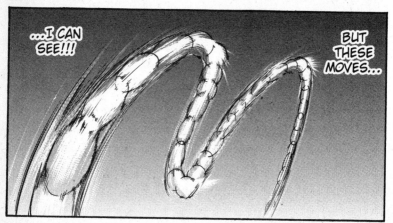

...I CAN SEE!!!

BUT THESE MOVES...

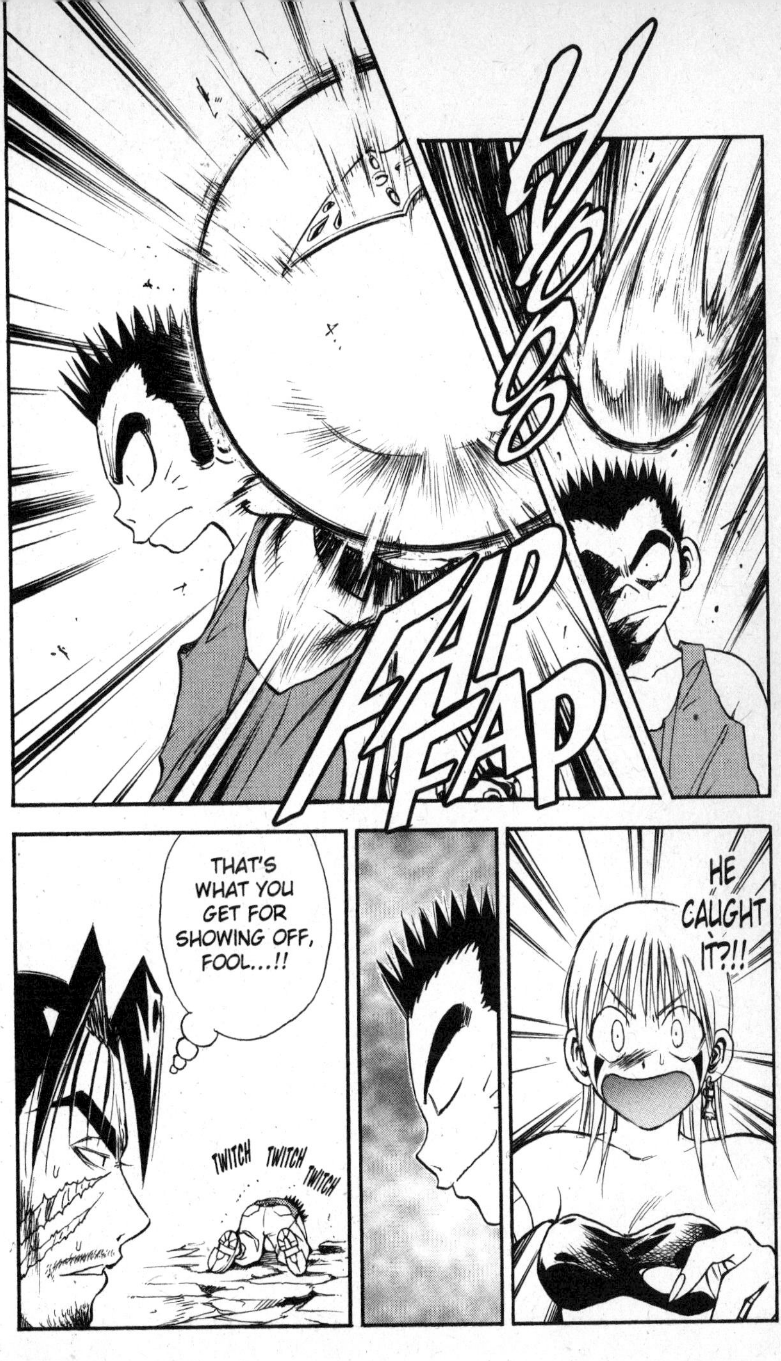
FAP FAP
HE CAUGHT IT?!!
THAT'S WHAT YOU GET FOR SHOWING OFF, FOOL...!!
TWITCH TWITCH TWITCH

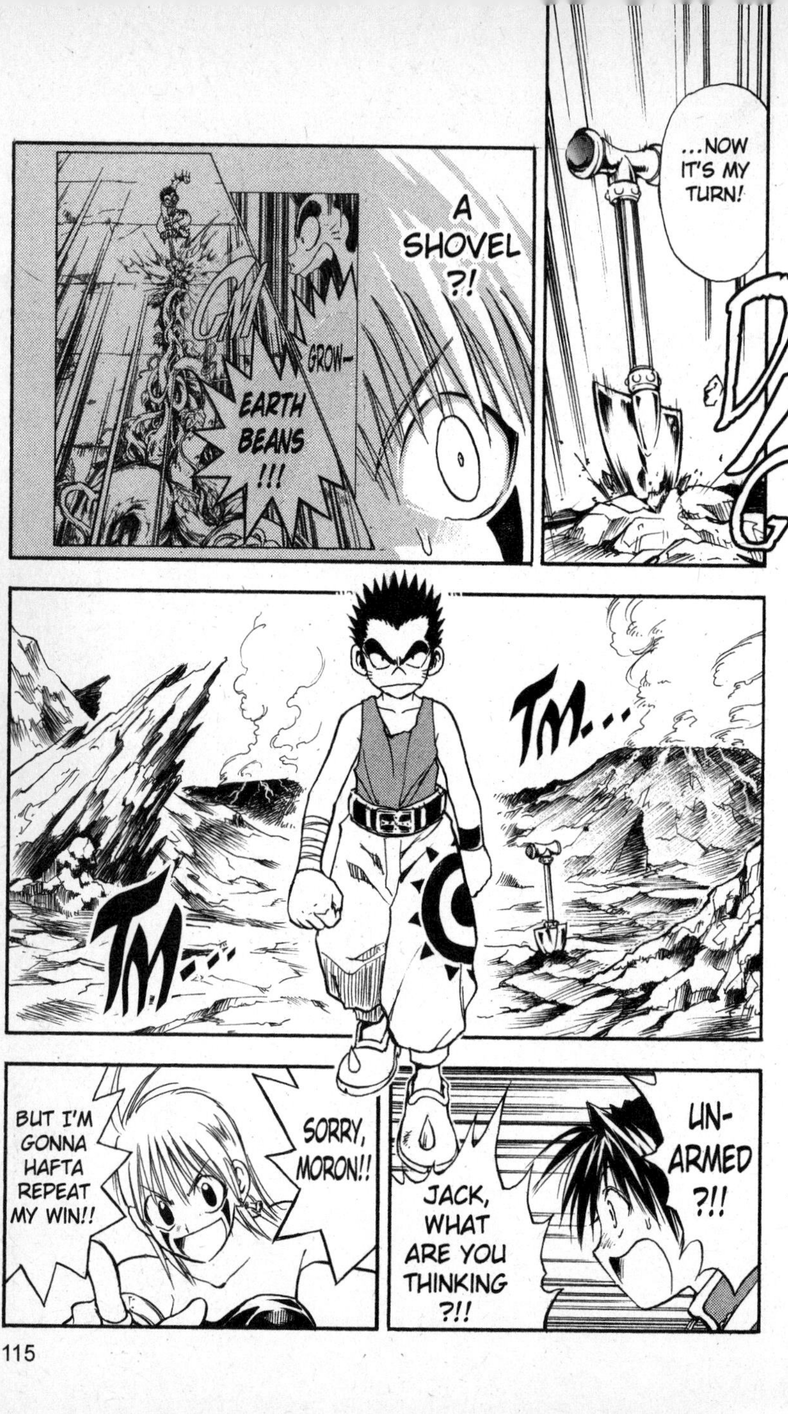
...NOW IT'S MY TURN!
A SHOVEL ?!
GROW-
EARTH BEANS !!!
TM...
TM...
UN-ARMED ?!!
JACK, WHAT ARE YOU THINKING ?!!
SORRY, MORON!!
BUT I'M GONNA HAFTA REPEAT MY WIN!!

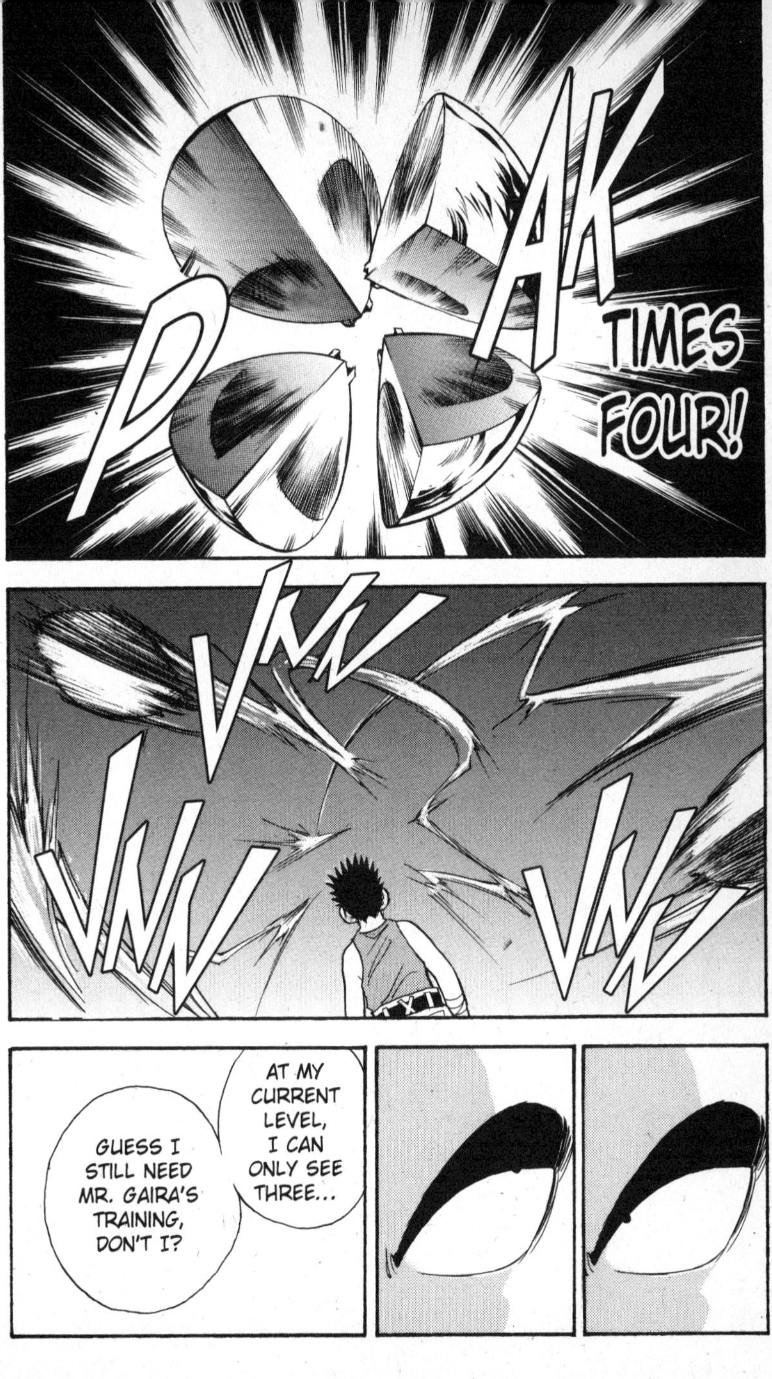
TIMES FOUR!
AT MY CURRENT LEVEL, I CAN ONLY SEE THREE...
GUESS I STILL NEED MR. GAIRA'S TRAINING, DON'T I?

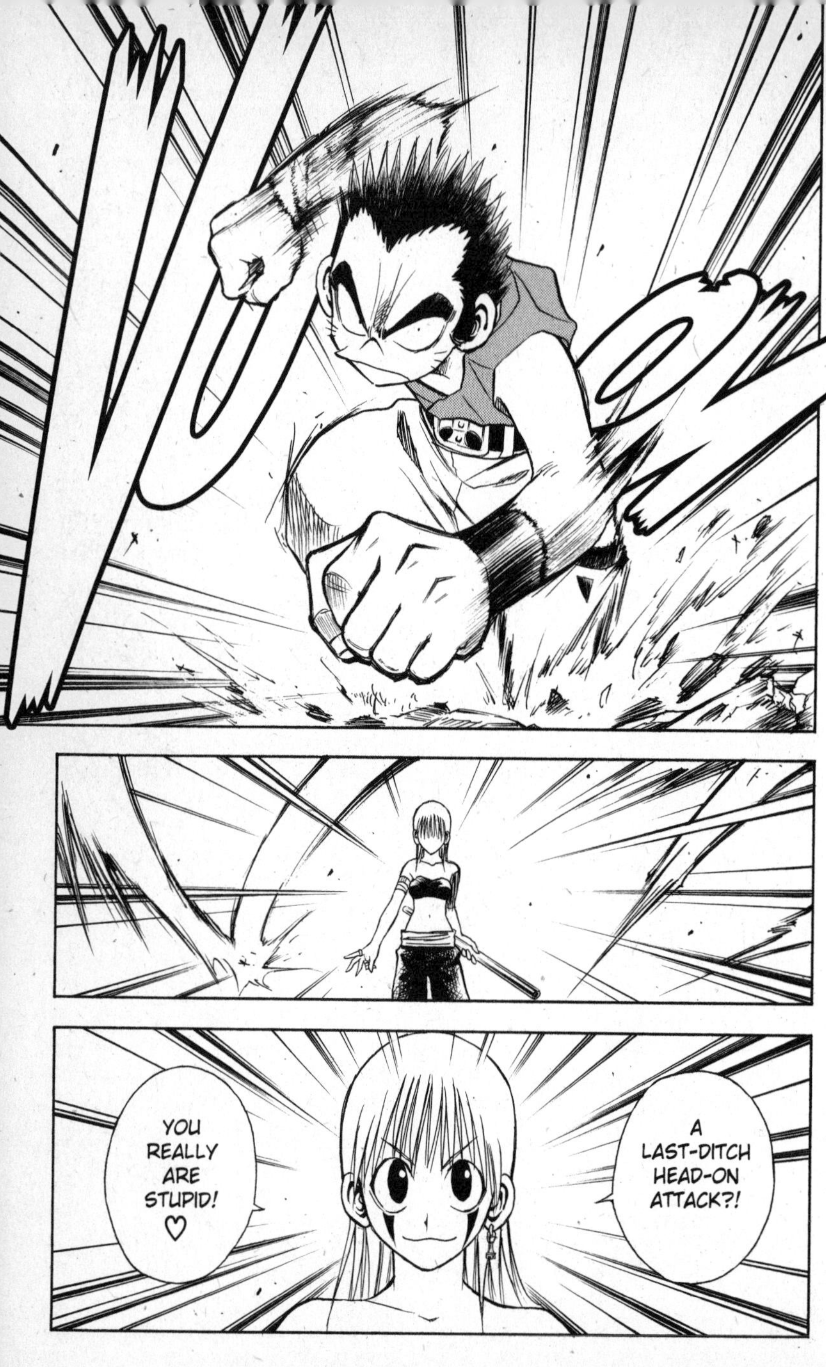
A LAST-DITCH HEAD-ON ATTACK?!
YOU REALLY ARE STUPID! ♡

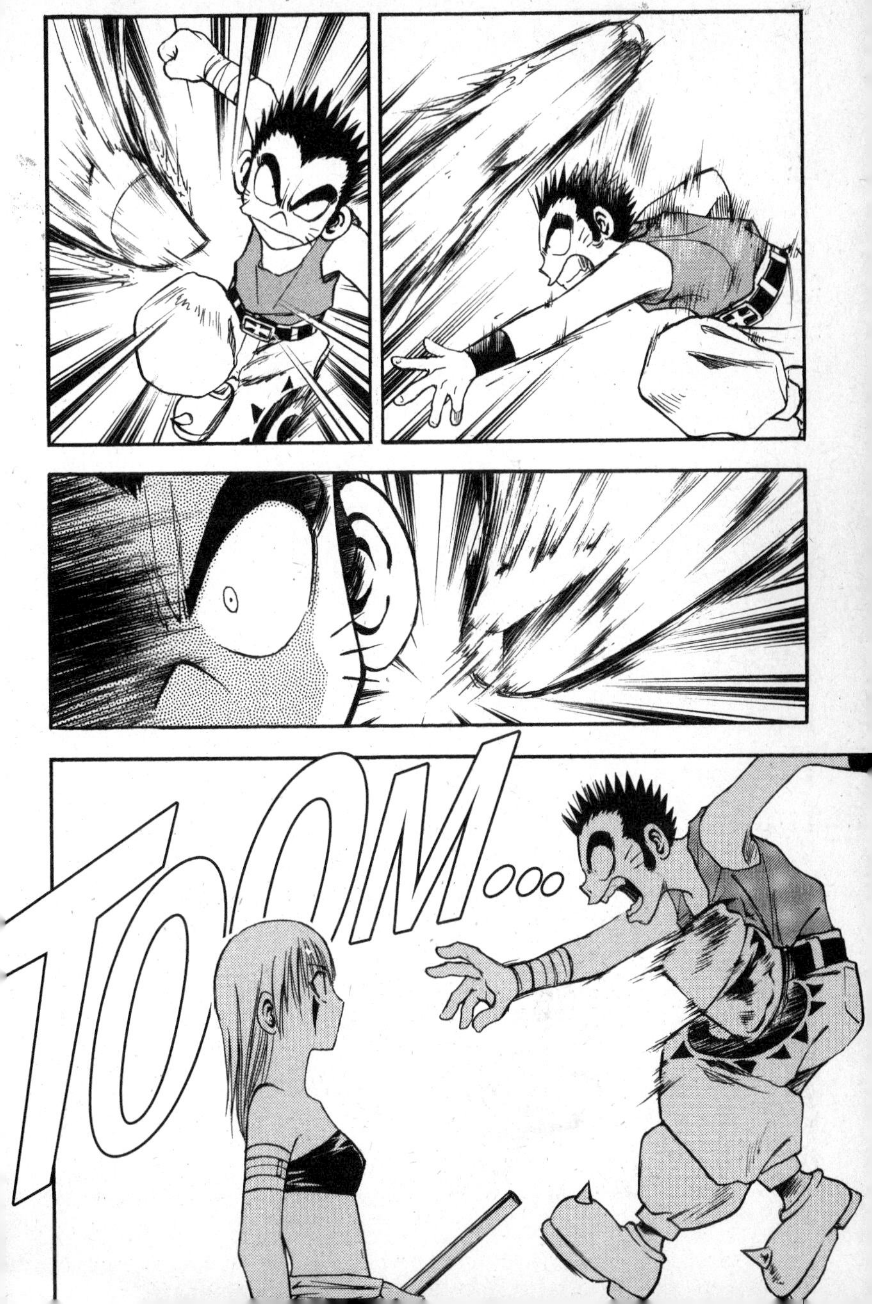
TOOOM...

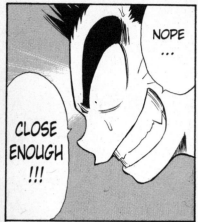

NOPE
...

CLOSE ENOUGH !!!

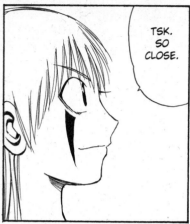

TSK. SO CLOSE.

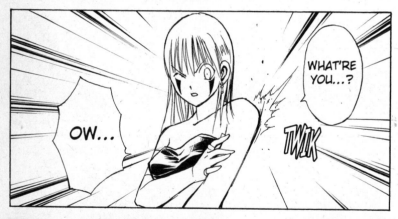

WHAT'RE YOU...?

OW...

TWIK

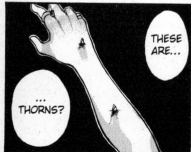

THESE ARE...

...? THORNS?

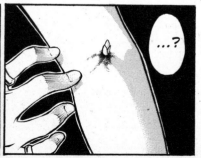

...?

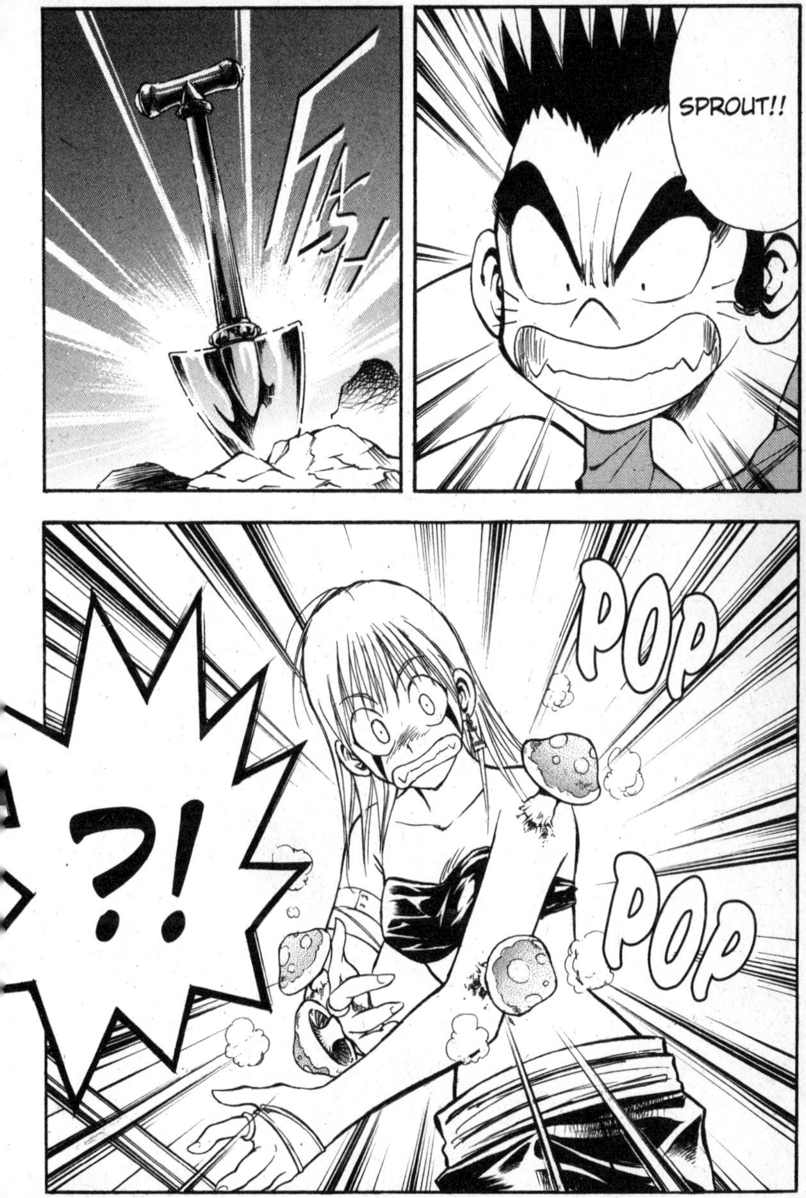
SPROUT!!
POP
POP
?!

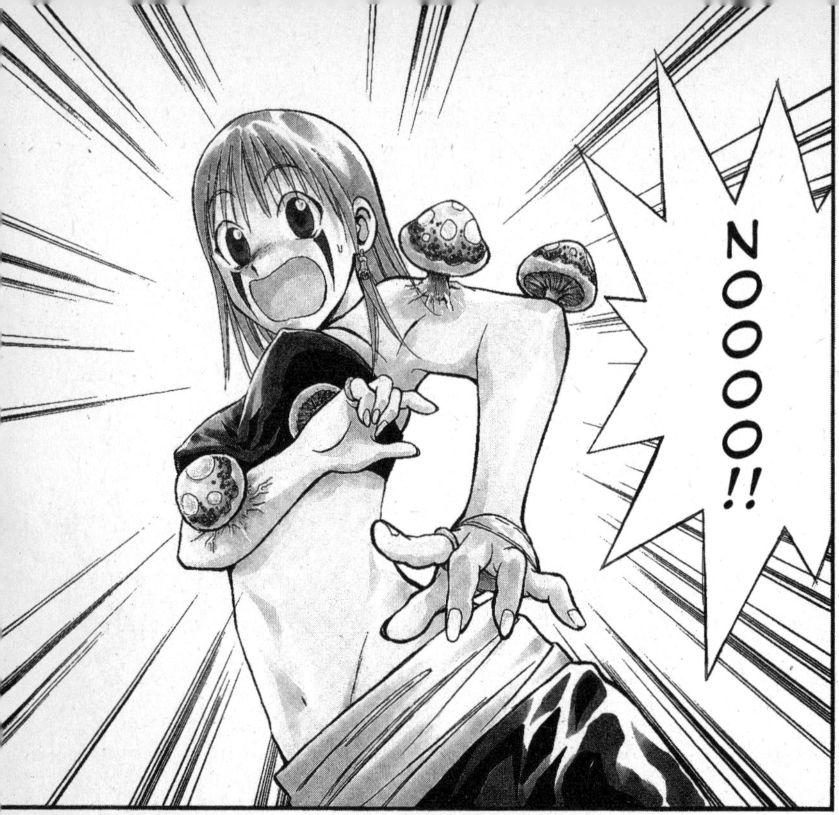
NOOOOO!!

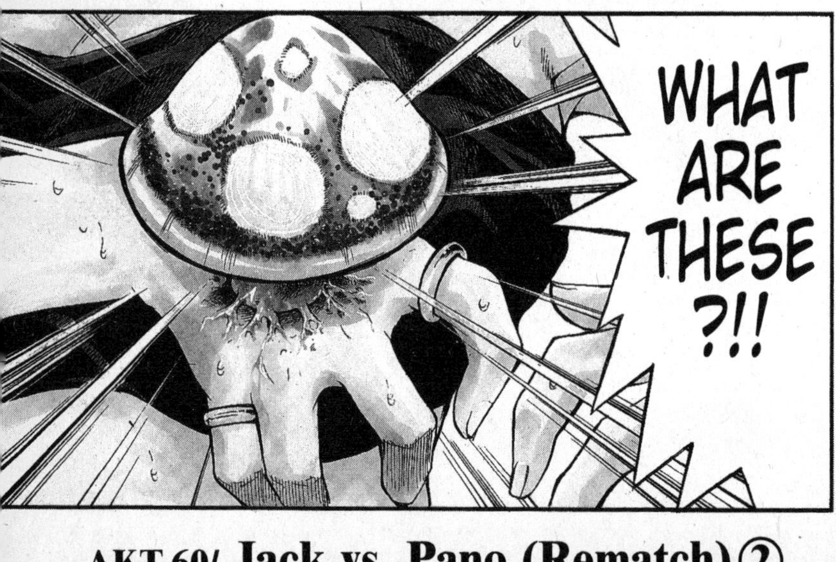
WHAT ARE THESE ?!!

AKT.60/ Jack vs. Pano (Rematch)②

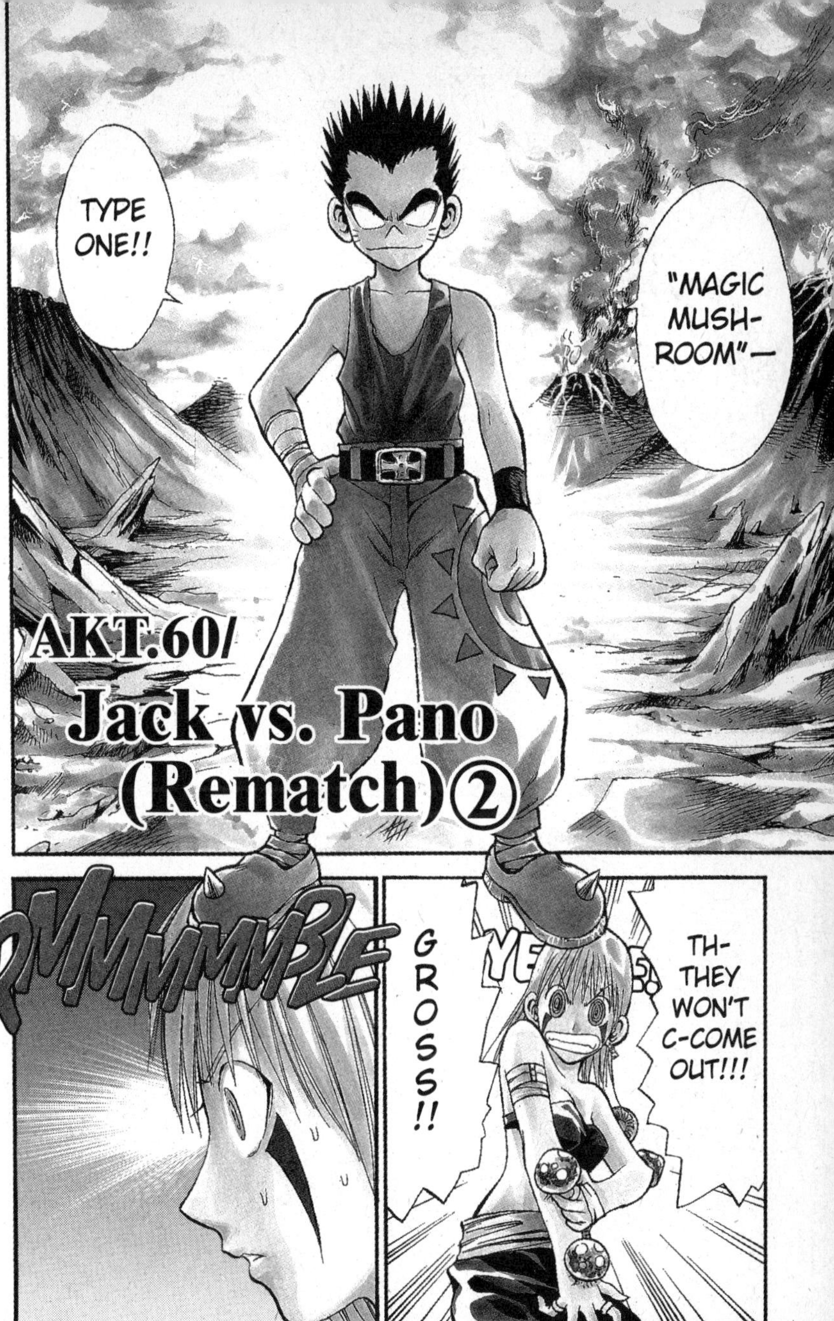
"MAGIC MUSHROOM"—
TYPE ONE!!
AKT.60/ Jack vs. Pano (Rematch) ②
TH-THEY WON'T C-COME OUT!!!
GROSS!!
RUMMMMBLE

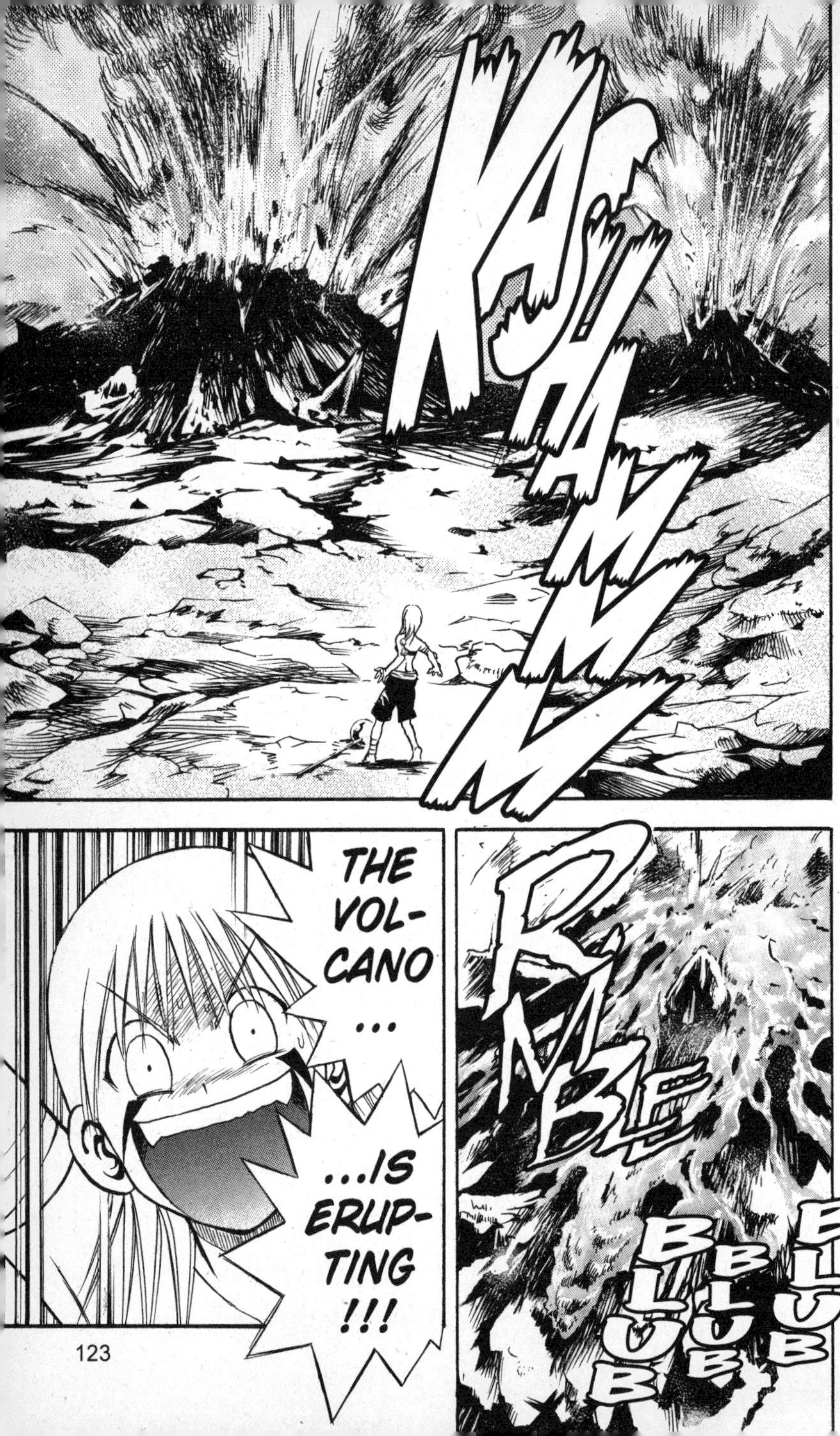
RUMBLE
BLUB BLUB BLUB
THE VOLCANO...
...IS ERUPTING!!!

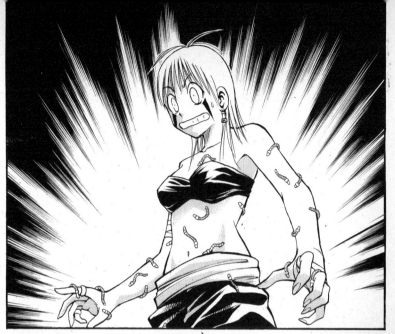

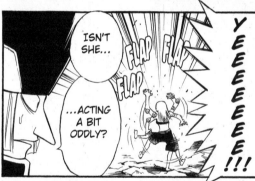

ISN'T SHE...

...ACTING A BIT ODDLY?

FLAP FLAP FLAP

YEEEEEEE!!!

AIIIIII...

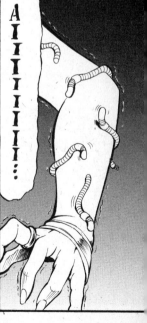

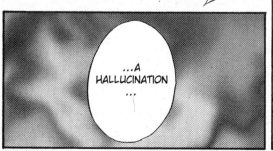

...A HALLUCINATION...

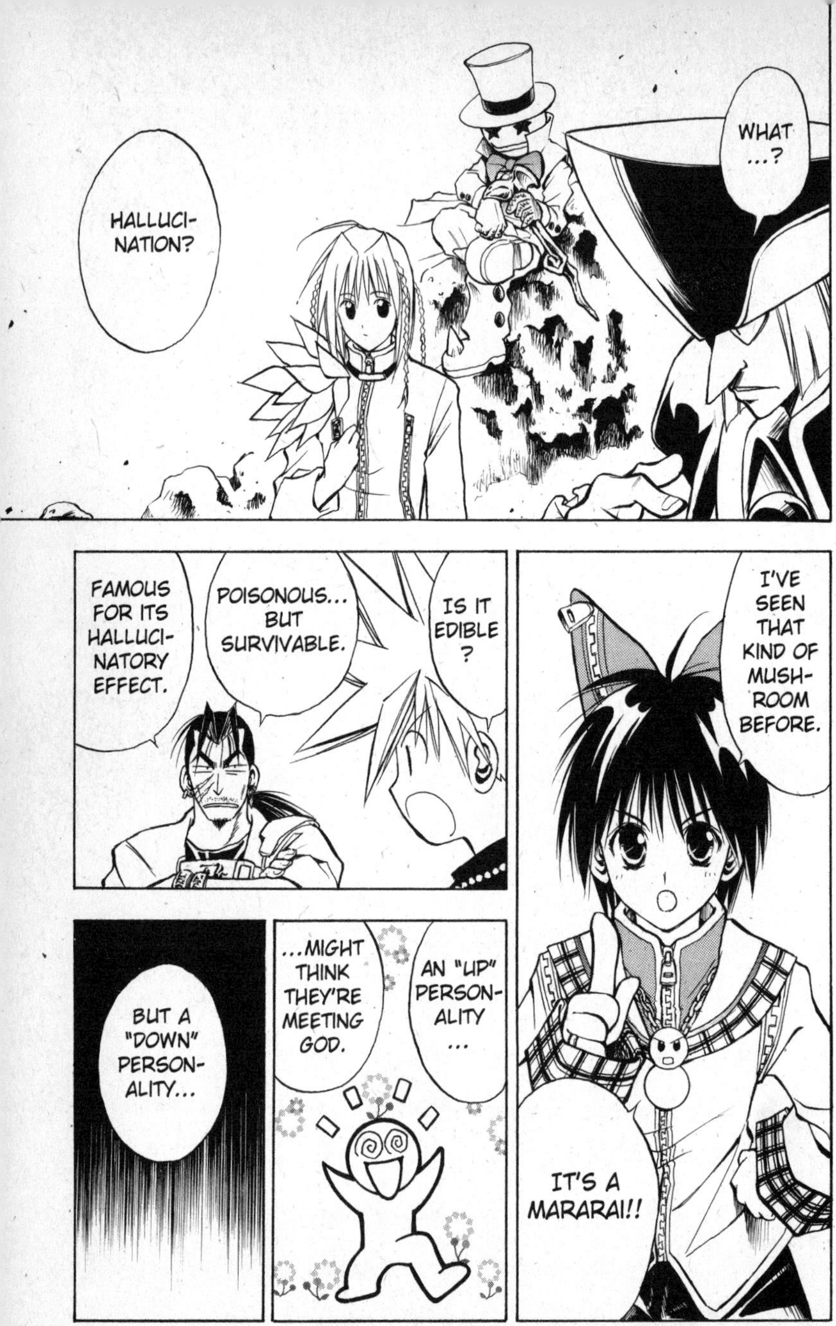
WHAT ...?
HALLUCINATION?
I'VE SEEN THAT KIND OF MUSHROOM BEFORE.
IT'S A MARARAI!!
IS IT EDIBLE?
POISONOUS... BUT SURVIVABLE.
FAMOUS FOR ITS HALLUCINATORY EFFECT.
AN "UP" PERSONALITY ...
...MIGHT THINK THEY'RE MEETING GOD.
BUT A "DOWN" PERSONALITY...

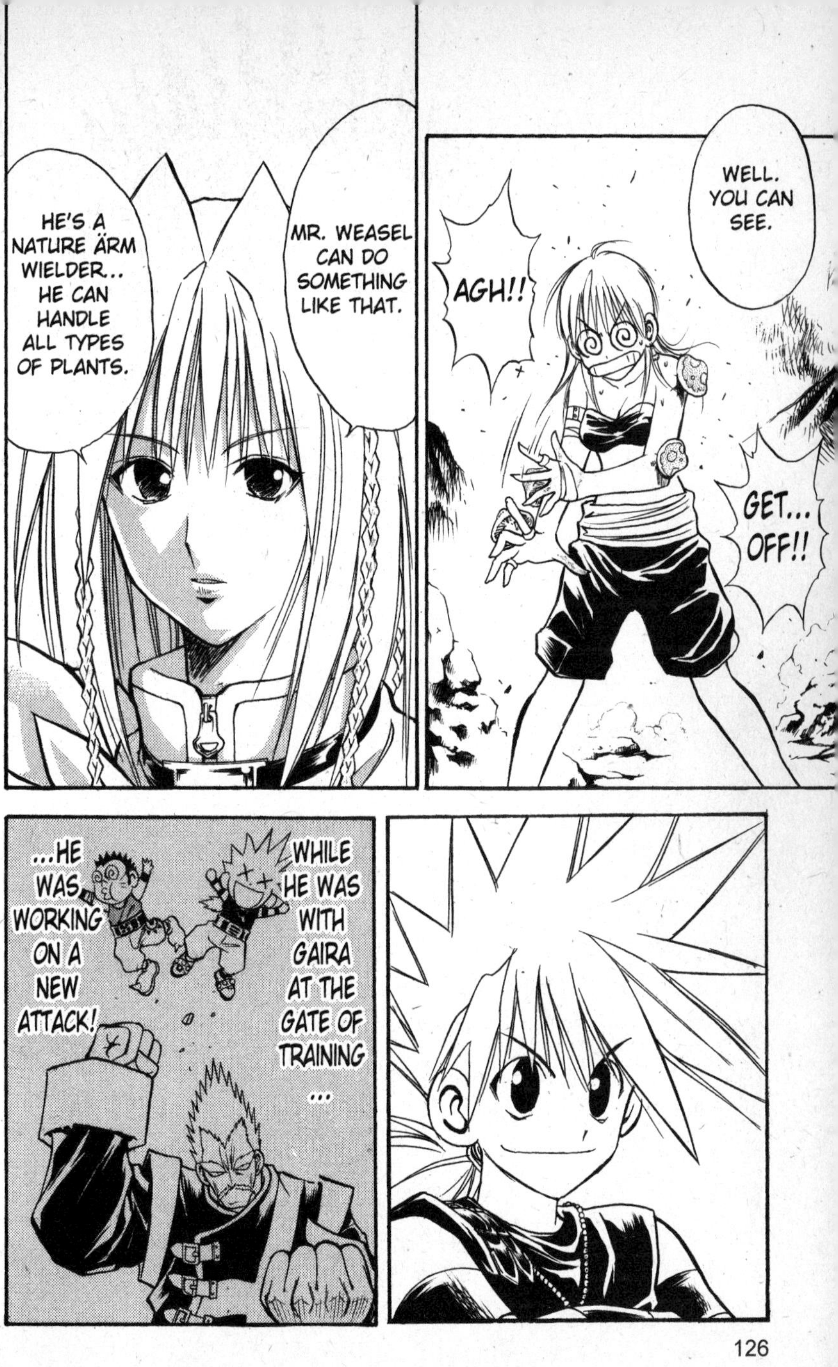
WELL. YOU CAN SEE.
AGH!!
GET... OFF!!
MR. WEASEL CAN DO SOMETHING LIKE THAT.
HE'S A NATURE ÄRM WIELDER... HE CAN HANDLE ALL TYPES OF PLANTS.
WHILE HE WAS WITH GAIRA AT THE GATE OF TRAINING...
...HE WAS WORKING ON A NEW ATTACK!

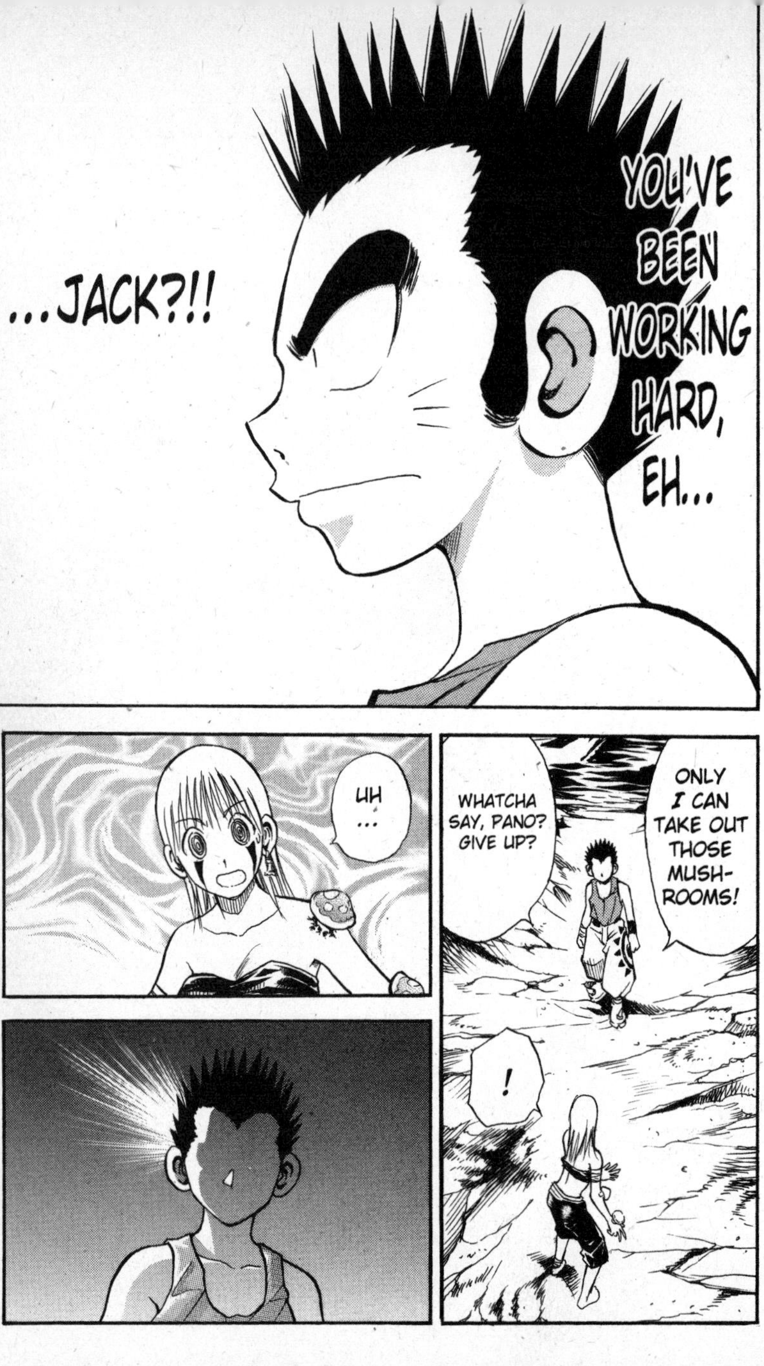
YOU'VE BEEN WORKING HARD, EH...
...JACK?!!
ONLY I CAN TAKE OUT THOSE MUSH-ROOMS!
WHATCHA SAY, PANO? GIVE UP?
!
UH ...

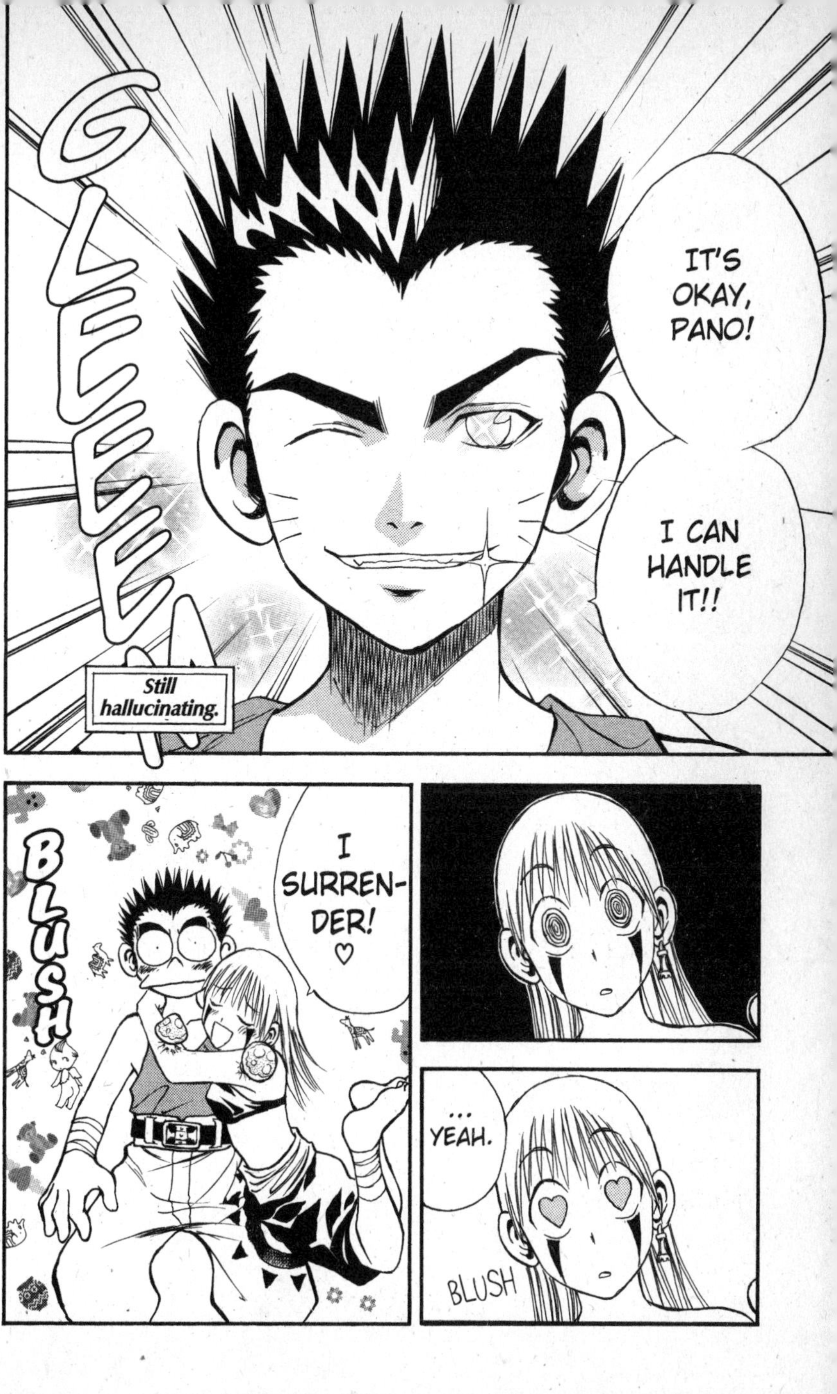
GLEEEE
IT'S OKAY, PANO!
I CAN HANDLE IT!!
Still hallucinating.
... YEAH.
BLUSH
I SURREN-DER! ♡
BLUSH

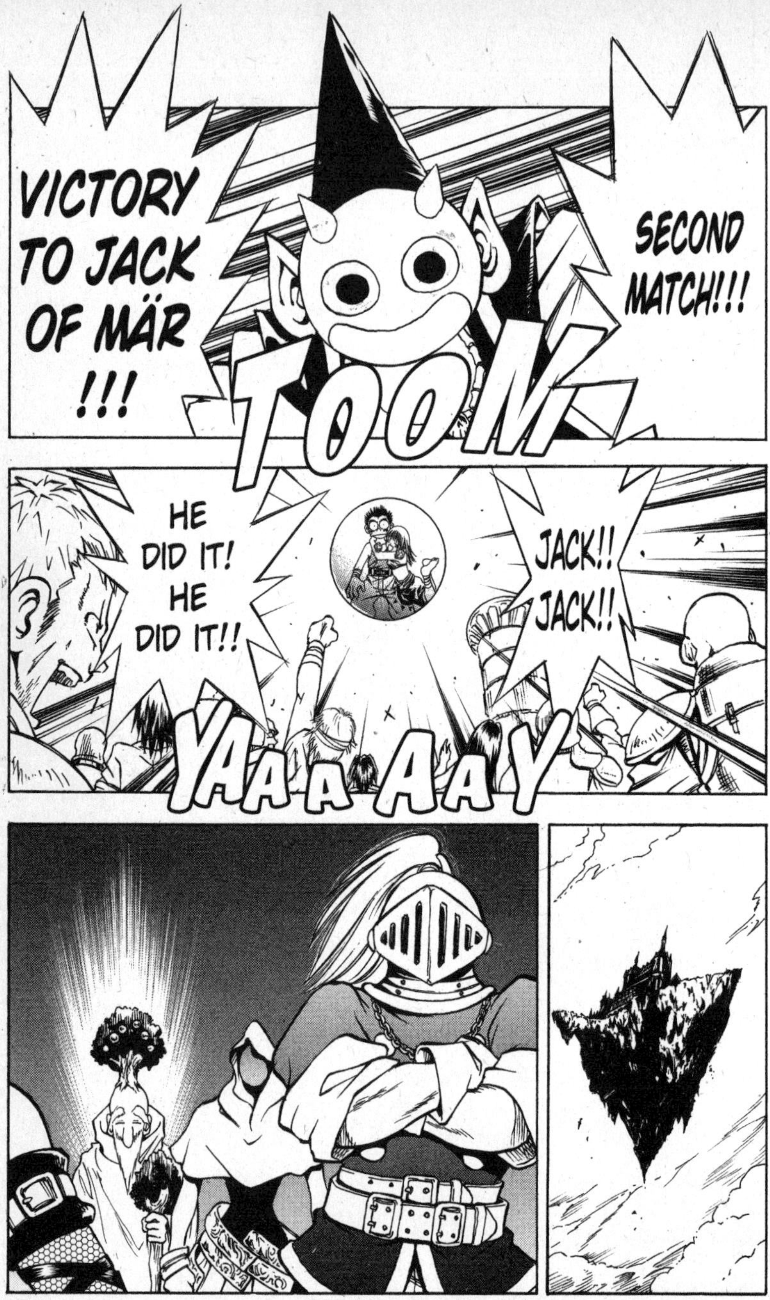
SECOND MATCH!!!
VICTORY TO JACK OF MÄR !!!
TOOM
JACK!! JACK!!
HE DID IT! HE DID IT!!
YAAAAAY

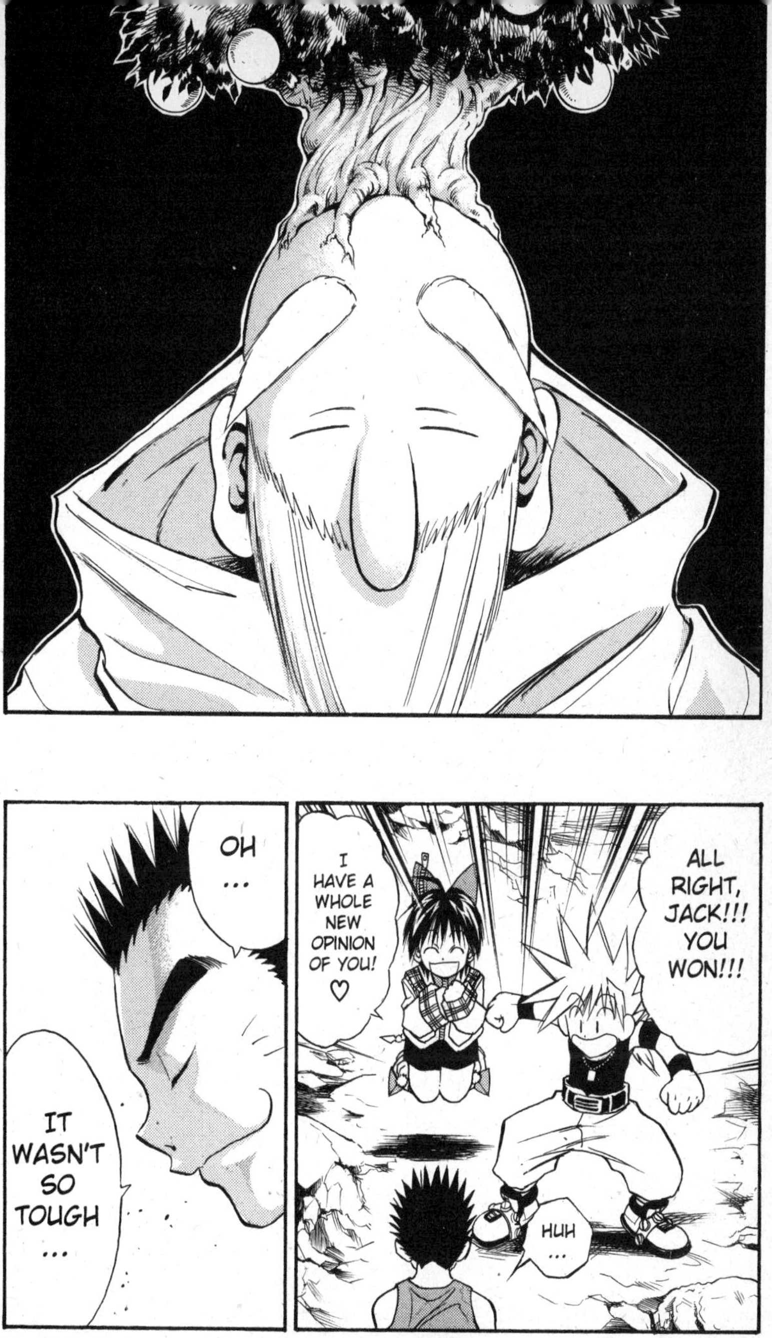
ALL RIGHT, JACK!!! YOU WON!!!
I HAVE A WHOLE NEW OPINION OF YOU! ♡
HUH ...
OH ...
IT WASN'T SO TOUGH ...

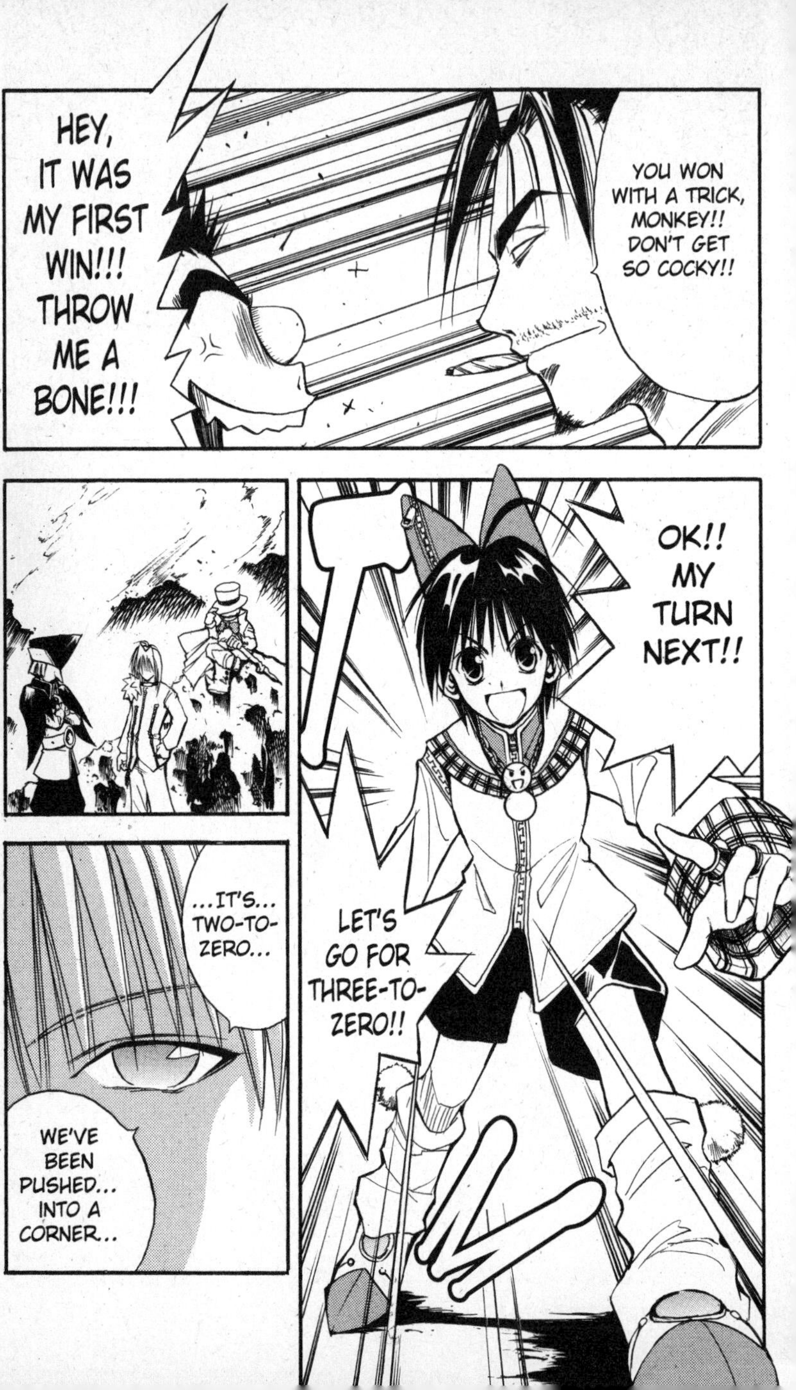
YOU WON WITH A TRICK, MONKEY!! DON'T GET SO COCKY!!
HEY, IT WAS MY FIRST WIN!!! THROW ME A BONE!!!
OK!! MY TURN NEXT!!
LET'S GO FOR THREE-TO-ZERO!!
...IT'S... TWO-TO-ZERO...
WE'VE BEEN PUSHED... INTO A CORNER...

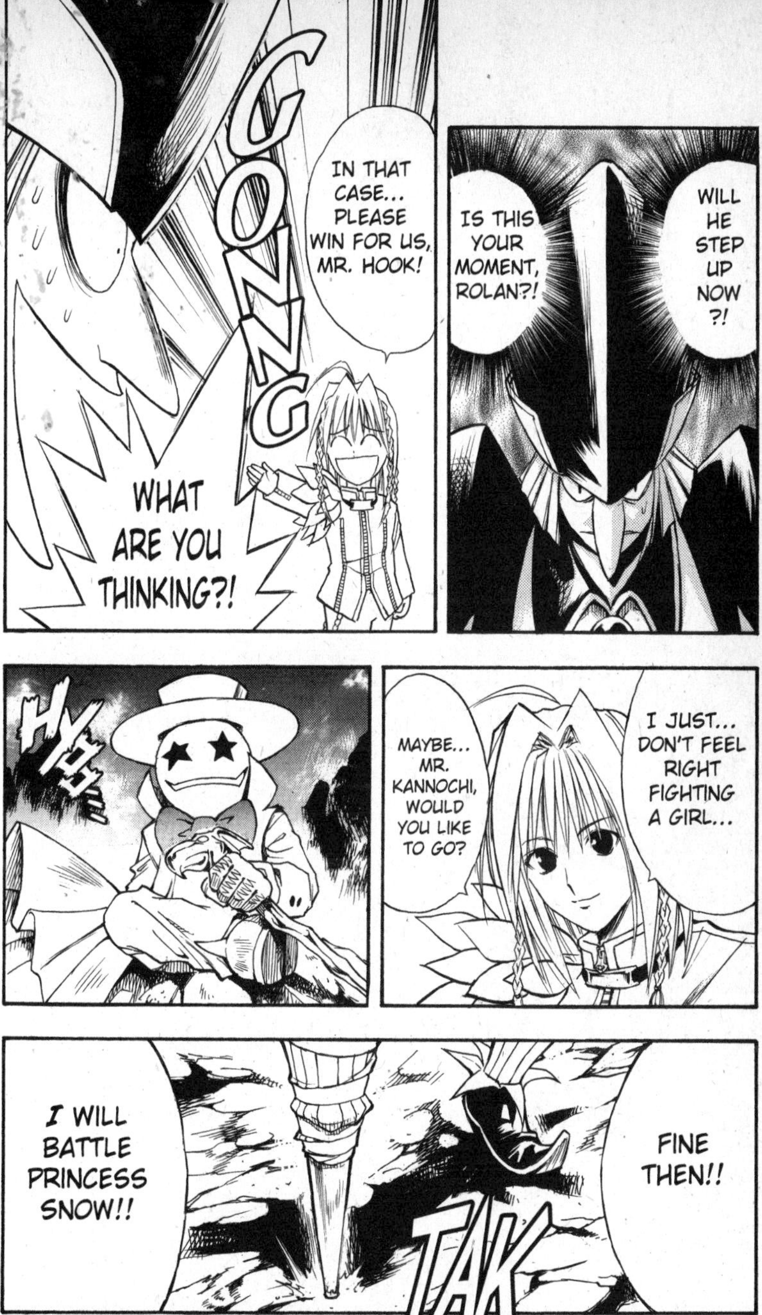
WILL HE STEP UP NOW?!
IS THIS YOUR MOMENT, ROLAN?!
IN THAT CASE... PLEASE WIN FOR US, MR. HOOK!
GONG
WHAT ARE YOU THINKING?!
I JUST... DON'T FEEL RIGHT FIGHTING A GIRL...
MAYBE... MR. KANNOCHI, WOULD YOU LIKE TO GO?
FINE THEN!!
TAK
I WILL BATTLE PRINCESS SNOW!!

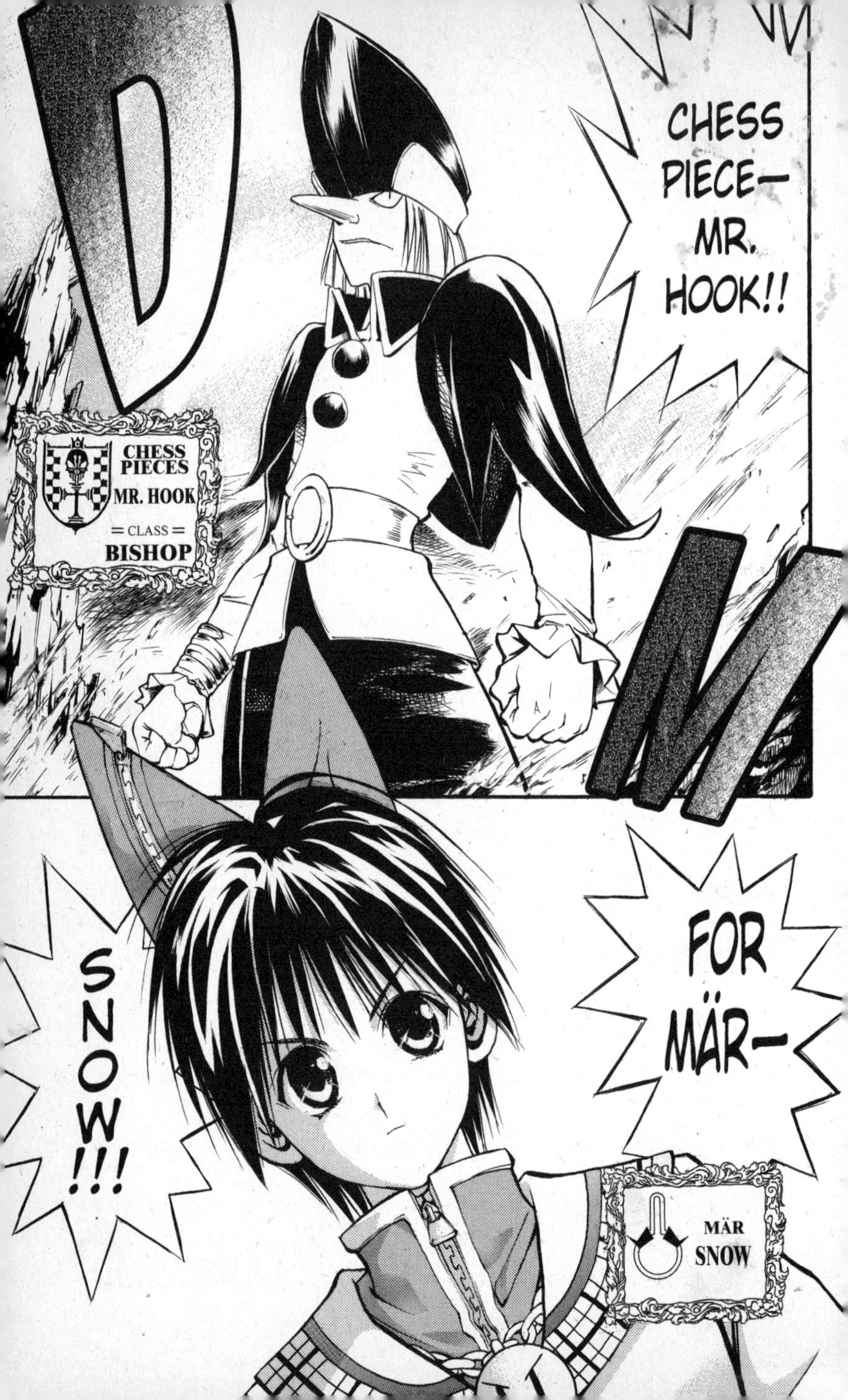
CHESS PIECE— MR. HOOK!!
CHESS PIECES
MR. HOOK
CLASS
BISHOP
D
MM
FOR MÄR—
SNOW!!!
MÄR
SNOW

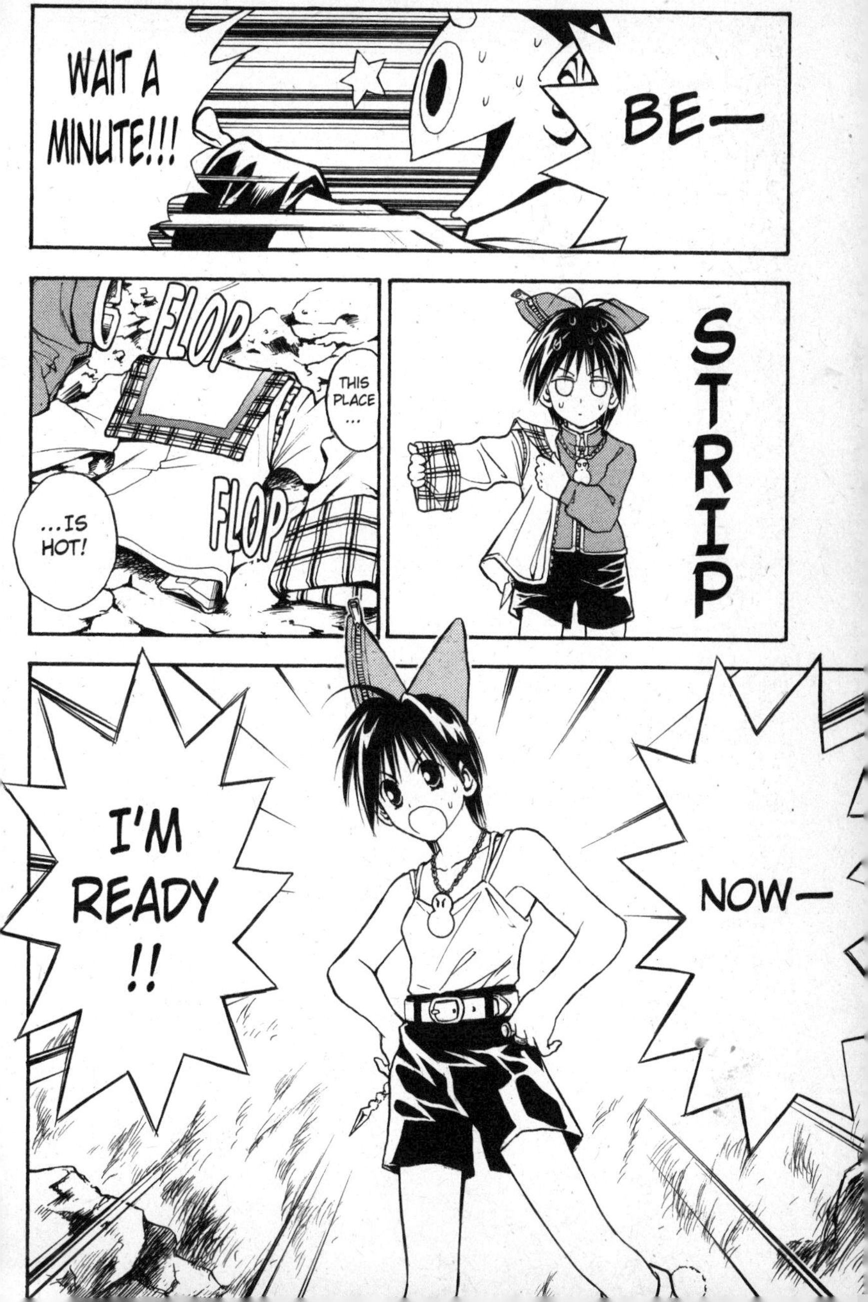
BE—
WAIT A MINUTE!!!
STRIP
THIS PLACE ...
FLOP
FLOP
...IS HOT!
NOW—
I'M READY !!

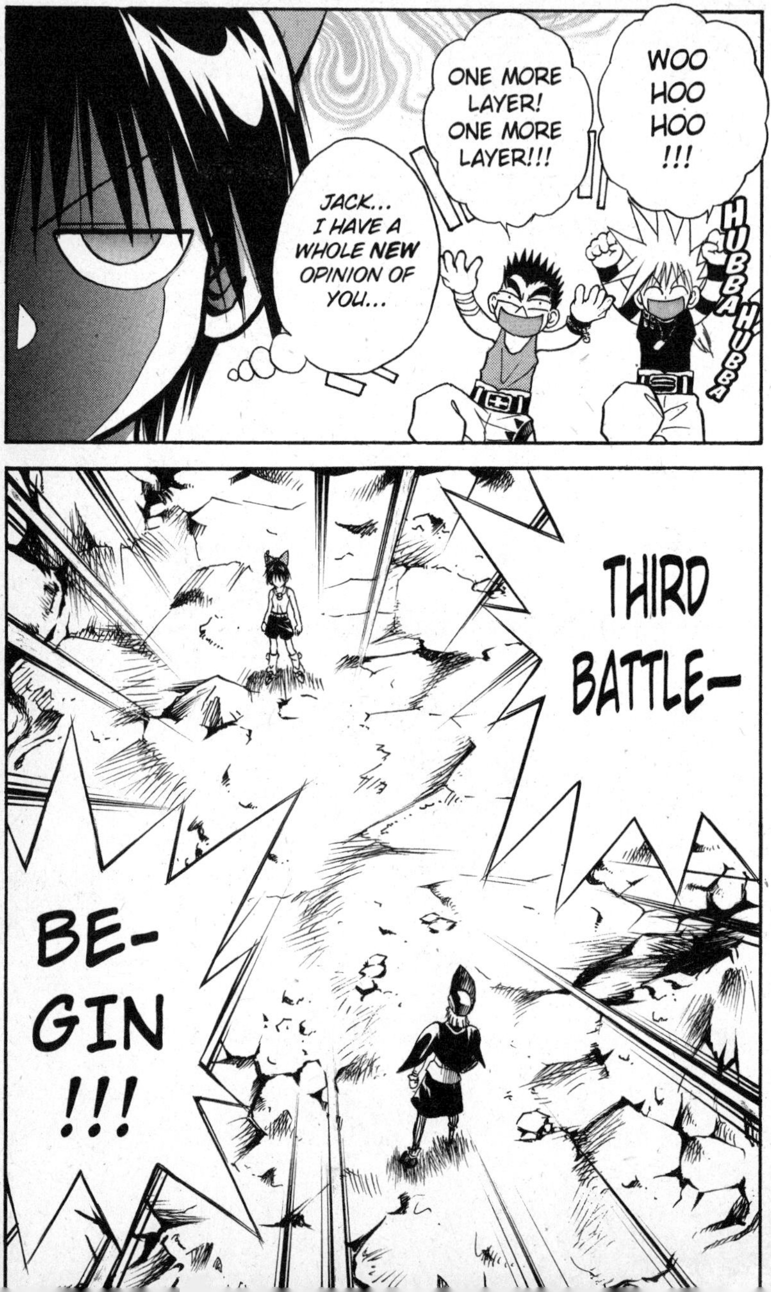
WOO HOO HOO!!!
HUBBA HUBBA
ONE MORE LAYER! ONE MORE LAYER!!!
JACK... I HAVE A WHOLE **NEW** OPINION OF YOU...
THIRD BATTLE—
BE-GIN!!!

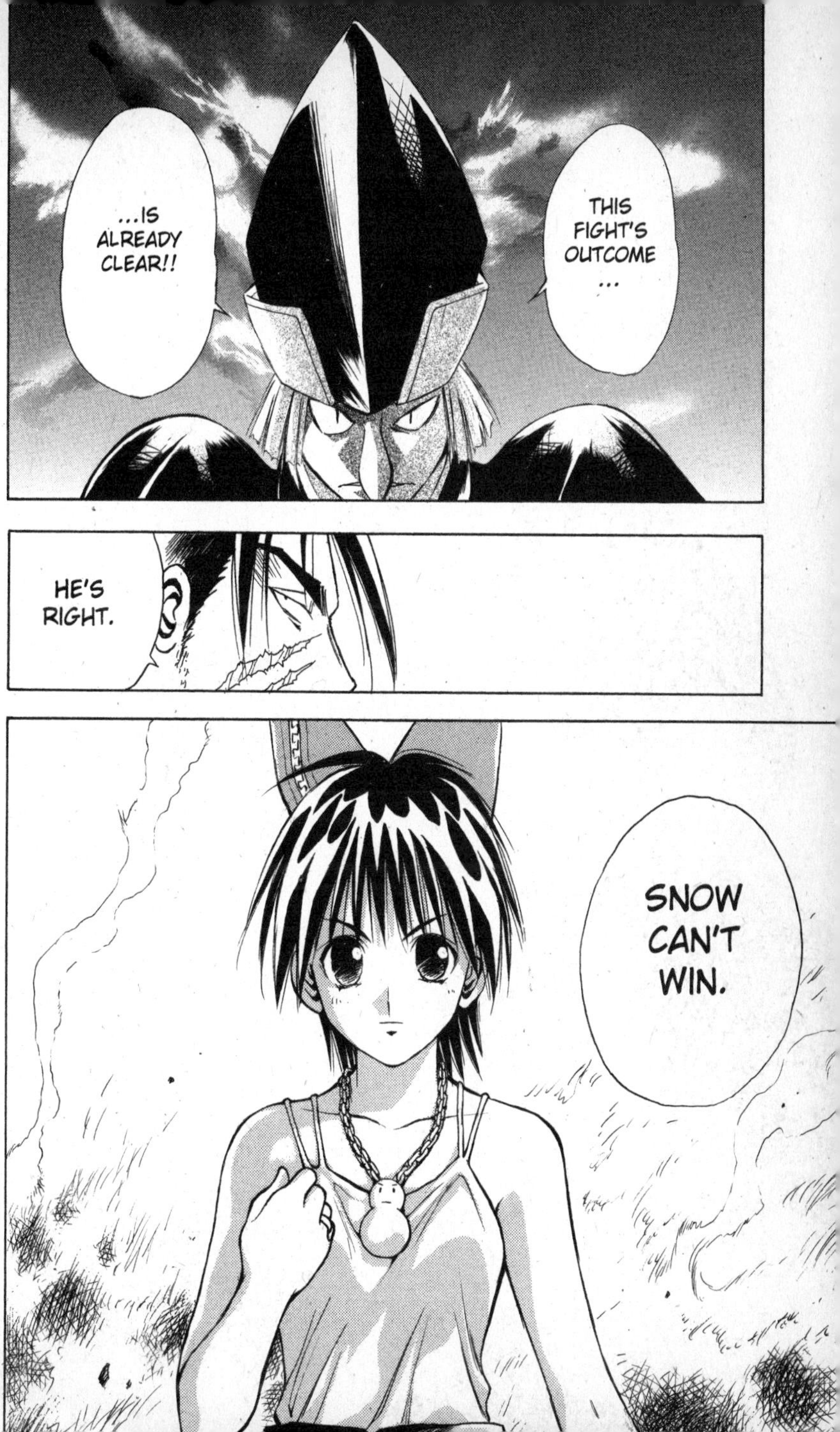
THIS FIGHT'S OUTCOME ...
...IS ALREADY CLEAR!!
HE'S RIGHT.
SNOW CAN'T WIN.

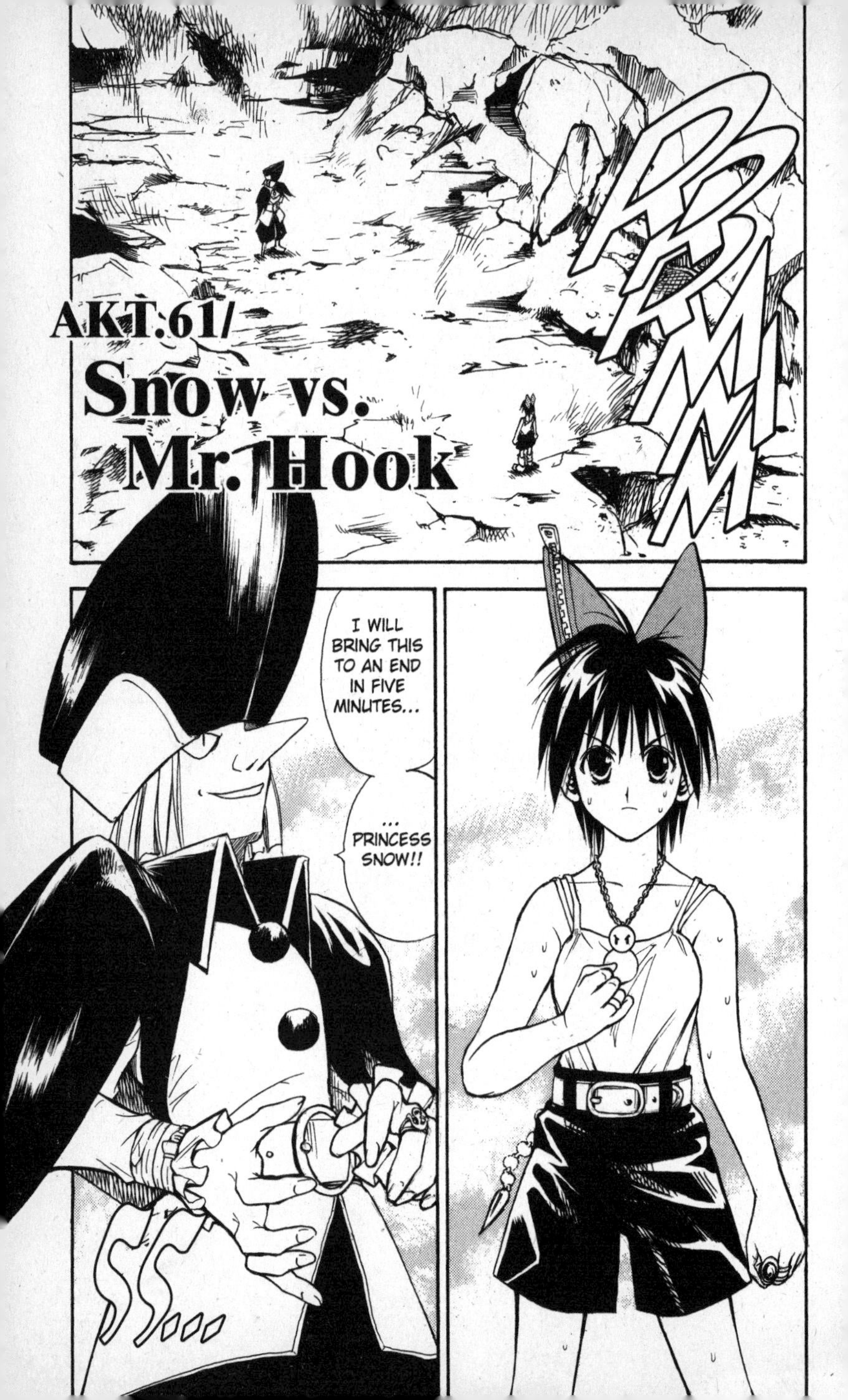
AKT.61/
Snow vs. Mr. Hook
I WILL BRING THIS TO AN END IN FIVE MINUTES...
...PRINCESS SNOW!!

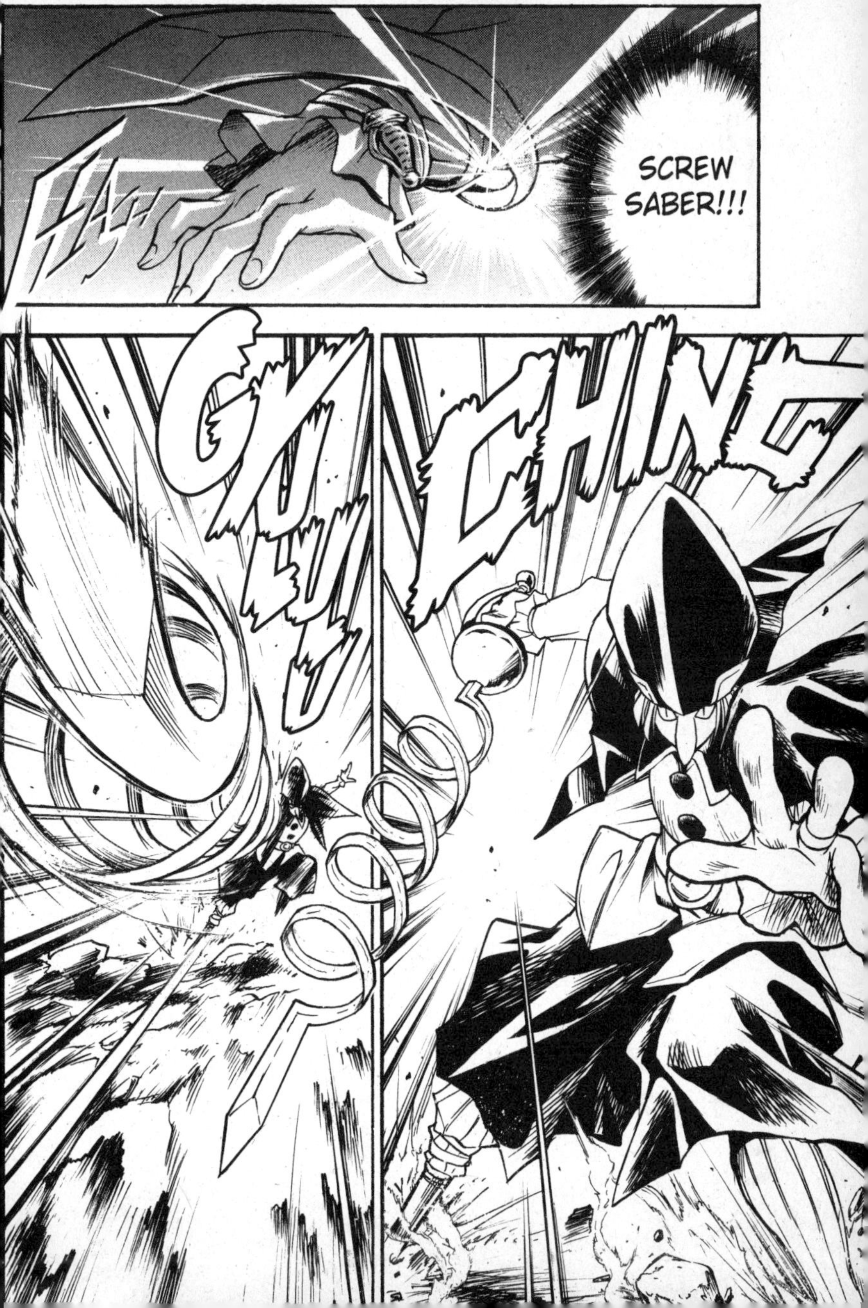
SCREW SABER!!!
CHING
GYU

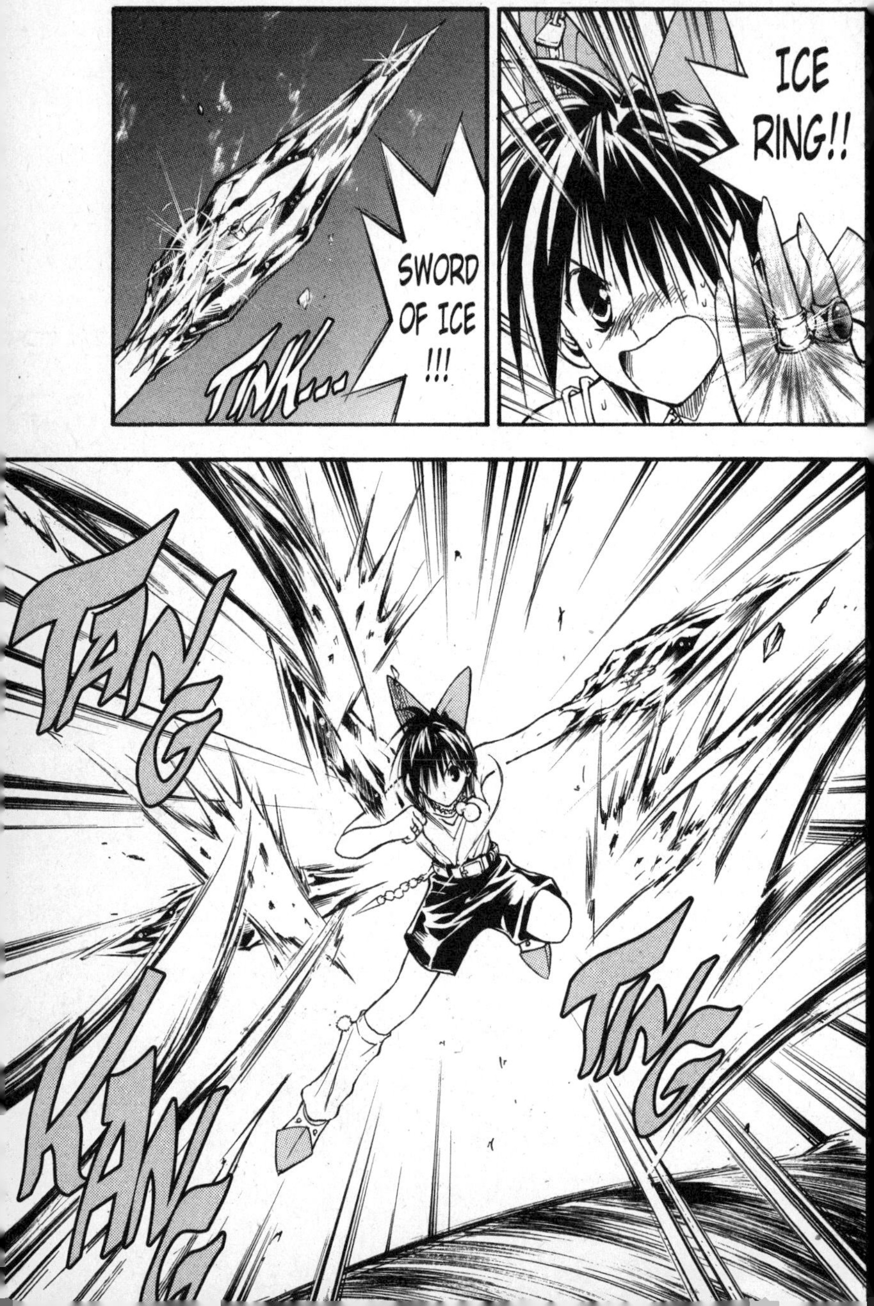
ICE RING!!
SWORD OF ICE !!!
TINK...
TANG
TING
KAN

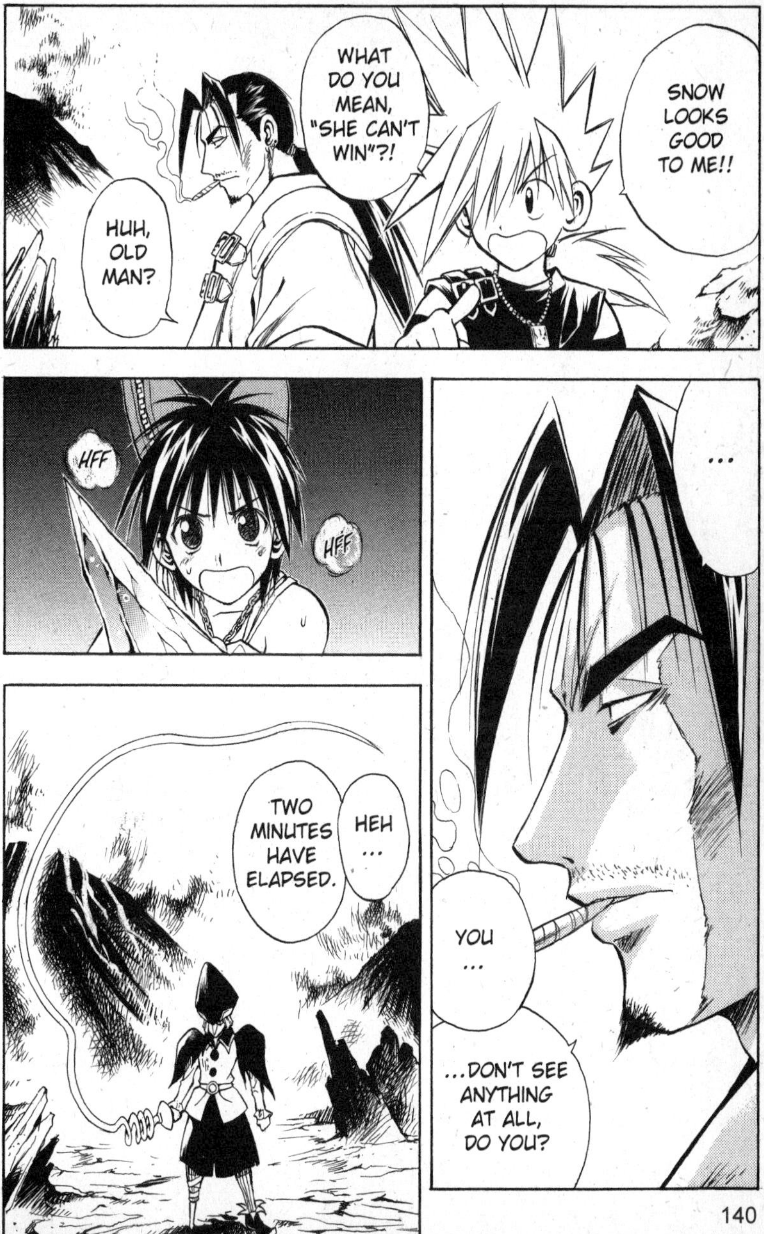
SNOW LOOKS GOOD TO ME!!
WHAT DO YOU MEAN, "SHE CAN'T WIN"?!
HUH, OLD MAN?
...
YOU ...
...DON'T SEE ANYTHING AT ALL, DO YOU?
HFF
HFF
HEH ...
TWO MINUTES HAVE ELAPSED.

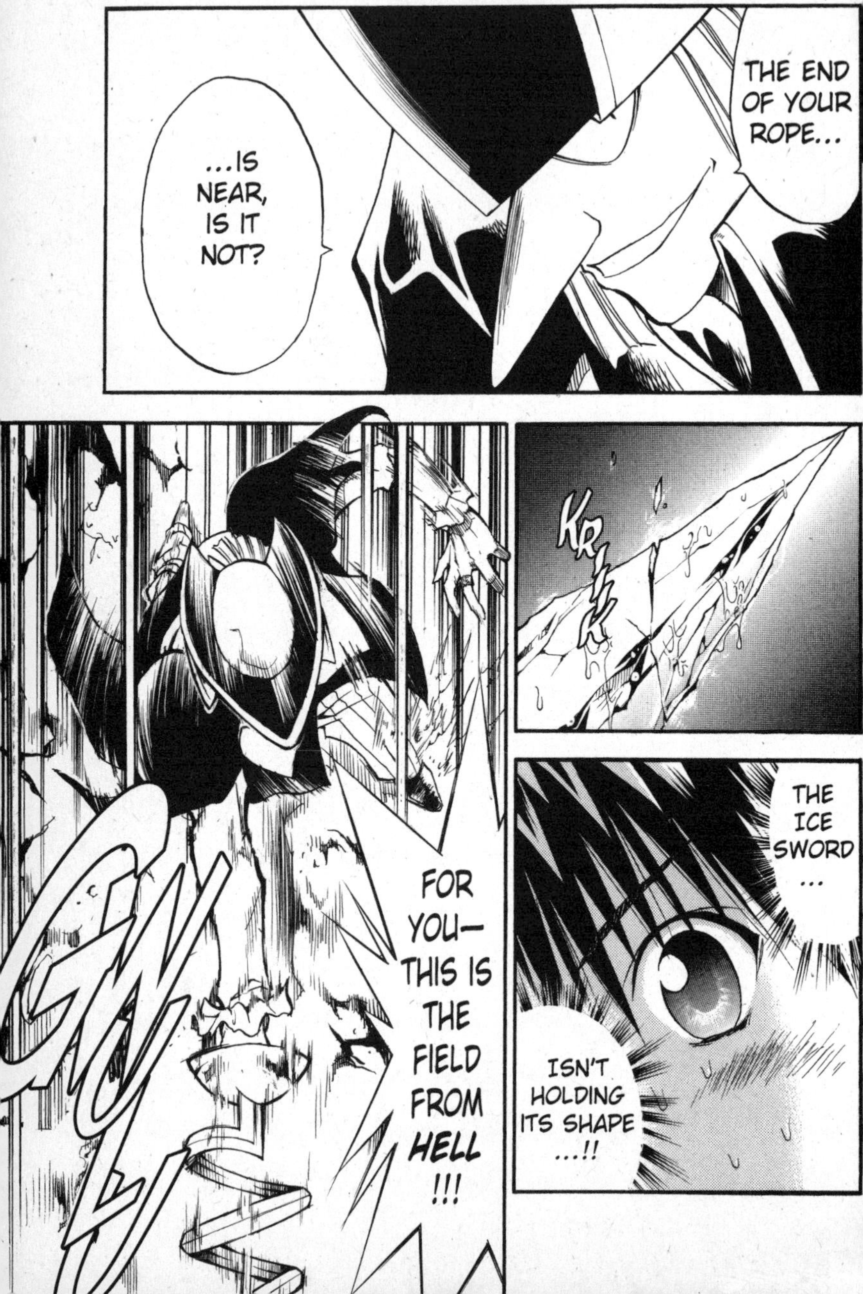
THE END OF YOUR ROPE...
...IS NEAR, IS IT NOT?
THE ICE SWORD ...
ISN'T HOLDING ITS SHAPE ...!!
FOR YOU— THIS IS THE FIELD FROM **HELL** !!!

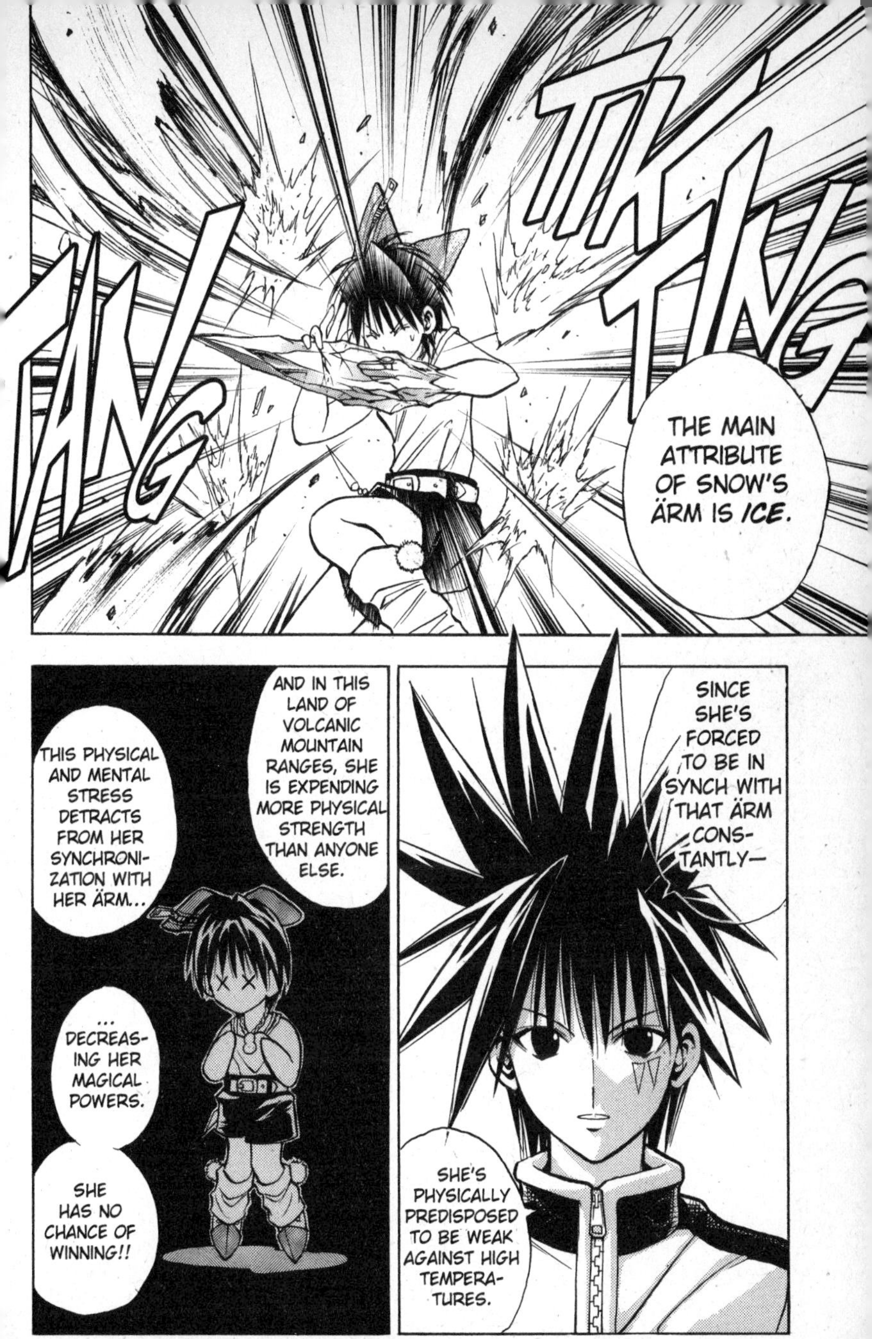
TIK TING
THE MAIN ATTRIBUTE OF SNOW'S ÄRM IS *ICE*.
TANG!
SINCE SHE'S FORCED TO BE IN SYNCH WITH THAT ÄRM CONS-TANTLY—
SHE'S PHYSICALLY PREDISPOSED TO BE WEAK AGAINST HIGH TEMPERA-TURES.
AND IN THIS LAND OF VOLCANIC MOUNTAIN RANGES, SHE IS EXPENDING MORE PHYSICAL STRENGTH THAN ANYONE ELSE.
THIS PHYSICAL AND MENTAL STRESS DETRACTS FROM HER SYNCHRONI-ZATION WITH HER ÄRM...
...DECREAS-ING HER MAGICAL POWERS.
SHE HAS NO CHANCE OF WINNING!!

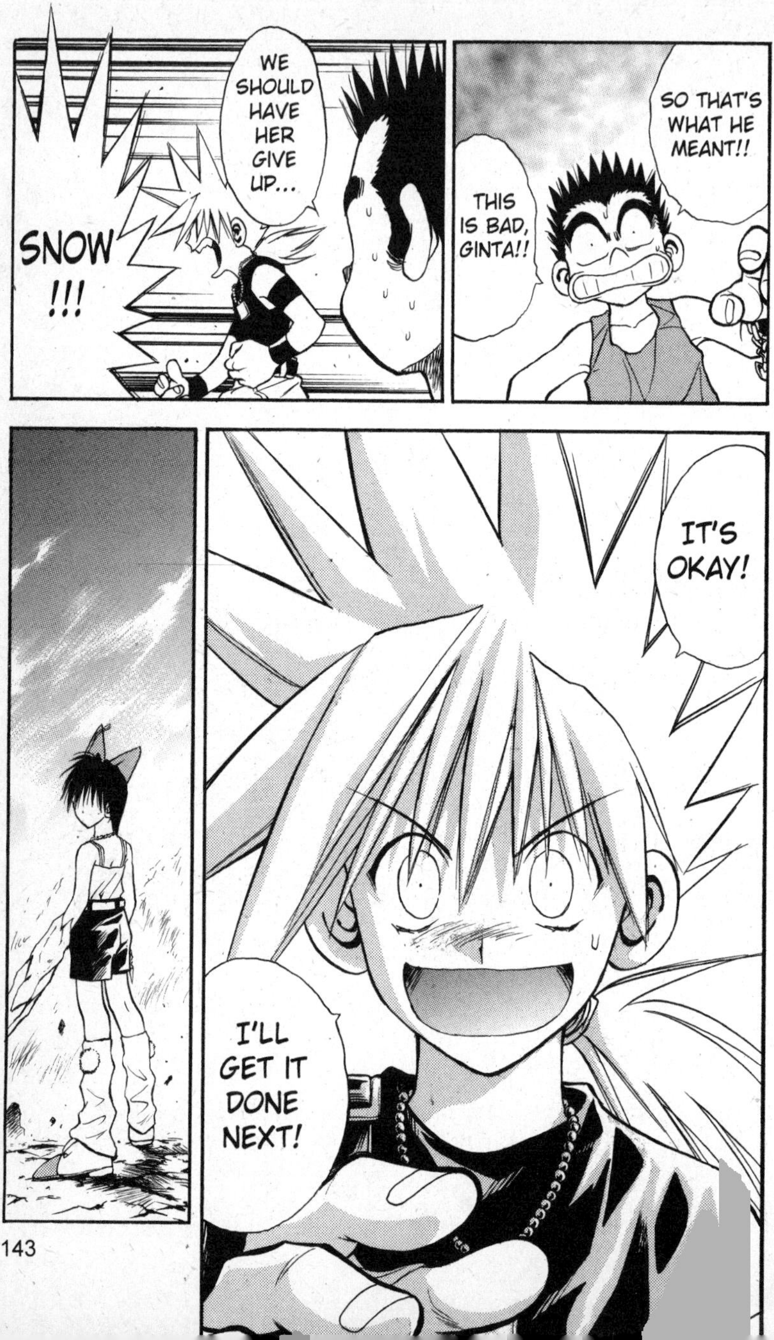
SO THAT'S WHAT HE MEANT!!
THIS IS BAD, GINTA!!
WE SHOULD HAVE HER GIVE UP...
SNOW!!!
IT'S OKAY!
I'LL GET IT DONE NEXT!

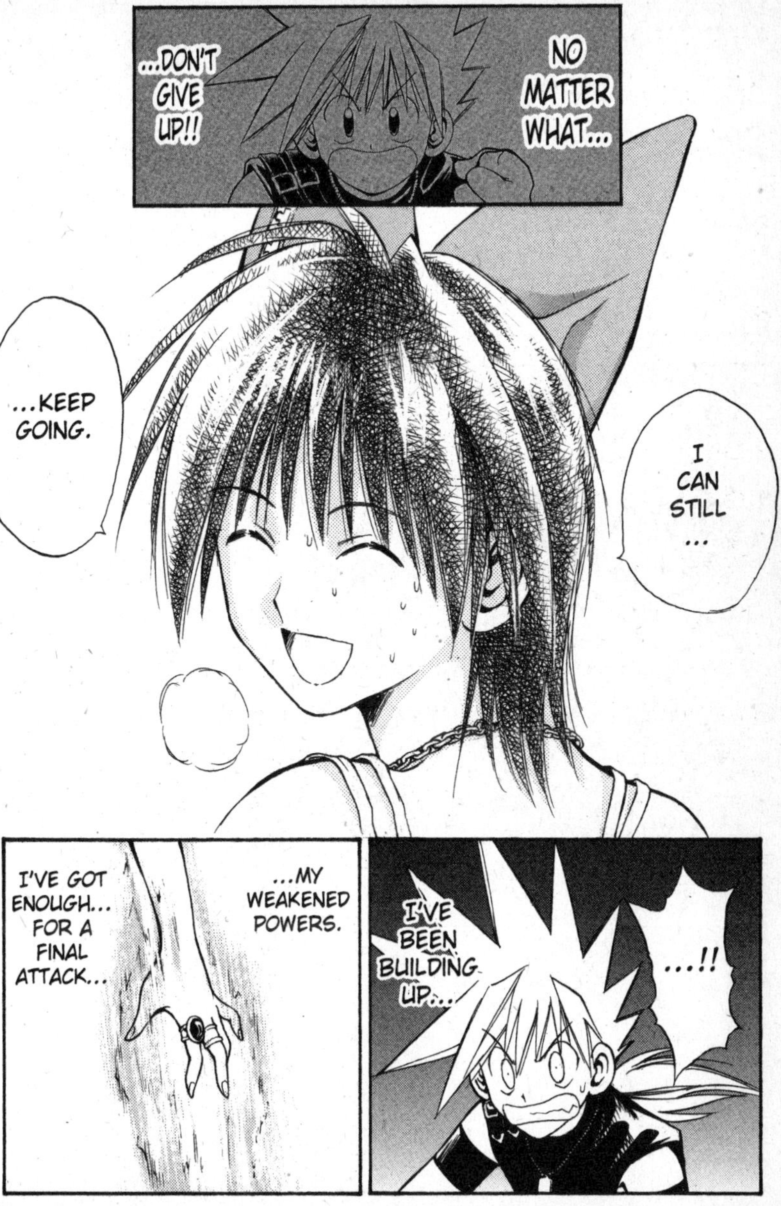
NO MATTER WHAT...
...DON'T GIVE UP!!
I CAN STILL ...
...KEEP GOING.
...!!
I'VE BEEN BUILDING UP...
...MY WEAKENED POWERS.
I'VE GOT ENOUGH... FOR A FINAL ATTACK...

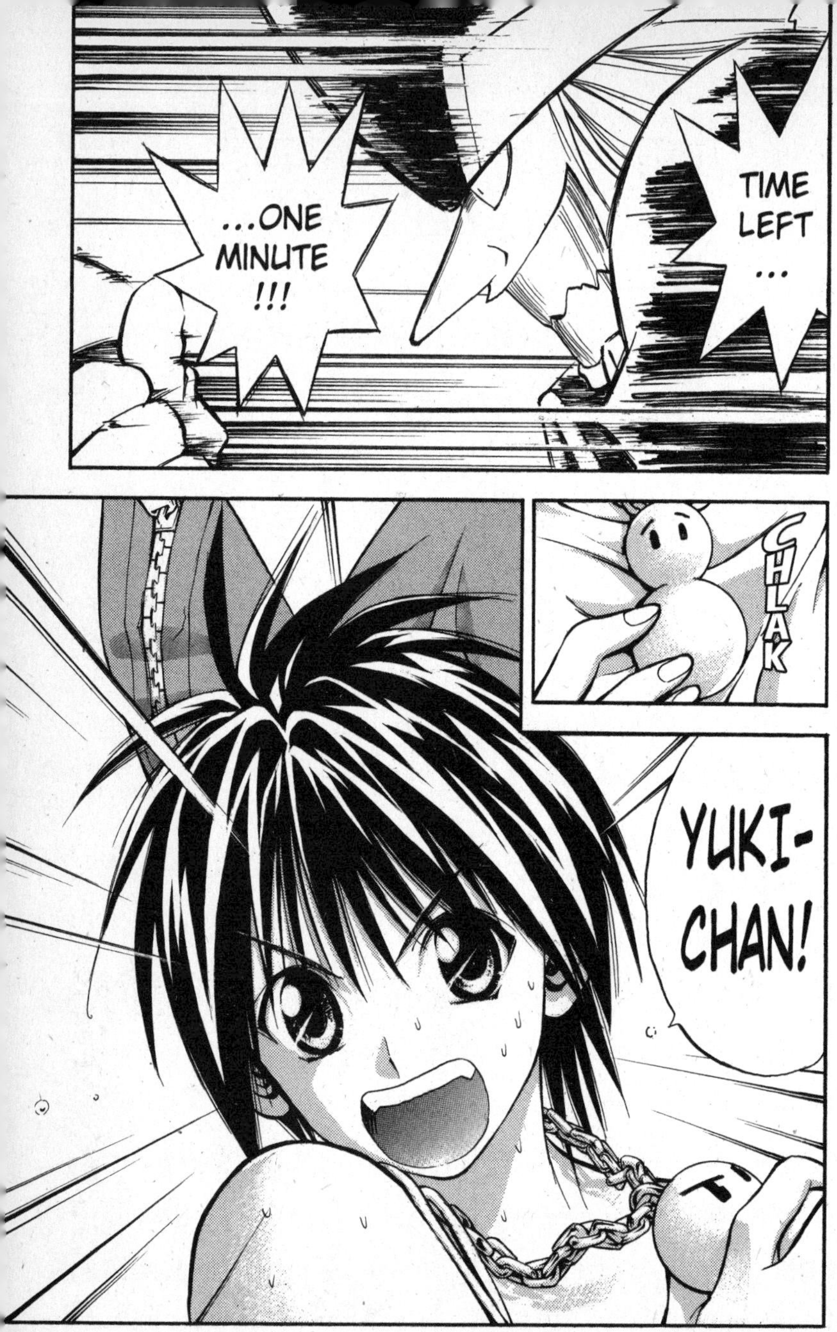
TIME LEFT...
...ONE MINUTE!!!
CHLAK
YUKI-CHAN!

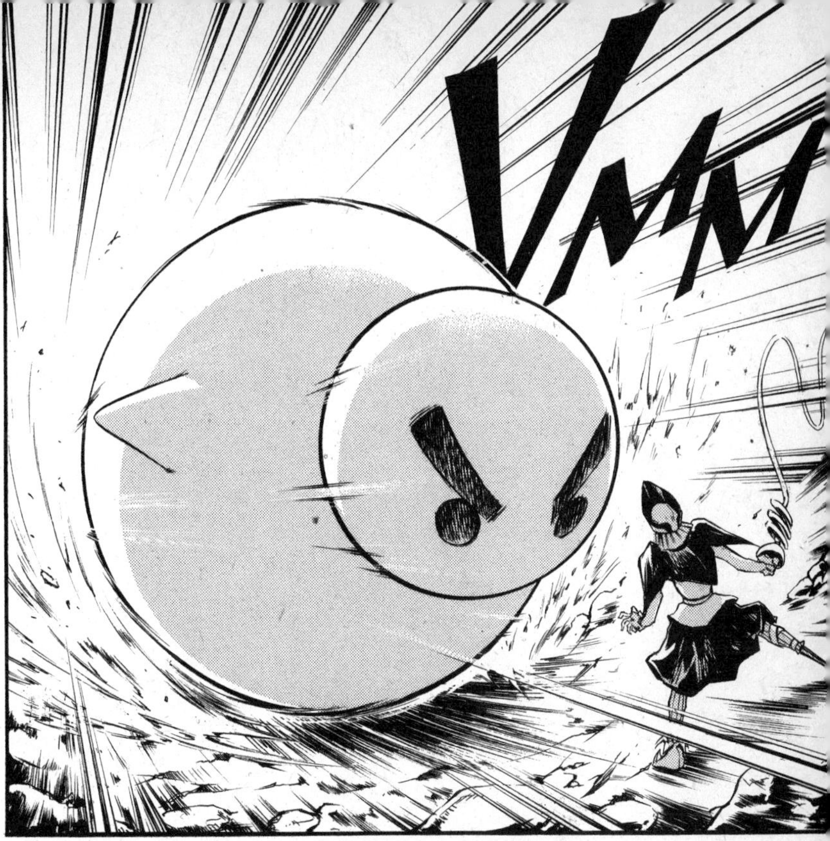
VMM
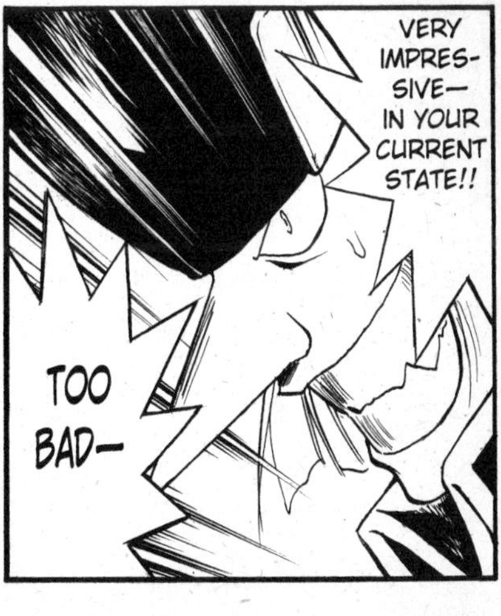
VERY IMPRES-SIVE— IN YOUR CURRENT STATE!!
TOO BAD—
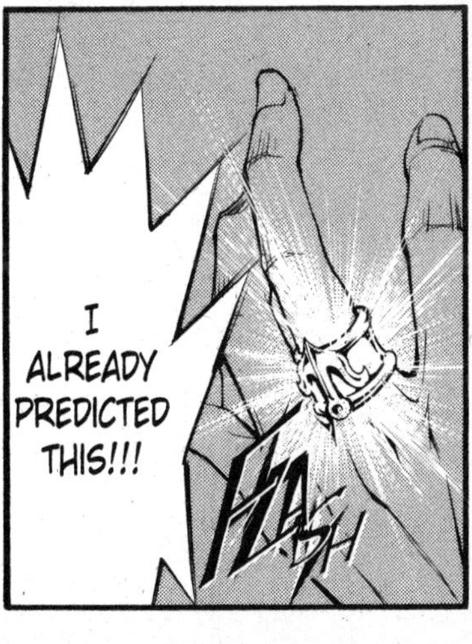
I ALREADY PREDICTED THIS!!!
FLASH

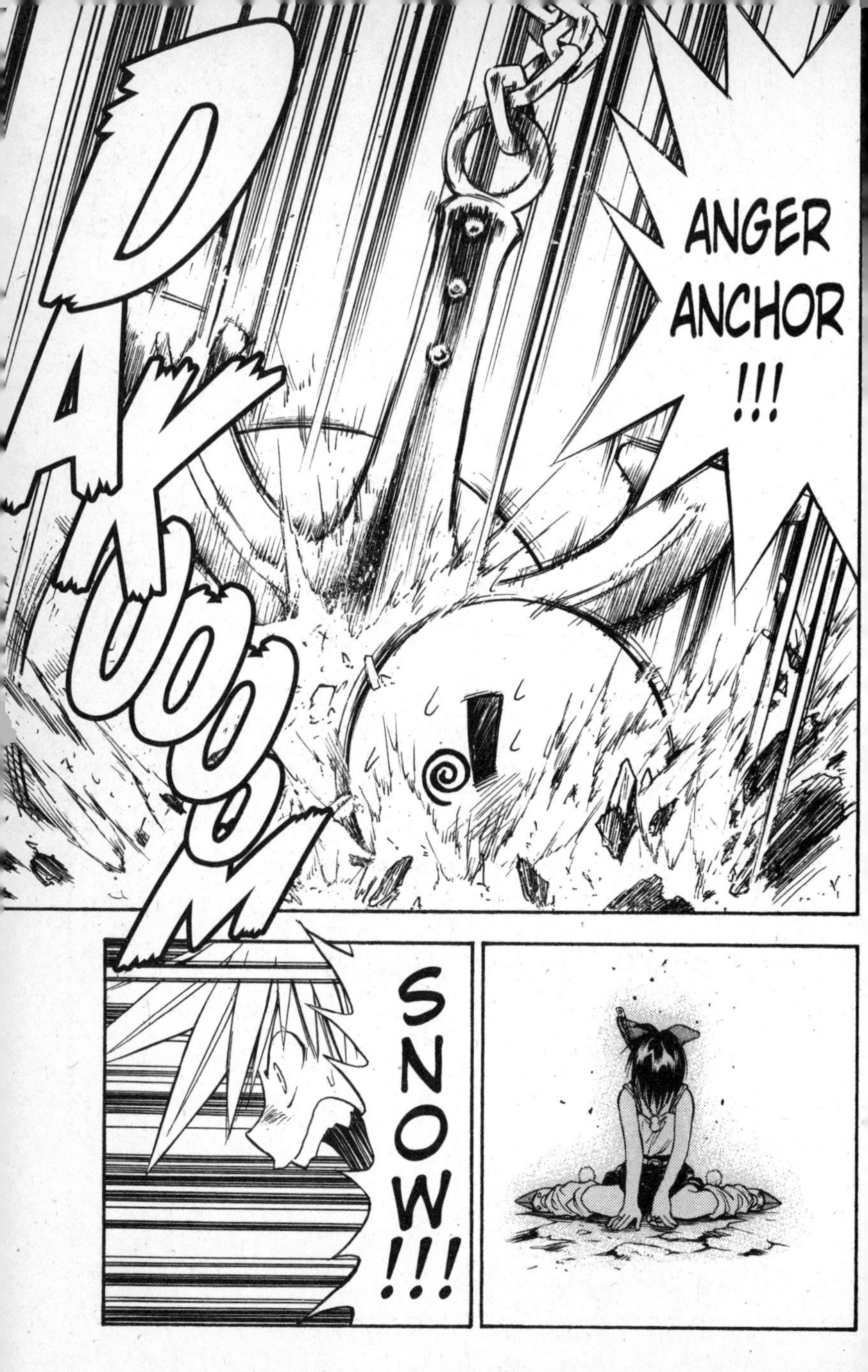
ANGER ANCHOR !!!
DAKOOOOM
SNOW!!!

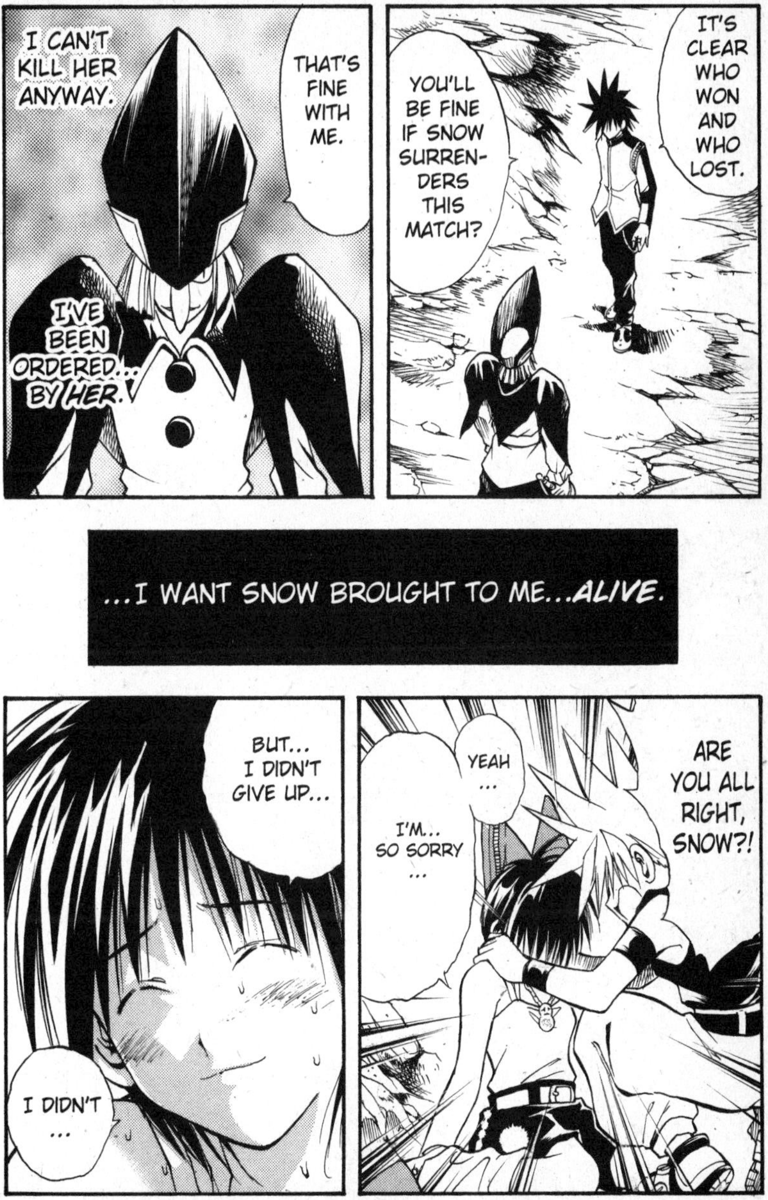
IT'S CLEAR WHO WON AND WHO LOST.
YOU'LL BE FINE IF SNOW SURRENDERS THIS MATCH?
THAT'S FINE WITH ME.
I CAN'T KILL HER ANYWAY.
I'VE BEEN ORDERED... BY HER.
...I WANT SNOW BROUGHT TO ME...ALIVE.
ARE YOU ALL RIGHT, SNOW?!
YEAH ...
I'M... SO SORRY ...
BUT... I DIDN'T GIVE UP...
I DIDN'T ...

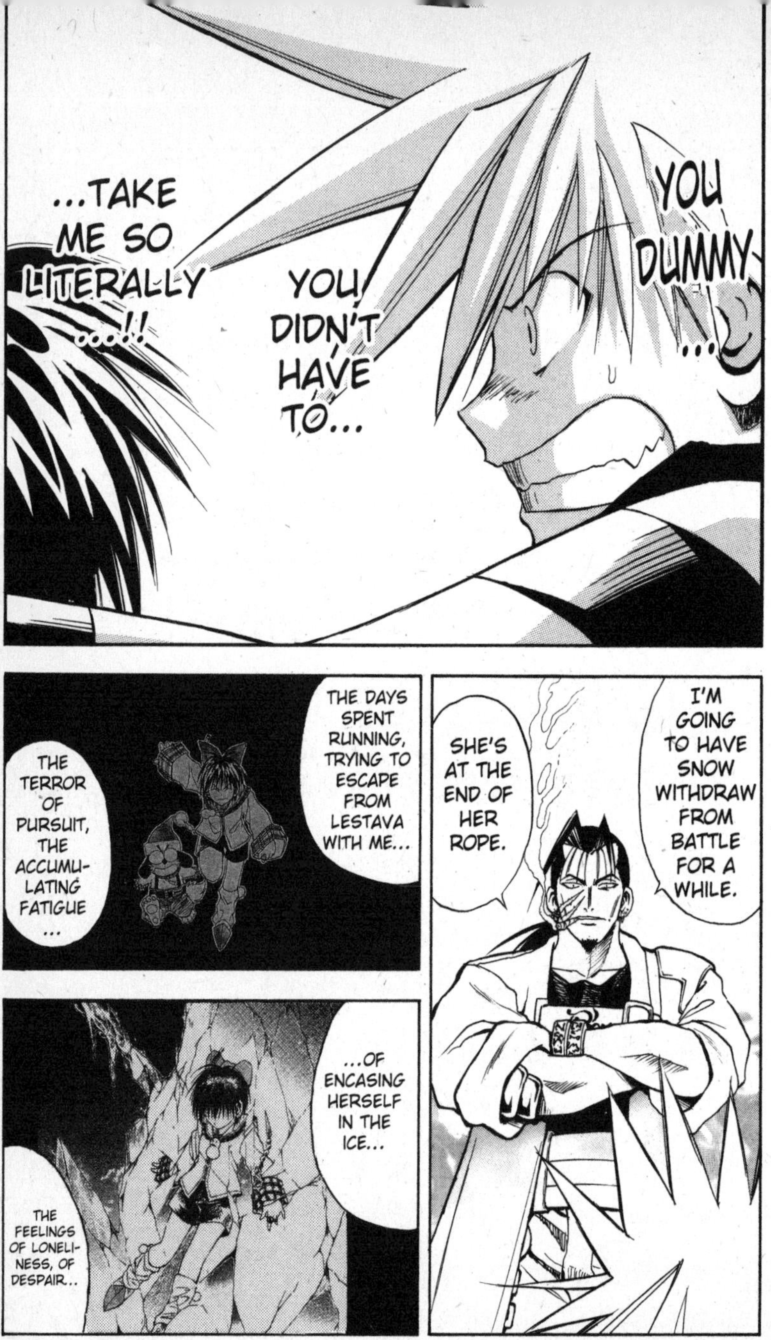
YOU DUMMY...
YOU DIDN'T HAVE TO...
...TAKE ME SO LITERALLY...!!
I'M GOING TO HAVE SNOW WITHDRAW FROM BATTLE FOR A WHILE.
SHE'S AT THE END OF HER ROPE.
THE DAYS SPENT RUNNING, TRYING TO ESCAPE FROM LESTAVA WITH ME...
THE TERROR OF PURSUIT, THE ACCUMULATING FATIGUE...
...OF ENCASING HERSELF IN THE ICE...
THE FEELINGS OF LONELINESS, OF DESPAIR...

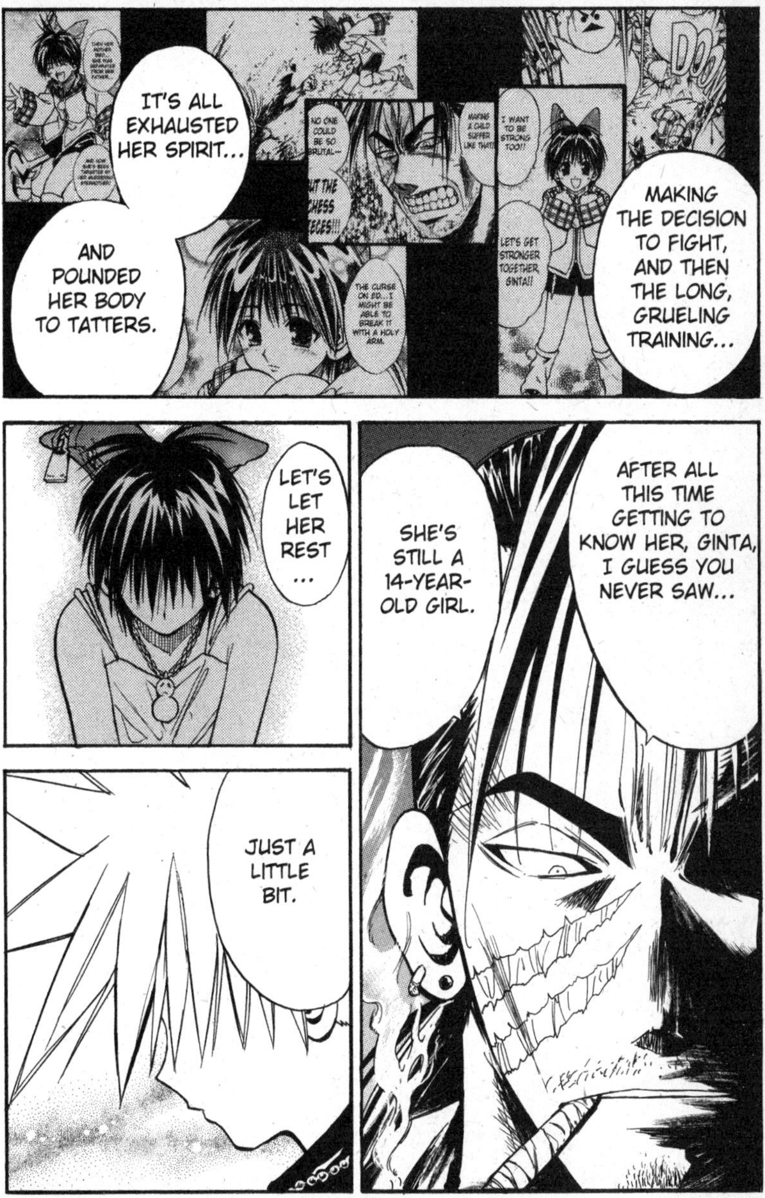
MAKING THE DECISION TO FIGHT, AND THEN THE LONG, GRUELING TRAINING...
I WANT TO BE STRONG TOO!!
LET'S GET STRONGER TOGETHER GINTA!!
MAKING A CHILD SUFFER LIKE THAT!
NO ONE COULD BE SO BRUTAL—
THE CURSE ON ED... I MIGHT BE ABLE TO BREAK IT WITH A HOLY ARM.
IT'S ALL EXHAUSTED HER SPIRIT...
AND POUNDED HER BODY TO TATTERS.
AFTER ALL THIS TIME GETTING TO KNOW HER, GINTA, I GUESS YOU NEVER SAW...
SHE'S STILL A 14-YEAR-OLD GIRL.
LET'S LET HER REST...
JUST A LITTLE BIT.

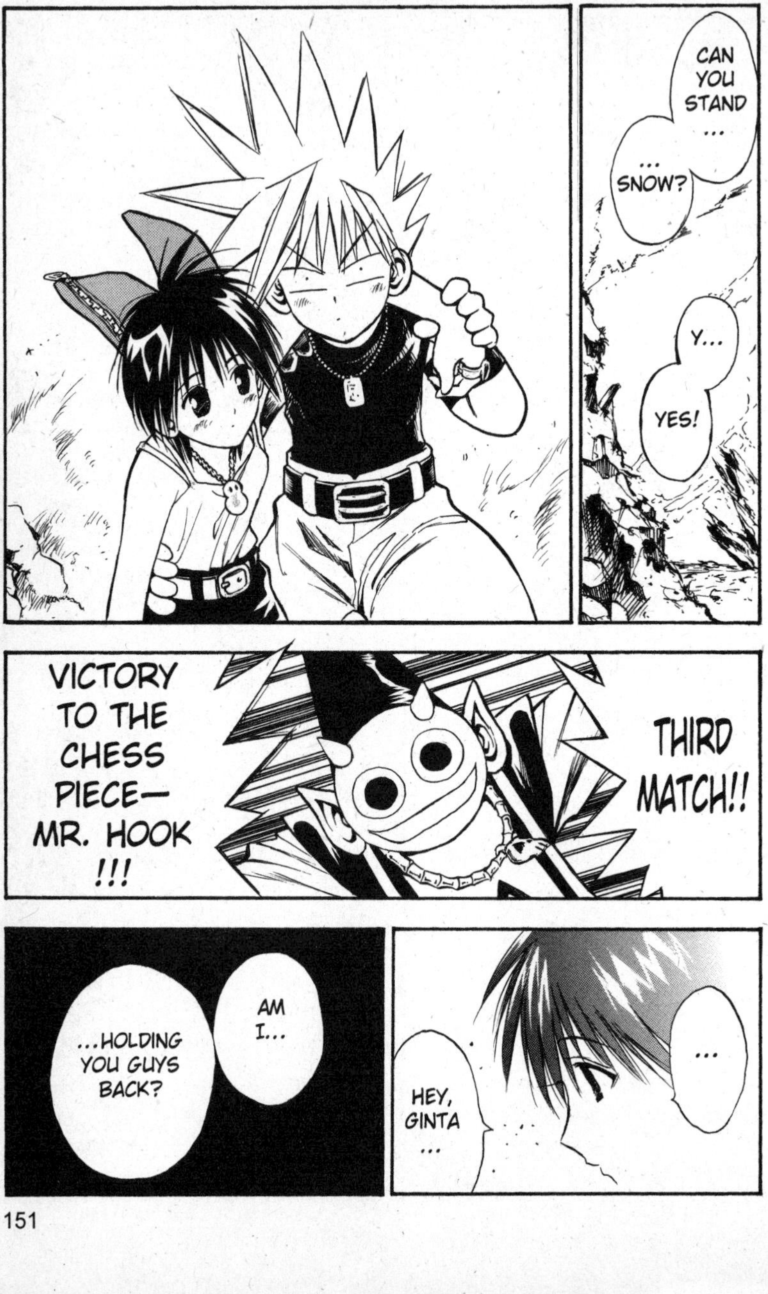
CAN YOU STAND ...
... SNOW?
Y...
YES!
THIRD MATCH!!
VICTORY TO THE CHESS PIECE— MR. HOOK !!!
...
HEY, GINTA ...
AM I...
...HOLDING YOU GUYS BACK?

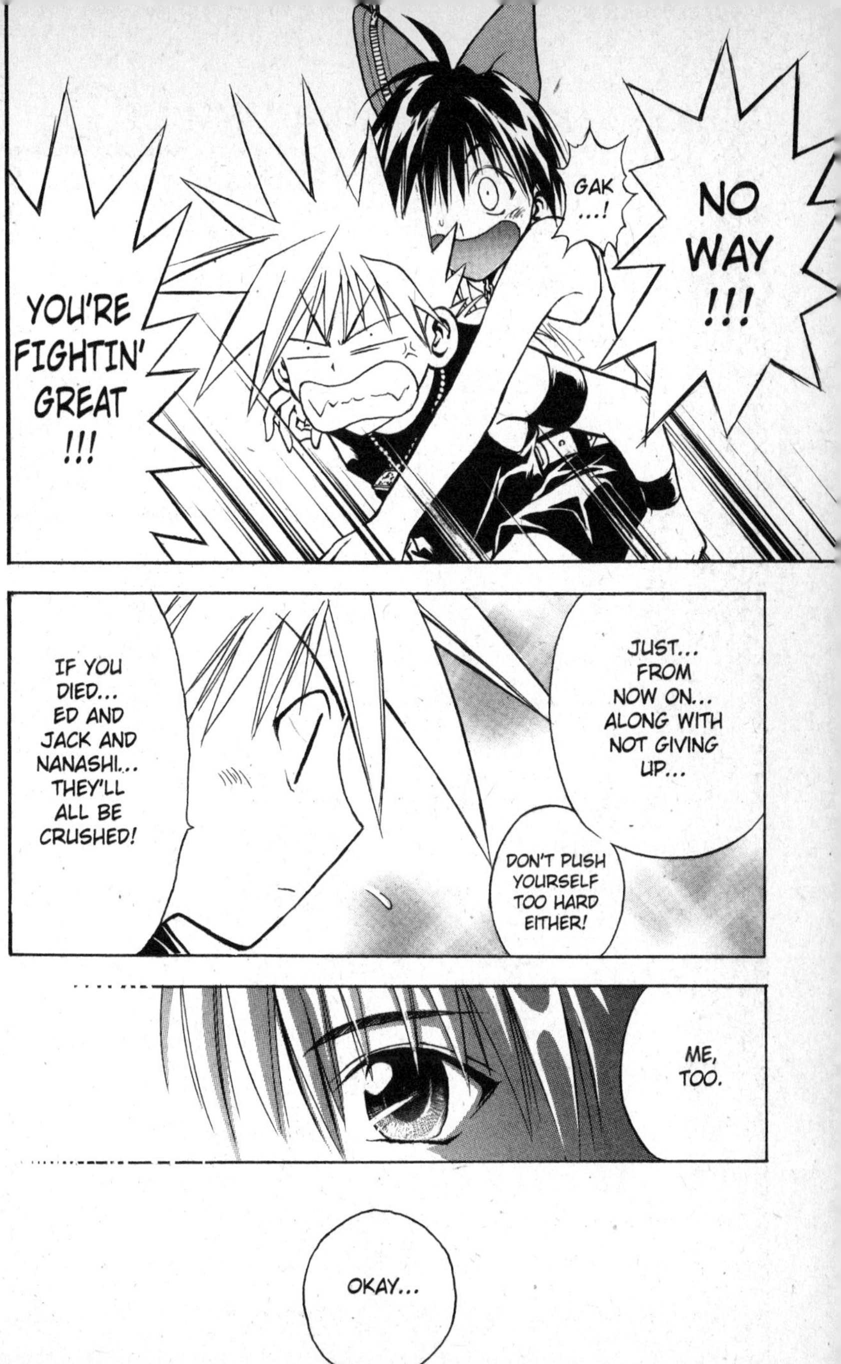
NO WAY !!!
GAK ...!
YOU'RE FIGHTIN' GREAT !!!
JUST... FROM NOW ON... ALONG WITH NOT GIVING UP...
DON'T PUSH YOURSELF TOO HARD EITHER!
IF YOU DIED... ED AND JACK AND NANASHI... THEY'LL ALL BE CRUSHED!
ME, TOO.
OKAY...

AKT.62/Ginta vs. Kannochi①

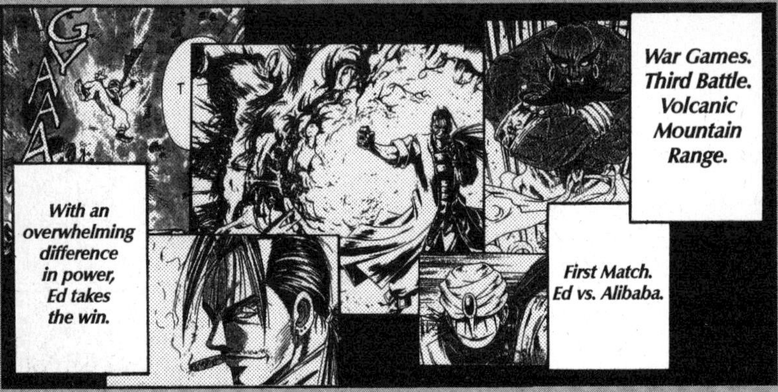
War Games. Third Battle. Volcanic Mountain Range.
First Match. Ed vs. Alibaba.
GYAAA
With an overwhelming difference in power, Ed takes the win.

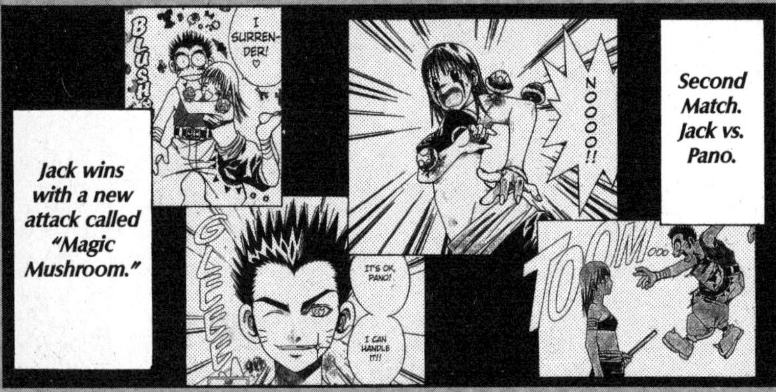
Second Match. Jack vs. Pano.
NOOOOO!!
I SURRENDER! ♡
BLUSH
TOOM...
IT'S OK, PANO!
I CAN HANDLE IT!
Jack wins with a new attack called "Magic Mushroom."

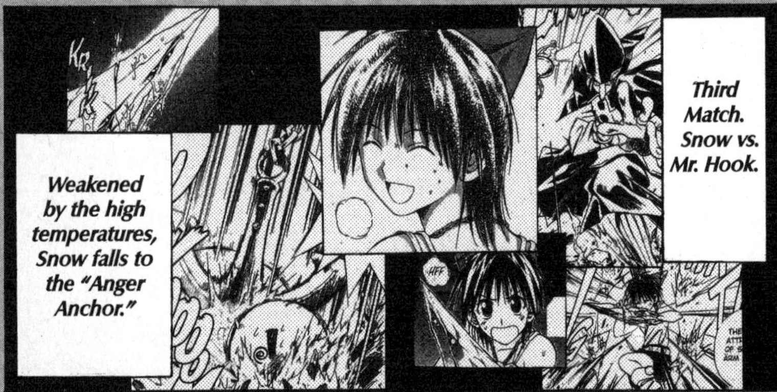
Third Match. Snow vs. Mr. Hook.
HFF
Weakened by the high temperatures, Snow falls to the "Anger Anchor."

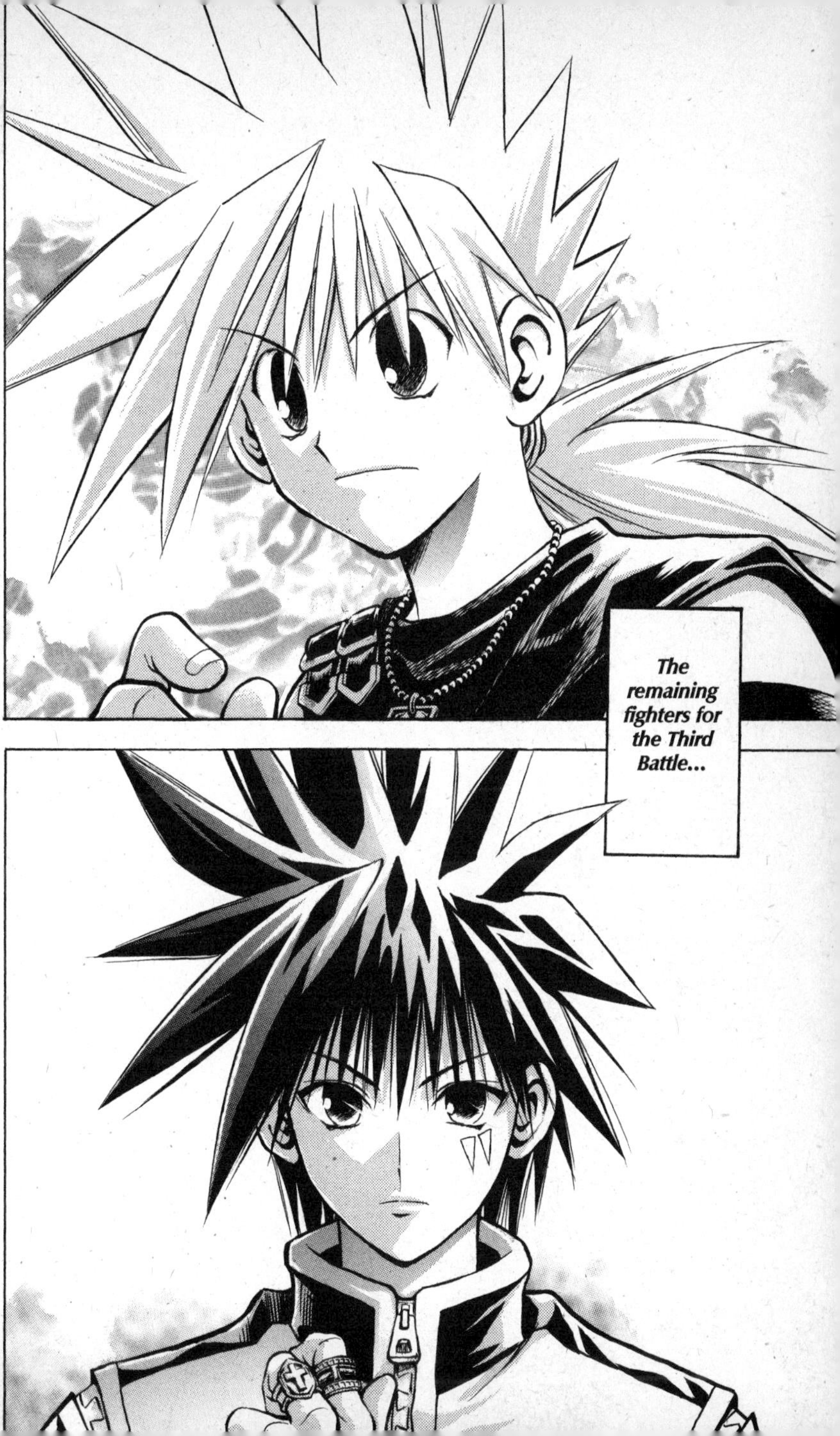
The remaining fighters for the Third Battle...

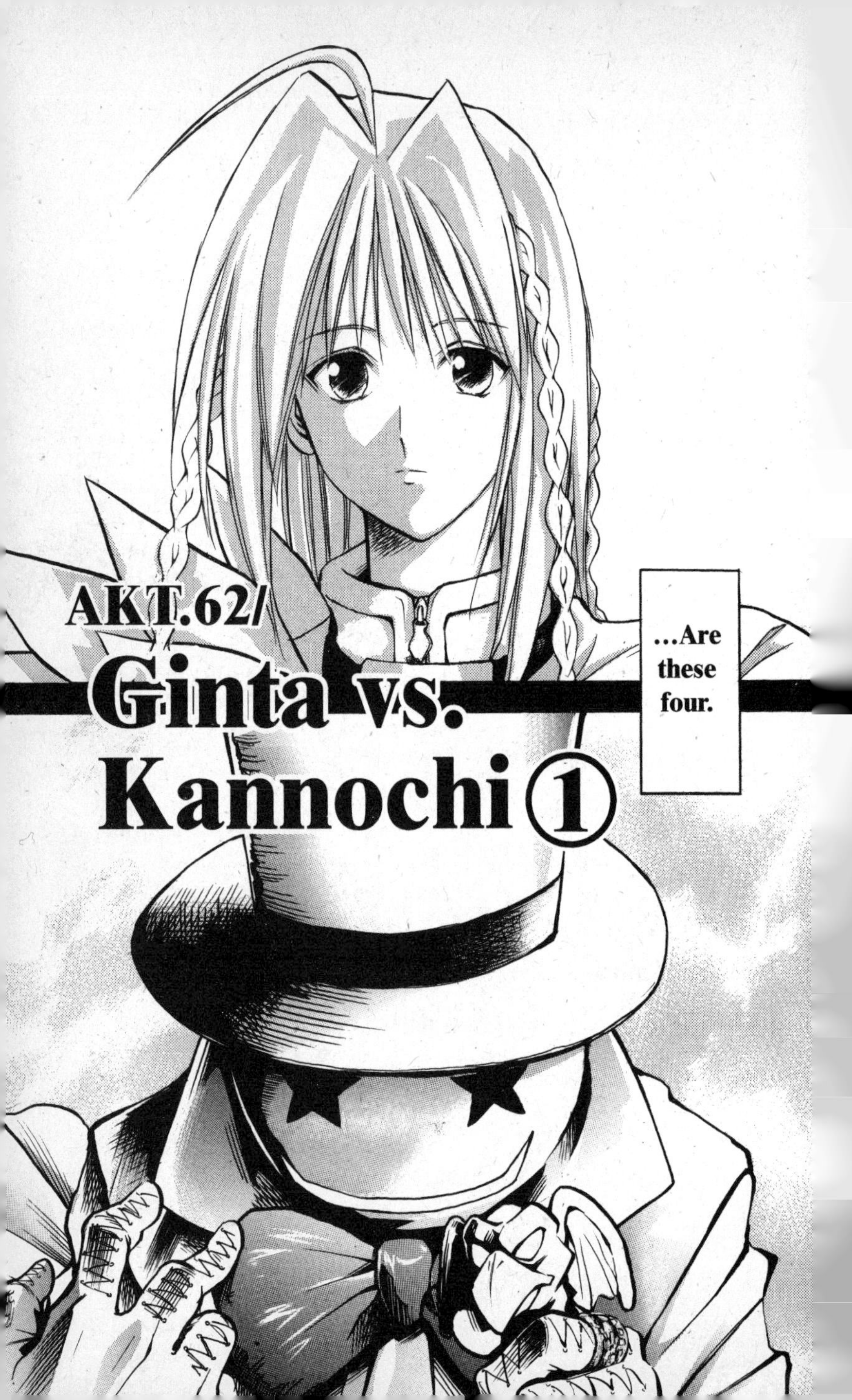
AKT.62/
Ginta vs. Kannochi ①
...Are these four.

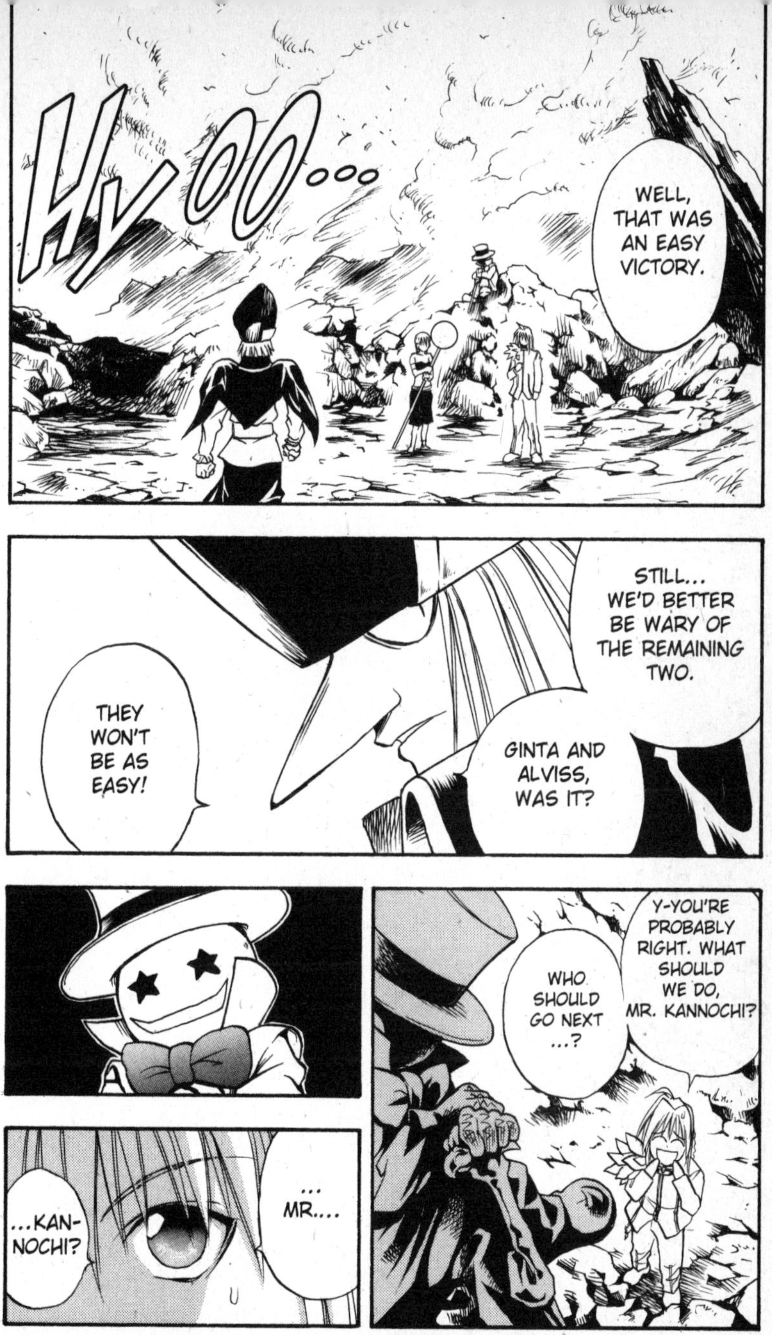
WELL, THAT WAS AN EASY VICTORY.
HYOOO...
STILL... WE'D BETTER BE WARY OF THE REMAINING TWO.
GINTA AND ALVISS, WAS IT?
THEY WON'T BE AS EASY!
Y-YOU'RE PROBABLY RIGHT. WHAT SHOULD WE DO, MR. KANNOCHI?
WHO SHOULD GO NEXT ...?
... MR....
...KAN-NOCHI?

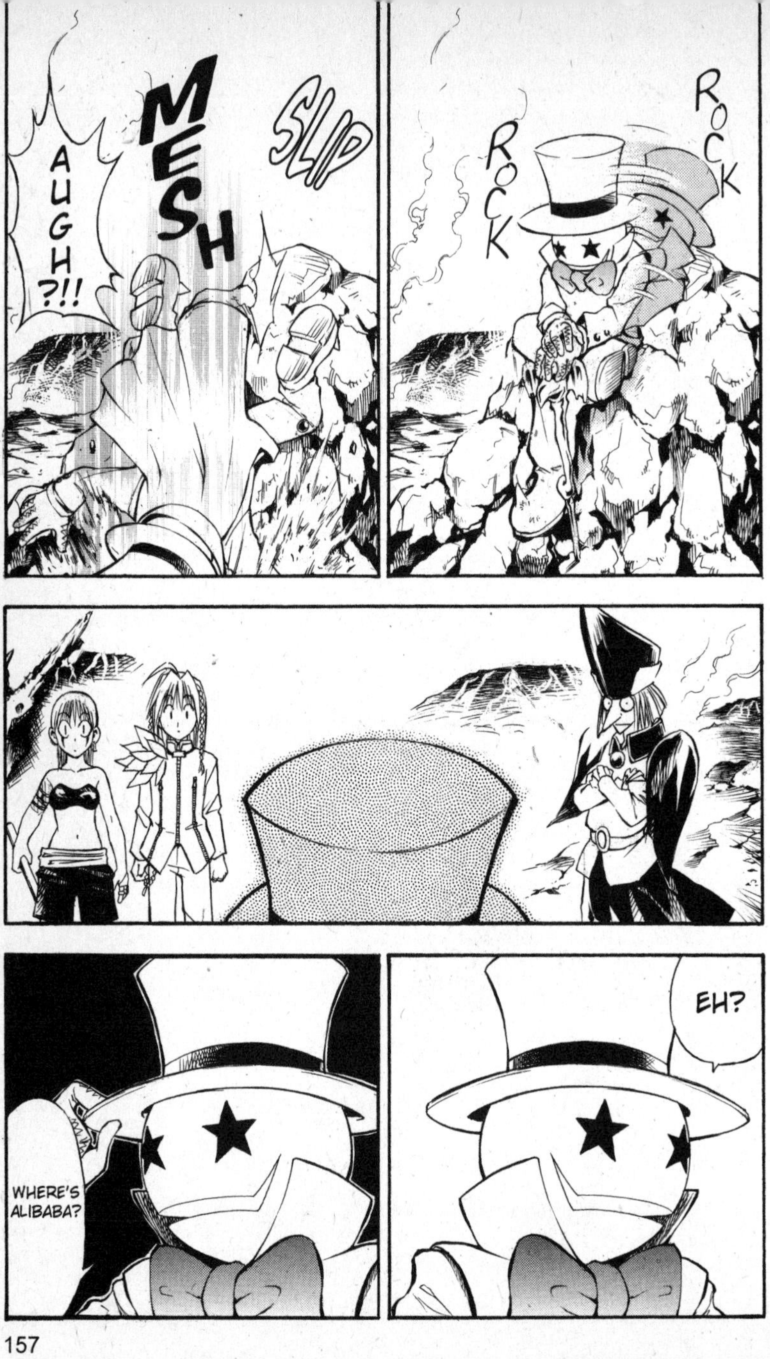
ROCK
ROCK
SLIP
MESH
AUGH?!!
EH?
WHERE'S ALIBABA?

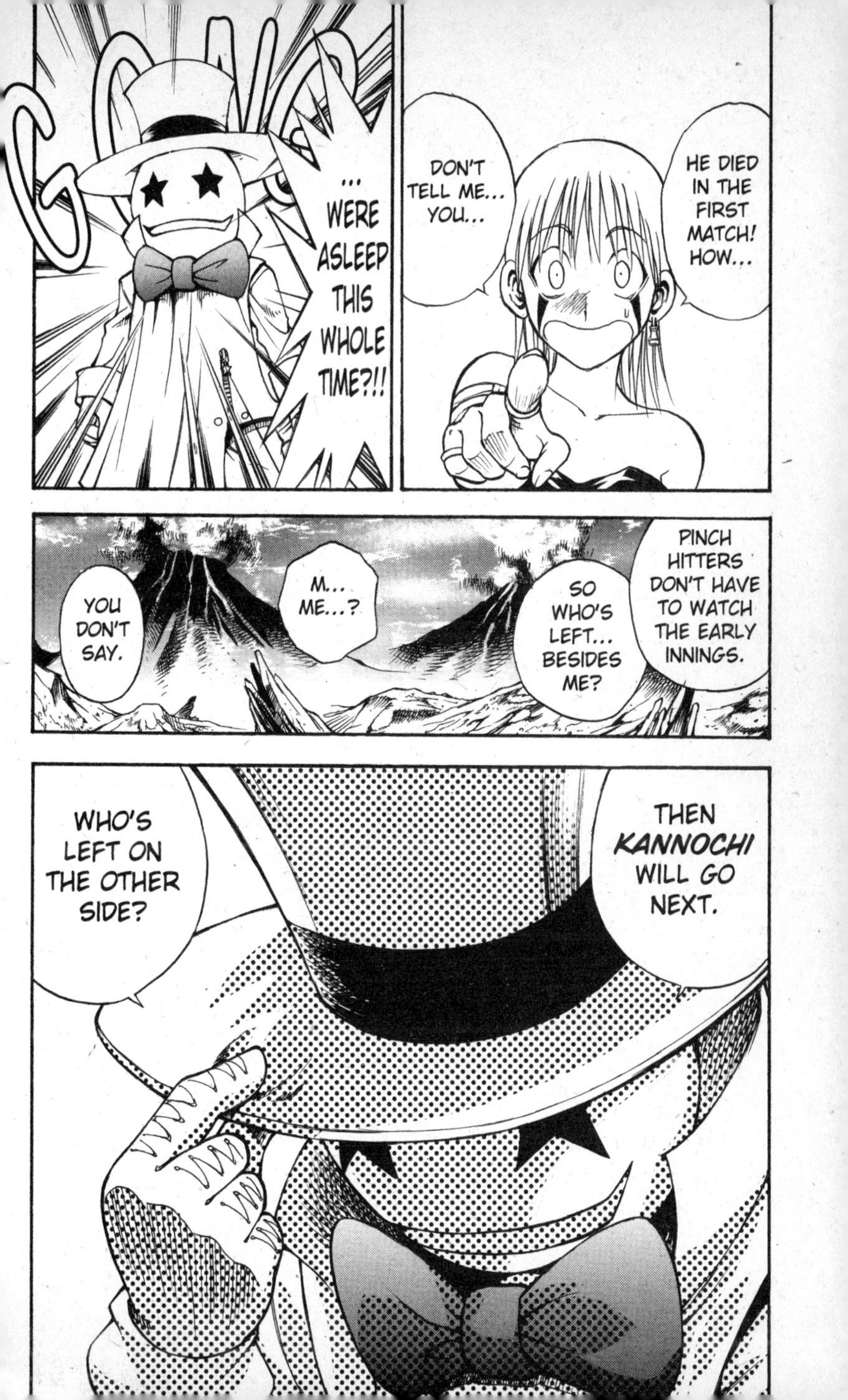
HE DIED IN THE FIRST MATCH! HOW...
DON'T TELL ME... YOU...
... WERE ASLEEP THIS WHOLE TIME?!!
PINCH HITTERS DON'T HAVE TO WATCH THE EARLY INNINGS.
SO WHO'S LEFT... BESIDES ME?
M... ME...?
YOU DON'T SAY.
THEN *KANNOCHI* WILL GO NEXT.
WHO'S LEFT ON THE OTHER SIDE?

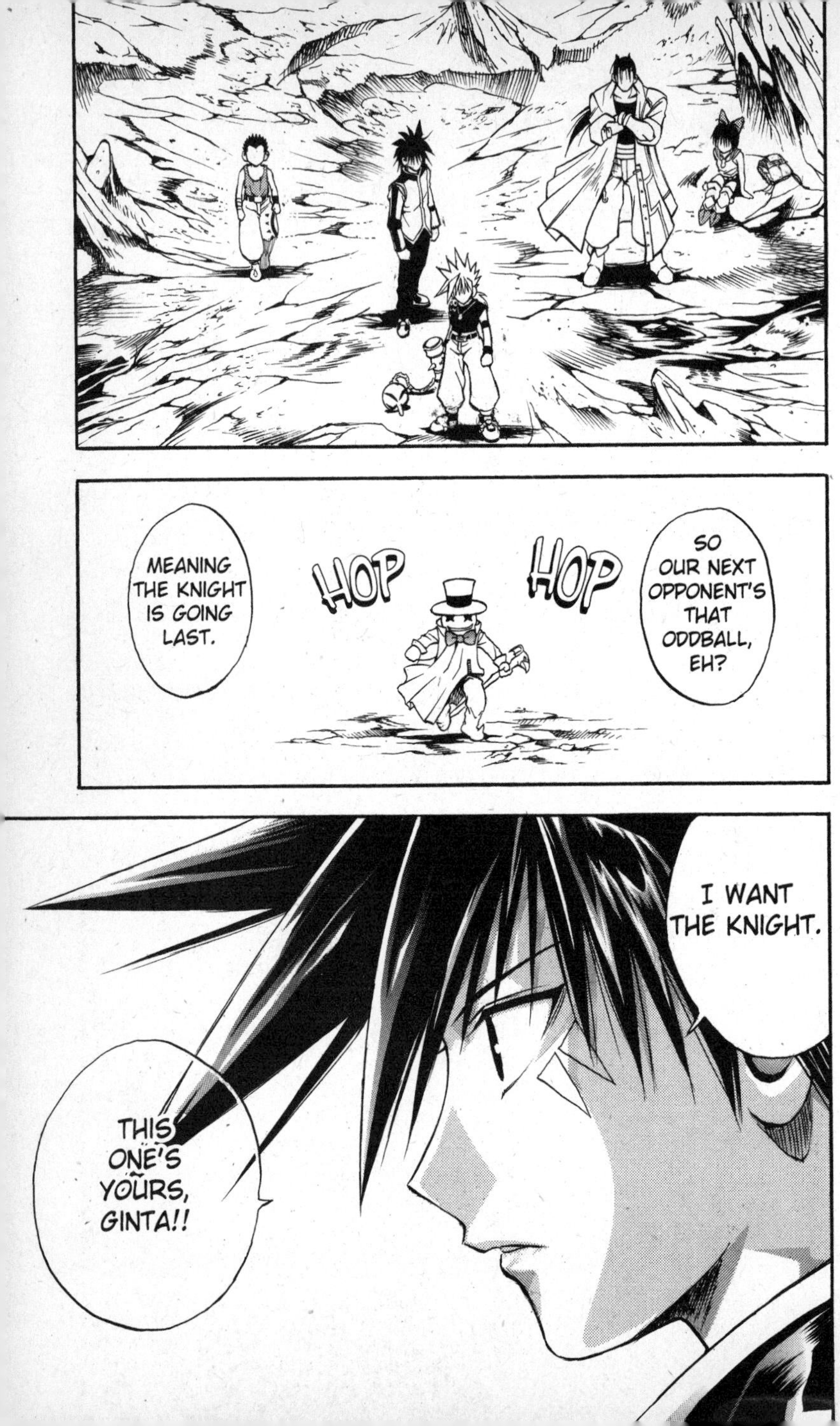
SO OUR NEXT OPPONENT'S THAT ODDBALL, EH?
HOP
HOP
MEANING THE KNIGHT IS GOING LAST.
I WANT THE KNIGHT.
THIS ONE'S YOURS, GINTA!!

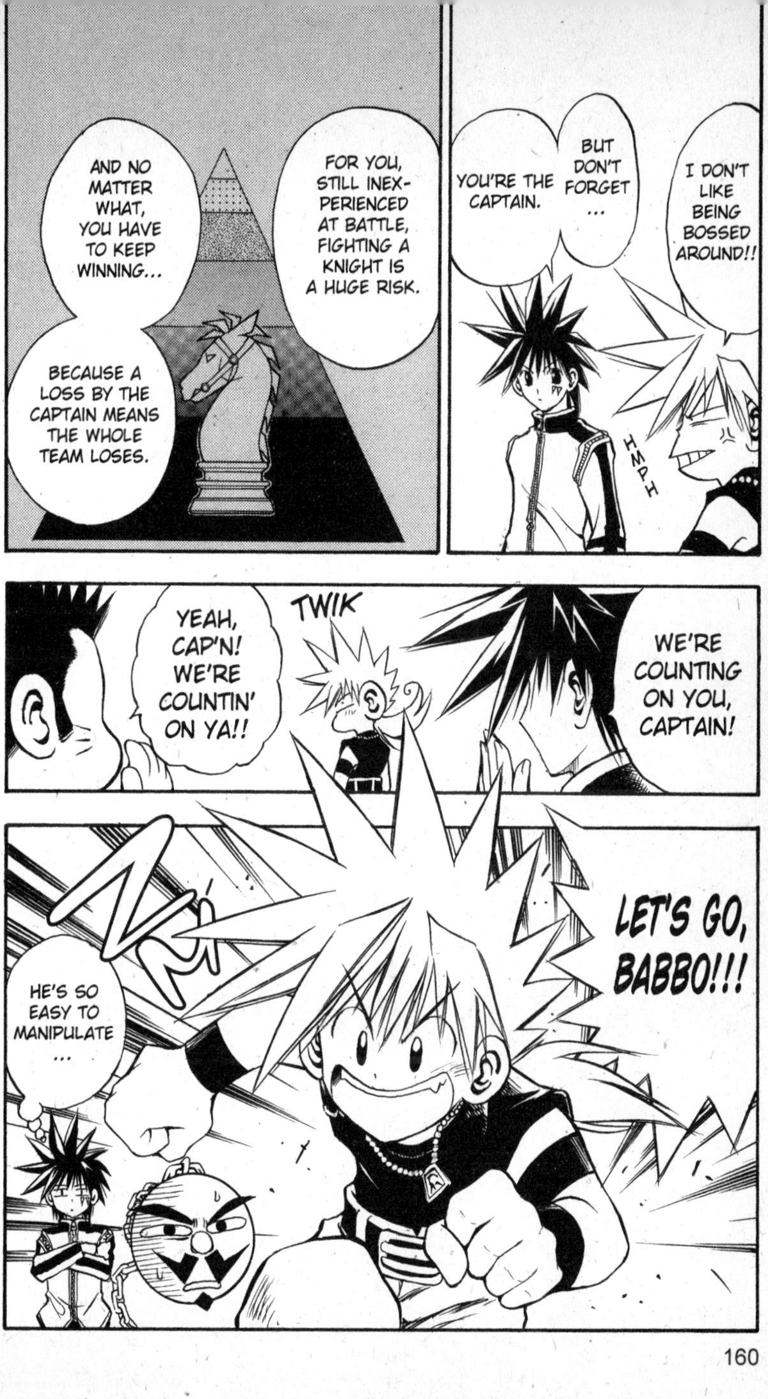
I DON'T LIKE BEING BOSSED AROUND!!
BUT DON'T FORGET ...
YOU'RE THE CAPTAIN.
HMPH
FOR YOU, STILL INEX-PERIENCED AT BATTLE, FIGHTING A KNIGHT IS A HUGE RISK.
AND NO MATTER WHAT, YOU HAVE TO KEEP WINNING...
BECAUSE A LOSS BY THE CAPTAIN MEANS THE WHOLE TEAM LOSES.
WE'RE COUNTING ON YOU, CAPTAIN!
TWIK
YEAH, CAP'N! WE'RE COUNTIN' ON YA!!
LET'S GO, BABBO!!!
HE'S SO EASY TO MANIPULATE ...

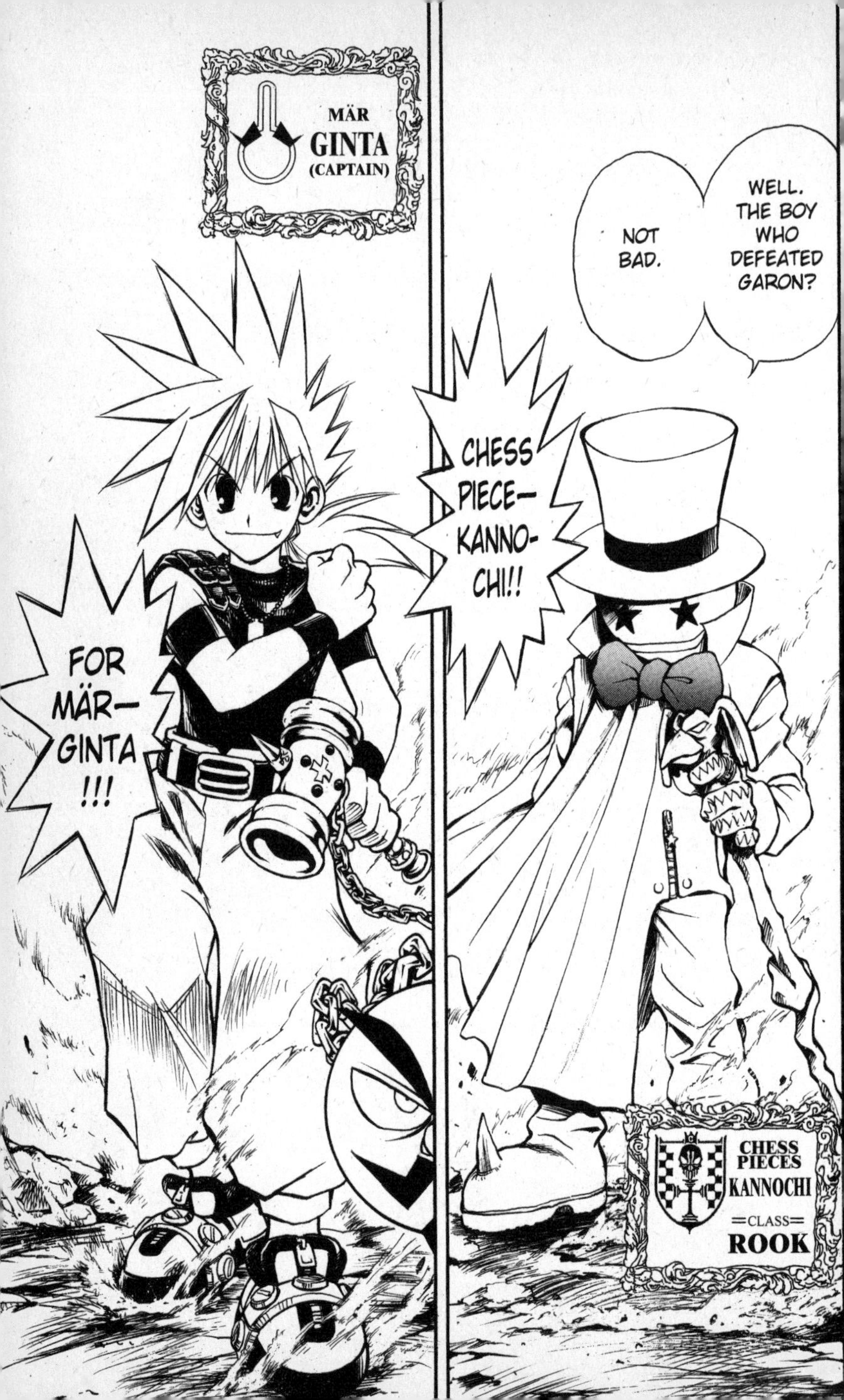
WELL. THE BOY WHO DEFEATED GARON?
NOT BAD.
CHESS PIECE— KANNO-CHI!!
CHESS PIECES
KANNOCHI
=CLASS=
ROOK
MÄR
GINTA
(CAPTAIN)
FOR MÄR-GINTA!!!

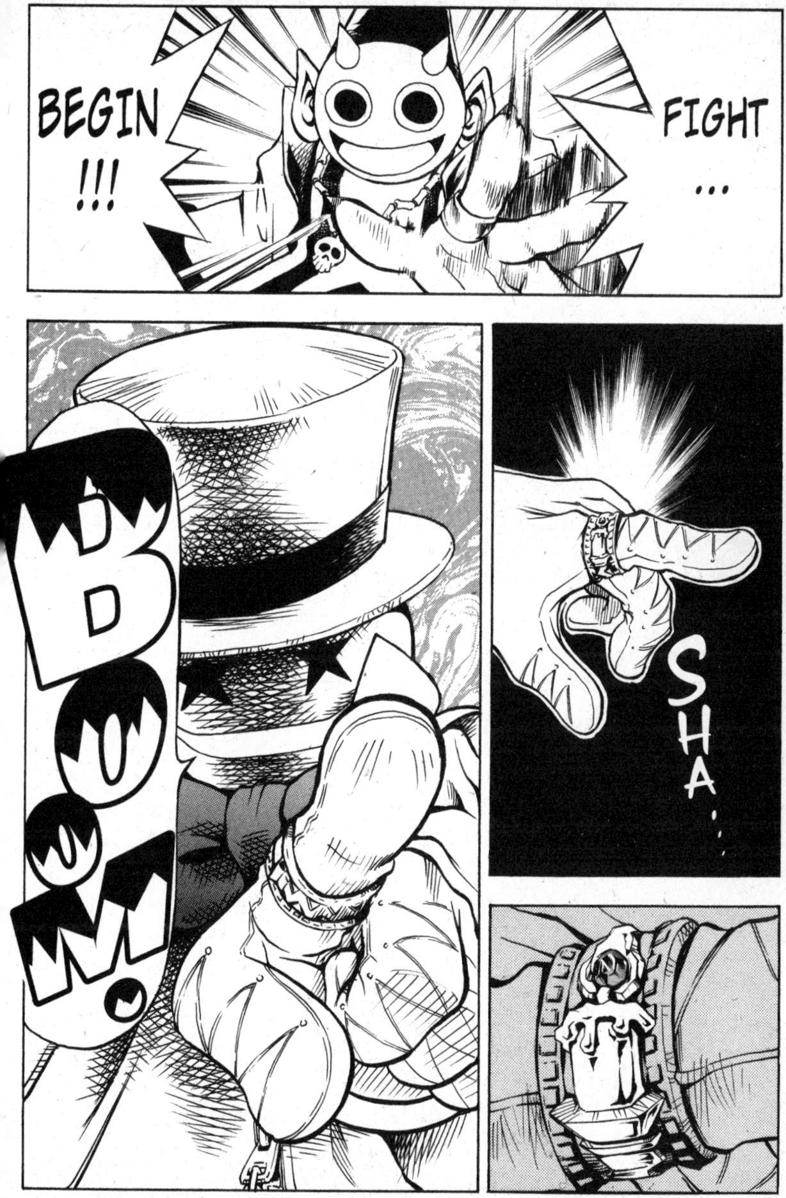

FIGHT ...
BEGIN !!!
SHA...
BDOOOM

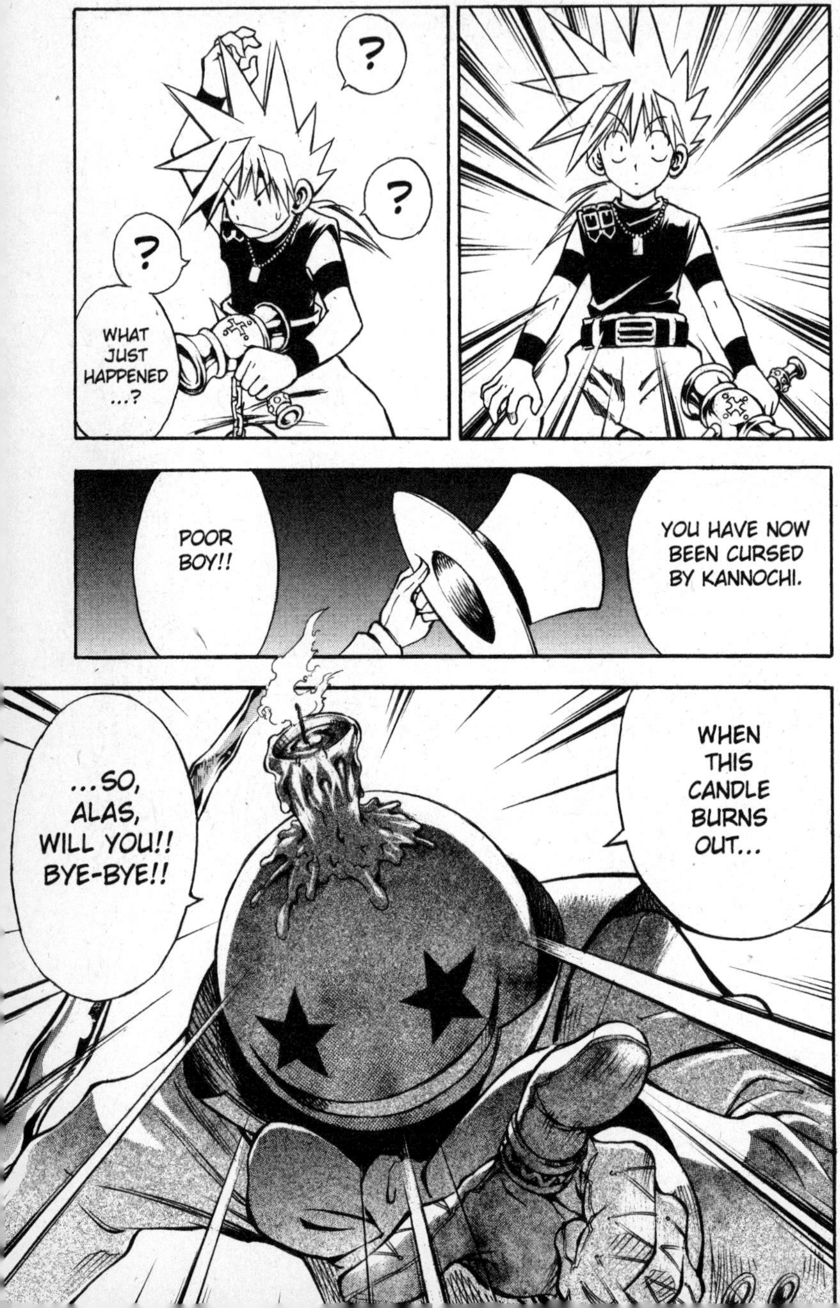
?
?
?
WHAT JUST HAPPENED ...?
YOU HAVE NOW BEEN CURSED BY KANNOCHI.
POOR BOY!!
WHEN THIS CANDLE BURNS OUT...
...SO, ALAS, WILL YOU!! BYE-BYE!!

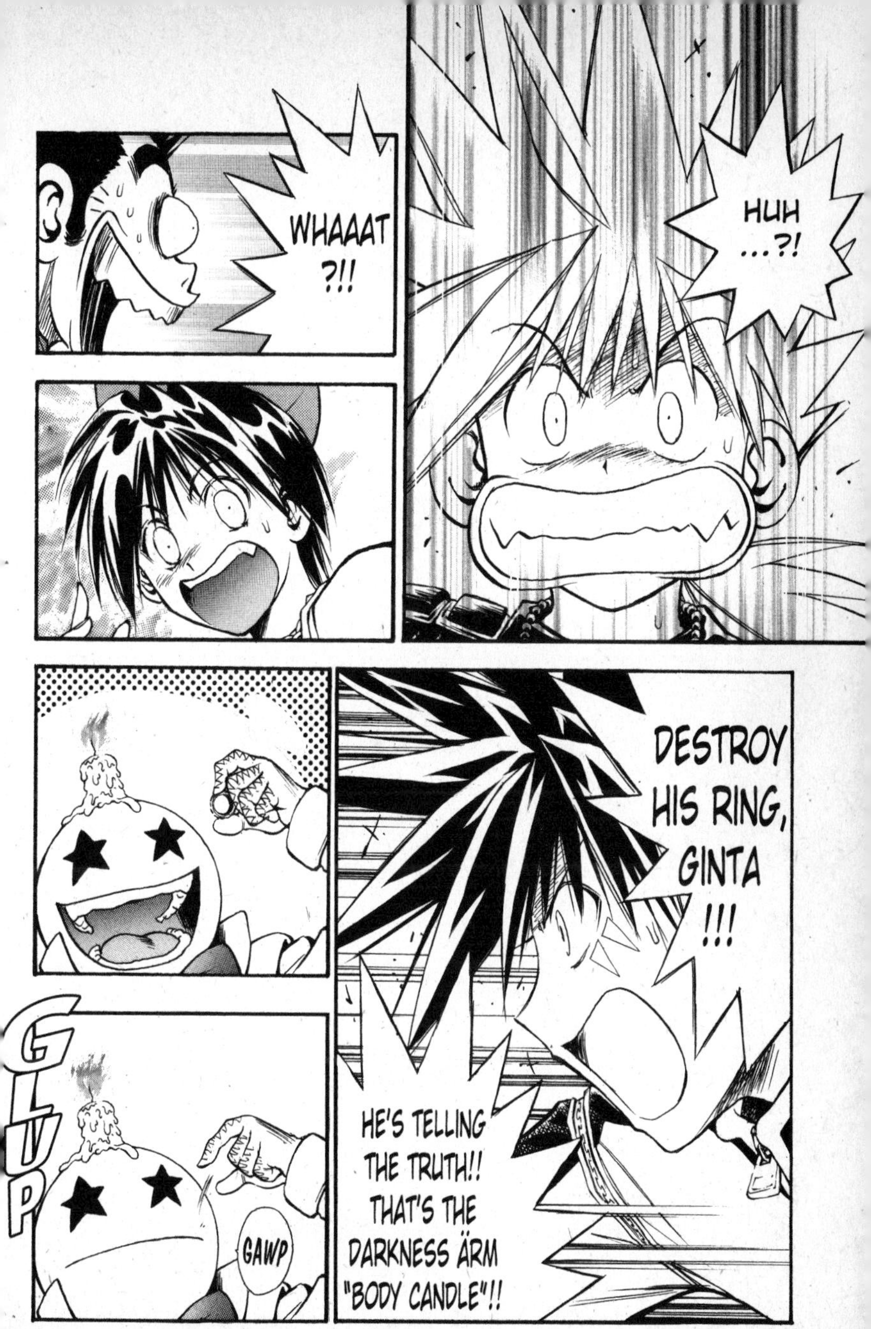
HUH ...?!
WHAAAT ?!!
DESTROY HIS RING, GINTA !!!
HE'S TELLING THE TRUTH!! THAT'S THE DARKNESS ÄRM "BODY CANDLE"!!
GLUP
GAWP

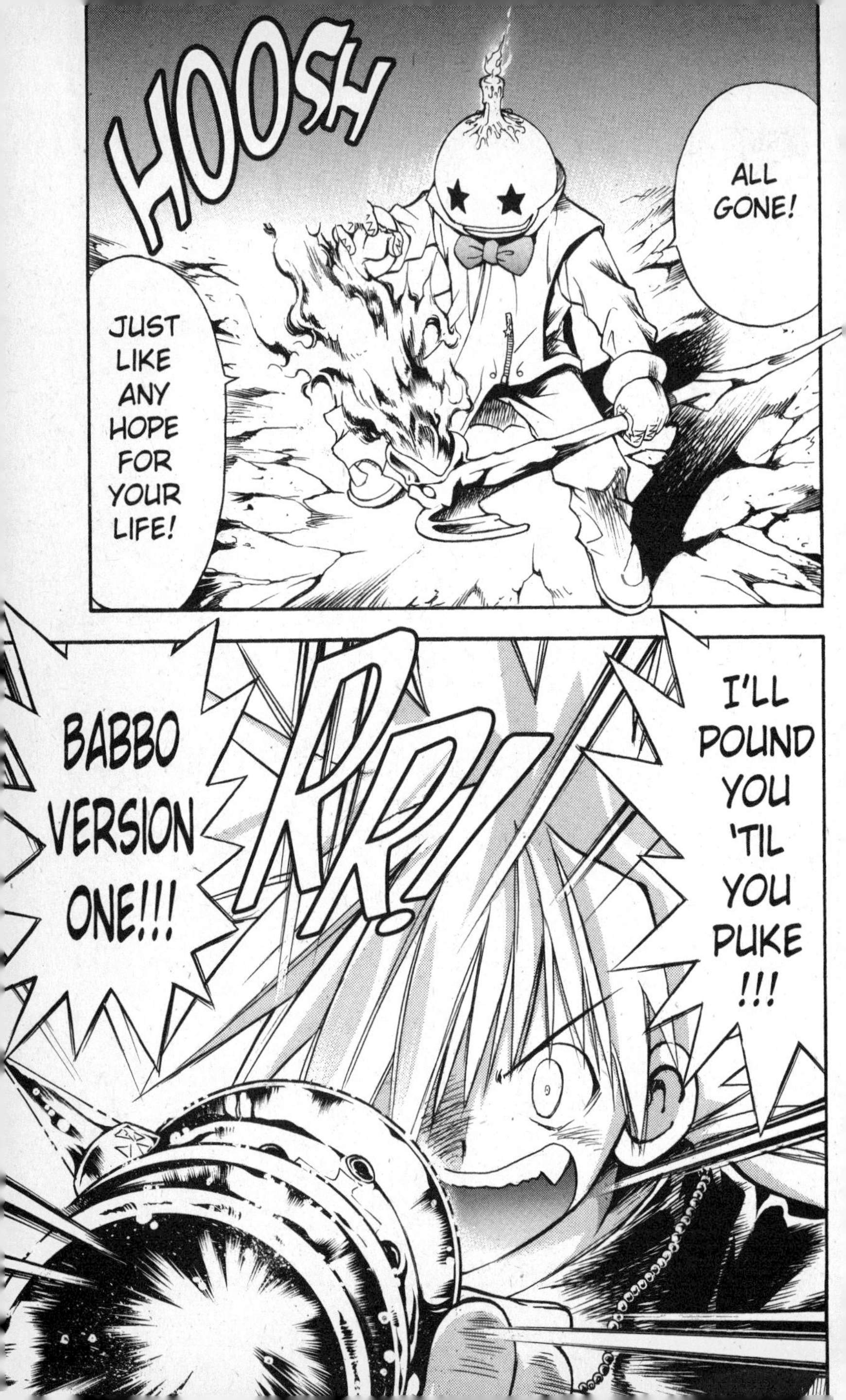
ALL GONE!
HOOSH
JUST LIKE ANY HOPE FOR YOUR LIFE!
I'LL POUND YOU 'TIL YOU PUKE!!!
BABBO VERSION ONE!!!

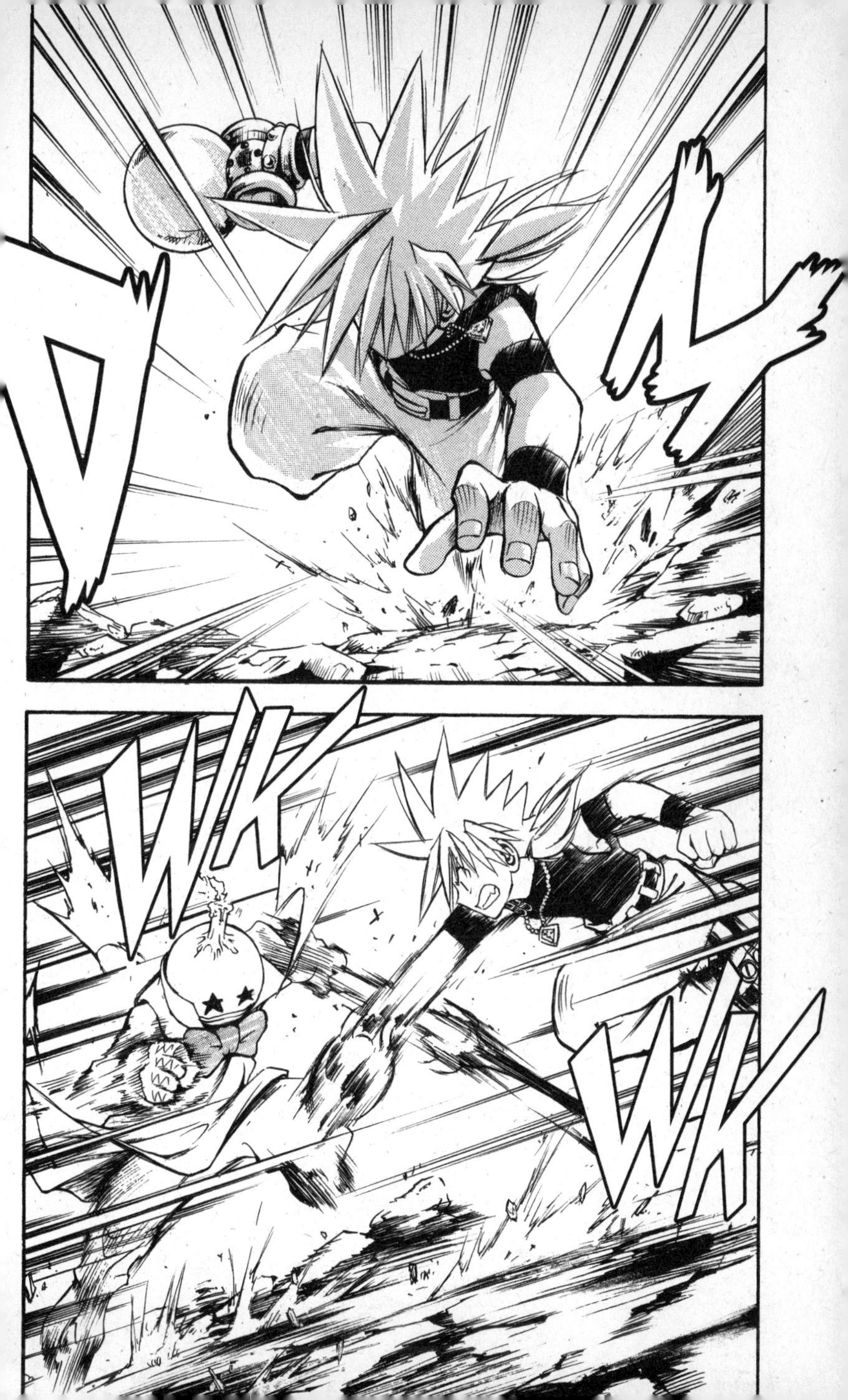
WAK
WAK

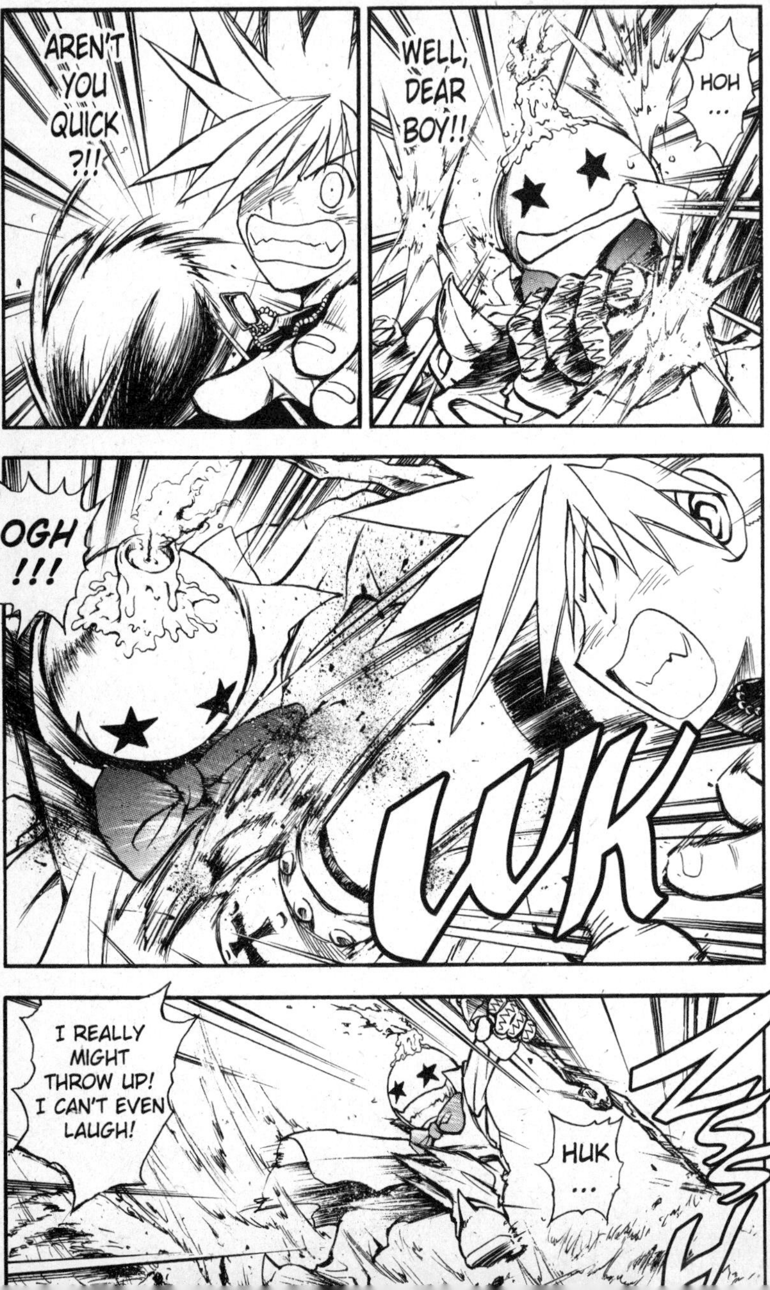
HOH ...
WELL, DEAR BOY!!
AREN'T YOU QUICK ?!!
OGH !!!
WUK
I REALLY MIGHT THROW UP! I CAN'T EVEN LAUGH!
HUK ...

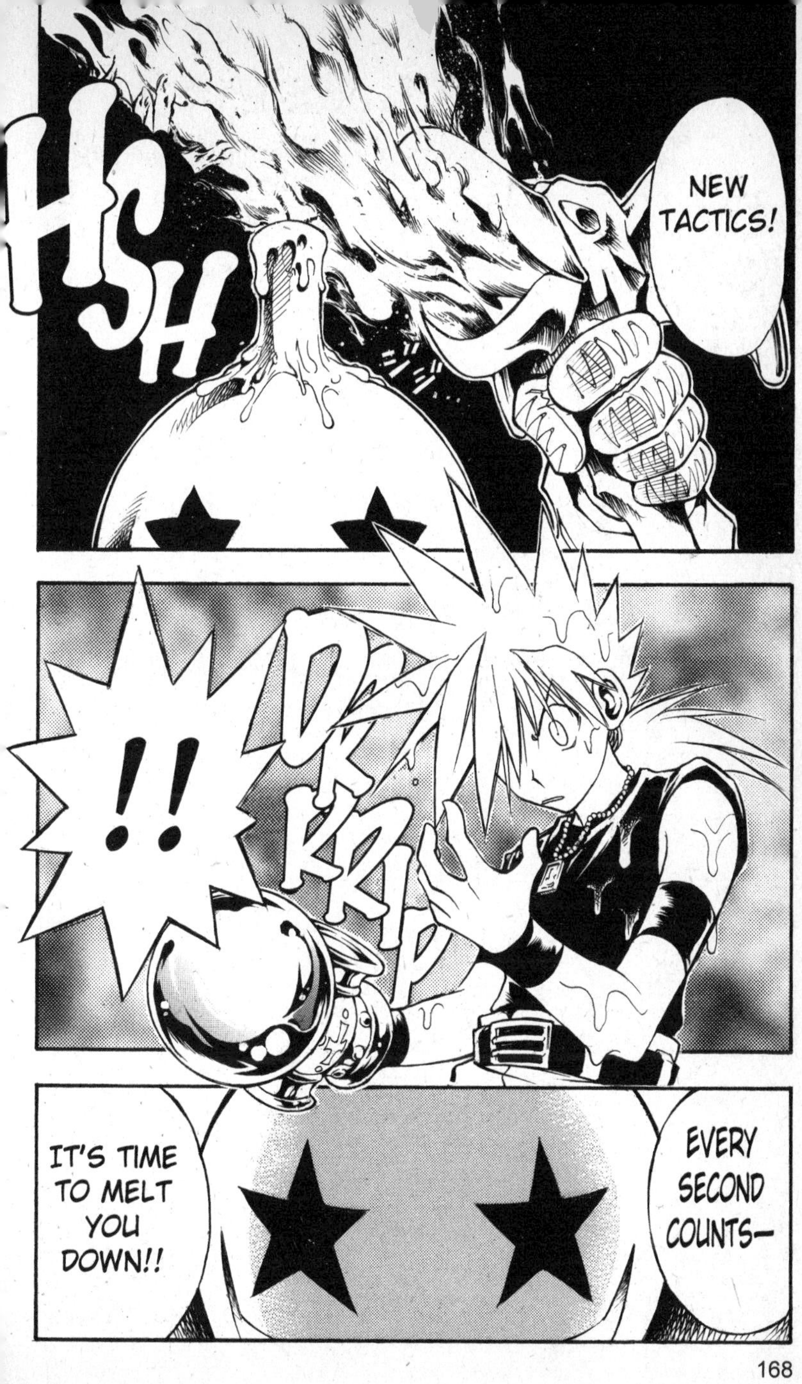
NEW TACTICS!
HSH
!!
DRKRIP
EVERY SECOND COUNTS—
IT'S TIME TO MELT YOU DOWN!!

AKT.62/ Ginta vs. Kannochi ②

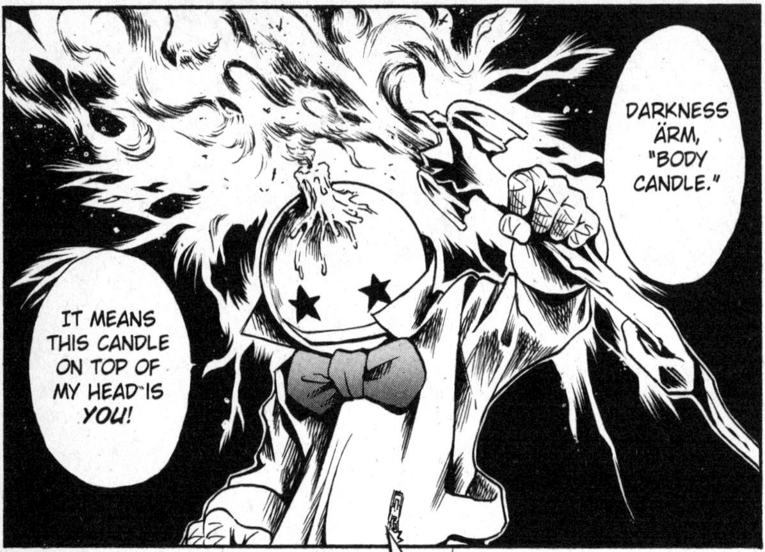
DARKNESS ÄRM, "BODY CANDLE."
IT MEANS THIS CANDLE ON TOP OF MY HEAD IS *YOU*!

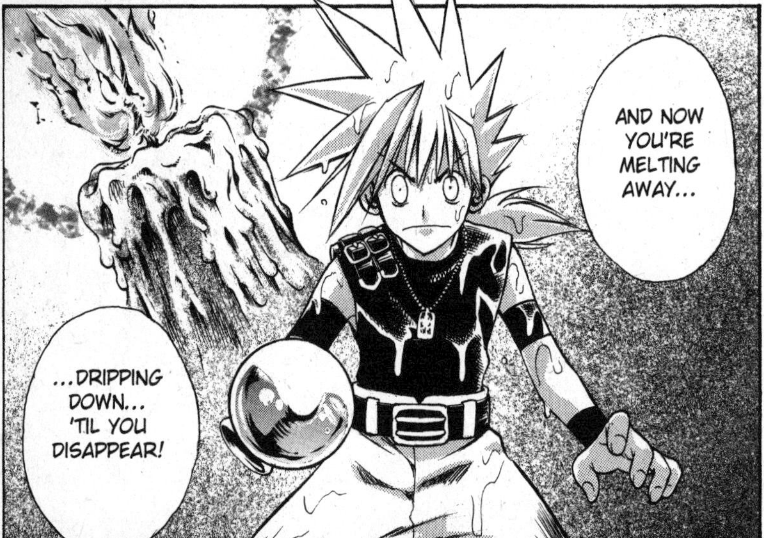
AND NOW YOU'RE MELTING AWAY...
...DRIPPING DOWN... 'TIL YOU DISAPPEAR!

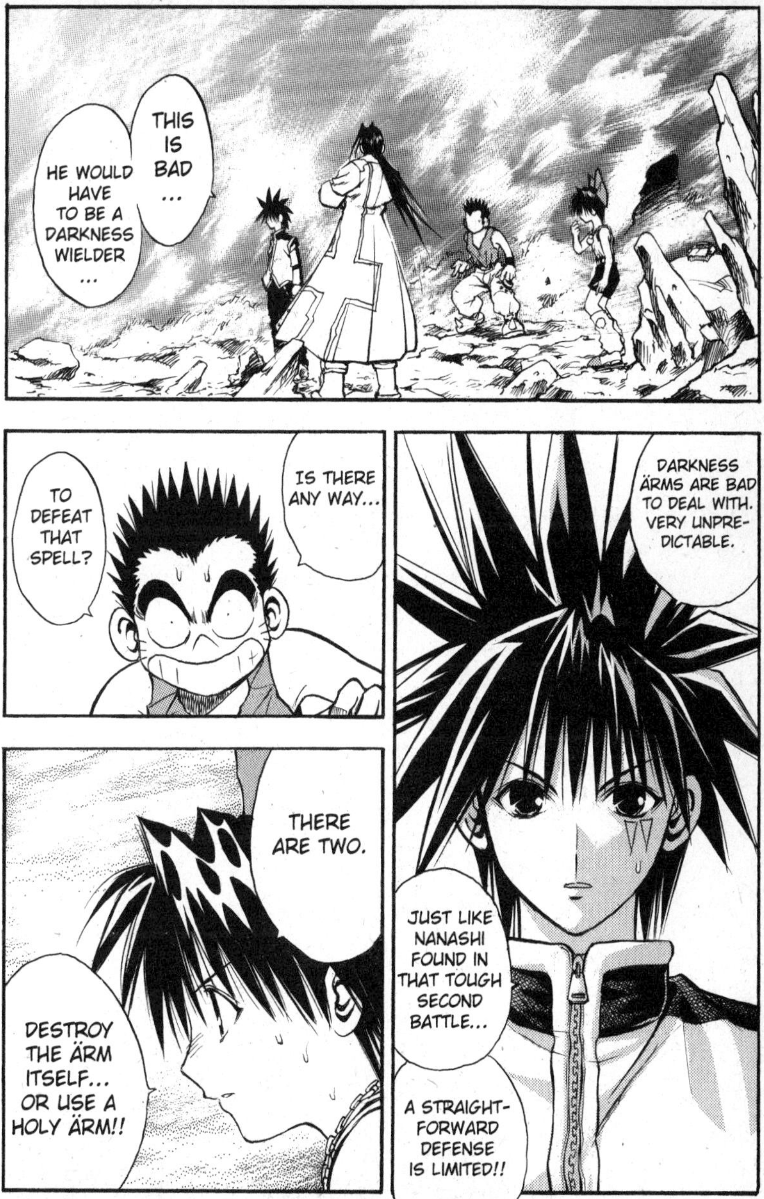
THIS IS BAD...
HE WOULD HAVE TO BE A DARKNESS WIELDER...
DARKNESS ÄRMS ARE BAD TO DEAL WITH. VERY UNPREDICTABLE.
JUST LIKE NANASHI FOUND IN THAT TOUGH SECOND BATTLE...
A STRAIGHT-FORWARD DEFENSE IS LIMITED!!
IS THERE ANY WAY...
TO DEFEAT THAT SPELL?
THERE ARE TWO.
DESTROY THE ÄRM ITSELF... OR USE A HOLY ÄRM!!

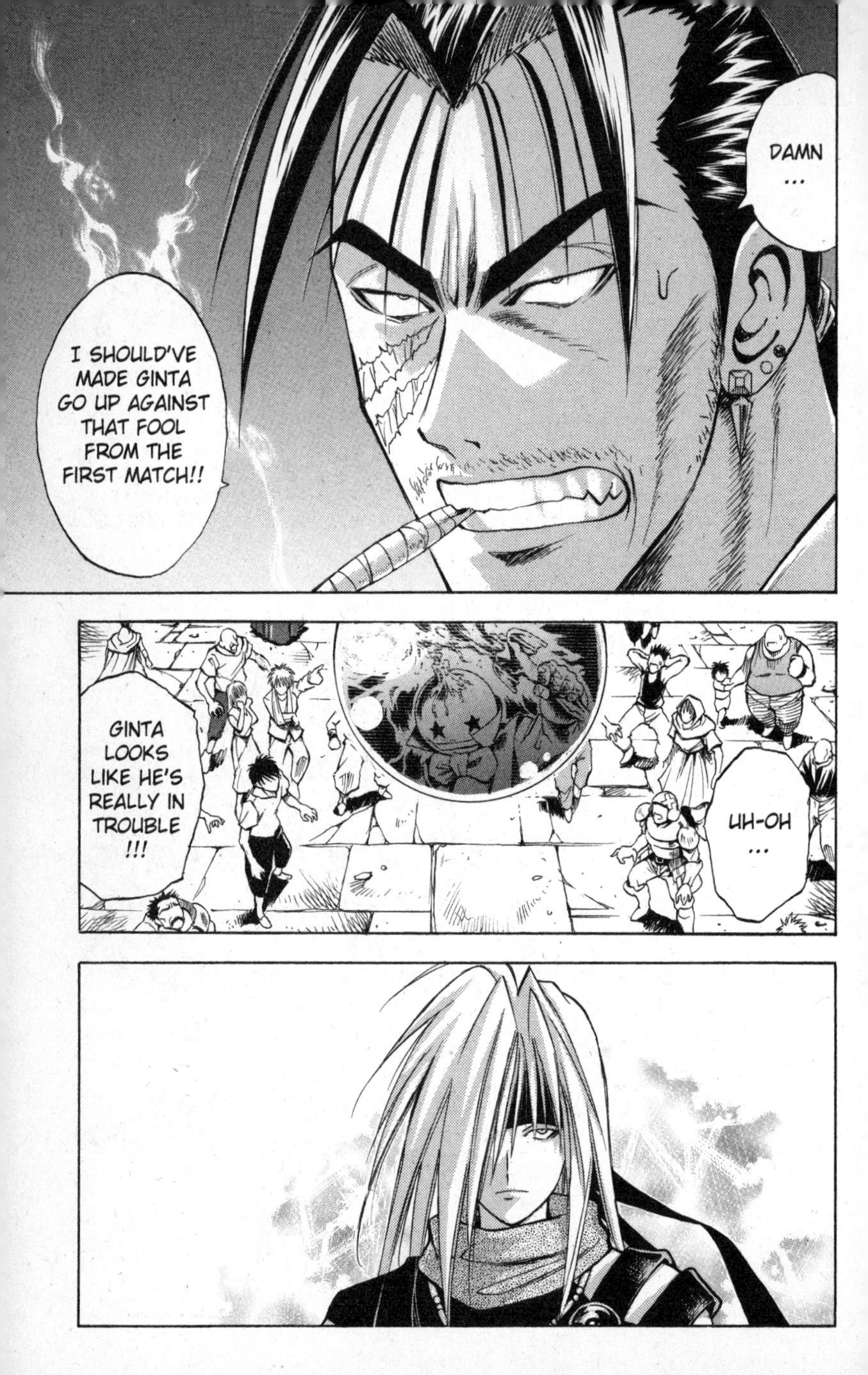
DAMN ...
I SHOULD'VE MADE GINTA GO UP AGAINST THAT FOOL FROM THE FIRST MATCH!!
UH-OH ...
GINTA LOOKS LIKE HE'S REALLY IN TROUBLE !!!

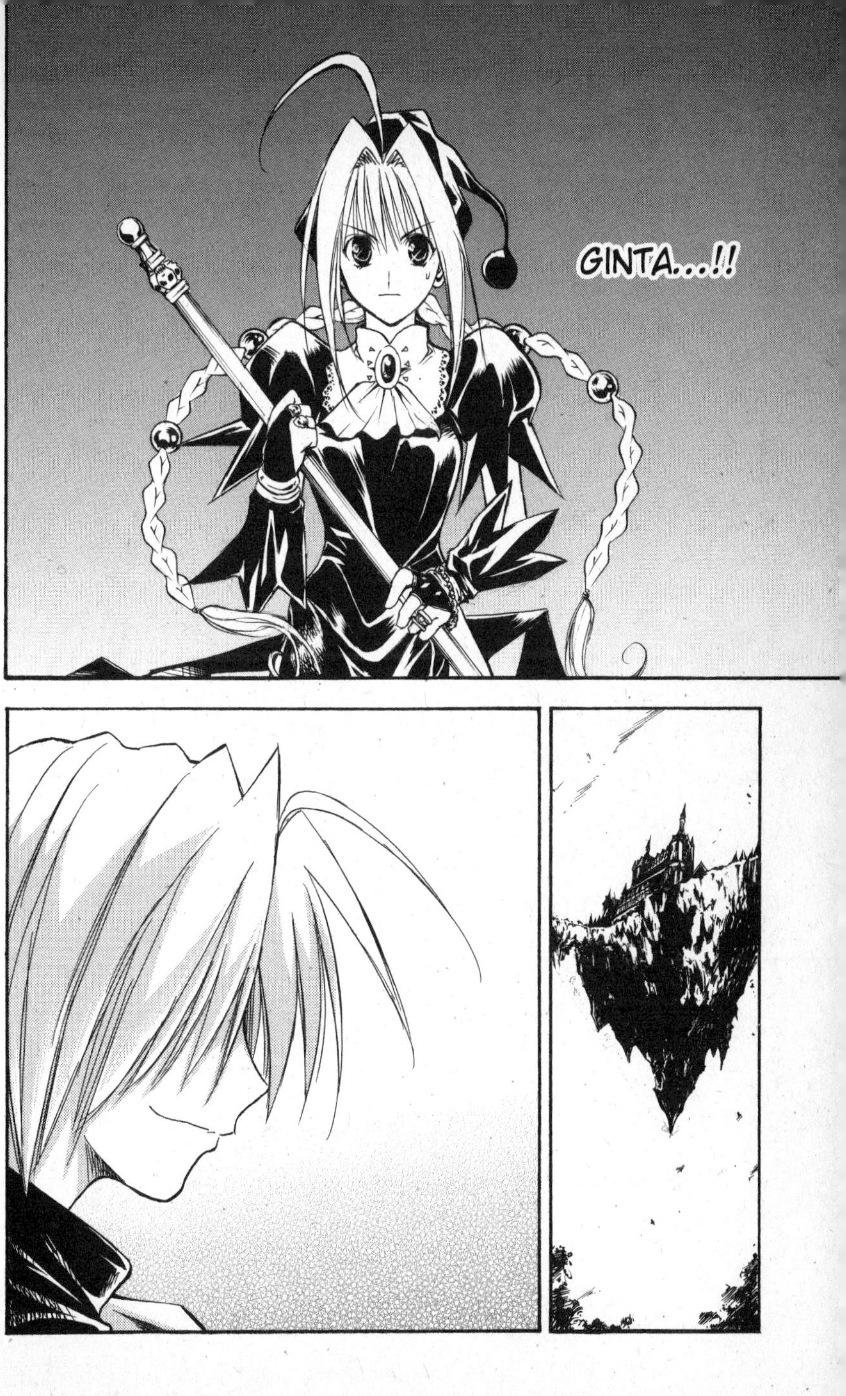
GINTA...!!

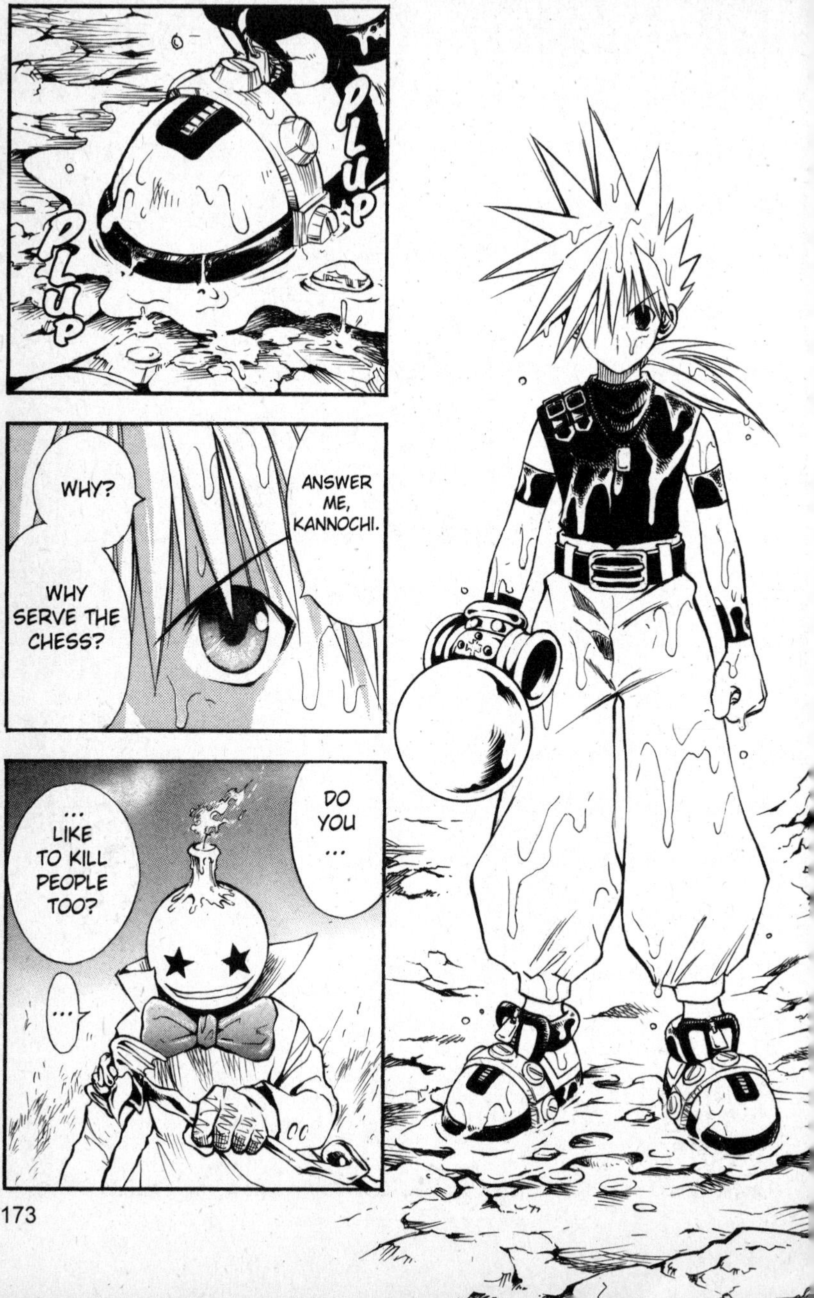
PLUP
PLUP
ANSWER ME, KANNOCHI.
WHY?
WHY SERVE THE CHESS?
DO YOU ...
... LIKE TO KILL PEOPLE TOO?
...

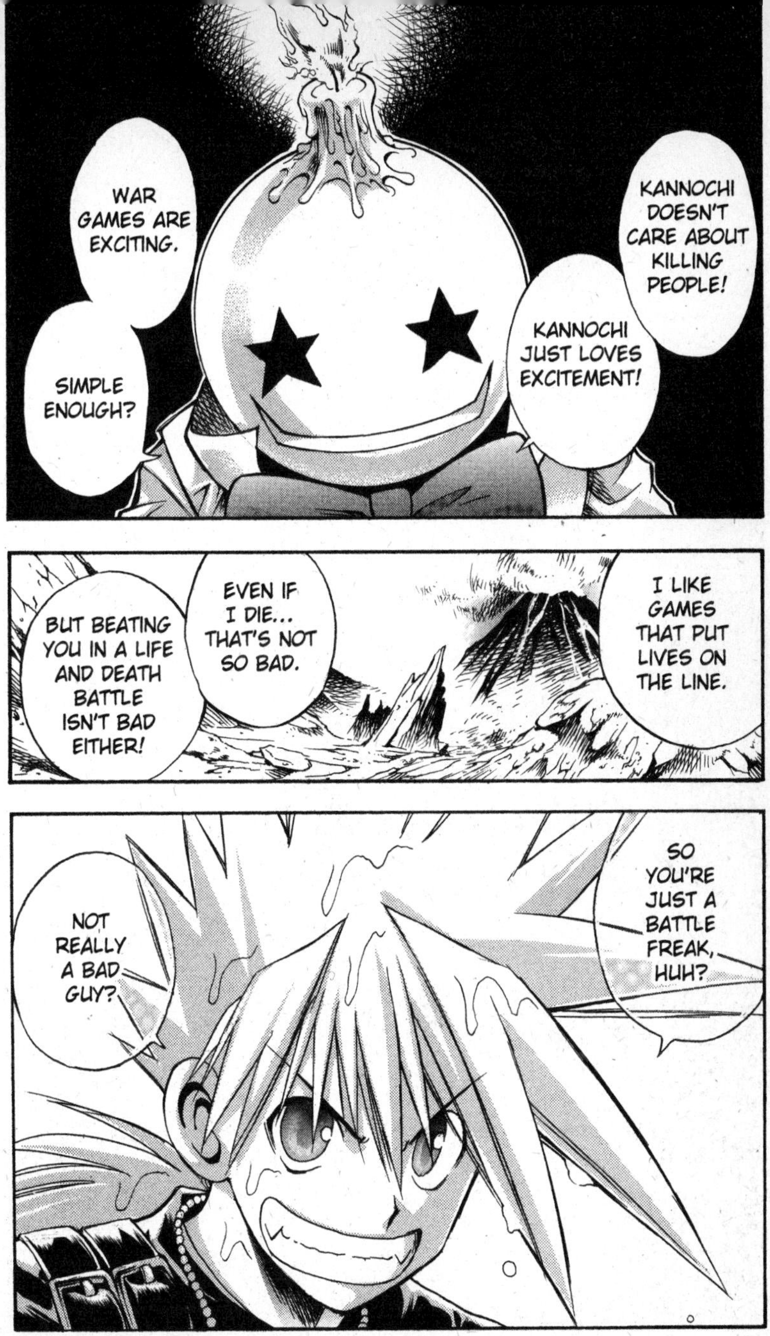
KANNOCHI DOESN'T CARE ABOUT KILLING PEOPLE!
KANNOCHI JUST LOVES EXCITEMENT!
WAR GAMES ARE EXCITING.
SIMPLE ENOUGH?
I LIKE GAMES THAT PUT LIVES ON THE LINE.
EVEN IF I DIE... THAT'S NOT SO BAD.
BUT BEATING YOU IN A LIFE AND DEATH BATTLE ISN'T BAD EITHER!
SO YOU'RE JUST A BATTLE FREAK, HUH?
NOT REALLY A BAD GUY?

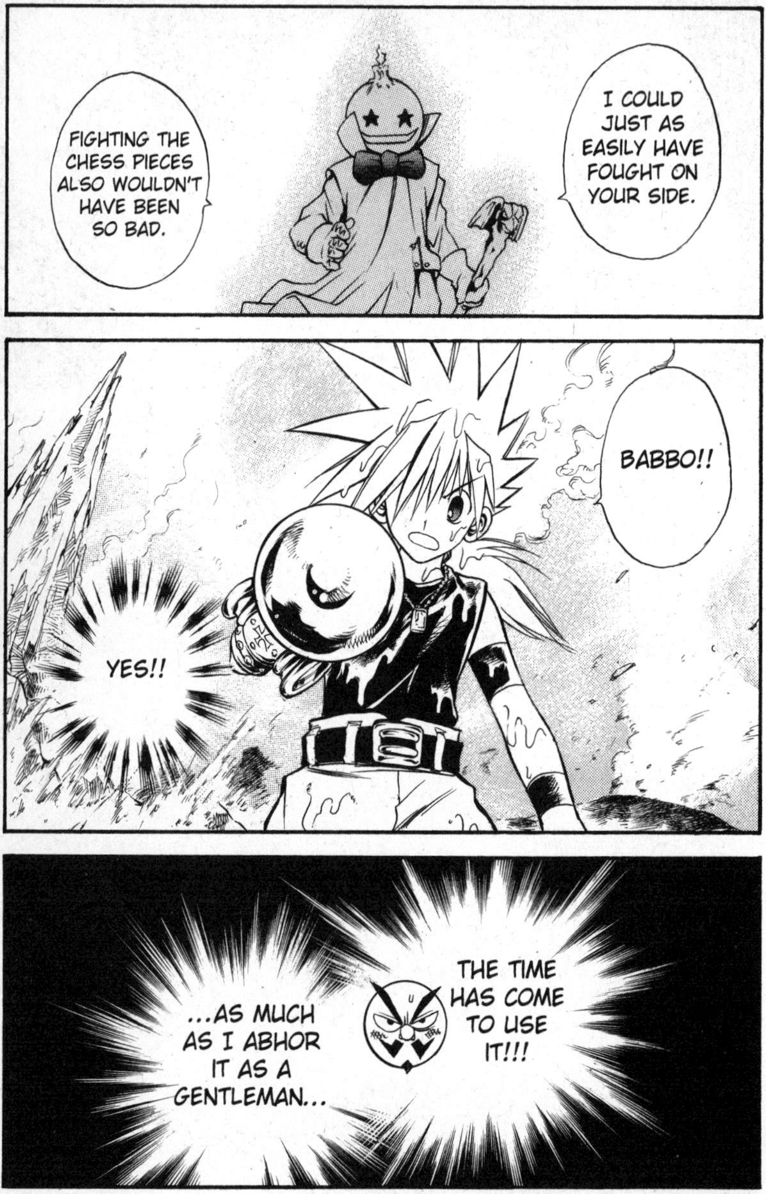
I COULD JUST AS EASILY HAVE FOUGHT ON YOUR SIDE.
FIGHTING THE CHESS PIECES ALSO WOULDN'T HAVE BEEN SO BAD.
BABBO!!
YES!!
THE TIME HAS COME TO USE IT!!!
...AS MUCH AS I ABHOR IT AS A GENTLEMAN...

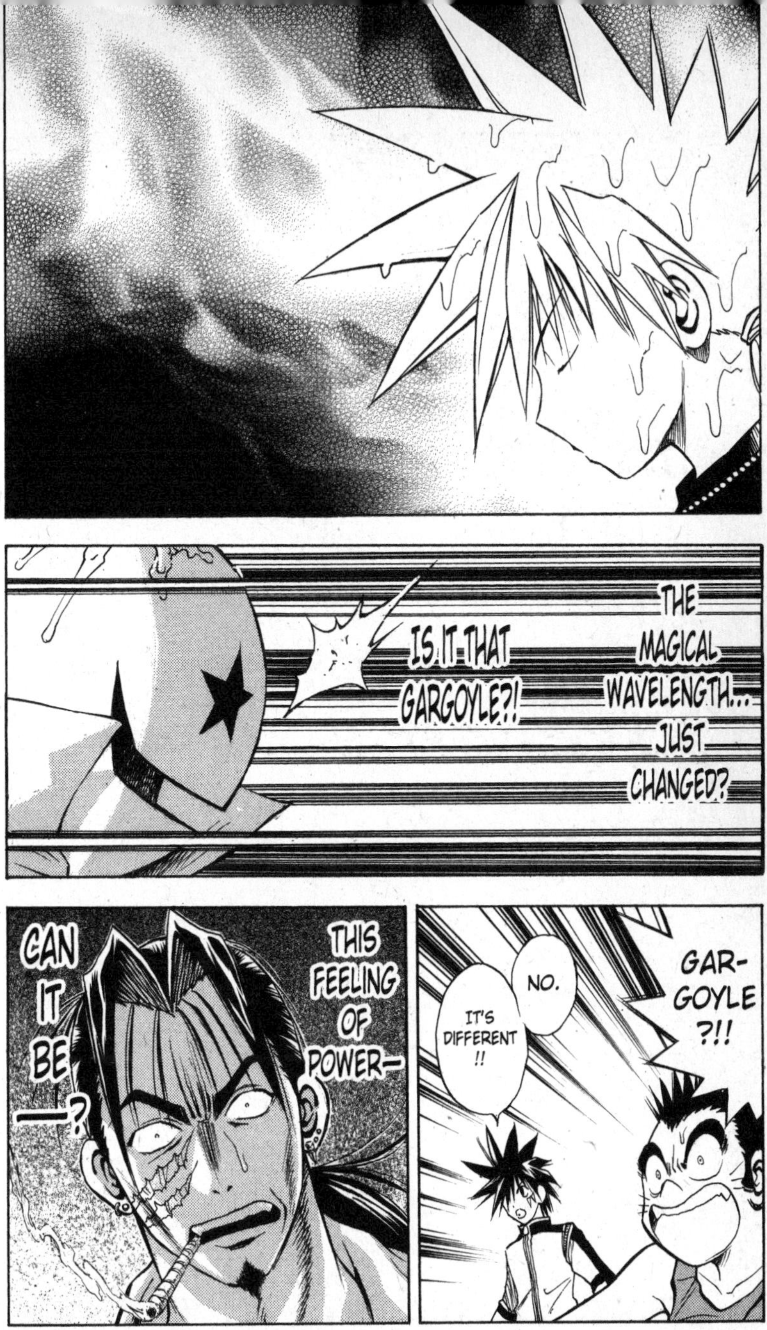
THE MAGICAL WAVELENGTH... JUST CHANGED?
IS IT THAT GARGOYLE?!
GAR-GOYLE?!!
NO.
IT'S DIFFERENT!!
THIS FEELING OF POWER—
CAN IT BE—?

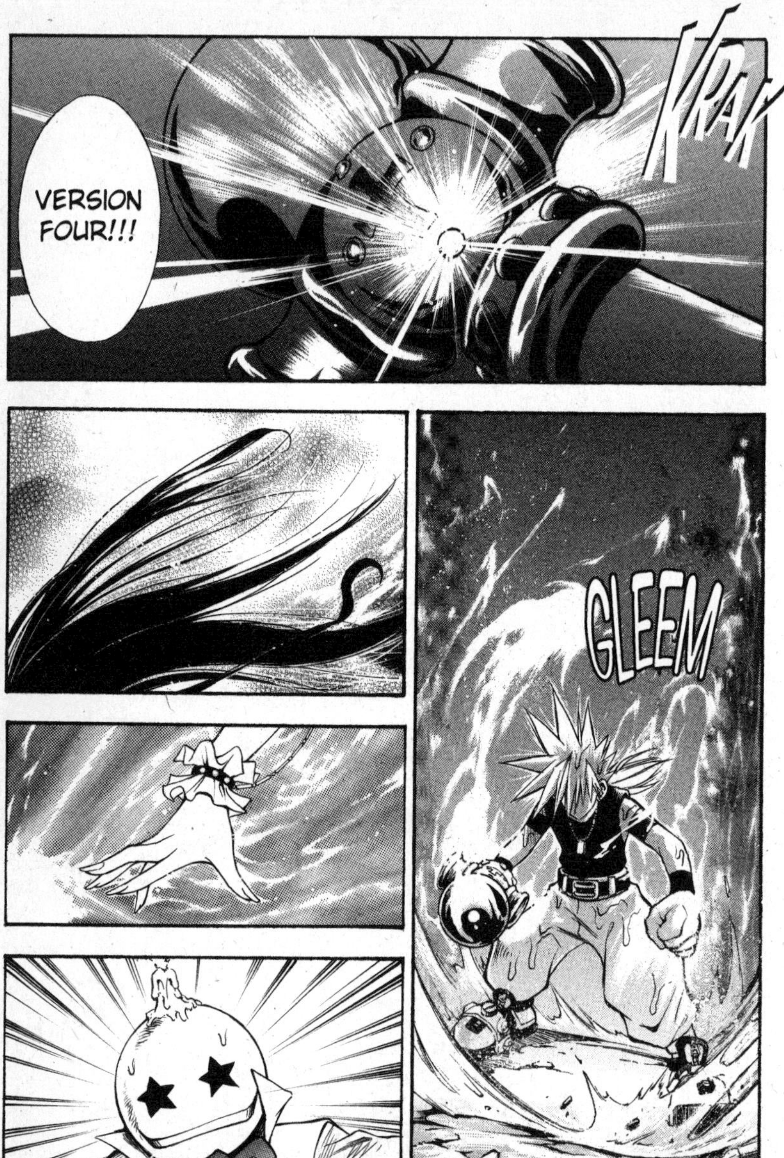
KRAK
VERSION FOUR!!!
GLEEM

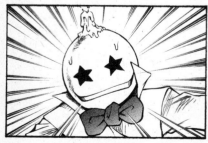

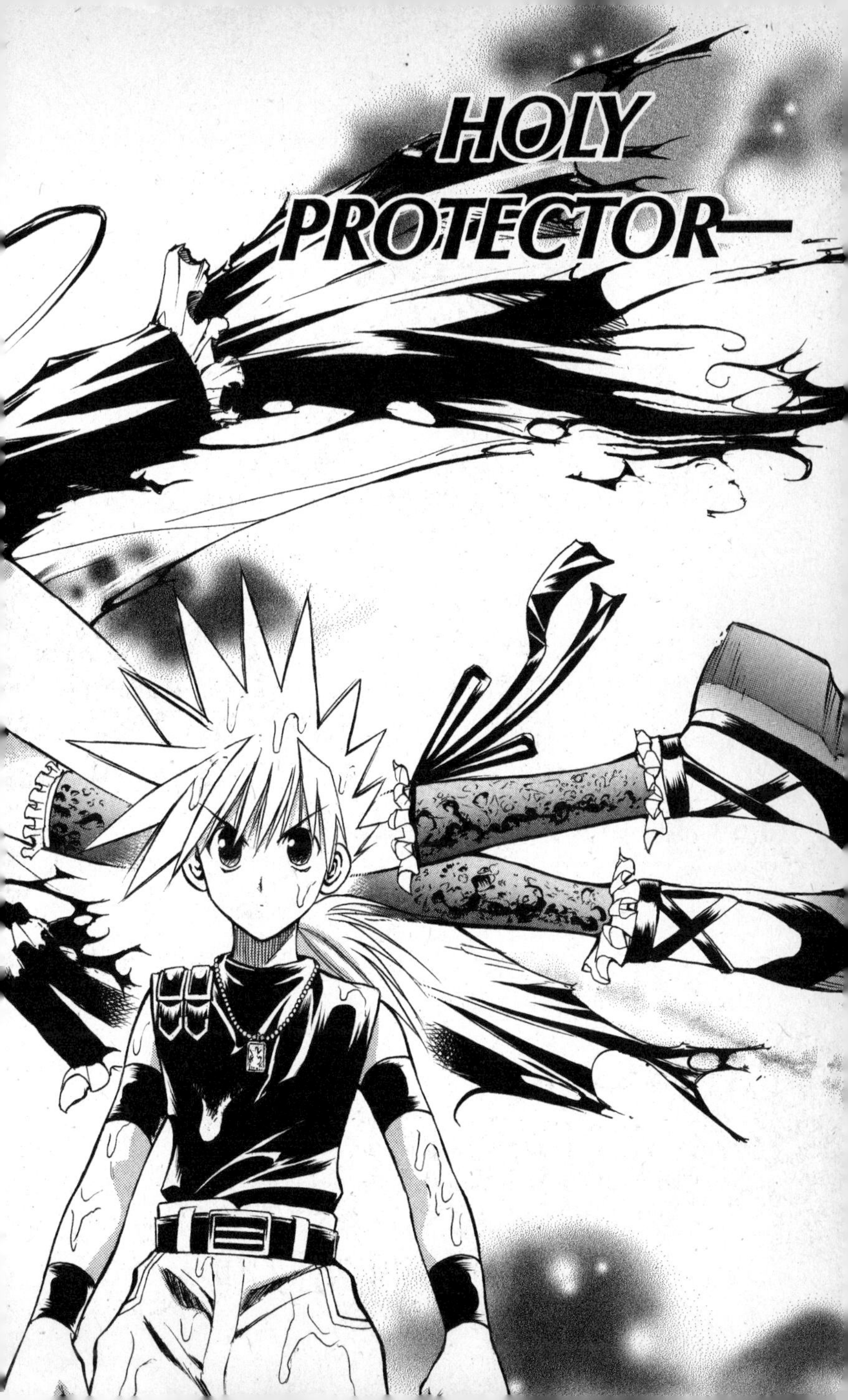
HOLY
PROTECTOR—

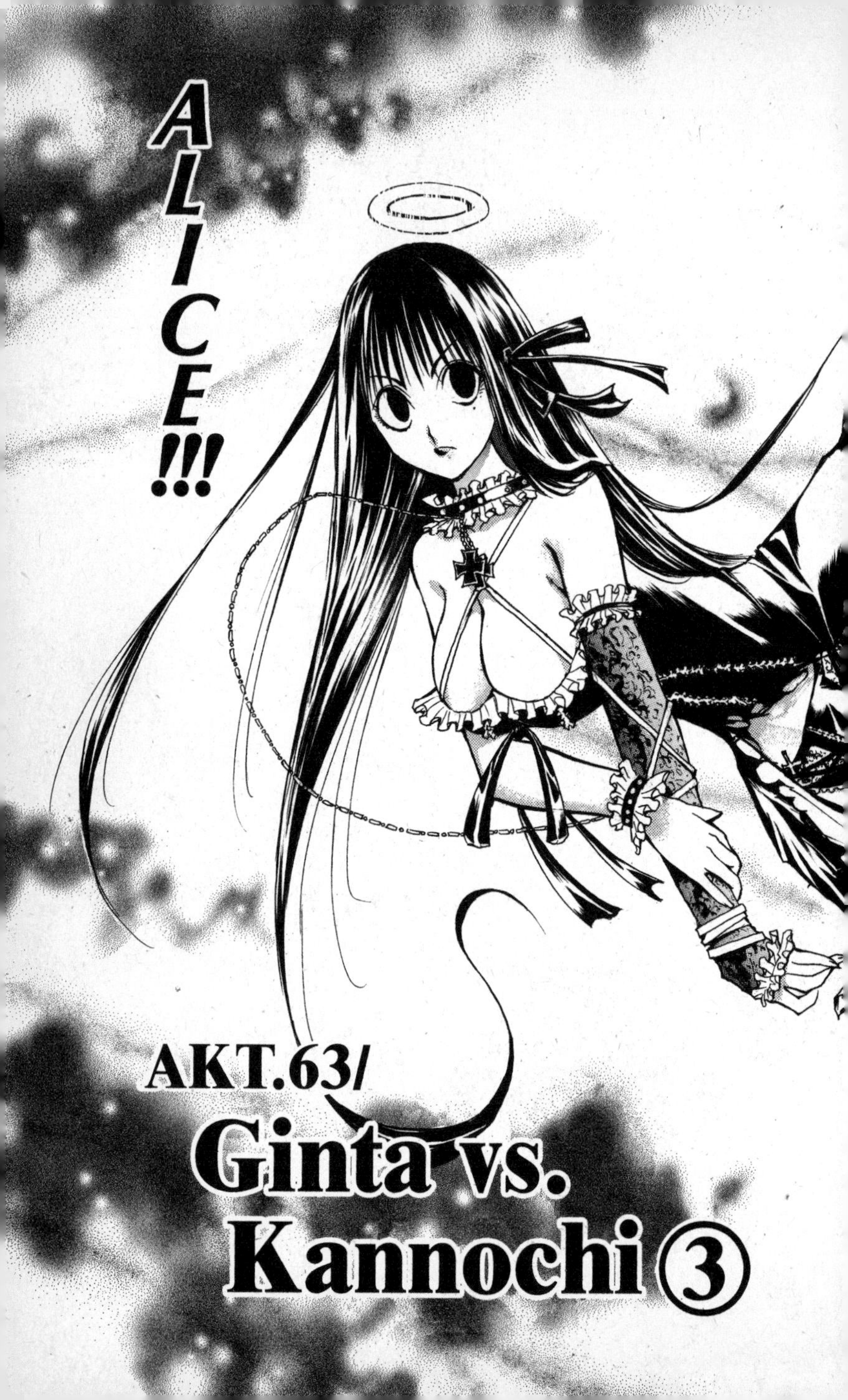
ALICE!!!

AKT.63/ Ginta vs. Kannochi ③

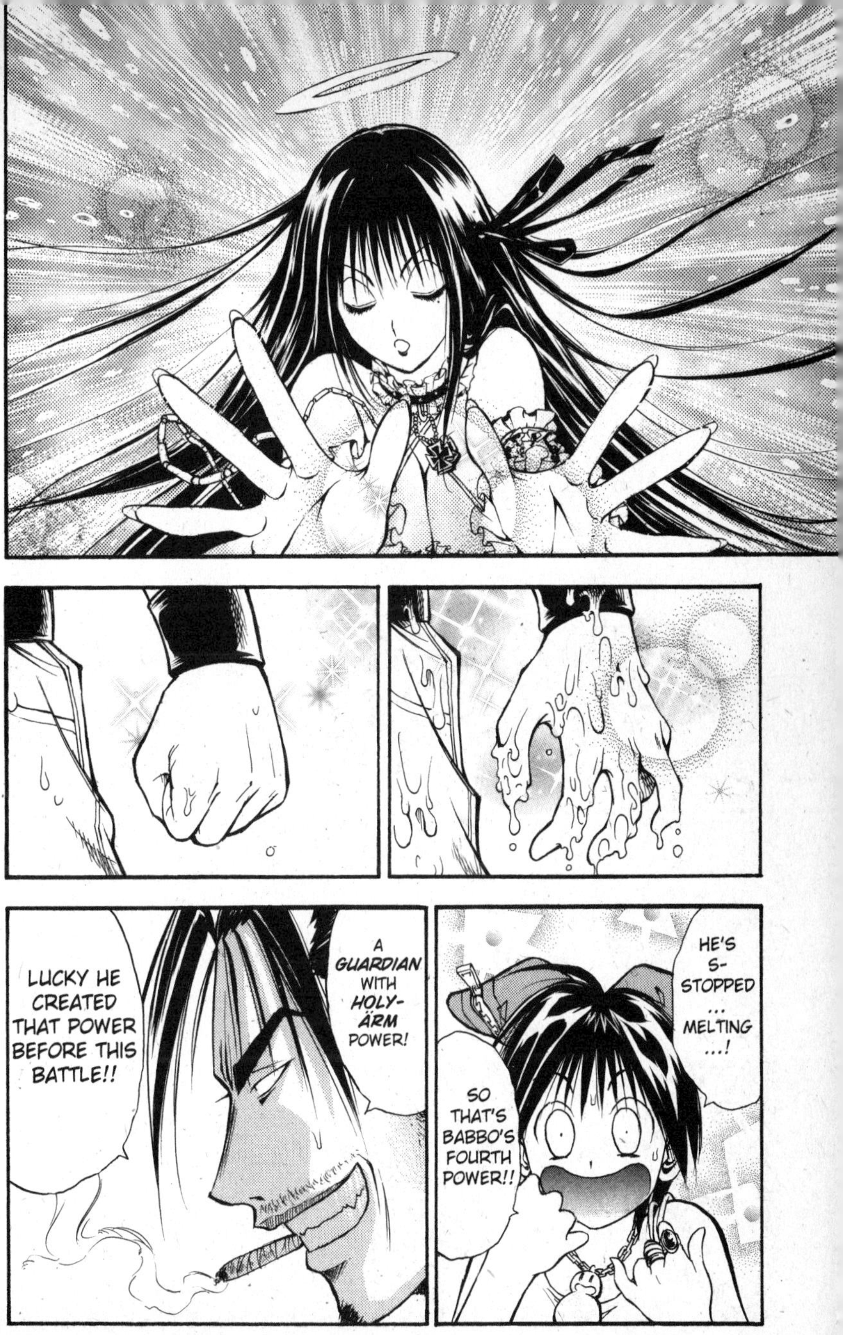
HE'S S-STOPPED ... MELTING ...!
SO THAT'S BABBO'S FOURTH POWER!!
A GUARDIAN WITH HOLY-ÄRM POWER!
LUCKY HE CREATED THAT POWER BEFORE THIS BATTLE!!

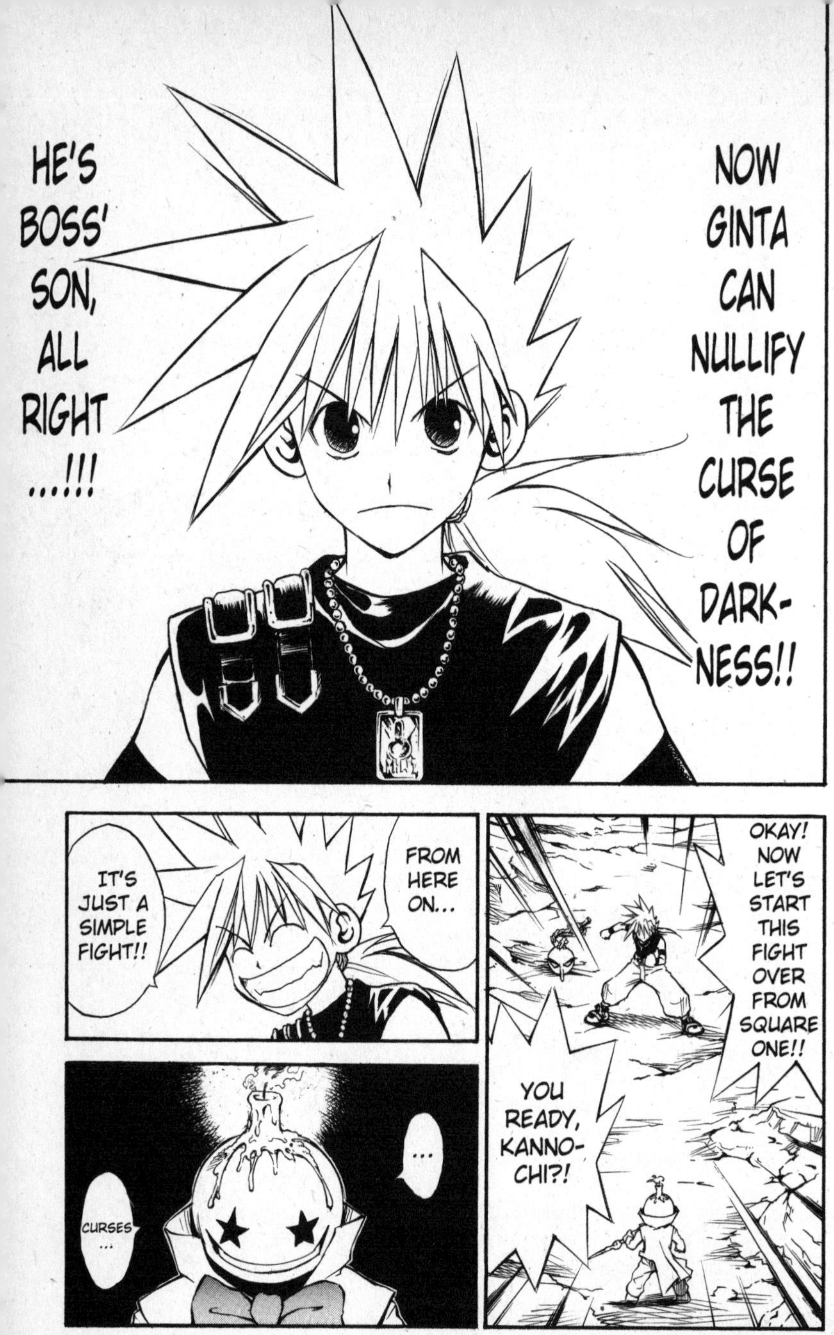
NOW GINTA CAN NULLIFY THE CURSE OF DARKNESS!!
HE'S BOSS' SON, ALL RIGHT ...!!!
OKAY! NOW LET'S START THIS FIGHT OVER FROM SQUARE ONE!!
YOU READY, KANNOCHI?!
FROM HERE ON...
IT'S JUST A SIMPLE FIGHT!!
...
CURSES ...

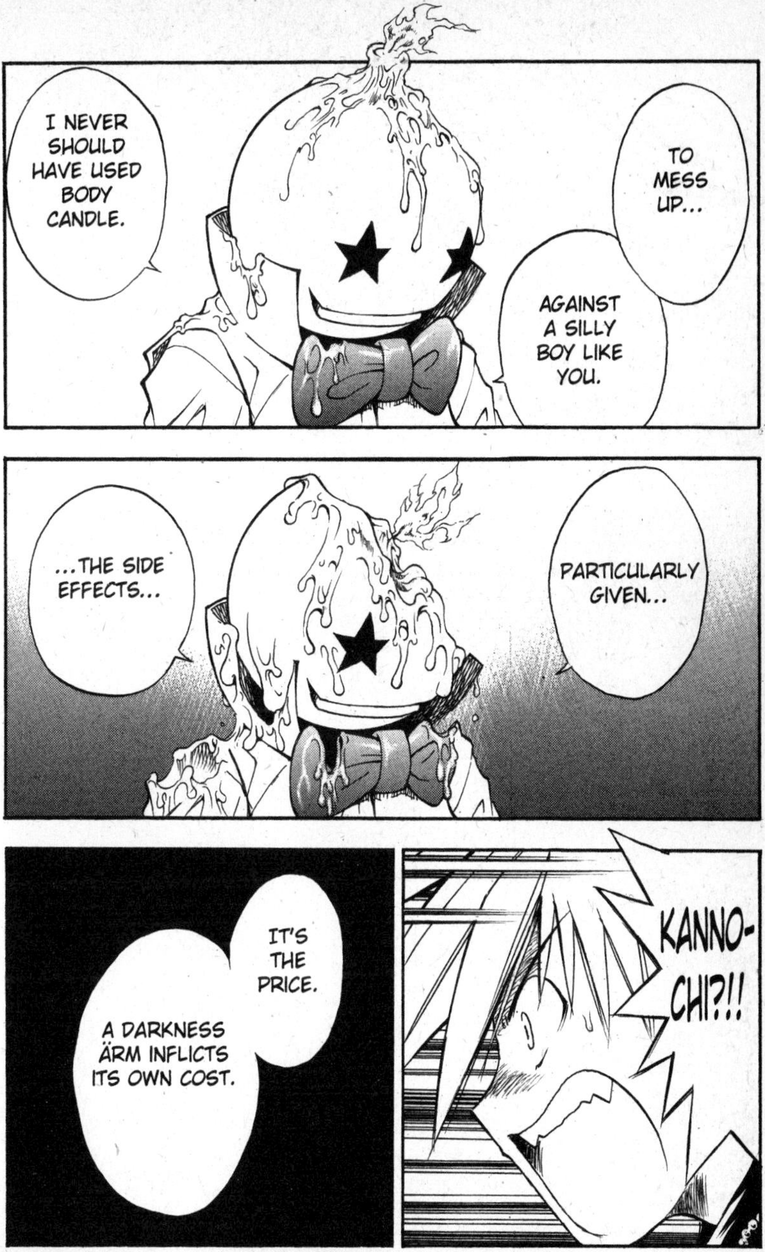
TO MESS UP...
AGAINST A SILLY BOY LIKE YOU.
I NEVER SHOULD HAVE USED BODY CANDLE.
PARTICULARLY GIVEN...
...THE SIDE EFFECTS...
KANNO-CHI?!!
IT'S THE PRICE.
A DARKNESS ÄRM INFLICTS ITS OWN COST.

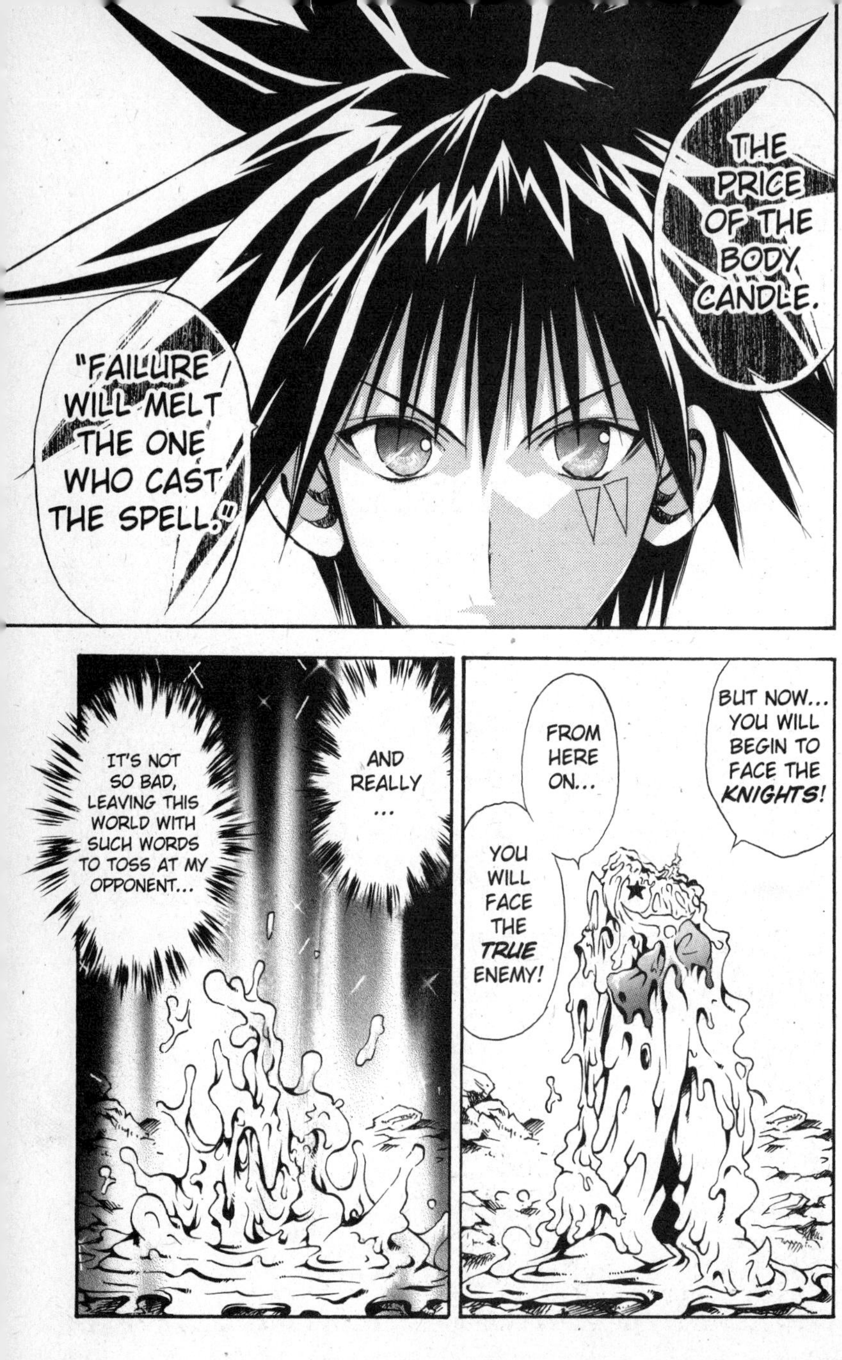
THE PRICE OF THE BODY CANDLE.
"FAILURE WILL MELT THE ONE WHO CAST THE SPELL."
BUT NOW... YOU WILL BEGIN TO FACE THE ***KNIGHTS***!
FROM HERE ON...
YOU WILL FACE THE ***TRUE*** ENEMY!
AND REALLY ...
IT'S NOT SO BAD, LEAVING THIS WORLD WITH SUCH WORDS TO TOSS AT MY OPPONENT...

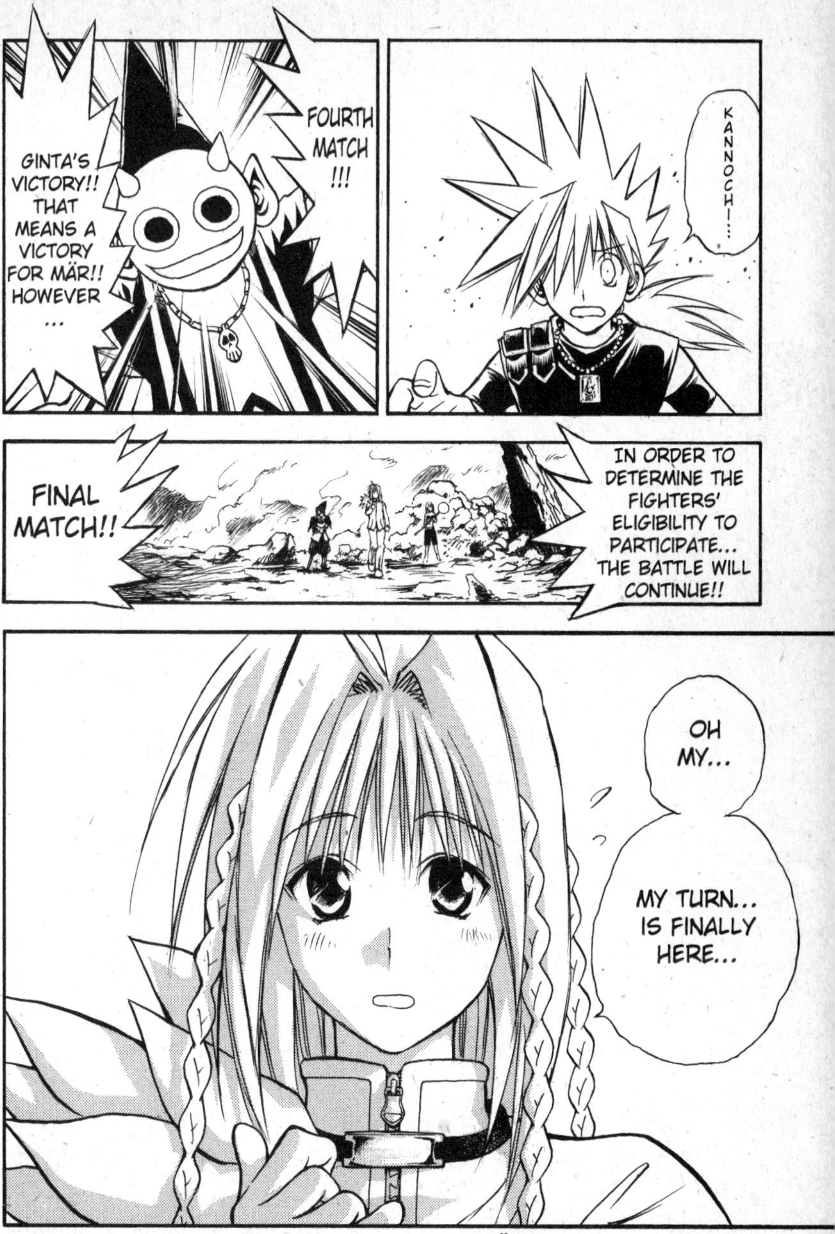
KANNOCHI...
FOURTH MATCH!!!
GINTA'S VICTORY!! THAT MEANS A VICTORY FOR MÄR!! HOWEVER...
IN ORDER TO DETERMINE THE FIGHTERS' ELIGIBILITY TO PARTICIPATE... THE BATTLE WILL CONTINUE!!
FINAL MATCH!!
OH MY...
MY TURN... IS FINALLY HERE...

MÄR Volume 6 – The End

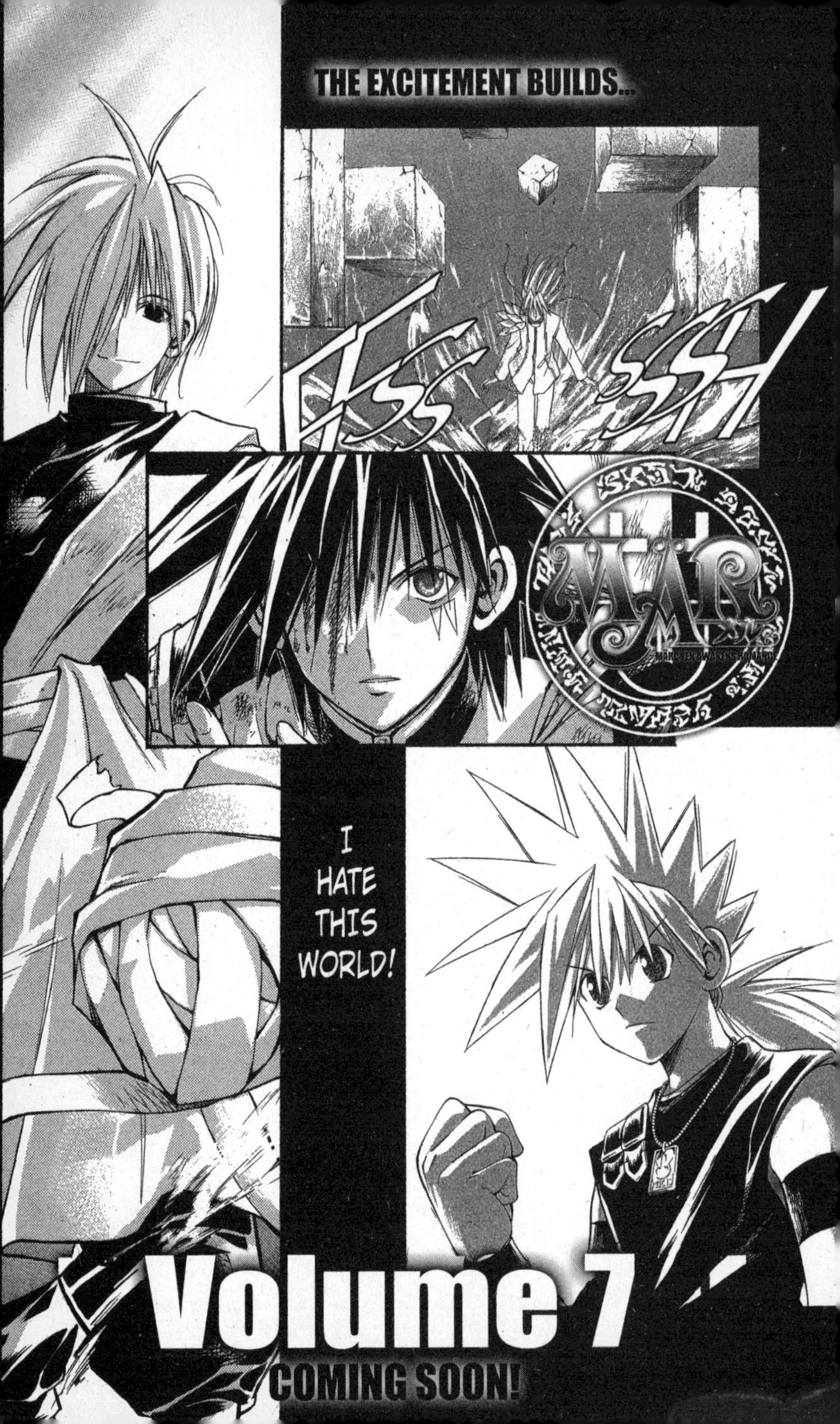
THE EXCITEMENT BUILDS...
FSSSSSH
MÄR
I HATE THIS WORLD!
Volume 7
COMING SOON!

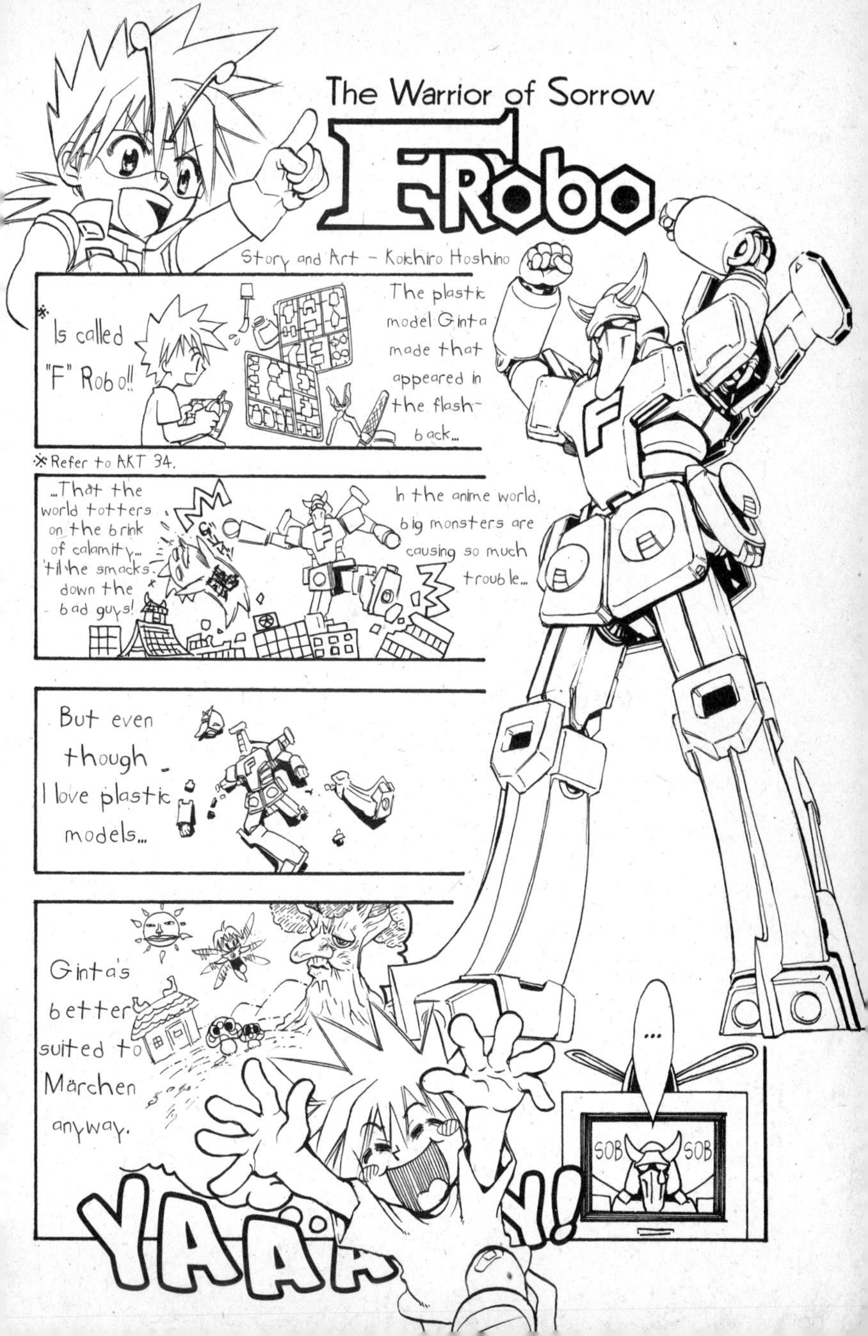
The Warrior of Sorrow
F-Robo
Story and Art - Koichiro Hoshino
The plastic model Ginta made that appeared in the flashback...
※ Is called "F" Robo!!
※Refer to AKT 34.
In the anime world, big monsters are causing so much trouble...
...That the world totters on the brink of calamity... 'til he smacks down the bad guys!
G'YAA!
But even though I love plastic models...
...
SOB SOB
Ginta's better suited to Märchen anyway.
YAAAAY!

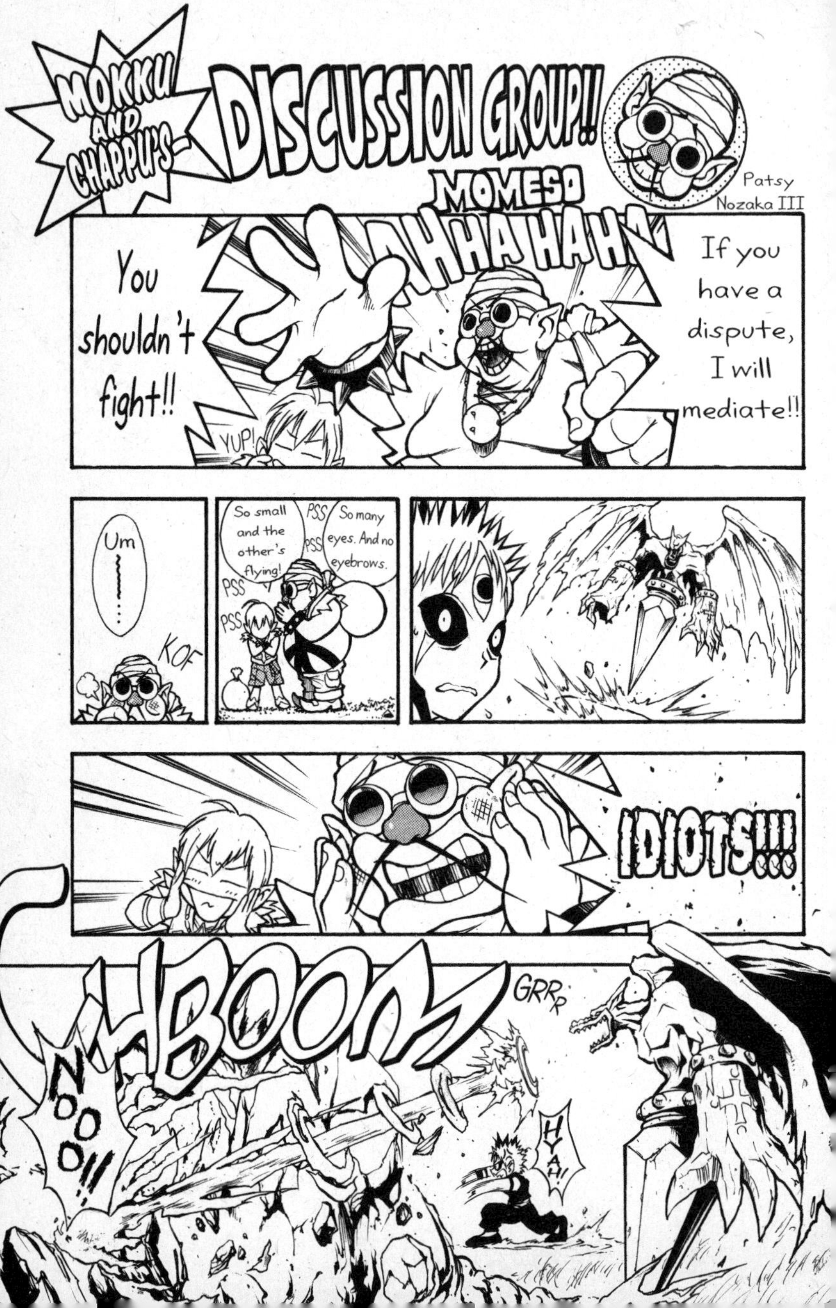

MOKKU AND CHAPPUP'S-
DISCUSSION GROUP!!
Patsy Nozaka III
MOMESO
AHHA HA HAH
If you have a dispute, I will mediate!!
You shouldn't fight!!
YUP!
So many eyes. And no eyebrows.
PSS
PSS
So small and the other's flying!
PSS
PSS
Um ~~~......
KOF
IDIOTS!!!
GRRR
BOOM
HYAH!
NOOO!!

ACID VOMIT

Written by: GB
Title lettering: Anzai

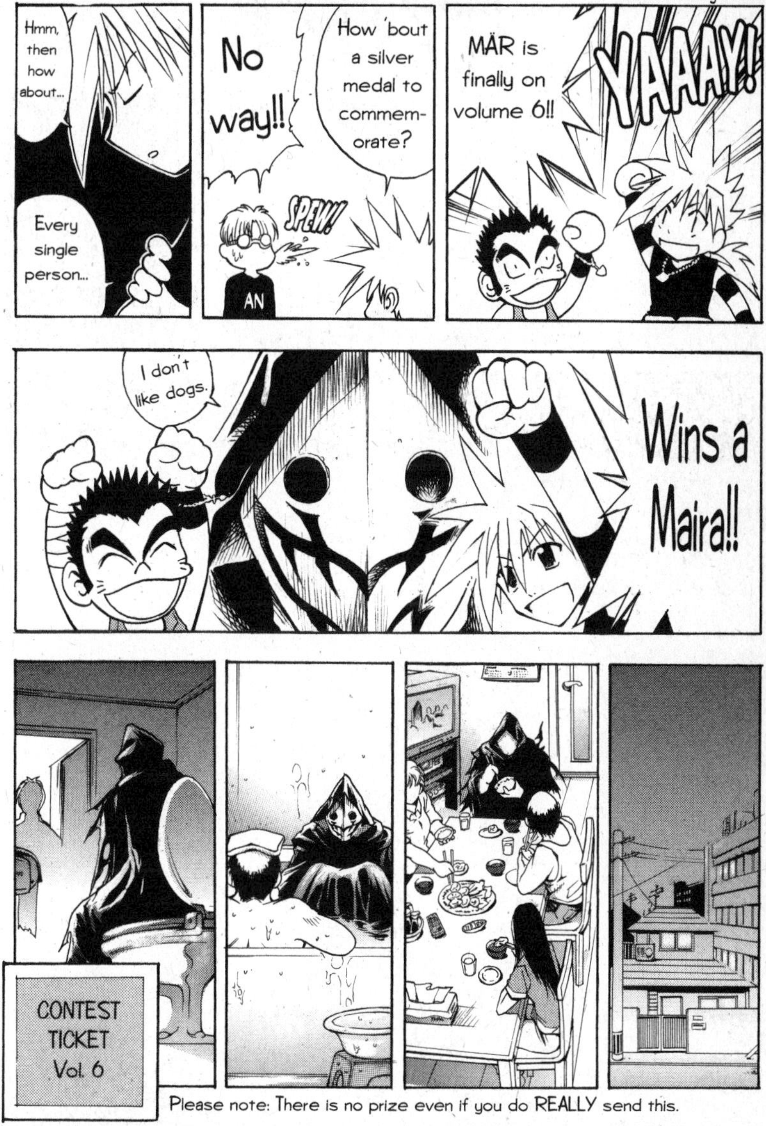
YAAAY!!
MÄR is finally on volume 6!!
How 'bout a silver medal to commem-orate?
No way!!
SPEW!
Hmm, then how about...
Every single person...
Wins a Maira!!
I don't like dogs.
AN
CONTEST TICKET Vol. 6

Please note: There is no prize even if you do REALLY send this.

BONUS—POP!

Nobuyuki Anzai

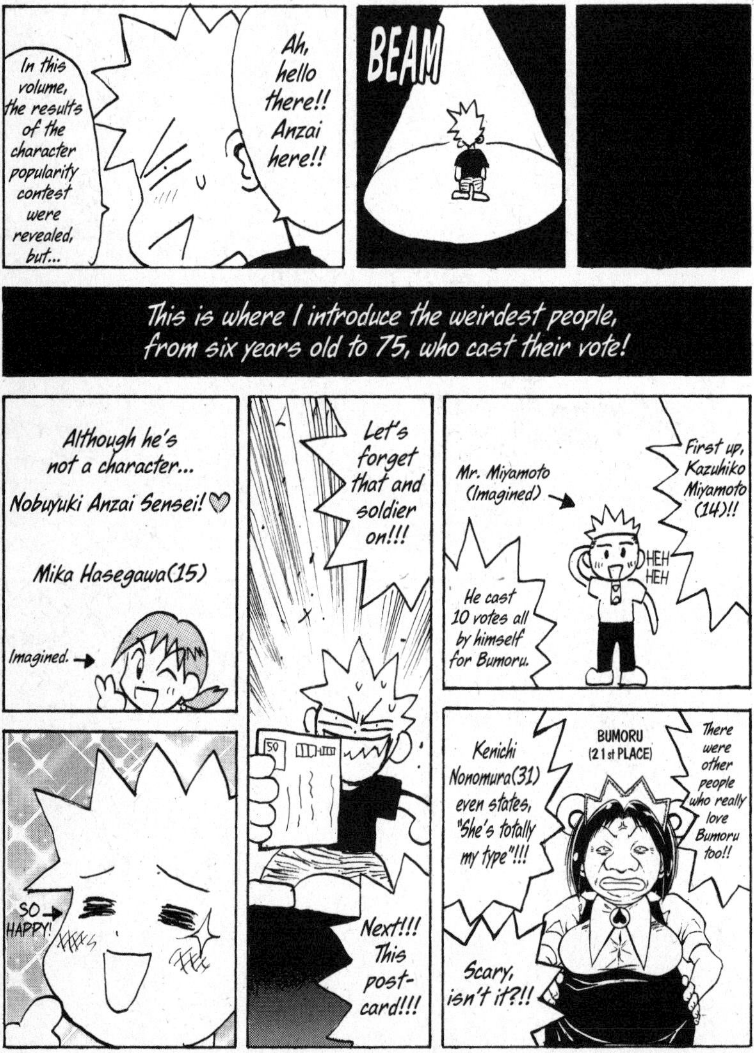
BEAM
Ah, hello there!! Anzai here!!
In this volume, the results of the character popularity contest were revealed, but...
This is where I introduce the weirdest people, from six years old to 75, who cast their vote!
First up, Kazuhiko Miyamoto (14)!!
Mr. Miyamoto (Imagined) →
HEH HEH
He cast 10 votes all by himself for Bumoru.
There were other people who really love Bumoru too!!
BUMORU (21st PLACE)
Kenichi Nonomura(31) even states, "She's totally my type"!!!
Scary, isn't it?!!
Let's forget that and soldier on!!!
50
Next!!! This post-card!!!
Although he's not a character...
Nobuyuki Anzai Sensei! ♡
Mika Hasegawa(15)
Imagined. →
SO HAPPY! →

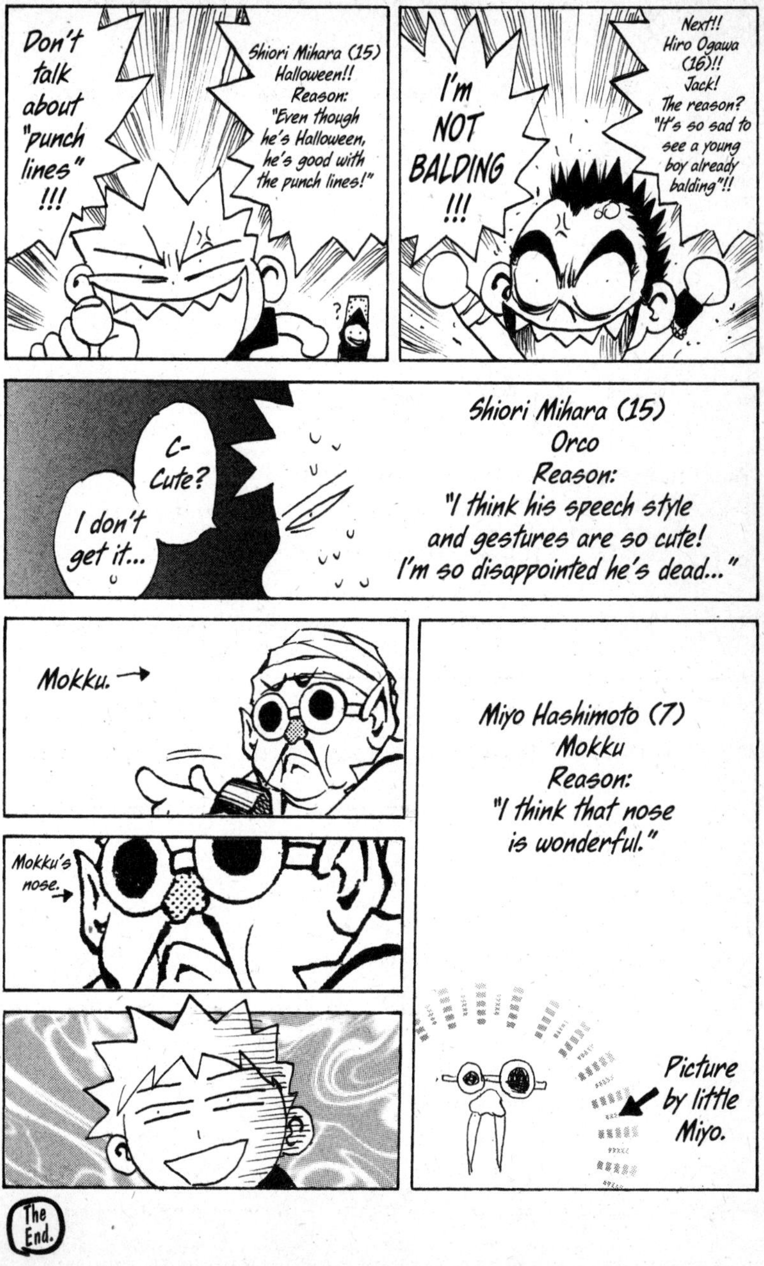
Next!! Hiro Ogawa (16)!! Jack! The reason? "It's so sad to see a young boy already balding"!!
I'm NOT BALDING !!!
Shiori Mihara (15) Halloween!! Reason: "Even though he's Halloween, he's good with the punch lines!"
Don't talk about "punch lines" !!!
Shiori Mihara (15) Orco Reason: "I think his speech style and gestures are so cute! I'm so disappointed he's dead..."
C-Cute?
I don't get it...
Miyo Hashimoto (7) Mokku Reason: "I think that nose is wonderful."
Picture by little Miyo.
Mokku.
Mokku's nose.
The End.

LOVE MANGA? LET US KNOW!

☐ Please do NOT send me information about VIZ Media products, news and events, special offers, or other information.

☐ Please do NOT send me information from VIZ Media's trusted business partners.

Name: _____

Address: _____

City: _____ State: _____ Zip: _____

E-mail: _____

☐ Male ☐ Female   Date of Birth (mm/dd/yyyy): ___ / ___ / _____ (Under 13? Parental consent required)

What race/ethnicity do you consider yourself? (check all that apply)

☐ White/Caucasian   ☐ Black/African American   ☐ Hispanic/Latino

☐ Asian/Pacific Islander   ☐ Native American/Alaskan Native ☐ Other: _____

What VIZ Media title(s) did you purchase? (indicate title(s) purchased) _____

_____

What other VIZ Media titles do you own? _____

_____

Reason for purchase: (check all that apply)

☐ Special offer   ☐ Favorite title / author / artist / genre

☐ Gift   ☐ Recommendation   ☐ Collection

☐ Read excerpt in VIZ Media manga sampler   ☐ Other _____

Where did you make your purchase? (please check one)

☐ Comic store   ☐ Bookstore   ☐ Grocery Store

☐ Convention   ☐ Newsstand   ☐ Video Game Store

☐ Online (site:_____)   ☐ Other _____

How many manga titles have you purchased in the last year? How many were VIZ Media titles?
(please check one from each column)

MANGA	VIZ Media
☐ None	☐
☐ 1 – 4	☐
☐ 5 – 10	☐
☐ 11+	☐

How much influence do special promoti... and gifts-with-purchase have on the titles you buy?
(please circle, with 5 being great influence and 1 being none)

1 2 3 4 5

Do you purchase every volume of your favorite series?

☐ Yes! Gotta have 'em as my own ☐ No. Please explain: ____________________

What kind of manga storylines do you most enjoy? **(check all that apply)**

☐ Action / Adventure ☐ Science Fiction ☐ Horror
☐ Comedy ☐ Romance (shojo) ☐ Fantasy (shojo)
☐ Fighting ☐ Sports ☐ Historical
☐ Artistic / Alternative ☐ Other ____________________

If you watch the anime or play a video or TCG game from a series, how likely are you to buy the manga? **(please circle, with 5 being very likely and 1 being unlikely)**

1 2 3 4 5

If unlikely, please explain: ____________________

Who are your favorite authors / artists? ____________________

____

What titles would like you translated and sold in English? ____________________

____

THANK YOU! Please send the completed form to:

VIZ media™

NJW Research
42 Catharine Street
Poughkeepsie, NY 12601

Your privacy is very important to us. All information provided will be used for internal purposes only and will not be sold or otherwise divulged.